*Climb Every
Mountain*

Climb Every Mountain

**498 Scottish mountains
in one continuous
self-propelled journey**

CRAIG CALDWELL

Macdonald

For family and friends who made a dream become reality

A Macdonald Book

Copyright © Craig Caldwell 1990

First published in Great Britain in 1990 by
Macdonald & Co (Publishers) Ltd
London & Sydney

Reprinted 1990

British Library Cataloguing in Publication Data

Caldwell, Craig, *1959–*
  Climb every mountain.
  1. Scotland. Highlands. Mountains. Mountains Munros
  I. Title
  796.522092

ISBN 0-356-18809-4

Typeset by Leaper & Gard Ltd, Bristol
Printed and bound in Great Britain by
Biddles Ltd, Guildford and King's Lynn

Macdonald & Co (Publishers) Ltd
Orbit House
1 New Fetter Lane
London EC4A 1AR
A member of Maxwell Macmillan Pergamon Publishing Corporation

Contents

List of Maps
and Illustrations

Acknowledgements

I am indebted first and foremost to my parents Tom and Doreen, who approved my mad plan and supported me through thick and thin during the course of the walk, and also to my friends, led by Alasdair Brown, who enthusiastically rallied to my support with countless visits and letters and eagerly helped raise funds for our charity, Erskine Hospital. My thanks also to Alastair Conkie, Simon Strachan, Angus Cameron and Graham Moss for their support on the hills, and to Geoff Payman who showed me the way to the mountains.

Grateful thanks are due to Peter and Eileen Daynes, of the Clachaigh Inn, Glen Coe, and to Mr Colin Turner, Rector of the Glasgow Academy, for their superb fund-raising efforts.

To the many new friends made in the course of my journey may I express my gratitude for their great generosity and much-appreciated cheerful company. And last, but not least, I must mention Munro, my faithful collie, the most stalwart and trusty of companions — what a pedigree chum!

The following companies kindly donated equipment for the trek: Berghaus, Epi Gas, Helly Hansen, Winter Gear and Polisox. Their products are explained in the equipment section.

The words of the song 'Thogail nam Bo' (Lifting the Cattle) on page 348 are reproduced by kind permission of Richard Drew Publishing, Glasgow.

The words of the poem 'Moment Musical in Assynt' on page 36 is from Completed Poems by Norman MacCraig and reproduced by kind permission of Chatto & Windus/The Hogarth Press, London.

For their help in the course of writing this book, I thank Max Hodes for his editing and patience, and Hamish and Janette Inglis for research.

Craig Caldwell

The Historical Background

Hillwalking as a sport is a fairly new game. Up to the eighteenth century, Scotland's mountains formed a defensive barrier from which warlike clans would raid the Lowlands and then melt back into their mountainous shield. Hills and remote passes were crossed for survival more than pleasure, after which the bare-footed clansmen would return to their glens with precious cattle for their hungry families. This Highland way of life ended on the bloody field of Culloden. Sadly the defeated clansmen and many of those who unwisely supported the Government were brutally evicted from their homes and sent to the colonies in leaking, disease-ridden ships. Their mountain homeland was turned into massive grazing grounds for sheep, and later deer forests for rich sportsmen to shoot in.

In the nineteenth century the popular image of the Highlands was that of a barren place, inhabited by cut-throats and cattle thieves. This was suddenly all changed with the romantic works of Sir Walter Scott, and the many royal visits by Queen Victoria who came to love the country dearly. From these early days started the now booming tourist industry. It became fashionable to visit the glens and tramp up heathery mountains. A new sportsman had been born: the hillwalker. In 1891 Sir Hugh Munro produced, in the Scottish Mountaineering Club (SMC) *Journal*, a list of Scottish peaks over 3,000 feet (914 metres) high. This grew and grew to the 277 now listed in the SMC book *Munro's Tables*. Climbing the Munros soon became a popular game, with the Rev. A.E. Robertson being the first to complete the round in 1901.

The fourth person to climb the Munros was J. Rooke Corbett, who, like many, after climbing all the 3,000-feet (914 metres) peaks, looked around for another challenge. He climbed and quietly listed all the Scottish peaks over 2,500 feet (762 metres) high but under 3,000 feet (914 metres). Because of the many hundreds of mountains in this category, he decided to thin the total down by adding a proviso that all the mountains must have 500 feet (152 metres) reascent on all sides. The result is a current list of 222 mountains. Because of the ruling regarding reascent, these hills tend to sit independently from their neighbours, unlike the Munros which are restricted to the Highlands and the islands of Mull and Skye. The Corbetts, as they became known, cover practically all the mountainous areas of Scotland, including the Border and Galloway Hills, the far north and the islands of Arran, Jura, Mull, Harris, Rhum and Skye.

Perhaps as a reaction against the soft life most of us are forced to live, we feel a pull back to our hunting instincts. Alas, exercise alone is rarely sufficient incentive to set off into the wilds, often in atrocious weather. While the botanist proves his sanity searching for rare plants, and the geologist seeks unusual rocks, the would-be Munroist and Corbetter holds proudly aloft his magic list, giving him a viable excuse to explore the Scottish wilds.

Introduction

It was now dark outside, and the hut's corrugated-iron roof creaked in the wind. The fire crackled loudly as we stared into the glowing embers, hands warming after a cold day on the hills. I turned to my companion, Simon Stewart, and said, 'Simon, have you ever thought about climbing the Munros in one continuous journey?'

'Och yes,' he replied, 'but in some ways I would rather attempt the Corbetts, as they cover a more varied area and in some ways create a greater challenge.'

'What about attempting them both?' I suggested.

Simon choked and spluttered on his tea, then said, 'Them *Both*? You would be away for years!'

I groaned at the thought of returning to work the next week, then dreamed for a while. Would it really be possible? 'Where are you bound for tomorrow, Simon?' But silence answered my question, for his was the sleep of the contented mountaineer.

Simon had implanted the seed of an idea which grew and grew. By the autumn I had decided to give up my small business as a manufacturer's agent selling sports equipment, and plan the adventure of a lifetime. My spare-time hours were spent dealing with the massive logistical problem of buying and packing a year's supply of food and equipment. The biggest job was certainly planning the route. Three factors were most important:

1. To avoid difficult mountains in winter conditions.
2. To avoid sensitive areas, during the deer-stalking season from mid-August to mid-October. A book called *Access* lists most of the estates and the restricted times. These were carefully noted and put on the planning map. My route was made round these restricted areas. Only later did I find the book's listings were slightly inaccurate. This could have led to the end of the journey, but for the kindness and patience of the Highland stalkers I encountered.
3. The easier hills of Perthshire and the Trossachs to be left for the final push home.

The objective of the walk was to climb all the 276 Munros (mountains over 3,000 feet, now 914 metres) and all the 223 Corbetts (mountains over 2,500 feet, now 762 metres, but under 3,000 feet). The total of 499 mountains were to be climbed in one continuous self-propelled journey. I would walk or cycle everywhere, no other form of transport would be allowed, except ferries between the mainland and the various islands. In the course of the walk, however, one Corbett, Cook's Cairn, was deducted from the official tables as it did not have the required 500 feet reascent on all sides. This reduced the total number of mountains to 498.

People of all shapes and sizes and from all backgrounds come on foot and ski, by cycle and canoe, to explore the Scottish hills. Those who come are rarely just hillwalkers with the blinkered objective of the summit in sight. For the mountains have rich treasures in flora and fauna, wildlife and rocks. As well as the delight of climbing the mountains there is a lifetime of exploration waiting in the maze of tracks that criss-cross the wilds, giving an inexhaustible supply of walks from a short day to one of a month's duration.

When I walk over the hills, my eyes are drawn to the glens below, where the ruined buildings remind me of the people who once lived among the now empty hills. I think of their happy days among the summer shielings, and the excitement as the fiery cross was sent round the glens to gather the clansmen, eager to prove their bravery in the forthcoming cattle raid.

The mountains we love to climb have been there longer than any historian can record. The rocky peaks sat silently while raiding Viking galleys explored the lochs at their feet. The hills stood mute as warring clans battled in their corries and whisky smugglers sneaked through the glens. Their caves became homes for wanted men like Bonnie Prince Charlie, who hid while thousands of Redcoats searched in vain below. Our mountains have seen things that man has long forgotten. All we are left with is a hint of a clue in a Gaelic name, which gives us an inkling of what may have happened in that wild and lonely spot.

This is how I see the mountains. So put an eagle feather in your bonnet, pick up your broadsword and targe, leave your dingy offices and factories behind and let this young MacGregor lead you on a yearlong adventure on the Scottish mountains!

Map 1 Scotland's major mountain regions

CHAPTER 1

February and March 1985

A Border raid

—

Over the hills to Gallowa'

—

Arran's peaks

—

Cowal

—

Always Argyll: Glen Fyne

—

Arrochar Alps

—

Jura

—

The Outer Hebrides

—

Inverpolly Nature Reserve

—

Assynt

A BORDER RAID, 16–18 FEBRUARY 1985

My father Tom drove south towards the snow-covered hills of the Southern Uplands. The tenements of Glasgow were far from our thoughts as the car purred along the road skirting the Talla Reservoir, whose still waters reflected the snowy hills above. The wheels slipped on an icy patch, then lurched forward to arrive at the Megget Stone, which marks the top of the pass between Tweedsmuir and St Mary's Loch. We were now in the heart of the Border Fells, and my adventure was fittingly about to begin in what had once been Scotland's front line. For 'The Marches', as the Borders were called, was once wild bandit country, forsaken by the Scottish monarchy, who could not control either the unruly Border reivers in their raids into England or the bitter feuds among themselves.

I took my bicycle out of the boot and laid it against the sign marking the district boundary. Little did I know that my last car journey was over for what was to be a year and two weeks. A lump filled my throat as Tom's car spluttered into life and drove off back to Glasgow, my father's hand waving from the window. I thought back to last night's farewell party and my friends' good luck wishes. It all seemed like a dream now as the stark reality of this mountain walk hit me. My mind was exhausted after the months of planning and training, and it was good at last to set foot on the hills. Although the dream was to climb all the 499 Scottish peaks over 2,500 feet high in one continuous self-propelled journey, today this seemed an intangible fantasy. For how could I, whose longest marathon walk had been limited to a few three-week-long treks, attempt an expedition which was planned to take just under a year? He who had worn his snow gaiters upside-down on his first winter outing on the hills was now about to spend a winter alone on the Scottish mountains.

A district boundary fence led up the hillside to the first of the 499 mountains I was to climb. It was good to start with an easy hill, Broad Law, 840 metres, the first of seven Corbetts in the

3

Southern Uplands. Spring usually comes early to these hills, so my plan was to concentrate on these peaks, island-hop through the Western Isles climbing the remote peaks there, then arrive in the far north of Scotland in late March, just in time for the coming of spring. However, this was to be a year which was to pay no respect to the calendar months' usual weather habits.

The sun shone benevolently for me as I crossed the snowy moorland. Grass and heather sprang out of the surrounding snow patches in blissful optimism that spring would soon be here. I felt the same way. The maze of partially snow-covered sheep tracks led like plough furrows towards the summit, as mountain hares hopped unconcernedly into the distance. Nearing the top, I tapped the posts of the district boundary fence with my ice axe, so that the ice wings formed by the wind crashed to the ground. On the summit is a radio beacon station. Some hills have to put up with these ugly intrusions, but this is nothing new to them, as the several Roman hill-top signal stations in the Borders bear witness.

Broad Law is the second highest mountain in the Southern Uplands, beaten by The Merrick by only 3 metres. She is however, the highest of the Manor Hills which offer easy, gentle hillwalking and in winter good cross-country skiing. To the north lay the Pentland Hills with Edinburgh beyond. But my eyes searched further north where my year-long adventure beckoned. There was a purging of Corbetts in this area when the maps were resurveyed before metrification, and sadly this mountain's shapely neighbour, Cramalt Craig, was struck off the list. The mountain makes an enjoyable horseshoe route with this peak, and gives a fine view down the Ettrick Valley. A line of fox tracks crossed my path as I jogged downhill over the springy turf. An icy wind was blowing from tomorrow's challenge, the snowy Moffat Hills.

It was exhilarating to be cycling down the steep hill towards Talla Reservoir, keeping an eye open for icy patches. It took some time to get used to the bike's heavy load of food and camping equipment. I was soon passed by an Edinburgh cycling club on their sleek machines.

> O, young Lochinvar is come out of the west,
> Through all the wide Border his steed was the best.
> Sir Walter Scott

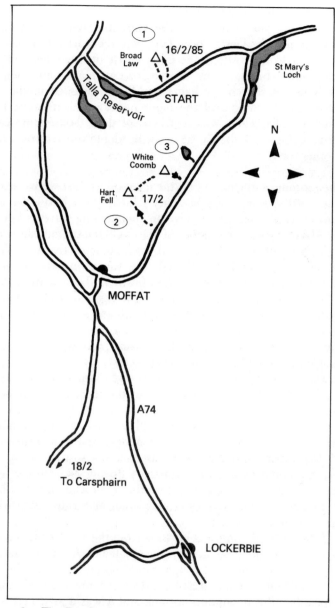

Map 2   The Borders

(Even if his chain did rattle a bit.)

Darkness was falling by the time the tent was pitched. Opposite lay the Devil's Beef Tub, where Border reivers used to hide their stolen cattle in the misty corrie of Annanhead Hill. It was grand to be snug in my sleeping bag, with a hot mug of tea in my hand, as the cheery lights of Moffat gleamed in the glen below. In the middle of the night I woke to hear some large animals walking by. Was it a herd of deer? Some stray cattle perhaps? Or was it the ghosts of the Border reivers returning from another fray?

The morning sun glittered on the icy road as the bike worked its way north-east towards St Mary's Loch. Two busy shepherds hard at work took time to give an encouraging wave as I cycled by. Above lay the scree slopes of Hart Fell, the summit showing a white band of snow. It was hard work climbing the steep slopes behind Capplegill Farm, though the sun shone kindly as the rabbits scurried in and out of their burrows. The summit plateau gave a magnificent view of the snow-covered, rolling hills of south-east Scotland. Farmers grow crops and graze their livestock on the Border hills — a shining example of what the Highlands could have been like had not the barbaric landowners cleared the people from their land in favour of sheep.

The A74 could be seen snaking its way south to the Solway. At nearby Lockerbie was fought one of the most ferocious of the Border feuds. Here the Johnstones, outnumbered five to one, were attacked by the Maxwells with 2,000 cavalry. Cunningly, the Johnstones lured them into an ambush and routed them. On 21 December 1988 the town was to know sorrow again, as a terrorist bomb blew up an American Boeing 747 airliner flying overhead, sending it crashing into the town, claiming 270 lives, all innocent victims cowardly murdered for a cause with which they had no connection.

A strong cold wind was blowing from the east, sending a mist of spindrift floating across the plateau. A storm seemed imminent. Four miles of rough moorland lay ahead to the next summit, White Coomb. If a blizzard started now it would make it impossible. But it came to nothing and it was a joy to cross the crisp, white wilderness. The plateau seemed alive with mountain hares, hardy creatures carving a life from the wilderness while avoiding the sportsman's gun and the foxes' clutch. Like snowy sand dunes the hills stretched endlessly to the north, quiet, lonely hills to wander through with only the sheep for company. White Coomb is one of the most dramatic hills in this part of the country. Loch Skeen nestles in her wild western corrie, spouting forth the waters that cascade down the Tail Burn into one of Scotland's most dramatic waterfalls, The Grey Mare's Tail, a sight well worth seeing. The falls have been ice-climbed by some hardy individuals, but a particularly cold winter is required to freeze the waterfall to a climbable condition. With darkness falling I crept down the mountain and was soon whizzing back to a warming meal at the tent.

It was a cold frosty morning and freezing mist clung to the glens. I was glad of my warm Gore-Tex-lined mitts as I started the 56-mile cycle west to Carsphairn in the Galloway Hills. My training programme had been biased towards long-distance walking. I had done no cycling whatsoever, so I was glad my leg muscles were coping with the bike's heavy load. At the village of Balmaclellan it was good to take a break and thaw out my frozen moustache. This village was once home to Elspeth McEwan, who was burnt at the stake for allegedly being a witch. King James VI of Scotland was obsessed with stamping out witchcraft. As a result, over 4,000 old women, for the most part innocent, were tortured and burnt at the stake during his reign. Scotland was second only to Germany in her brutal treatment of suspected witches.

The bleak weather continued until at last the cheery lights of the village of Carsphairn could be seen in the distance. A food parcel and a welcome were waiting at the Salutation Hotel. As icy rain fell outside it was good to enjoy a warming dram by the bar's roaring fire.

OVER THE HILLS TO GALLOWA'

> Oh the Gallowa' hills are covered wi' broom
> And heather bells in bonny bloom,
> Wi' heather bells and rivers a'
> I'll tak it o'er the hills tae Gallowa'.

Cold sleet stung my eyes as I walked out of Carsphairn next morning. A snow-covered Land Rover track led up past the Green Well of Scotland, an ancient healing well. Ahead, somewhere through the swirling snowstorm, was Cairnsmore of Carsphairn, 797 metres, highest of the lonely hills of the Carsphairn Forest. The mountain is rich in minerals, for geologists have found precious metals on her barren eastern slopes. The hills to the north-east rise from a sea of forestry, offering all sorts of interesting long-distance routes over these small mountains or through the glens. Visibility was reduced to a few feet as I climbed the mountain's bleak snowy slopes, the hook-shaped ridge curving slowly to the summit. Head-down against the biting wind racing over the ridge, I suddenly realised I was descending. Only after double-checking my bearing did I realise I had walked past the trig point that marks the top of the mountain.

Nearby was a handy wall that gave some shelter from the driving wind and snow. Luckily the wall was exactly in line with my bearing down to the glen. The spindrift towered twenty feet high around me. Some fresh fox tracks crossed my route ahead in a perfect line. Foxes are very active at this time of year as it is the mating season.

Carsphairn is steeped in Covenanting history. The hills are full of cairns commemorating Covenanters who died for the freedom to worship as they pleased. As they dared not worship in church, for fear of their lives, they held services called Coventicles on the moors. Often the sound of curlews and lapwings would betray their hiding place to the Dragoons hunting them. If nothing else, it kept the sermons short!

It was a cold morning, and freezing mist clung to my Dachstein mitts as the bike worked its way south down Glen Ken towards Forrest Lodge. Roe deer scuttled across the road then disappeared into the mist in seconds. Near the lodge stands a figurehead of a Black Watch officer, which once stood on the bows of a now sunken Fred Olsen liner. It was salvaged from the depths and returned to a drier existence at the lodge.

A forestry road led through the blanket of mist that clung to the woodland. After a couple of miles I was still in a sea of fog when a path branched off, weaving between young trees, as it climbed uphill. Suddenly I broke through the mist to a bright

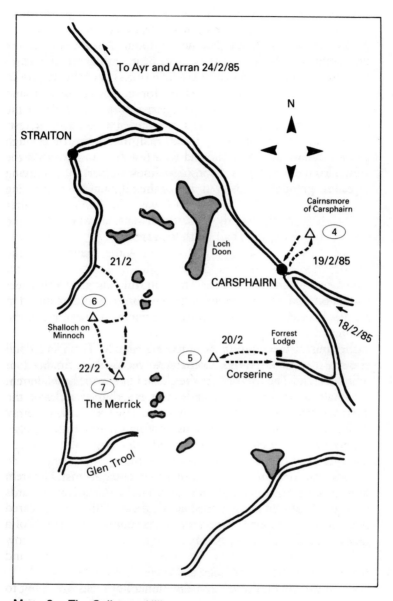

Map 3   The Galloway Hills

exciting world, leaving the fog below to shroud the glens. Ahead lay Corserine, to my mind the most beautiful of the Galloway peaks, her snowy slopes gleaming in the morning sunlight. The mountain is the highest point of an eight-mile ridge running north from Clatteringshaws Loch to Loch Doon. This enchanting ridge is known as the Rhinns of Kells. A gentle, if rock-strewn, slope led to the table-top summit of Corserine. Near by lies the neighbouring summit, Carlins Cairn, marked by a cairn built in memory of Robert the Bruce. I nestled down by the trig point in the warm sun, ate some chocolate and took in the breathtaking views. To the west lay the heart of roughest Galloway. This area's awesome grandeur rivals even that of the Highlands.

> Whilst o'er those Catcliffs where they lie,
> The wolf shall snarl, the eagle cry.
>   Sir Walter Scott

The Government planned to use these hills as a nuclear-waste dump, but thankfully public outcry put a stop to their plans. With names like Mullwharchar and Loch Enoch, these are not the gentle hills portrayed in the novel *The Thirty-Nine Steps*, but rather mirror the ruggedness of the Highlands. Towering above the sea of mist lay future Corbetts to be climbed: Shalloch on Minnoch and The Merrick. My eagle's-eye view of the wilderness of small rocky mountains and strangely shaped lochans was spectacular. But I shuddered when my eyes fixed on Loch Neldricken, with its murder hole at the western end. Once, a family living in a cottage there would offer hospitality to weary travellers and pedlars, murder them for their goods, weight their bodies and lower them into the murder hole. A least fifty such killings were said to have been carried out by the family.

The mist stayed in the glens below all day. This had one drawback: when I climbed down from Corserine to the misty forest below, I couldn't find my bike!

It was a bright sunny morning as I cycled north-west towards the pretty village of Straiton, a conservation village and which boasts spotless streets and white-washed cottages, whose window-boxes blossom delightfully in the warmer months. A minor road leading to Glen Trool took me south, and the bike was soon struggling on the steep pass leading to Stinchar Bridge. The ruins of Craiglure Lodge were an ideal place to leave the bike, and all the necessary kit for an overnight stay in the hills was transferred to my pack.

A pleasant path led towards Cornish Loch, where greylag geese were enjoying a break during their long journey north. The path south-east of the loch, shown clearly on the old maps, quickly gets lost in the forest, and eventually I was floundering in the woodland. Perhaps the Roman legion believed to have dis-appeared in the Galloway Hills also had my map. The mystery of the lost legion has puzzled historians for centuries. Imagine 10,000 legionnaires wandering through these wild lands when suddenly, flowing over the mountain tops, came a sea of wild Galloway tribesmen. Clad in deer and goat skins, wielding swords and spears, they crashed into the unprepared ranks, leaving none alive to tell the tale. That at least is the Scots' theory. There is another: that they found a good pub and decided to desert. Certainly the abundance of Italian cafés down the Ayrshire coast would tend to support the idea.

At last I hit a Land Rover track, leading from Balloch Beatties, the sensible approach to this part of Galloway, unless you're in training for a future trip to the Indonesian jungle. Tunskeen bothy was deserted. It was the first of its type to be renovated by the Mountain Bothy Association, whose members are a dedicated band of enthusiasts who maintain simple, unlocked shelters in remote country for the use of all who venture there. They are maintained by the people who use them, and are left open with the owner's permission. Therefore good relations are important: they should be kept tidy, and those in deer-stalking areas should be avoided during the stalking season, usually from mid-August to mid-October. The bothy had one room, although the cottage was once bigger. There was an amusing entry in the visitors' book from two soldiers taking part in an army exercise. They had been ordered to stay overnight in the bothy, pretending to be prisoners of war. They were not allowed to go beyond fifty yards from the hut and were assured that the following day they would be rescued by friendly forces. Unfortunately this did not happen for a further twelve days, by which time their comments in the visitors' book were getting very rude indeed!

Snuggling down in my sleeping bag, I felt an air of content-ment as the candle flickered in the draught. The trip was going well. Apart from the wild day on Cairnsmore the weather had been kind, and so far the bike was taking the strain. But there was still a long, long way to go.

It was exciting to be starting off from a remote bothy and to weave through the mist to the Nick of Carclach which, like a siege machine, breaches the long ridge forming the west flank of the Galloway Hills. Known as 'the Awful Hand', its northern peaks form the fingers while to the south the thumb and hand form this area's showpiece mountain, The Merrick.

There are two Corbetts in the range. A bearing led me through the mist easily to the first of these, Shalloch on Minnoch, which rises like a pyramid from the ocean of trees around her. At the foot of her south-eastern crags is a flat rock, once used by the Covenanters to hold services. It is significant that they were forced to use one of the remotest parts of the Galloway Hills for worship, in order to be free from the sabres of Graham of Claverhouse and his murderous Dragoons. I spent some time searching for the top and found three separate cairns before reaching the trig point. There was no view today, which was a pity as I was on top of the highest hill in Ayrshire.

Wind and rain buffeted the rocky hillside as I skirted over Kirriereoch Hill, which until recently was a Corbett, and on towards The Merrick, meaning 'the Branched Finger'. The mountain's black Gairey Corrie looked impressive in the stern dark winter mood of today's hills. I was glad of my ice axe on the climb up her frozen northern ridge, keeping well clear of her steep eastern side which plummets to the cauldron burn below. At the huge cairn that marks the summit I met a father and son who had camped the previous night in pretty Glen Trool, a favourite base for these hills. Forestry there has swallowed up what little remains of the 'Deil's Dyke', a strange fortified wall, built from Dumfries to Stranraer, believed to have been constructed by Galloway tribesmen to keep out their enemies invading from Strathclyde.

It was disappointing to have been cheated of a view down to Loch Trool, one of the most scenic spots in the Southern Uplands. It was in 1307 that 2,000 English and Border troops were walking in single file along her peaceful shores when suddenly the silence was broken by the strange blowing of horns and rumbling of rocks, as Robert the Bruce's tiny 200-man army sent boulders rolling down the hillside on to their enemies. The clansmen soon followed with their fearsome swords. Believing their foes to be far more numerous, the invading army retreated, leaving many dead behind.

Although Galloway has some fine mountains she has much more than that to offer, with many paths creeping out of the forestry either to cross the wild moorland or visit a strangely named loch: there is something for everyone. Burns turn into 'lanes', the name given to rivers in this area, and it was the Tunskeen Lane that led me back to the bothy. It was a very cold night. My efforts at lighting a fire were limited, as smoke gushed out of the holes in the chimney, sending me dashing outside choking for breath. Later it was grand to be cosy in my sleeping bag, as the cold wind roared outside, rattling the bothy's corrugated iron roof.

It had snowed overnight. I cycled back to Straiton and on to Ardrossan, the busy ferry port for the Isle of Arran. As the *Glen Sannox's* engines shuddered into life, it was refreshing to stand on the bow while she ploughed through the waves. Ahead, looking dark and forbidding in the mist and rain, lay Arran, 'the High Island'. The four Corbetts I had come to climb lay well hidden under nature's misty cloak. On landing you could sense the difference: gone was the rush and bustle of the mainland. Despite being less than fifty miles from Glasgow, here was an atmosphere of Hebridean calm.

One of the first persons I met was an old friend, Gavin Bell, who invited me to his farm. It was fun next day to help him worm his sheep, while the goats looked out suspiciously from the byre. Gavin has an unusual selection of sheepdogs. Jaff, the undisputed leader, delights in chasing the horse and biting his tail. Then there is Brae, who must rank as the world's keenest sheepdog. She reckoned it was her duty to gather not only the sheep but the cats and goats as well. Gavin's spaniel Jake tried to be helpful and fit into this strange life, but really excelled only at digging for rabbits. We had spent about an hour gathering all the flock together when Jake suddenly saw a hare and charged. His route unfortunately went straight through the sheep, who scattered in panic, with Gavin muttering angrily in the background.

It was still dark when I left Gavin's farm, the moonlight sweeping across his land to the hillock lying south. It is not everyone who can boast of having a Pictish hill fort in his back garden. With the first successful week of the walk completed, I was raring to go. In past marathon walks, I have found the first week to be crucial, for that is when any unsuspected problems are ironed out. The bike's dynamo buzzed as I whizzed through the sleepy main street of Brodick; the island's highest mountain, Goat Fell, drew me like a magnet. A light covering of morning mist soon evaporated as I pulled up the fine tourist track from behind Brodick Castle. Goat Fell derives from *Geita Fjek*, named by the Vikings who once had a stronghold there. An easy two and a quarter hours led to the top. Sitting near the trig point was a viewfinder, pointing to the panoramic view of the Arran ridges with Kintyre and the Argyll mountains to the north. You can usually see the Arran hills from most mountains in south Argyll, so it was a pleasant change to turn the tables.

The dramatic granite mountains of Arran rival even the Cuillins of Skye. Only six miles separate the four highest peaks on the island, but they offer some of the finest ridge-walking and scrambling in the country. Only on parts of the A'Chir ridge and Ceum na Caillich, 'the Witch's Step', does the scrambling become more testing and then the adrenalin flows.

The sea stretched out like a sheet of glass, the water ruffled only by a container ship sailing on her long journey home to the Clyde. Arran was in a peaceful mood today, though she has a violent past. The Lord of the Isles sailed here and his men ravaged the Island.

> Mackinnon's chief in warfare grey,
> Had charge to muster their array,
> And guide their barks to Brodick bay.
> Sir Walter Scott

Later the English and the Campbells were to take over.

A series of playful rocky towers led over North Goat Fell, and crept respectfully above Coire nam Fuaran, meaning 'the Corrie of the Spring'. It was here one fine summer's day in 1889 that John Laurie murdered his companion, Edwin Rose. What followed was a manhunt through the country which led to the

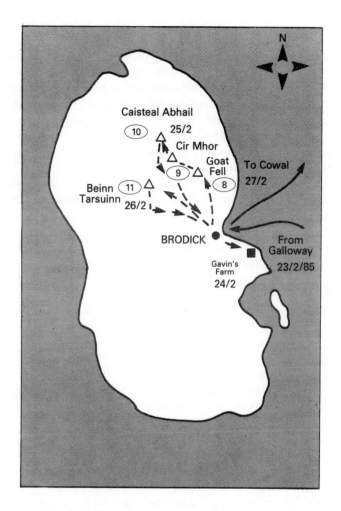

Map 4   The Isle of Arran

murderer's eventual capture. At his trial he was found insane and locked away for forty-one years. Strangely, to the day he died he proclaimed his innocence, and took to his grave the macabre secret of what really happened that summer's day.

I was soon bounding up the grassy scree slopes of Cir Mhor, 'the Great Comb'. It has a beautifully pointed summit and some breathtaking cliffs on the north face. A gentle ridge led north to Caisteal Abhail, meaning 'the Ptarmigan's Castle', which was well garrisoned by those hardy birds today. The top has several summit tors, the central one being the highest. To the west lie Arran's western hills, Beinn Bharrain and Beinn Bhreac, beautiful wild tiny mountains you are almost assured of having to yourself.

With darkness creeping in there wasn't time to push on over the A'Chir ridge for Beinn Tarsuinn, the last of the island's four mountains to be climbed. I crossed over Cir Mhor's shoulder once more and descended to Glen Rosa. A welcoming light drew me towards Gavin's croft. Soon I heard a well-known voice, a friendly bark, and smelt the appetising aroma of mince and tatties cooking on the stove.

Early morning found me back in Glen Rosa as the mist clung to the jagged mountains and the cheerful sun lit up the short green grass by the camp site. The rock-strewn heathery slopes of Beinn a'Chliabhain tested temper and patience, but it was well worth it, as I was treated to an eagle's-eye view of a huge herd of deer grazing below in Coire a'Bhradain. The magical Isle of Arran is really Scotland in miniature, though only about twenty miles long and ten wide. As the old Scots used to say: 'Guid things go intae small bulk.' And good things there certainly are, for apart from her spectacular mountains she has interesting glens to explore and hill lochs to fish. Small wonder it was a favourite hunting ground for the legendary King Fionn. To the south of the island are several chambered cairns which have been excavated. Arrow heads, flints and human remains have been found, reminding us that man has lived here for almost 10,000 years.

From the rim of Coire Daingean I admired the saw-blade-like A'Chir ridge before a blanket of mist obscured it from view. With compass in hand I pushed on up the mountain's steep northern slopes and was soon enjoying the game of 'find the summit cairn'. Finally it was located and Beinn Tarsuinn, the last of the Arran peaks conquered. The ridge led south to Beinn Nuis, where it was a pleasant surprise to pick up a path leading down to join the trunk road track in Glen Rosa. Islands, especially mountainous ones, always seem to interest people. Arran is a very special island — the Hebrides scaled down.

Cowal, 27–28 February

Sad though it was to be leaving Arran's friendly shores, new adventures in Argyll lay ahead. It was strange to be cycling up the busy coastal road towards Greenock as lorries with stinking exhaust fumes squeezed by. I caught another ferry, this time to Dunoon, a holiday town nestling among the foothills of the wild Argyll mountains.

I was away early, as dawn broke over narrow Loch Eck. Curiously a green car lay floating on the water. It belonged to a local man who, returning from a recent *ceilidh*, had misjudged a corner and driven into the loch ... now known locally as 'Donald's car wash'. At Invernoaden I took the steep forestry track up the north side of Allt Audainn, the smell of pines lingering in the air. Ahead lay pretty Beinn Bheula, the only Corbett in the Cowal peninsula. Never have I seen grass look so golden as it did that day in the warm spring sunshine when I pushed up the gentle slopes into Coire Audainn, disturbing a sleepy adder sunbathing on a boulder.

The bonny lands of Cowal were once the stronghold of Clan Lamont, known as 'the Law makers'. Eventually the Campbells overwhelmed their kingdom. The beleagured Lamonts made a last-ditch stand at Dunoon Castle, but eventually were tempted to surrender, on condition that they would be well treated. The Campbells disarmed them, then murdered the entire garrison of 200 men.

A short two-hour climb led to the pillar trig point that marks the top. Before my eyes was the beautiful Ardgoil peninsula, a wild tract of small mountains known strangely as Argyll's bowling green. Piercing this landscape are the sea lochs of Loch Long and Loch Goil, once a familiar haunt of raiding Viking longships ... now Royal Naval submarines plough the waves. Beinn Bheula is the highest point of the long twelve-mile ridge, extending from Creachan Mor, overlooking Loch Long, till it plummets to the dramatically named 'Hell's Glen' to the north. She boasts a fine corrie, and wild crags known as Caisteal Dubh, meaning 'the Black Castle'. The mountain's wildness is probably best appreciated from Loch Goil-side. A visit to the remote Curra Lochain is a pleasure since it has a real 'Lost World' feel to it, as its waterfalls cascade down to the Lettermay Burn. There are the

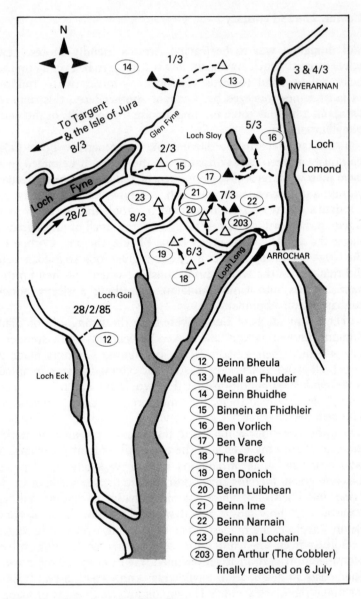

Map 5   Arrochar and Glen Fyne

sad remnants of a crashed aircraft nearby, and the SMC (Scottish Mountaineering Club) guide tells of some caves on the north-west crags of Carnach Mor. As with so many mountains, there is much more to do than just climb to the top.

Seagulls swooped on a fishing boat as I cycled north to the top of Loch Fyne. I camped beyond Glen Fyne Lodge, passing the dramatic gorge known as Eagle's Fell on the way. The tent was pitched just as the winter darkness fell. My nylon home was a Vango Zephyr solo, weighing just 3 lb. It packed neatly into the bulk of a couple of sugar bags. It was smaller inside than I would have liked, but was ideal for my nomadic existence, where accommodation varied from caves to youth hostels and bothies.

After a glorious feed I read myself to sleep by candlelight. *The Great Escape* was, I thought, a rather apt title in my present situation. There was not a sound in the glen except for the river flowing gently beside the tent. I wondered what the wildlife in the glen would be doing tonight. Would the foxes be out on the hunt for a careless mountain hare? Would the wild cat be sheltering in his rocky cave, or making the most of the now ever-shortening winter nights and be out stalking his prey? These were my thoughts as the last night of February came to a peaceful close.

ALWAYS ARGYLL: GLEN FYNE, 1–4 MARCH

The tent shook violently as, outside, sleet and icy cold winds raked the glen, while inside the stove roared with an early morning brew-up. A tarmac road led to the Lairgh reservoir, launching pad for Meall an Fhudair, my 13th hill of the walk — all Corbetts so far. With rock and heather underfoot, I climbed higher into the mist while, below, the white waves of the reservoir crashed over the dam. A grouse sprang from my feet, cackling loudly.

A feature of the Corbetts is that their summits often have bumpy knolls, each little hillock having a tiny cairn — a test of your compass work and patience. This mountain, wild and so remote in the worsening weather, ran to type. Battling head-down against the wind, I found the correct cairn at last and placed my card among the rocks, as the wind howled round the snowy summit.

All was white and blurred, till eventually the reservoir came into sight. I enjoyed cycling down the steep hill past the tent, then further up Glen Fyne for an assault on lonely Beinn Bhuidhe, the first Munro of the trip. It was an intriguing coincidence, for Martin Moran — the first person to climb the Munros in winter in one trip (using a motorised caravenette as a mobile bothy) — combined Ben Lomond with Beinn Bhuidhe for his first day.

My route from Glen Fyne is one of the quickest ways to climb this solitary, whaleback-shaped Munro. The Inverchorachan burn roared angrily, and a fierce snowstorm soon blanked out the view. A maze of snow-covered boulders slowed my progress considerably.

On the summit ridge, winter was at war. I knelt and took a bearing, as my goggles became covered in snow and my face cringed painfully against the storm. Head-down, I battled southeast, expecting every snowy bump to be the summit, but alas, it wasn't. Mountains humble a man. My progress slowed to a crawl. It was with relief and a sense of triumph that I finally leant up and touched the trig point. It was comforting to be in the lee of the wind, though my ears still hummed.

At last, snow underfoot gave way to heather and grass, and as I returned to the normal world, Glen Fyne appeared out of the mist.

A storm had passed through in the night: twigs and branches were strewn across the road. The sleeping bag dried over a stone bridge while the tea brewed. I was soon whizzing down Glen Fyne on my bike, first passing the remnants of an ancient hill fort, then the Cairndow Inn, whose distinguished guests in the past have included Keats and Wordsworth.

Binnein an Fhidhleir, 817 metres, was today's challenge. Her steep slopes guard the north of Glen Kinglas. A steep three-quarters of a mile pull took me to the long summit range. Despite this mountain's steep southern slopes, her northern ones are just the opposite. It is almost as if nature had used up all her energy. To the north, gentle barren slopes stretch for four miles before plummeting to Glen Fyne. The misty curtain unveiled to give a brief glimpse of the Arrochar Alps and Ben Lui beyond, all in their winter coats. The Ordnance Survey plays a cruel game with this mountain. Having reached the trig point — my 15th hill of the trip — I studied the map and realised the actual summit was 6 metres higher, a mile further east of the trig point. It took an age to get there through the thick mist. The pointed summit towers above Butterbridge where Glen Kinglas takes a left turn on its long journey to Loch Sloy.

What a disappointment it was not to be able to see further up Glen Kinglas, for here lie some wild crags opposite the ruin, with a name that aptly describes the glen: Abyssinia. The cars in the glen below looked like beetles as they scurried along.

In contrast, the bike slowly made its way over this 'Pass of the Black Waterfall' to Arrochar. There, Tom — head of the super-efficient support team — relieved me of heavy cycle bags. Without them, the bike fair raced to Inverarnan Hotel, at the head of Loch Lomond. This is a genuine Highland clachan, built in the heart of MacGregor country. There's a friendly, comfortable bar, where they don't mind your dog, nor boots drying by the fire. Duncan MacGregor, the landlord, and his friendly family and staff looked after us royally.

Rest days came as something of a shock to the system. Far from being restful, they became a frantic race of planning, packing and dealing with the mail. It was a relief to get back to the hills!

ARROCHAR ALPS, 5–9 MARCH

A wild storm had blown through, leaving behind a morning of peace and sunshine. I was like a caged lion, itching to get up the two Munros planned for today. Saying goodbye to Daisy, the cook, I took my bike out of the side door. As I yanked it open, part of the ceiling collapsed, covering me in plaster. I apologised to Daisy, who simply said, 'Och, don't worry, Craig. That's always happening!'

At Inveruglas, I had to lift the bike over the locked gate, then hid my pannier bags in some bracken before cycling up the hill to Loch Sloy dam, which provides the water for the Inveruglas power station. Plans to build a similar dam recently at Craig Rostan, on the east shore of Loch Lomond, were thankfully defeated following a public outcry led by The Friends of Loch Lomond Society and Tom Weir.

The steep slopes of Ben Vorlich were a glorious mixture of russet bracken, golden grass and large boulders. Climbing higher, I could see over the dam. Loch Sloy can be very wild at times; the wind roars down it like a wind tunnel. Behind it lay a lonely wilderness of mountains and lochans. The MacFarlanes took the loch's name as their battle cry, aptly reflecting that wild clan of cattle-thieving fame. Ben Vorlich is a huge mountain and can give a full day if climbed from Loch Lomond-side. But the Loch Sloy route is, if less scenic, best for combining Vorlich with her sister mountain, Ben Vane. At 943 metres, Vorlich has several deep fissures in the crags and boulders high above the dam, some suitable as rough overnight shelters. She is the most northerly of the Arrochar Alps, as my next group of hills are called.

I had the mountain to myself. Only a raven cawed from the misty corrie below the bumpy ridge that led to the summit. Alas, the mist rolled in to obscure my view. It was 3 p.m. by the time I was back at the dam. It would be a frantic rush to climb Ben Vane before darkness fell. I pushed up her slopes and jogged through the flat plateau halfway up her northern slopes, a place of little lochans and peat hags. Here I got my first good ice-axe work of the trip, cutting steps up the steep slopes to the summit ridge. In the fading daylight of a winter's afternoon, I was treated to the magnificent sight of the northern corries of the Arrochar Alps.

Ben Lomond was sitting proudly, just managing to keep its head under the clouds. This was planned to be the last mountain of my trip, though it would be almost a year before I would climb it.

Darkness fell as the bike tackled the bends of the Loch Lomond road. The normally busy Ardgartan Youth Hostel had only a few 'gangrels' as guests. We gathered round the fire as dark clouds gathered over the Arrochar Alps.

The mist was well below the treeline. A miserable downpour of rain soaked everything in minutes. The path ahead disappeared into a jungle of fallen timber. Through the mist lay The Brack, a fine Corbett whose northern crags fall steeply to Glen Croe. There, near the forest, lies a rough natural shelter among the boulders called The Cobbler View. A confusing, bumpy plateau eventually rose steeply, testing navigational skills in the thick mist.

The rain poured down the final steep slopes that led to the summit. A long ridge down took me to the col of Ben Donich (847 metres). A hill fox jumped from his soaking cover and, with a cheeky grin, disappeared into the mist. Both these mountains tend to be forgotten, since most hillwalkers head off, with mounting anticipation, for their higher and more accessible neighbours. This is unfortunate for they are well worth the effort. I recalled a school trip to climb Donich. At the summit I told a prefect that I had snow in my boots, and what should I do? He advised me thus: 'Oh, just pour coffee down the back of your boot — that'll sort it out.' I did as he said, thinking that hillwalkers must be a pretty crazy bunch ...

The best way to climb Ben Donich is from the Rest and Be Thankful at the top end of Glen Croe. Here a gentle ridge leads to the summit with fine views into Ben Donich's wild northern slopes, strewn with crags and boulders. The path down into Glen Croe is delightful, and with the rain easing it was a pleasant walk back to the youth hostel after an exhilarating day in the wilds of Argyll.

High above, the sunlight danced on the snow patches of the Arrochar Alps. The next day's bright weather rejuvenated body and mind, as I planned a horseshoe of the fine peaks above. One and a half hours took me up the long, grassy slopes to the top of Beinn Luibhean (857 metres), where I was treated to a spectacular view of Beinn an Lochain. For once, she was clear of mist and standing guard over the Rest and Be Thankful pass. That was for tomorrow. Today felt like a holiday, as snow patches melted in the sunshine. Ptarmigan, caught out of their winter coats, scurried for cover. A raven was sitting on the cairn at Beinn Ime. Ravens are common in the area. At times, you can have a conversation with them, as they reply to your deep caws. The mountain is said to be haunted by the ghost of a man in a tweed jacket, carrying a parcel.

The eastern ridge offers a more sporting route up this splendid mountain. My next Munro, Beinn Narnain, is easily climbed from Bealach a'Mhaim. How grand to take in the spectacular views and enjoy a feast at the summit. Climbing from Arrochar to Narnain in the mist can be quite a shock close to the summit: the Spearhead Buttress blocks your way, but by going round its south-western side all problems are avoided.

I descended to the bealach (pass) and headed up Ben Arthur, The Cobbler — so called because its three rocky peaks resemble an old man working on a last. On the summit there is a pleasant scramble on to a large block of rock. You can go through a hole in the rock, along a ledge, and scramble easily to the top. Unfortunately my way was barred: the exposed summit was coated with ice and my crampons were back at base. Although only a couple of feet from the summit I turned back. It just wasn't worth risking an injury at this stage of the trip, so I left it till July, when I would be at Inverarnan again. Feeling angry and despondent, I worked my way down to Glen Croe. But one couldn't stay in that mood for long, not with the fine weather and prospects of adventures in the Western Isles ahead.

Fitness was now at a high level as the bike, despite its heavy load, glided up Glen Croe to the Rest and Be Thankful, summit of the pass. Below me, the old road twisted and turned its way in a more tortuous manner; rally drivers are its only users now. High in the mist, towering above the top of the pass, was the sad mountain of Beinn an Lochain, the mountain nobody wanted. The Ordnance Survey couldn't make up its mind about its height. It has been demoted to Corbett countless times, only to be promoted to Munro. Now it lies firmly in the ranks of Corbett, listed at 901 metres. It's a fine mountain, with steep, western-facing crags that plummet towards Loch Restil. A long ridge leading up from Butterbridge offers some spectacular walking and scrambling.

The steep, misty slopes grew alarmingly steeper, and I was soon messing about in a rocky gully. A rush of wind flowed down it like a wind tunnel. With my adrenalin flowing, it was a surprise to arrive on a gentle ridge leading over several bumps to the summit.

A hard cycle ride of some 55 miles lay ahead to Tarbert, Loch Fyne. The rain pelted down near Inveraray, with Dundarave Castle living up to author Neil Munro's description in *Castle Doom*. Sadly, time did not allow a visit to Inveraray Castle, nor the town's Commando museum. Years ago, a crofter called McPhun was hanged here for sheep-stealing. As soon as it was dusk, his wife was allowed to take her husband's body home in her boat. Then she heard him moan, and revived him with whisky and her own milk — she was pregnant at the time. He survived and, as he could not be tried for the same offence twice, he was pardoned and became known locally as Half Hung McPhun.

It was a long and weary cycle to Tarbert in the dark, but a warm welcome and a food parcel was waiting at the Victoria Hotel.

The friendly ferry chugged sleepily to life, and the prominent Paps of Jura, towering above the gleaming still waters, could soon be seen. A highly enjoyable though long journey was needed to climb Jura's only Corbett, Beinn an Oir. After catching the little connecting ferry from Islay, I jauntily cycled along the quiet, single-track road. There is only one road on the isle, known locally as the 'M1½'. Jura is shaped like a wedge, though almost cut in half by Loch Tarbert, a deep, penetrating sea loch. Her population of roughly 200 is heavily outnumbered by over 5,000 deer, several thousand goats, and countless adders.

JURA, 10–11 MARCH

The morning sunlight shone gently on my back, as the cool breeze ahead sifted through the misty mountains towering in the distance. Looking over my shoulder, I gazed at Lowlandman Bay, a magnificent natural harbour, believed to have been used by the Vikings as a dry dock.

At Loch an t-Siob, some swans were resting as the strong breeze produced whirlwinds of water across the loch. The grey scree slopes of Beinn an Oir lay ahead. The western slopes of this solitary Corbett were very rocky. Climbing up it, you wondered whether you were actually ascending, or just putting a lot of effort into staying still on the scree. Its north-east ridge from Cnoc an Oir is recommended, rather than the south-east one which I floundered up. At the top were several ruined buildings, originally put up by the Ordnance Survey in 1812 when they were conducting experiments on boiling water at altitude. They also built a useful causeway over the rocky summit, where a tin box contained a visitors' book, somewhat waterlogged.

Jura is my favourite island. Every corner has a new surprise, like fertile Glen Garrisdale, scene of a remote battle between the MacLeans and the Campbells. Nature reaches a climax at the most northerly tip of the island, where the roaring Corryvreckan whirlpool can be heard in full swing, sixty miles away.

> And verdant Ilay call'd her host,
> And the clans of Jura's rugged coast,
> Lord Ronald's call obey,
> And Scarba's Isle, whose tortured snore,
> Still rings to the Corrievrecken's roar.
>   Sir Walter Scott, *Lord of the Isles*

Sweet revenge was had on the scree slopes by running down them. Small wonder the Paps of Jura are a popular venue for a fell-running event every May. I was sad to be leaving Jura so quickly, but three days had been spent visiting and climbing her solitary Corbett. The first boat wasn't till the afternoon, so I enjoyed the locals' company in the Craighouse bar ... and subsequently almost missed the ferry!

Back on the mainland by 5 p.m., my plan was to get to Mull the next day, and I resolved to cycle north as far as possible before dark. As I was passing through Ardrishaig, a large retriever chased the bike, sank its teeth into the pannier, and almost pulled the machine over!

With the cloak of darkness firmly around, the tent was pitched, using a headtorch.

A light tailwind was a help on the long cycle north to Oban. This part of Argyll is rich in Iron Age settlements, with several standing stones and the famous burial cairns at Kilmartin. To the west lay the three remote Garvellach islands, where a reporter from the TV programme 'Nationwide' tried to survive living off the land in a wet, miserable October some years ago.

It was strange to arrive at a very busy Oban, just in time to catch the ferry to Mull. On a training walk in December, the Mull ferry had been full of people going home for Christmas ... there was even a Christmas tree outside the ticket office.

It felt good to be back on another favourite island, although the strong headwind made cycling progress slow. A rough Land Rover track led up Glen Forsa. Tomorrow's hills lay at the head

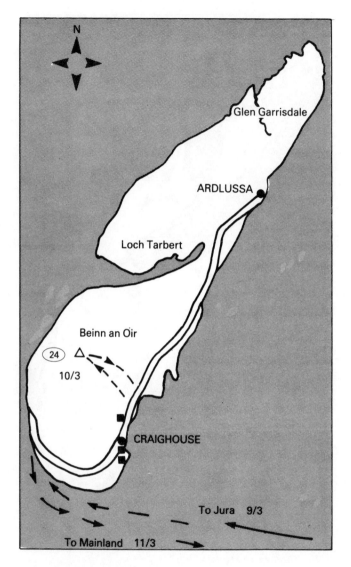

Map 6 The Isle of Jura

of the glen. I'd donned overtrousers to cycle through a deep ford, then, at the end of the track I collected wood and got a fire going as darkness cast its shadow over Mull's mountain domain.

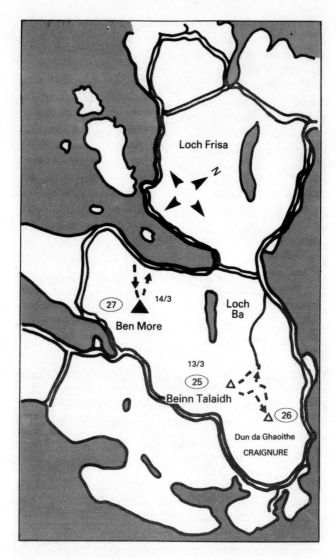

Map 7   The Isle of Mull

My footprints spoilt the virgin covering of fresh snow over the slopes of Beinn Talaidh, the first of Mull's two Corbetts. On 1 February 1945 an RAF DC3 plane crashed into the mountain. All the crew were killed.

There was a terrific view from the summit. All of Mull was spread out around me. Despite the island's short length, it has almost 300 miles of coastline, with many peninsulas.

One of the most memorable walks I ever did was to tramp around Mull's coastline in early April. Today, Ben More and her neighbouring hills looked magnificent in their new white coats. Historically, Mull largely belonged to the MacLeans, who were great warriors. Alas, their loyalty to the Stuart cause cost them their beautiful lands which were then given to the Campbells.

The mist came in, and I descended west to try and find the crashed DC3. It was in a steep gully a few hundred yards down Gleann Lean. Most of the wreckage lay covered in vegetation, though the wheels were still bright with their black rubber tyres. With the mist coming in, it was a ghostly place. I said a prayer for the unfortunate crew, and descended west down some steep slopes to Glen Forsa.

Two eagles soared above my next hill, Dun da Ghaoithe, but an electric deer fence stood in my way. I managed to cross it with difficulty, using gloves and holding a thermal jacket round one hand and a waterproof jacket round the other. Such monstrous barriers belong to the Berlin Wall, not the Highlands and Islands.

My route up the mountain was a headlong battle against a fierce sleet storm. A side wind on top blew me about like a rag doll. Dun da Ghaoithe is well-named, 'the Hillock of the Two Winds'. A huge cairn marks the top, though I was deprived of a view of Morvern today. On the way down the electric deer fence was avoided by crawling along a river bed.

In the morning the bike clanked its way down the frosty Land Rover track to Salen. There I rested and read of Martin Moran's brilliant success in climbing all the Munros in winter, supported by his wife Joy in their caravanette. The cycle ride to Loch na Keal was a blur, as blinding sleet storms raked the road. Beside me now lay the snow-covered slopes of today's conquest, Ben More — Mull's only Munro. Stormclouds gathered over the Treshnish Isles to the west. It was here that some brave MacLeans made a gallant last stand against hordes of invading Campbells. Opposite lay the island of Ulva — MacQuarrie land. Legend has it that the chieftain had the right of the first night with any bride married on the island. As compensation, the groom would receive a sheep — some consolation!

I was glad of my ice axe on the steep, snowy slopes of Corrie nam Fuaran. Ben More, 966 metres, is all that is left of a 15,000-foot-high volcano. Every five minutes, in would come a snowstorm, whiting out everything and disappearing as quickly as it had come. The summit gave a brief view of Ben More's western ridge and the Cioch, the mountain's most sporting route, before winter cast its white cloak over the views. Following a bearing on the way down, I stumbled across a well-cairned path. So much for the experience of a previous round of Munros under your belt!

It was a cold cycle back to the tent in Glen Forsa, but I was warmed by the knowledge that the mountains of Mull had been secured. Mystery surrounds the glen regarding a low-flying small aircraft that went missing recently. No wreckage was found, only the body of pilot Peter Gibbs, who flew Spitfires in the Second World War.

The next hill to be climbed was Clisham on Harris. But Harris was a long way away, and the quickest route there was to get a boat to Uist and, from North Uist, catch the boat to Harris. The only problem was that the boat was not till Sunday and today was Friday. So it was an ideal time to have a rest day and see the support team in Oban.

I was away early, about 6.30 a.m. It was snowing, and I was loath to leave the warm tent and venture out into the inhospitable weather. Cycling down the rough Land Rover track, my wheels left tell-tale signs of my progress. An hour and a quarter later, I had covered the four rough miles to the road. In the process I had broken a brake cable and toe clip. At 11 a.m. the Cal Mac (Caledonian MacBrayne) ferry shuddered into life. We passed Lady's Rock, where a MacLean chieftain tried unsuccessfully to murder his Campbell wife by leaving her stranded on the rock, which is covered by high tide. But a Campbell boat passed by and saved her, after which the barbaric chieftain was reputedly murdered in revenge. As we docked, an Arctic storm blasted the town and everyone took shelter. I had left the mountains of Mull just in time.

The rest days were the usual panic of fixing the bike, packing, and dealing with my mail. All too soon it was time to board the ferry for South Uist. Leaving at midnight on the sacred Sabbath was permitted.

We sailed past the hotel and saw the lights of the lounge flash on and off three times. It was the support team saying farewell as the ship sailed into the darkness.

THE OUTER HEBRIDES, 18–20 MARCH

The ship rolling in the gale-force winds was better than any alarm clock. It was 5.30 a.m., yet the canteen was busy. A bacon sandwich and a steaming mug of tea was comforting as wind and rain lashed the windows. Cattle lowed eerily from the car deck. The rolling eased as we neared South Uist. The island had a light covering of snow — an unusual sight. To the south lay the island of Eriskay, the 'Whisky Galore' setting for Sir Compton Mackenzie's famous novel, on which the film was based. We prepared to dock in tiny Loch Boisdale. A strong wind was blowing up the island, which was to be of great help to me. Even with my heavy load, I cycled almost effortlessly. Today's journey would take me through South Uist, which has a straight west coast, but a wild and rugged coastline on the east, with a labyrinth of rocks and bays. The deep and narrow sea lochs still have the chains which were used to secure submarines during the Second World War.

Here was the kingdom of MacDonald, Lord of the Isles. This Hebridean island empire was a separate kingdom from Scotland. Their 10,000-man army and navy was a formidable force, and dreams of ruling the Kingdom of Ross resulted in an invasion of Scotland that ended on the bloody field of Harlaw in Aberdeenshire.

To my left lay the snowy Bheinn Mhor and Hecla, wild, rugged hills that are particularly impressive when climbed from the untamed and spectacular east coast, rivalling anywhere in the Hebrides.

Loch Drudibeg, the wildlife nature reserve, is an oasis among the lunar landscapes of the Uists. The population suffered little during the Clearances, as the land was not considered worth clearing. I crossed over to the Dark Isle of Benbecula, then reached Loch Maddy, 'Loch of the Wolves' or 'Foxes', where I

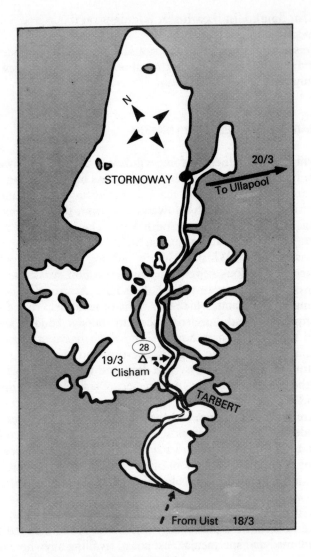

Map 8   The Isle of Lewis and Harris

made ferry enquiries. It was now 10.45 a.m., and although there
was a boat to Skye at 1 p.m. there was not another boat to Harris
until 4 p.m. the next day, so I phoned the boatman of the smaller,
alternative, ferry service. 'When will you be sailing?' I asked.

'What time can you get here?' he replied.

At 3 p.m. I boarded his small fishing boat, he helped me on with my bike, and we headed out into the stormy seas. The boat rolled about, and the boatman eyed my white face with a smile. 'Don't worry,' he said, 'we've never sunk yet!'

As I finally staggered off, he said that he was thinking of having a wee bar fitted. 'Great,' I thought, 'next time I'll book for a world cruise ...!'

It was marvellous to be cycling round Harris's beautiful coast-line, with her magnificent beaches, even if progress was slowed by a strong headwind and collie sheepdogs coming down from the crofts to practice their gathering on me. But the steep hills before Tarbert were a cruel end to a long day. Seventy miles with a heavy load on a single-track road were enough to make anyone sleep soundly!

I left the bed-and-breakfast at 9 a.m. Some children waved from the back window of the school bus. Thankfully, a snow plough had packed the fresh fall of snow into the verge.

Yesterday's strenuous efforts had left me with a pulled muscle which gave the odd painful twinge. Above in the mist lay Clisham, Harris's highest mountain, at 799 metres. The bridge over the Maaruig River was ideal for hiding the bike. Brown heather gave way to snow as I climbed Clisham's gentle eastern slopes. Harris and Lewis are spoken of as two separate islands when, in fact, they are actually one. It is only when you climb high that you can see it is the difference in terrain that causes the division. To the north of Loch Langavat lie the moors and thousands of lochans. This is Lewis; Harris's wild landscape is full of deep glens amid wild, jagged mountains that fall steeply to deep, penetrating sea lochs.

As if by magic the mist cleared close to the top, and sunlight sparkled over West Loch Tarbert. The rock-strewn ridge led to the narrow summit, just wide enough for the trig point and surrounding wall. The mountains of North Harris lay to the west — ridge after ridge of spectacular little mountains, shining in their white winter glory.

On a winter walk from Harris to Glasgow, I spent four days exploring this area. The unforgettable sights included the steeple-like peak of Taran Mor and the huge, overhanging cliffs of Sron

Ulladale, seen in the gloaming of a winter's evening. This land belonged to the MacLeods, whose territory also stretched to the north-west coastline and some of Skye. Their terrible feuds with the MacDonalds are legendary.

While I was descending, a huge herd of deer — at least a hundred strong — charged away over to the safe sanctuary of Loch Vistem. In some ways I wished I was going with them, free of the timetable pressure of a marathon walk.

To the east lies the remarkable Pairc peninsula, and this wild, forgotten land is almost cut off as a separate island, as the moat-like Loch Seaforth joins up with Loch Erisort. By 1887 most of the area had been cleared for deer forest, and the poor evicted Highland families were forced to face starvation and deprivations of all sorts. They fought back, with 700 men raiding the wild mountains of the Pairc to bring back a hundred dead deer in order to feed their families. They were ill equipped, with only fifty old guns between them, no match for the large force of Government troops sent to capture them. After three days they melted into the wilderness.

The barbaric Clearances continued in the Western Isles well into the twentieth century; the tragedy is that if only these clansmen's ancestors had supported Prince Charlie they would never have been 'cleared' in such a manner, if at all.

The miles soon sped by until the bustling fishing port of Stornoway could be seen in the distance.

INVERPOLLY NATURE RESERVE, 20–22 MARCH

The *Suilven*, Cal Mac's Stornoway to Ullapool ferry, sailed into Loch Broom, passing the Eastern Bloc factory ships and berthing at Ullapool. My last sail on the ferry was a memorable one. Thinking that I had missed the boat, I ran down the pier shouting 'Wait for me!', only to be told: 'But laddie, we're only just coming in!'

Vicious storms forced me to turn back from a foray north on the day I arrived, but the next morning was more encouraging. Cycling north to Ardmair Point, I was treated to a view of some seals playing in the bay. Here lies the Isle of Martin, where St Martin, a disciple of St Columba, is reputed to have had a church

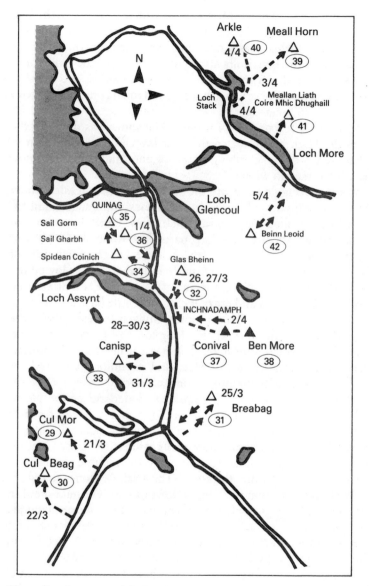

Map 9   Assynt and Coigach

and settlement. The wild, steep, craggy slopes of Ben Mor Coigach were reflected in the calm bay. She is a beautiful mountain but, alas, under the magic 762-metre mark. There are many hills in the Inverpolly area that are famous little mountains, like Stac Pollaidh, with its fairytale-like pinnacles, and Suilven, rising above Lochinver like a giant sugar loaf. Yet neither is above the level of 762 metres.

Suddenly I felt unsure of myself. The snow was down to the roadside. High above me in the mist lay Cul Mor, 849 metres. What was I doing climbing some of the Highlands' remotest peaks by myself in winter?

It was a struggle to locate the stalking track concealed under the snow. Behind me lay the Knockan rock, a popular haunt for geologists. I waded through the thick snow, crawling at times to spread my weight over the deep parts. The route ahead lay over Meallan Diomhain to a little frozen lochan to the north-west of the summit ridge. The mist cleared, and what a view lay before me of the Inverpolly Nature Reserve! This really is a pioneering area — wild hillocks and crazy lochs, with little bays and a tortu-ous, twisted coastline. To the north, Suilven towered above the empty moors. In between lay the long lochs of Loch Veyatie and Fionn Loch, which almost reach the sea. They form an eleven-mile barrier — quite uncrossable, and an unfortunate find for anyone coming on them after a compass error.

This is the magic of Sutherland, or Suderland as the Norse called it: a delightful mountain paradise and a haven for hill-walkers, fishermen, geologists and a host of others who like to spend their time exploring Scotland's wilder domains. Concen-tration was needed on the steep slopes to the summit, as treacher-ous icy rocks penetrated the snow. The circle of stones that gave shelter to the trig point was almost full of snow. The mist sifted in and out, unveiling the wilds of Assynt in a sombre winter's mood.

> Wagnerian devil signed the Coigach score,
> And God was Mozart when he wrote Cul Mor.
>   Norman MacCaig

I was heading downwards as a fierce wind got up, and I floundered into several snowdrifts, emerging with wet feet from the burns hidden below.

Cycling north to the car park at Knockan, I joined in a snow-ball fight with some geology students. My night was spent in a tiny hut normally used as an information centre on the geological features of Knockan — a welcome base. It was so small that you couldn't lie out straight. Several times I leant against the door and fell out into the snow!

The next day I set off and cycled south in miserable weather to Loch Lurgainn in the heart of Coigach. Icy rain fell in the glen; snowstorms were certain to be raking the ragged slopes of Cul Beag (769 metres), today's misty challenge. I looked around the beautiful mountains, with Stac Pollaidh lying three miles to the west. The fine northerly crags of Ben Mor Coigach made me feel insignificant, humble, and just a little scared. No cars were moving on the roads, another snow flurry came in, and I had to ask myself the question which solo hillwalkers often have to face: 'Is it really safe to go for it?' To which the answer usually is: 'Let's get a bit of height, and see what it's like further up the hill.'

Wild slopes led up to Creag Dubh. From there, mist and snow showers blocked the views. Cul Beag is best seen farther west from Stac Pollaidh, where she shows her stern, western crags to the full. The ice axe was put to good use on the steep climb to the summit ridge, where the mountain's cliffs could be felt, if not seen ... Lack of concentration on the way down resulted in my coming off the compass-bearing I had taken. I floundered about on the gentle eastern slopes till the bearing 'felt' right.

Back at the bike, I hungrily tucked into the last of the rations, then cycled south to Ullapool to meet a member of the support team. I welcomed a restful weekend with little reorganising required. A bonus was that the weather was lousy. Batteries were recharged by Monday morning.

ASSYNT, 25 MARCH–2 APRIL

A long campaign lay ahead. Would the weather be kind? Cycling north, it seemed to be on my side.

Assynt is famous for its caves, particularly those around Inchnadamph, where the first hunters appeared after the Ice Age. At Lyne I left the bike at the crofthouse, and soon the slopes of

Breabag (800 metres) were in sight. Leaving the croft of Lyne, spring seemed really to be in the air. The Feur Loch grew tiny as I climbed higher and stopped at a little lochan for a welcome brew, feeling at peace with the world. As the wind rippled the water of the small lochan, a couple of noisy hoodies (hooded crows) chased a buzzard out of their territory.

The Ordnance Survey lists Breabag summit to be 715 metres, but the actual summit of 800 metres lies one and a half miles to the south. A broad ridge starts at the summit, and, skirting her wild eastern cliffs, continues for twelve miles, crossing some of Scotland's loveliest and wildest wilderness areas. They include Conival — Ben More's sister mountain — and reach Glas Bheinn, standing guardian over Eas a' Chual Aluinn, Britain's highest waterfall. Here is the most sparsely populated county in Britain — only 13,000 inhabitants, or 99 square miles per person.

The mist rolled in, accompanied by a fierce sleet storm. My descent was faster than I would have liked, owing to the strong roaring wind at my back. It is scarcely believable how a warm spring day can turn to winter in a few seconds — that's the Highlands for you!

I cycled north to the heart of Assynt which is Inchnadamph, or 'the Pasture of the Stags', where a parcel awaited me at the Inchnadamph Hotel. Mr Morrison's friendly hotel was bursting at the seams with geologists from Hull Polytechnic. What a luxury it was to relax in a hot, steaming bath — bliss!

I was first down to breakfast, as the grey dawn silhouetted the huge bulk of Quinag, the group of three peaks to the north of Loch Assynt. Sheepdogs from a nearby farm growled as I cycled up the rough Land Rover track to Glen Bain House. After crossing a river, the track became very steep. The rear wheel lost its grip and slithered, biting into the pebbles, as slowly the bike and its heavy load clawed its way up the slopes. Leaving the bike in a small hayshed, I took the stalker's trail that leads from Inchnadamph over the shoulder of Glas Bheinn. It started to snow slightly. At the Loch Fleodach Coire the wind had increased and the snow was much heavier, so I sheltered behind some boulders in the hope it would recede. After about ten minutes, however, conditions worsened, and it was sadly necessary to retreat downhill. It was only 12.30 p.m., and the glens were covered with a new coat of white.

At about 2 p.m. the weather cleared, so I raced off back up the hill. The snow returned even worse than before, so there was nothing for it but to go back to the hayshed. There, I chatted to a geologist about local folklore and the dawn of history in that area. Two famous scientists, Peach and Horne, found here remains of Ice Age man; lynx and Arctic fox have been discovered in the locality, and during the actual Ice Age, auk, bear and wolf were also common. The River Traligill disappears through an underground network of caves, only to reappear a mile downstream, leaving a dried-up river bed. More than one water-seeking camper has been left scratching his head.

The wind roared and some snow sifted through the gaps at the bottom of the walls of the shed. But it didn't take long for me to fall into a deep sleep. It had been a wasted day, but at least spring would soon be here.

I awoke to the chilly sight of horizontal snow shooting past the door, so I opted for a leisurely breakfast. About mid-morning, the snow stopped. Here was my chance for another assault on Glas Bheinn. The deer were being sensible and staying in the glen, or perhaps they knew something that I didn't. At Loch Fleodach Coire, my turning point of yesterday, the weather was as bad as ever. But then it was only one small mountain ... it could be climbed safely. I was alone, yes, but isn't this always a game of risks? The wind roared and the spindrift spiralled to the sky on the summit plateau. Here winter was at war indeed! The wind froze my jacket and the snow stung my eyes. I shouted 'Caberfeidh' (antlers) and, head down, struggled to reach the correct summit. As the wind howled around the cairn, I stuffed a frozen Mars Bar into my mouth. This is the life!

In clear weather, Glas Bheinn is a real gem. A two- to three-hour climb to the summit rewards you with one of the most spectacular views in the Highlands. Then you can fully appreciate the wilds of Sutherland.

Assynt would be a tough nut to crack if the weather stayed like this. It was a contented walker who descended to his four-star hayshed.

In the morning, the farmer looked in to give out hay to the sheep. He glanced at a half bottle of whisky in the corner and asked if I took a wee drop. I replied that I had been tempted, but his need was greater than mine! 'It's just as well,' he said. 'There's many a person has been caught out with that — it's full of Dettol!'

After the previous day's icy blasts, this morning seemed quiet and peaceful. Two Edinburgh climbers, Rory and Alan, passed, complete with sunglasses, going for Ben More. It was now 9 a.m. and I was soon bombing down the track on the bike, bound for Canisp. The rough moorland on the approach to the mountain was hard going in the deep snow. Sinister clouds gathered over Canisp, and I could see that we were in for a fight. Nature paralysed my efforts at the small lochan between Meallan Liathn Mor and the summit ridge of Canisp. It was impossible to continue. The wind howled, and fierce sleet and snow stung my eyes … I was temporarily blinded several times. On Canisp, towers of snow spiralled skywards for hundreds of feet, as the wind seemed to rock the mountain. It was tempting to battle on, but quite impossible since I couldn't even stand up. I cycled back to the hayshed, feeling despondent and frustrated. Rory and Alan, who had been forced off Ben More, were coming down the track.

The snow flurried under the walls of the shed again. It was bitterly cold. I cooked a feast of dehydrated chicken, Angel Delight, tea and compo biscuits. Then, snug in the sleeping bag with my boots for company, I wrote a short letter: 'Dear support team … HELP!'

The plan to climb the trio of Corbetts, the Quinag, was abandoned. It was snowing heavily, backed up by a strong wind — a deadly combination. It might just be possible to climb one solitary mountain in the lea of the storm. However, with the weather deteriorating rapidly, I was grounded.

After another freezing night in the shed, the weather was worse than ever. Expedition HQ was abandoned and re-established in the Inchnadamph Hotel. It was a treat to sleep between clean sheets and wake to the prospect of a full breakfast.

The forecast was encouraging for the following day, and the weather prophets got it right. The sun was in the sky as I cycled south to attempt Canisp yet again. It was hard work wading through the snowy moors. Canisp is a deceptively long way from the road. It looks like a pleasant afternoon's walk, but it is eight miles there and back. The wind still sent spirals of snow towering skywards, and the freezing blast burnt your ears. But it stayed clear — that was the all-important factor. Height means little in Assynt: small mountains rise steeply from the low moors to give a full day's outing. But we shouldn't be blinkered into just climbing mountains. Equally as challenging are the many paths that penetrate and criss-cross the wilds of Sutherland. The summit just failed to give a view, which I felt was rough justice, considering the conditions of the last few days.

I had now been 'out' for a month and a half. Yet, despite strenuous efforts, only 33 summits had been climbed, though some of those were remote peaks in the Western Isles. But surely spring had just turned, and lost time would soon be made up? You have to be an optimist to be a hillwalker!

A huge snowdrift provided half an hour of fun, climbing its vertical slopes, before descending for an end-of-the-month celebration of a good meal and the luxury of a hot bath.

CHAPTER 2

April 1985

The Quinag (The Milk Churn)

—

The Reay Forest

—

Loch Naver

—

North-west Sutherland (The Land of MacKay)

—

Easter Ross

—

Dundonnell to Beinn Dearg and back again

—

Dundonnell, Loch a'Bhraoin to Kinlochewe

THE QUINAG (THE MILK CHURN)

It was comforting at breakfast to hold a warm cup of tea between my hands. It was still dark. The only sound was the purring of a generator outside, and the tap-tapping of rain against the window panes.

Through the inky dawn I could make out today's conquest, The Quinag, 'the Milk Churn', a rare combination of three Corbetts close together. The heavy rain overnight had all but washed away her mantle of snow, and only grey streaks were shining dimly through the dark. Today was the first of April, surely the start of spring. Darkness turned to daylight as I cycled north. Quinag was certainly living up to her name, her milky-white foaming burns gushing down to Loch Assynt below.

Gentle slopes led up to the summit of Spidean Coinich. The cairn is beautifully exposed. From there, a jaunty little path wriggled its way in and out of the steep, rocky slopes to Bealach a'Chornaidh, 'the Pass of the Folded Cloth'. An easy scramble took me to the south ridge of Sail Ghorm. These hills reminded me very much of the Arran hills which had been so pleasant six weeks ago. How I longed for that spring-like weather, as I leaned at an incredible angle against the gale-force winds just to keep walking straight. The wind roared around the cairn, tearing the mist to shreds. The return trip along the ridge was a lot faster than I would have liked, as the wind threatened to despatch me to Canada. Weatherbeaten ptarmigan scurried for cover among the rocks. Dozens of fresh footsteps in the snow led to the group's highest summit, Sail Gharbh, 'the Rough Heel'. As a violent squall shifted the damp mist from the summit, I found I was not alone. The owners of the footprints were enjoying a picnic! I worry about some people, they don't seem to take mountaineering seriously enough. But what a view it was, the stern but beautiful mountains of Assynt rewarding us for our patience of the last few days with a brief glimpse of their beauty.

The nearest road to the west lay ten miles away, yet it would be a much longer journey than that by the time one had circum-navigated some of the 245 hill lochs which blocked your way. Small wonder the district is renowned for its fishing. A long snow patch gave a great bum-slide down towards the stalking track at Lochan Bealach Chornaidh, leading down to the road. Sheep scattered as I sang happily at the top of my voice, content that, after the disappointment of the last few days, I had enjoyed a successful day on the hills, with three more summits climbed. Only Assynt's two highest mountains, Ben More and Conival, remained unclimbed.

Morning light glinted off the puddles on the now familiar track up to Gleann Dubh. The hayshed that had been my home was empty, though some comedian had fixed a note to the door, marked: 'Room to Let'.

The River Traligill was in a violent mood, her foamy waters gurgling through her network of underground caverns. The river enthusiastically led uphill, but soon became choked with snow. Soon I was in a misty world. Snow fell silently around a huge, lonely boulder on the shoulder of Conival, overlooking Coire a'Mhadaidh, 'Corrie of the Wolf'. Visibility was restricted to a few feet; if winter was still with us, gone at least were the ferocious winds of the last few days. An easy ridge led up to Conival's summit, 987 metres. The snow had covered the shattered quartzite rocks for which this mountain is renowned. I double-checked my compass-bearing for the eastern ridge leading to Ben More Assynt, the only peak that stood in the way of my plans to advance further into the wilds of Sutherland.

The mist cleared briefly to allow a glimpse of the lonely, barren wilderness to the north, land of fiord-like sea lochs, small craggy mountains and crazily shaped lochans. It was in this inhospitable area that Graham of Montrose spent his last days of freedom, fleeing from the disastrous battle of Carbisdale. In desperation, he fell on the mercy of the MacLeods, who treacherously betrayed Scotland's finest general to the enemy.

Almost everyone will climb Ben More by this route. However, many other spectacular routes exist for those with imagination. An energetic walk from the south by Carn nan Conbhairean will leave you with a lifetime of memories. At the summit, a miserable-looking ptarmigan, lying in the lee of a snowy rock, was singularly unimpressed by my proud boast that this was my 38th mountain. I was almost seven weeks into the walk, with some 260 miles of walking and 880 miles of cycling. It occurred to me that speaking to birds was not a good sign; perhaps I had already been on the hills too long!

THE REAY FOREST, 3–5 APRIL

It was great to stand at the top of the pass between Inchnadamph and Kylesku and enjoy the freshness of a Sutherland morning. Far below, on stormy Loch Assynt, white horses ran neck and neck to be the first to crash on to its lonely southern shore. It was very satisfying to look south at range after range of misty mountains, knowing every one of them over 762 metres high had been climbed.

It was a day for gales to harass the north-west, as burns like fountains rose vertically from the hillsides. The cross-winds roared over the new Kylesku bridge, forcing me to cycle at a ridiculous angle into the wind to prevent being blown into the crash barrier. The 35-mile ride north to Loch Stack was painfully slow, as the bike struggled with the wind to keep on the road. While making camp on the loch shore, I was treated to an extraordinary sight. Two dead crows, caught in a downdraught of wind, floated above me as if caught in a whirlwind. They circled round and round, hundreds of feet above, resembling a free-fall parachute team. Then, suddenly, they plummeted into the dark stormy waters of the loch. I was deeply concerned lest my smelly socks may have been to blame, but a leading orni-thologist assured me later this was not the case! The crows had probably been caught in a ferocious gust of wind that was roaring up the cliffs of Ben Stack and were dashed against the rocks, killing them.

From the tent a pleasant hill track took me north by the side of a gurgling burn. The path led over the shoulder of Meall Horn, a lonely Corbett. From the windy summit, it was thrilling to see my first view of the northern coastline, Loch Eriboll penetrating the wilds like an accusing finger. Thoughts of my first innocent day in the Borders seemed far away, as were my memories of my first ever winter's day on the hills years ago, proudly showing off my new compass and advising everyone that the bubble trapped inside indicated the north. Instructions for use of the ice axe were tucked into my top pocket should they be required when falling.

Spring seemed to have arrived at last, as the evening sun sparkled on the snowy slopes of nearby Foinaven. Back down at the tent, I got tucked into a celebratory feast, while a contingent of stalking ponies with a keen interest in tent design nibbled playfully at the guy ropes.

Any dreams of waking to a blissful, clear spring day were dashed, as another Icelandic low pressure area crossed the Atlantic and dropped its entire contents on top of my tent. The cheeky stalking ponies eyed me suspiciously as I squelched up the previous day's stalking track, not daring to look around in case the sight was of them rolling over my nylon home.

Above in a misty world lay a gem of a peak, Arkle, 787 metres. Her steep south-western slopes, that give such a stern and craggy appearance from the roadside, were easily avoided by a gentle brae which rose to the smaller of the mountain's two summits. The mist lifted to reveal Arkle's sickle-shaped ridge. The steep drops on each side were soon forgotten as I enjoyed the fun, with some easy scrambling leading up to the summit cairn. The inky black Loch an Easain Uaine looked as dark and foreboding as the steep, craggy slopes of Foinaven that plummet straight into it. To the west lay 'the Empty Quarter', a wild maze of small hills and lochans, once populated by wolves. Fierce Vikings raided and eventually settled here; now only their names remain. Imagine the sight of a hundred longships leaving Loch Inchard with horns echoing around the glens, 15,000 warriors confident of an easy victory against the Scots to the south — a dream shattered by a tiny Scots army at the Battle of Largs, helped tremendously by a terrible storm that scattered the enemy fleet.

After a comforting brew at the tent, I cycled back along the very rocky Land Rover track that led to the main road. A puncture slowed the progress, but I was determined to climb another mountain before dark: the race was on to 'clear' this area and meet the support team the next night. It felt so good to reach a tarmac road. The bike seemed to glide along to Loch More. Here lies what has got to be one of the Corbetts' biggest mouthfuls: Meallan Liath Coire Mhic Dhughaill. It's a big hill, too, at 801 metres. Unfortunately it was a race to be up and down before dark. Progress was delayed by a minefield of peat hags at the back of Meall Reinidh. It was good to shelter from the cold winds at the trig point, which was surrounded by a circular wall; my cold red nose peeked out to enjoy the superb mountainous view to the north.

It had turned into a nice evening, the sun slowly following my descent. A twelve-pointer (Royal) stag was silhouetted against the crimson background. People ask us, 'Why climb?.'

Cycling back to the tent, I disturbed a huge herd of deer who raced and panicked in all directions over and through a flimsy wire fence nearby.

Today was to be a long one. The tent was packed while the tea boiled, and the gentle light of dawn carpeted around the cliffs of Ben Stack, another of Sutherland's magnificent little peaks. First obstacle of the day was getting through the gate with a loaded bike and preventing the ponies from escaping at the same time. After fixing another puncture, I once more reached the bliss of a tarmac road. Pedalling through the sleepy hamlet of Achfray, nothing stirred and only the sweet smell of wet fir trees lingered in the air. One mile south of Kinloch, I hid the bike and strode up a well-defined stalking track. This disappeared at the top of a small pass like a worm cut in half.

Descending into Gleann Dubh, one gets the impression one is really entering an inner kingdom of Sutherland. Here lies Beinn Leoid (Hill of the MacLeods'), 792 metres, one of the most remote Corbetts. A long grassy ridge led to the summit. From here you realise the true meaning of the wilderness of Sutherland: to the south, far across Glen Coul, lies Glas Bheinn, in a peaceful mood today compared to the winter tantrum she had thrown at me the week before. From her watershed, white burns raced down and crashed spectacularly over Eas a'Chual Aluinn, Britain's highest waterfall, four times the size of Niagara. The seething burns raced down to Loch Glencoul, which joins another sea loch, Loch Glendhu. They resembled a giant shaft of an arrow, straining to shoot across the Atlantic, where most of the former inhabitants of the glens were forced to live. It is a land of great beauty and sadness. In Glen Coul there is a war memorial in memory of two brothers who left this remote glen to fight in the First World war, never to return.

My mad race continued. The support team would be at Altnaharra that evening. It was three weeks since I had seen them at Oban. I walked and ran the four hilly miles back to the bike. Thoughts of a change of clothes and a relaxing rest day tomorrow filled my mind. The bicycle struggled against the wind. It was forty long miles to Altnaharra. White horses charged across Loch Shin, adding reality to the superstition that the loch is home to a giant sea horse. Here the rocky terrain of the west becomes that of the east: wild, deserted moorland littered with bogs and lochans. Doubtless it has changed little since the days when the MacKays and MacLeods had a furious battle close to the loch ... each clan, no doubt, wanting a little more bogland to add to its collection! Cycling north, the wind began to help instead of hinder my journey. At the Altnaharra Hotel it was great to meet up with Tom, Doreen and Munro, who delighted in sprinting up and down the hotel stairs like the mad collie he is.

LOCH NAVER, 6–8 APRIL

Rest days were strange things. They were looked forward to tremendously, but sometimes I was glad to get back to the hills for a rest. The mad dash to update routes, replace kit and pack and repack equipment often left me more tired than the longest day on the hills. But it was always good to see the team and get fresh clothes and a hot bath.

Easter Sunday was like a dream come true. Sunshine danced on Loch Naver, and flowers peeped out of the soaking moorland that rose steeply to my 43rd mountain, Ben Klibreck, 961 metres. Munro was reliving puppyhood, racing in and out of the bogs, ensuring himself a month's ban from the hotel. After a steep pull to the summit ridge we enjoyed a grand snowball fight, till Munro lost his temper and pushed me down a snow slope. At the summit, a shiny new trig point replaced the old shattered one, which was lying on its side.

Although easily accessible, Ben Klibreck has a great sense of remoteness. Rising from the moorland like a great pyramid, she towers above her neighbours. To the east lies a wilderness of almost totally uninhabited bogs and moorland, stretching forty miles to the sea.

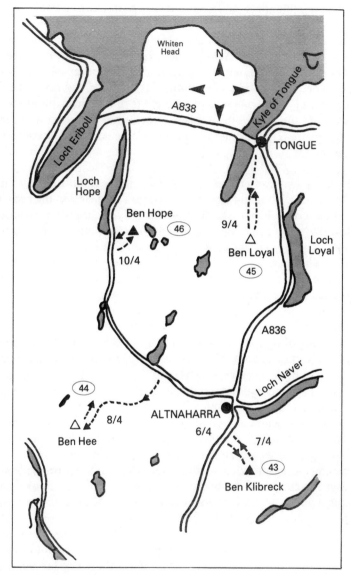

Map 10   The Far North

The Highlanders suffered terribly here during Blibha nan Caorach ('The Year of the Sheep'). Those who chose not to emigrate had their houses burnt. Many vicious battles took place between crofters and the lairds, who were supported by the authorities. Back down at the loch side, we bumped into Tom and Doreen. Tom, who is an industrial diamond engineer, was in disgrace. He had spun a story in the bar that he had found some diamonds on the shore of Loch Hope, and produced a simple rough gem. This emptied the bar and created a mass exodus to the loch.

The glorious weather was short lived. The next morning icy rain fell in sheets. Tom and Doreen waved goodbye, and as the red car became a distant blur on the horizon only the muffled sound of Munro's bark could be heard. I looked around the miserable scene. The bridge ahead was threatening to be swept away. A collie whimpered at the door of a cottage and a truck raced through a puddle, soaking my nice dry waterproofs. While the support team's visits and words of encouragement were very welcome, they seemed to be under the illusion that I was going to complete this mad walk. I took heart that the snow would soon be disappearing from the tops and so I would not need to cart my ice axe and crampons around with me. Frankly, I had only the faintest of notions how to use them!

Tufts of soaking wet grass plunged out of the tarmac road leading to Loch Hope. One mile south of Loch Meadie, among a forestry plantation, a good stalking track led me towards today's goal: Ben Hee, 873 metres, meaning 'the Fairies' Hill'. I was glad of my gloves as freezing rain pelted the glen, and the white foaming burns growled a challenge. Three fox snares were set along the track, no doubt rarely inspected, and just as likely to catch a dog as a fox. Our wild canine friends deserve a better end, and won themselves an ally that day.

Today was a perfect example of my planning capabilities, or how not to do a mountain marathon walk. Ben Hee could have been easily climbed from Loch Merkland the week before — a two-mile walk to the summit. But, lacking time and energy, I decided to leave it to today's mad eighteen-mile epic. Loch Coire na Saidhe Duibhe was like an icy cauldron, which promised a full winter's storm on the tops. The only way this mountain would be climbed today would be in the lee of the storm. A promising gap among the crags, marked on the map opposite Loch a'Choire Leacaich, looked encouraging. But on closer inspection it was impossible. Icy water plummeted down the steep crags which resembled a giant, greasy staircase. It had all the horrors of a tourist route on Skye.

There was only one alternative. An hour later, I was at the south of Loch a'Ghorm-choire, where easy slopes led up the mountain's south-east flank. The loch below looked black and deadly, like the eyes of a cobra. There was something about Ben Hee that gave me the creeps. The weather, of course, was terrible, and the terrain wild and remote. But there was more to it than that. Friends who have climbed her on separate occasions have expressed the same feeling. Perhaps the Hill of the Fairies holds a sad and dark secret. I was glad of my snow goggles, as snow whirled around the mountain and the icy wind froze my jacket. At last the summit cairn appeared out the mist. Huddled against it, I hungrily scoffed a Mars Bar, hoping in vain the storm would ease and give me a view of Bealach nam Meirleach, meaning 'the Pass of the Robbers'. Although the story behind the name is lost, like much of the history of the north, doubtless it refers to the MacKays and their long, bloody feuds with their neighbours.

It was a relief to climb down out of the storm and eat the last of the food at the lochan. This gave me enough 'zoom' to walk back to the bicycle — it had been an eighteen-mile walk just to climb one hill! Evening light was fading as the bike started its long, 21-mile journey north to Tongue. As if to rub salt into the wound, a fierce northern gale reduced my cycling to a crawl.

Some two and a half hours later, Mrs Mackay gave me a warm welcome to Tongue Youth Hostel. The friendly kitchen was full of steaming kettles and laughing voices. The bitter cold outside froze the dormitory window while I snuggled down under warm blankets. The cold snowy slopes of Ben Hee were soon forgotten.

NORTH-WEST SUTHERLAND (THE LAND OF MACKAY), 9–13 APRIL

Tired legs floundered in the muddy track leading south from the village to Cunside. Ahead lay the queen of Scottish mountains, Beinn Loyal, magnificently situated overlooking the Kyle of

Tongue. At 764 metres, she is a small Corbett, but height matters little in Sutherland. One can have a grand long day traversing her many tops, which protrude with the regularity of the prickles on a hedgehog. At Bealach Clais nan Ceap it was sad to pass the tortured, mangled wreckage of an aircraft that crashed in 1942, killing the Duke of Kent. The plane's compass was said to have been affected by the mountain's magnetic rock.

The summit, An Caisteal, meaning 'the Castle', towered out of the mist with all the splendour and challenge of a Himalayan peak. The mist was clear two feet above the summit, so I lay down and enjoyed the view. The empty wilderness stretched for miles to the east. Here lurks the 'Beast of Skerray', a large puma or lynx that marauds the crofts which scrape a living on the barren north coast. Tongue is rich in history, with ancient Pictish settlements and the MacKay's ruined fortress of Castle Bharraich, yet it is Beinn Loyal that stirs the imagination. On her northern slopes lies Loch Hakel, reputed hiding place for Prince Charlie's £12,000 treasure chest of gold coins. Not far from the loch lies the site of the MacKays' most desperate battle. In 1427 they were invaded by hordes of Sutherlands and their allies. Heavily outnumbered, the battling MacKays fell back on the slopes of Druim na Coup. After hours of furious fighting they turned the tide and swept their enemies south.

Back at the youth hostel, Mrs Mackay's incredible collie put a damper on the day by beating me 6–0 at football. Spirits were revived, however, thanks to a great after-dinner singsong with a group from the Birmingham Christian Society.

It is customary in a youth hostel to perform a helpful duty before leaving in the morning. Mine was to clean the shower room. Alas, the Caldwell touch causes innocent destruction wherever it goes: such was the fate of the shower, the nozzle broke off in my hand. Mrs Mackay took the news well and refused payment, though she did look pleased I was leaving.

It was a long pull west over the Kyle of Tongue. During the '45 Rebellion, a Jacobite ship landed in the loch and started unloading badly needed gold coins to pay the clans. They were captured by the MacKays, who supported the Hanoverians. Mystery, however, still surrounds the whereabouts of the gold.

A herd of deer raced across the road that traverses the dark and peaty Moine peninsula. The shore road of Loch Hope was a delight to cycle along. Towering in the distance soared a snow-splattered Ben Hope, at 927 metres the most northerly of the Munros. Her steep crags overlooking the road looked intimidating.

The route from Alltnacaillich is easy walking. However, my route, one and a half miles to the north, is a lot steeper but quicker. This was to be the busiest hill of the walk so far. I met three parties! For the many dedicated English Munro climbers, Ben Hope is their longest journey. Incredibly, some even succeed in doing it in a weekend.

To the west, Foinaven and Arkle were getting a real drubbing, though for once we seemed to avoid the storms. Be warned: Ben Hope has two summit cairns, the most northerly being the higher. This 'Hill of the Bay' has something for everyone: gentle hill-walking or exciting scrambling up her fine north ridge.

As the evening light faded in Strath Beag I pitched the tent. It amazed me how it was a different shape every time. Tonight it was like a lunar module. It was good to snuggle down in the sleeping bag and enjoy this, the most northerly camp of the walk, with only the call of the gulls and the lapping of the waves to ease me to sleep.

A path of sorts wound its way through the damp, fresh-smelling woodland. High above towered the impressive cliffs of Creag Shomhairle. My goal, Foinaven, 908 metres, lay far away. Sutherland's most spectacular Corbett was living up to her name, 'the White Hill'. Her four high summits stood like lonely sentries, awaiting the return of Fionn, or some other bygone hero. It was breathtaking to stand at the top of the Bealach na h-Imrich. This 'Pass of the Flitting' is named in memory of the 15,000 MacKays evicted by the hated George Leveson, supported by the authorities. Such was the clan's reward for supporting the Hanoverians during the 1745 Rebellion (or 'Quarter to Six', as it's sometimes known).

Crossing boggy Strath Dionard, I disturbed a herd of over a hundred deer charging in panic into Foinaven's lonely corries. Enjoying a breather at Cnoc Duail, my eyes caught sight of an eagle to the west. Her great wings soared over the Moors of Parph, which stretched from Kinlochbervie to Cape Wrath:

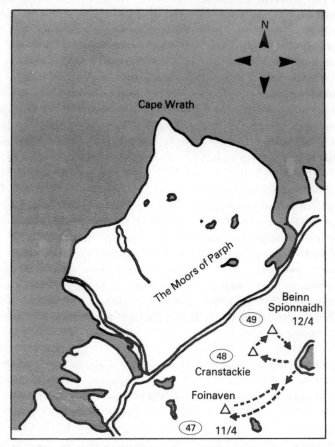

Map 11   North-west Sutherland

almost a hundred square miles of wilderness, changed little since
the days when it was inhabited by wolves. The interior has only
one resident, a recluse, who lives in a remote bothy with the deer
and gulls for company.

Weak sunshine faded under a blanket of mist. The mountain
seemed to shudder in the icy cold wind as the pink scree gave way
to snow-covered, shattered rocks that made progress slow. It was
with great relief that I arrived at the summit of Ganu Mor, the
highest of Foinaven's six summits. I was thankful that the
weather had been kind, for this remote mountain could be a real
brute if the weather was wild.

Back at the tent, a piece of old iron fence post was put to good use on an emergency boot repair. I was dismayed to find shrimp curry on the menu again — 'Yugh' — with a cheerful note attached from Angus: 'Rather you than me, mate.' However, a warm cup of coffee and endless packets of Compo biscuits satisfied the inner man. By candlelight my fingers lovingly caressed the pages of OS Sheet no. 9. The crags and close contours excited the reader just like a good adventure yarn. Ideas for the future sprang to mind, while old tea stains and candle wax were reminders of many previous visits. This had the same effect as counting sheep to lull me to sleep.

A raven croaked good morning as I struggled to push my laden bike through the boggy ditches and riverbeds that dominate Strath Beag. My poor battered bike was now something of an embarrassment, covered in mud and with grass poking out of the mudguards. Leaving it at the croft of Polla, it was great to stride up the pleasant grass slopes that led towards Cranstackie, 800 metres. Spring seemed to fill the air, with birds singing and optimistic blossoms standing out among the heather. The variety of flowers and colours changed with the altitude, so behind the next boulder was a new welcoming patch of radiant blooms. A hill fox crossed ahead, oblivious of my presence, its tongue hanging out, seemingly enjoying a good joke. Perhaps I was that joke.

The summit cairn was beautifully positioned, sitting like a throne over her boulder-strewn summit plateau. My eyes turned towards Cape Wrath, the start and finishing point for many a long-distance walk. An enthusiastic walking friend once arrived triumphantly at the lighthouse in perfect time to catch a mini tourist bus that operates in the summer. An elderly passenger asked if he had come far, to which he proudly replied, 'Yes, I have walked all they way from the Lizard. It has taken ten weeks.'

She replied: 'Well, I'm glad you're here now, laddie, because I think it's going to rain!'

My second hill of the day was Beinn Spionnaidh ('Mountain of Strength'). It is our most northerly Corbett and the 49th hill of the walk. In the short, two-month period since leaving home, I had now climbed The Merrick in Galloway, furthest south, Clisham on Harris, the most westerly hill, and now the furthest north. Little did I think it would be ten months before reaching

Mount Keen, the most easterly hill of the walk.

Legend has it that local bard, Robb Dunn, buried his beloved gun among the rocks of nearby Carn an Righ (overlooking Loch na Seilg, 'the Loch of the Hunting') when his poaching days were over. Perhaps it's still there?

Making a beeline from the summit to the bike soon had me in a minefield of scree and boulders. At last reunited, and in a ravenous mood, I attacked the food panniers like a demented timber wolf and found a packet of 'food' that looked and tasted exactly like Polyfilla. A 25-mile cycle took a very hungry cyclist to Tongue Youth Hostel, whose stores seemed full of delicious food. A couple of fit young Germans were signed up in my football team and faced up to Mrs Mackay's spring-loaded collie, whose rubber body and turbo-charged ambidextrous paws made mincemeat of us.

It was a cold, wet morning as I cycled south, determined to reach the Dornoch Firth. A pit stop at the public bar of the Altnaharra Hotel proved to be fatal to my plans. A party were celebrating a wake. Highland funerals being the best of all parties, the whisky flowed as the bar rocked to the singing of 'Lads amongst Heather' and other classics. Suddenly, cycling to Dornoch seemed an awfully silly idea, hic!

EASTER ROSS, 14–19 APRIL

It was early morning as I left a very wet Altnaharra. The heavy rain taunted me, for it stopped as soon as I put my waterproofs on, and if I was tempted to take them off, it would start pouring a few minutes later. Someone up there has a very warped sense of humour.

Twenty-five miles later at Invershin, Carbisdale Castle loomed out of the morning mist. Now a beautiful youth hostel, it's sometimes unkindly referred to as Colditz. Near the castle at Creag a'Choineachain was the site of the gallant Montrose's last battle, where his ragtag army of mercenaries were cut to ribbons or drowned fleeing from Strachan's dragoons.

It was great to get help from some tailwind, cycling up Strathcarron. A detour was made to visit the church at Croick. Here the

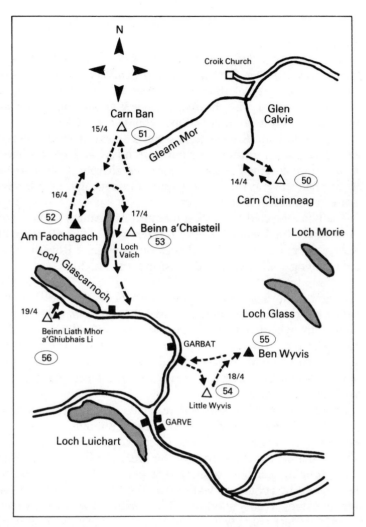

Map 12 Easter Ross

people of Glen Calvie came for sanctuary when their glens were being cleared, but the doors were barred to them. They scratched pathetic names and signatures, beautifully written, on the window, and believed that they were the wicked generation and deserved the punishment of eviction and deportation.

At Glen Calvie Lodge a flock of lambs, bleating madly, raced over towards me as I tried to hide my heavy cycle luggage before pedalling further up Glen Calvie. Here lies the twin-topped hill, Carn Chuinneag, 838 metres. This lonely Corbett lies in the empty lands between Strathcarron and Ben Wyvis. It was surprising to see a party of three walkers on the even more remote Diebidale Ridge. I was cheated of a view at the summit by an unpleasant snowstorm that had me running for cover.

Cycling on Land Rover tracks seemed an excellent idea until I started venturing further west into Gleann Mor. Here the nice, firm, well-maintained tracks deteriorated sharply. I went flying off the bike several times, once quite dramatically, as I somersaulted to land feet first in a burn.

The bike objected to fording the burn at Deanich Lodge. The Land Rover track ended a little further west. After 60 miles of cycling, 20 miles of which had been on slow Land Rover tracks, and climbing a hill, I was ready to stop for the night.

The sight of horizontal snow going past the tent in the morning was, to say the least, discouraging. My plans for a long day on the hill had just whistled down the glen with the snowflakes. A stalking track led up to Loch Sruban Mora. The visibility was poor, so bearings were double-checked for the assault on Carn Ban, 845 metres. Ptarmigan seemed to have the right idea, huddling for cover under the rocks.

At last the fourth bump was reached, which is the summit. Plans to traverse west to include Seana Bhraigh, one of the remotest Munros, were dropped, since I couldn't even stand up. What a shame, for the corries of the Freevater Forest and Coire Mor are a magnificent sight, giving good winter climbing for those energetic enough to walk there. Potential panoramic views were one thing, reality another. With visibility down to a few feet, the only scenery going was a snowy cairn, four feet away, and if I was lucky, my boots! It was one of those days when you could descend out of the mist and easily imagine you had gone back in time — which isn't as daft as it sounds. A party near Braemaer recently got the fright of their lives when they bumped into a crowd of whisky smugglers, complete with ponies laden with barrels. The men looked menacing with their kilts and weapons. They turned out to be a group re-enacting the journey of a freebooters' trail from Speyside to Angus!

It was a relief to find the stalking track, descend to the tent and celebrate the 51st, and possibly remotest, hill of the walk.

The morning mist was right down to the hut, so a leisurely breakfast was called for, in the hope that the weather would clear. Such developments, however, exist only in fairytales.

Gleann Beag soon disappeared in the mist as I followed the snow choked Allt a'Chrom uillt that led to the gentle, northern slopes of Am Faochagach, 954 metres, meaning 'the Place of Seashells'. This Munro lies cast out from the other members of the Beinn Dearg group, as if they disapproved of her gentle shape, compared to their stern and rugged appearance.

Many walkers, I fear, sadly throw this hill in on an off day, which is a mistake, as the views are among the finest in Scotland. If climbing in wet weather, the Abhainn a'Gharbhrain should be treated with respect, as a few hours of heavy rain could block your way to the south.

At the summit, visibility was restricted to a few feet, but memories came flooding back of a perfect June evening the previous summer. Then the lochan in Choire Ghranda was glinting like an emerald, and the only sound was the gentle flowing of the rivers gliding from one lochan to the next.

My ambitious plans to have climbed the four remaining Munros in the Beinn Dearg range and far-off Seana Bhraigh had been thwarted by the weather. I had arranged to meet Angus and Neil, from the support team, in Garve the following evening. It was impossible for me to contact them, so it would be necessary to make the long journey out of this special mountain kingdom to meet them. However, efforts wouldn't necessarily be wasted, as Beinn a'Chaisteil, a Corbett, lay *en route*.

A heavy thaw was well under way and, as if to prove it, a huge lump of hard-packed snow, the size of a transit van, took off downstream.

Down in Gleann Beag dozens of white, roaring burns were echoing a violent chorus. This wild land was home for Clan MacKenzie, whose warriors won fame fighting in Scotland's countless wars and rebellions, and were eventually to form the basis of the legendary Seaforth Highlanders.

These hills were no doubt a great training ground, too, for Sir Alexander MacKenzie, who explored the wilderness of North-

West Canada and gave his name to the Mackenzie River.

The morning's activities got off to an exciting start, as the front pannier leapt off its carrier, jamming the front wheel, and sending me flying. Some Land Rover tracks can be a cyclist's nightmare, but the road south through the Tollomuick Deer Forest was an unexpected pleasure. At Loch Vaich, meaning 'Loch of the Byre', it even stopped raining.

At Lubachlaggan, sheep came out of the shelter of the ruins to graze where children used to play. Golden sunshine danced on the slopes of Beinn a'Chaisteil, 787 metres, meaning 'Castle Mountain'. The summit looked deceptively near, but what was the hurry? Body and soul had a chance to dry out and recharge, climbing under the precious rays. From the rounded summit it was the eastward view that fired the imagination. The sea was twenty-five miles away but in between lay the peaceful hills of the Wyvis and the Kildermorie deer forests, little visited outside the stalking season.

Retrieving the bike from the croft, I rescued a sheep from a ditch, only to find it had hurt its legs. At Lubriach I met the shepherd, who promised to go and see the poor animal, his wife cheerfully adding that snow was forecast for the weekend! My dream of phoning the support team to bring up shorts and a sunhat next visit had just gone down the chute.

At Garve it was great to meet support-team stalwarts Angus and Neil, who had just completed a lucky day at Perth races and were in a celebratory mood. We had last met at my leaving party, over two months ago. There was a lot of chat to catch up on as the whisky flowed, and poor Garve shuddered as our strangled vocal chords murdered 'Come by the Hills'.

Yesterday's spring-like weather seemed short-lived as the rain came tumbling down. Neil and Angus waved cheerily from the train leaving for far-off Kyle of Lochalsh. The line boasts fine mountain scenery, but the view of that would be sorely limited today. I concluded, after years of suspecting it, that my friends must be quite mad!

The bike aqua-slid along the soaking road towards Garbat, a fine starting point for Ben Wyvis, 1,046 metres, and her sister mountain Little Wyvis, 764 metres. It was a deceptively long pull to the top of this little Corbett. The rain had stopped and the mist was a clear three feet above the summit, so I lay down on rock and enjoyed the view! Cars and lorries scurried like worker ants to and from Dingwall.

It was here, in 1411, that a small army of MacKays were totally overwhelmed trying to stop the advance of the Lord of the Isles and his massive army, marching to Aberdeen to contest the Earldom of Ross. Of course the MacKays fought everyone, including themselves. They fought against Bonnie Prince Charlie, won fame as mercenaries for Sweden, and later formed the Reay Fencible Regiment.

Ben Wyvis is a massive mountain which sadly sometimes lives up to her name 'Mountain of Terror'. Her slopes are prone to avalanche. A skier had been killed on the mountain only a few weeks earlier.

Martin Moran's assault on the Munros in winter almost came to an end on Wyvis. In atrocious visibility he and his wife Joy stepped over a cornice and were avalanched into the Coire na Feola, cryptically named the 'Corrie of Carnage' or 'Slaughter'. Thankfully both were unhurt. My climb today was a piece of cake compared to their brave battle. The summit ridge resembled a golf fairway that gently led to the large summit cairn.

Some strange traditions existed in this area. The MacKenzie Earls of Cromarty, owing to past services, had only to pay rent to the Crown of a snowball from Ben Wyvis. In Dingwall, if the court of justice sentenced you to death, you would receive pardon ... if you could escape through the crowd and touch the church steeple.

I had camouflaged the bike so well it took ages to find. Cycling west, a perfect pitch for the tent was found on the shores of Loch Glascarnoch, well sheltered from any prevailing winds. I rarely managed to pitch the tent perfectly; this evening it resembled a flattened pyramid.

The rosy sun sank sleepily into the west. The cold wintry days of the last six weeks seemed far away. At last spring had arrived.

Nature was my alarm clock as, early in the morning, the tent shook violently. Peeking out cautiously, cold rain lashed my face. Whirlwinds raced across the loch, and everywhere white burns crashed down the hillside, their roaring echoing around the glens.

Obviously spring had been by-passed in favour of summer! Just as the tea was boiling, a gust knocked it for six. This was not amusing. A second attempt was more successful. Every conceivable thing, from boots to boulders, was used to keep the stove steady.

The tent was packed up before it could disappear over the horizon, with sleeping bag and clothes carefully packed in several poly bags. Behind me lay a big mouthful of a Corbett, Beinn Liath Mhor a'Ghiubhais Li, 766 metres, meaning 'the Big Grey Mountain of the Coloured Pine'. This was planned to be an easy morning hill, but the day's weather was to change that. Crossing a burn of any size was proving to be a problem. The flat rocky summit was raked with hurricane-like winds that blew me about like a crisp packet. It was a slow business, crouching from one boulder to another, as my ears buzzed. This was a nightmare: just like watching Partick Thistle on their sixth defeat in a row. The situation suddenly became annoying. The cairn appeared in the distance through the fast-moving mist. It was the middle of April — 'Where the heck is spring?' With a shout of 'Caberfeidh!', I charged the last thirty yards to the wind-torn, rocky, summit cairn.

Descending was easy: all you had to do was flap your arms. One down, one to go, as the bike struggled to cycle west against the gale. The Corrieshalloch Gorge was excelling itself today, as the spray of its falls seemed to fill the air.

A Land Rover track led me to the north of the main road. While passing a lodge house, a sheepdog sprang from its kennel, snarling at the bike. I found some incredible resources of energy and my speed increased to a rate any Olympic cyclist would have been proud of.

A stalking track led up towards Beinn Enaiglair, 889 metres, meaning 'Hill of the Timid Birds'. What was I doing trying to climb a lonely peak most people have never heard of in terrible weather conditions? Information gleaned from guide books told me this fine mountain sits apart from its neighbours, giving one of Scotland's finest viewpoints. Given today's weather, I might as well have been climbing a Lanarkshire slag heap.

The wind and rain pelted down relentlessly. Close to the summit, it was strange to hear the eerie, wailing sound of the wind howling up the mountain's steep northern slopes. On the

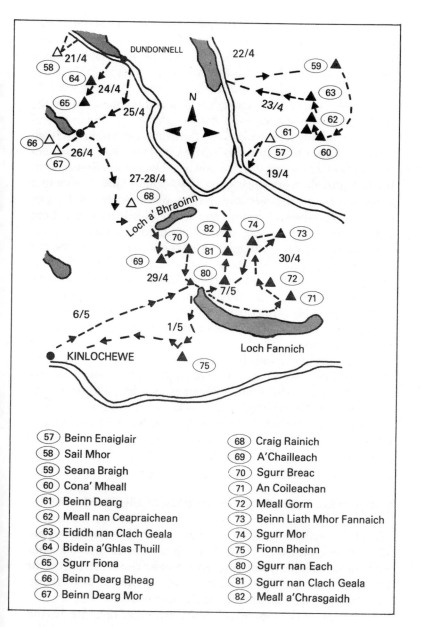

57 Beinn Enaiglair	68 Craig Rainich
58 Sail Mhor	69 A'Chailleach
59 Seana Braigh	70 Sgurr Breac
60 Cona' Mheall	71 An Coileachan
61 Beinn Dearg	72 Meall Gorm
62 Meall nan Ceapraichean	73 Beinn Liath Mhor Fannaich
63 Eididh nan Clach Geala	74 Sgurr Mor
64 Bidein a'Ghlas Thuill	75 Fionn Bheinn
65 Sgurr Fiona	80 Sgurr nan Each
66 Beinn Dearg Bheag	81 Sgurr nan Clach Geala
67 Beinn Dearg Mor	82 Meall a'Chrasgaidh

Map 13   Wester Ross

summit, ridge-crawling was the only effective method of travel. A snowstorm came in and turned the hill white in seconds. It was a relief to turn away from my 57th summit cairn and descend quickly away from the fierce weather.

Cycling silently down the track, I whizzed past the watchful collie, who jumped into action, lurching on his chain, threatening to chase me with kennel towed behind.

The Dundonnell Hotel lay only thirteen miles away; it felt like a hundred and thirty in today's weather. The A832 to Gairloch rises to over 1,000 feet and is known as Destitution Road. It was built to provide work during the 1840 potato famine. The high moorland gave no cover and cycling was reduced to a crawl, often to a standstill. A heavy snowstorm added to the fun. Long poles marked the passing places, about forty yards apart. To reach each one was a struggle, but was one stage nearer the pint of lager waiting at the bar of the hotel. At last the lights of Dundonnell could be seen in the distance. 'Whore of a night,' called a voice from the Smiddy Mountain Hut.

Sweeping snow off my pannier bags I entered the palace of the Dundonnell Hotel: electric lights, hot baths and, best of all, endless supplies of lager! The following morning I enjoyed the luxury of a full breakfast, for today was a rest day. My once tidy, sweet-smelling room had degenerated into what looked like the scene of a successful crime. Waterproofs and cycle bags were strewn everywhere. Clothes and socks dried while my cooking pots steeped in boiling water. On the floor lay a tattered map in eight pieces. Such was the welcoming scene when Tom, Doreen and Alastair arrived from Glasgow.

DUNDONNELL TO BEINN DEARG AND BACK AGAIN, 21–24 APRIL

Morning sunshine beamed on Little Loch Broom, making it sparkle with pleasure. From Ardessie a pleasant stalking track took me up the side of the Allt Airdeasaidh. The heavy rain of the last few weeks had filled it to the brim. It bored and twisted its way through many gorges and pools, adding a refreshing spray to the freshness of the morning. Despite the recent rain, the heather was now tinder dry.

My collie dog Munro who, as always, had come up with Tom

and Doreen, raced ahead. Above lay Sail Mhor, 767 metres, meaning 'the Big Heel'. Her easy-looking eastern slopes proved to be steep and hard work, but rewarding too, as pretty flowers seemed to peep out from under every rock. The summit ridge felt like a walk in the park in comparison.

Since Corbetts tended to be by themselves, the views are often superb. This summit was no exception. The Western Isles basked in the sunlight. The panoramic views of the Fisherfield Forest disappeared in a maze of lochans and mountains — wild empty land, at peace today. Only a cold wind from the snow-covered slopes of An Teallach disturbed the serenity.

I felt like a newborn lamb, and wished to run and run and never stop. But, alas, back at the hotel, routes had to be replanned and equipment double-checked, since an energetic fortnight lay ahead.

The previous day's brilliant weather was short lived as I steered my bike out of Dundonnell in the early morning light, cycling east to join the main Ullapool road. Soft rain fell instead of the wintry blast I had endured the previous Friday. A 21-mile ride took me to Inverlael. Today's plan was again to enter the MacKenzie country, climb Seana Bhraigh, and come out over the Beinn Dearg range tomorrow, then return to Dundonnell and continue my southward campaign.

Happily, I wasn't going to be alone. Tom and Doreen dropped off Alastair Conkie. I had met Alastair the year before, and he had been a great help nursing me over some of Skye's more difficult peaks. Alastair's slim build belied his endless energy and enthusiasm. While I had been tucked up in a warm bed in the Dundonnell Hotel, Alastair had been bivvying out close to the snowy summit of Beinn a'Chlaidheimh in the heart of the Fisherfield Forest. 'Och, it was a wee bit cold, but I had a fine early start the next day.' Such is the admirable spirit of a hardy mountaineer.

Alastair was my first companion on 'the hill' since leaving home in February, and soon the glen was echoing with jokes and laughter. A fine stalking track led over Druim na Saobhaidhe, meaning 'Slopes of the Fox's Lair', and struck east towards one of Scotland's remotest Munros, Seana Bhraigh, 927 metres. The path ended, like a worm cut in half, among a wilderness of lochans. Navigation in the mist was tricky, taking a bearing from one lochan to the next. This magnificent mountain has three summits, the most westerly being the highest. From here the northern cliffs plummet to the lonely Loch Luchd Choire. However, it is the smaller eastern top that steals the glory. From the south, in total contrast to her gentle sloping neighbours, Creag an Duine resembles a fine sharp peak that gives an exciting scramble to its rocky summit tower. Some walkers may welcome the use of a rope here; I know I would!

The day's constant drizzle had helped to top up the already full burns. Alastair was most impressed by my concern for his welfare as he waded the River Beag, until he realised he was carrying my precious camera. We settled down for the night and mixed both our dehydrated meals together, producing something quite appetising ... providing you didn't look at or smell it, of course.

My plans to climb 'The Deargs', the four remaining Munros in the Inverlael Forest, got off to a good start. We were away at 6.30 a.m., which was perhaps a bit of overkill on my part, but the hills had to be climbed today. As usual, mist was right down to the glen. Our compass-bearing took us to Loch Tuath, which is the start of the beautiful string of lochans that eventually feed Loch Glascarnoch. From the air it must appear like an elaborate group of garden ponds.

Climbing Cona'Mheall, 980 metres, from the east was a bonus, as we avoided the unpleasant scree on its more popular western side. The ice axe came in handy during the last hundred feet to the summit. From the col of Beinn Dearg we looked deep into Loch a'Choire Ghranda. Memories came flooding back of a camp near the lochan one freezing July evening on a trans-Scotland trip with Glen More Lodge.

We were both impressed with the wall that led us uphill, close to the summit of Beinn Dearg, 1,084 metres. Alastair commented that he never thought the Romans had got this far.

The weather was clearing now, and we crossed Meall nan Ceapraichean, 977 metres, with ease. Unknowingly, today was giving the biggest bag of summits of the walk so far. Alastair had left most of his kit at the tent and was lightly laden, so he pushed on ahead for Eididh nan Clach Geala, 925 metres, while I with the heavier load followed some way behind. Lying down sleepily at the summit, he heard footsteps approaching. Assuming it was me, he put on a hippy accent and said, 'Hi! Peace, man, what's new?" A southern accent replied with an awkward 'Good Morning' and rushed off, muttering something about bringing back conscription.

The crags on Beinn Dearg's western ridge had a perfect band of snow along the top, just like a whitewashed wall. It was sad to say goodbye, but I had to get back to Dundonnell, while Alastair was determined to investigate the spectacular Creag an Duine. After swopping rations, we arranged to meet in Skye in about eighty hills' time. The western slopes were springy, and I was soon enjoying a bouncy descent. Cycling back to Dundonnell, I hoped for a spell of settled weather. The BBC settled it all for me: it was going to snow.

Icy rain poured down on a waterlogged Dundonnell, meaning 'Field of the Two Donalds'. Disillusionment at the terrible weather conditions affected my judgement. High above, no doubt experiencing fierce winter weather, lay the two main summits of An Teallach. Although they can be climbed from the north quite easily, the real fun is traversing the narrow ridge and pinnacles to the east. However, my plans to do this, and descend to a bothy in the heart of the Fisherfield Forest, were thwarted by warnings of strong winds and wet snow on the summit. So, leaving the bulk of the kit at the hotel, and with only a day-sack, I ventured out on what seemed an insane journey. It took ages to climb up the rocky terracing that forms the lower slopes of the mountain.

The rain hammered down relentlessly, turning even the smallest burns into an Icelandic torrent. Boots were soon soaking, pockets filled with water, and icy drips disappeared down my back. Bidein a'Ghlas Thuill, 1,062 metres, wasn't in the friendliest frame of mind. After gobbling a soaking Mars Bar it was good to get moving, whistling 'Sing a Happy Song' and bombing on for Sgurr Fiona, 1,059 metres.

The mist cleared for a second, to reveal a sullen Loch Toll an Lochain, resembling a black widow spider in its sunken lair. The summit ridge was covered in wet slippery snow. I was glad of my decision not to attempt it. An Teallach is a spectacular mountain, but it demands respect and reasonable weather. For here is surely home of the Valkyrie. The BBC TV film 'Duel on An Teallach' told the true story of a young man's dramatic rescue attempt on the mountain.

It was a relief to climb down out of the storm, with ears buzzing from the excitement of the day, and heaven to jump into a hot bath, while the burns roared outside the hotel, and our weather prophets promised the same or worse tomorrow.

DUNDONNELL, LOCH A'BHRAOIN TO KINLOCHEWE, 25 APRIL–1 MAY

The contents of the breakfast table provided a perfect relief map for next week's foray. The goal was Kinlochewe, 27 miles to the south, represented by the marmalade pot. The napkin and condiment set were the hills to be climbed this week. Shaped like a giant meat hook, my route was to climb the mountains, south of yesterday's An Teallach, by Loch a'Bhraoinn, through the dense cluster of summits in the Fannichs; then via Fionn Bheinn to Kinlochewe, skirting the more forbidding peaks of the wild Fisherfield and Letterewe forests, like a respectful timber wolf encircling its prey. The problems suddenly disappeared: the waitress had cleared the table of this week's mountains. I wished it was that easy.

I was delighted to find the often troublesome Allt Gleann Chaorachain crossable, and was soon enjoying the twisting track into a land little changed since the Ice Age. Stern, towering mountains dominated the view, as hundreds of deer eyed me suspiciously from the misty heights. A cheerful puff of smoke came from the chimney of a nearby bothy. An elderly lady who once lived here used to walk every day the sixteen-mile round trip to and from work at the Dundonnell Hotel.

Keith and David were inside. After a wood-collecting foray, we settled down by the fireside and mixed all our food together, while Keith started a jovial *ceilidh* with his penny whistle. A good time was had by all.

The morning was as bleak as ever. Rain hammered across Loch na Sealga under the austere gaze of today's challenge, Beinn Dearg Mor, 908 metres.

After carefully wading across the two full rivers that feed the loch, I tripped and landed headlong into a peat bog. A wild burn led up to Loch Toll an Lochain and a perfect corrie, nestling between today's peaks: Beinn Dearg Bheag and her larger and more dramatic sister, Beinn Dearg Mor. Dumbstruck with the raw beauty before my eyes, I watched the strong wind pluck water from the lochan and glide around the loch, then swore as it dropped the entire contents on my head.

Gentle slopes led up the summit of Beinn Dearg Bheag. The sun made a weak attempt to shine, the grey light glittering on the maze of lochans that saturated the empty moorland stretching to lonely Greenstone Point. Here at Loch na Beiste, a monster can be found, often seen on Hogmanay or after a good *ceilidh*.

Beinn Dearg Mor charged my childish imagination. She seemed like a fairytale mountain, where goblins and dragons might live. Her massive summit cairn sits dramatically at the edge of an outcrop. Inches away, steep cliffs plummet down to the glen far below. Yes, she wins my prize as our most beautiful Corbett. Despite her stern appearance, she can be easily climbed by today's route from the south or by her north-east ridge.

A deceptively easy-looking descent to Gleann na Muice Beag, meaning 'Glen of the Little Pig', soon had me messing about on the edge of some crumbling crags, while hoodie crows soared above, amused at my predicament.

Back at the bothy, it was a pleasure to meet three lads from Ulster, and Celtic humour was soon in good swing, with whisky being a fair trade for my compo biscuits. Curtains of rain swept across the mountains and the bothy rocked in the wind, as one of the Irish lads took a spade in hand and, with a purposeful look on his face, repeated Captain Oates' famous words, 'I'm just going outside.'

It had snowed heavily overnight. We were now paying the price of an exceptionally mild winter. Putting on frozen boots was a painful experience. A rowan tree beside the bothy, planted by Hamish Brown, looked sorry for itself, laden with snow. I said cheerio to my Irish friends with a friendly snowball fight.

My route headed east into an icy wind, under the shadow of the roaring Eas Ban waterfall. This would be the most spectacular way to climb today's peak, Creag Rainich, meaning 'Rock of the Ferns'. This remote Corbett is well worth a visit, if only for her dramatic views to the west, and is easiest climbed from the stalking track by Loch a'Bhraoin.

The summit promised a view, but just on arriving at the cairn, a snowstorm blasted the mountain, sending me running for cover. Falling knee-deep into an icy burn added to the misery. The shores of Loch a'Bhraoin were a welcome sight, and soon the stove was simmering and the appetising smell of dehydrated Beef Bourguignon filled the air.

I woke to the sight of horizontal snow shooting past the tent. It felt more like January than the end of April. My diary read: 'Impossible to climb today, cannot see the hills through the snowstorms.' It is in circumstances like this that the eternal optimism of a Partick Thistle supporter comes in so handy, for surely it can't get any worse.

It was good to nestle down in a warm sleeping bag and dream of long summer days on the hills. I chuckled to myself about a local story. The previous Christmas Eve a walker from East Kilbride jumped off a bus at the road end, four miles to the east, and plunged straight into a pool of icy water, right up to his chin. I felt quite lucky in comparison.

The wet, misty morning had been successful in pushing the snowline further uphill, but the two Munros opposite were still in winter condition. It was great to be winding my way between the mass of burns that flood from A'Chailleach, 999 metres, meaning 'the Old Woman'.

The effect of mist on snow made navigation a slow, careful business to her sister peak, Sgurr Breac, 1,000 metres, meaning 'the Speckled Peak'. Both are very pleasant hills, but the latter, with its many crags and hollows, offers much more to fire the imagination.

The two Munros combined gave an easy day usually climbed from the road end, if weather allows. They are sometimes thrown in as a long hike with the seven other Fannich Munros to the east. The ice axe came in handy for the steep descent to a very full Loch Fannich.

A delightful stalking track wove its way between burns and hillocks to arrive suddenly at the loch where the tent was pitched. Tomorrow promised to give me a fine horseshoe round of the seven other Fannich Munros. There seemed little point in climb-ing hills in what was left of today, in poor conditions, that simply would have been revisited on the morrow. Unfortunately the hammering of the last few weeks was beginning to affect my judgement and confidence. Later that night, I found I had severe logistic problems as a result of running a day behind schedule, and food was very short. My Irish friends had given me an old bag of cereal which they explained was the most horrible thing they had ever eaten, rather like hamster food. While admitting that it was a bit tasteless, it really got me out of trouble.

It was a relief to be away at 7.00 a.m. and enjoy dry weather. The Land Rover track skirted the northern shore of a peaceful Loch Fannich and penetrated some sweet-smelling woods, abundant with wildlife, owing to the sensible planting of the trees, with enough living space for all. Five miles later, I was champing at the bit, racing up the slopes of An Coileachan, 923 metres, meaning 'Little Cock', the first of today's planned seven Munros. 'The Fannichs' are a long walk in anybody's books, but so rewarding. Apart from the pleasures of the summits, the range is a mass of hidden corries and lochans, abundant wild flowers and ice-cool springs on hot summer days. It cheered me to look north as mountain after mountain disappeared into the horizon, and know each one had been climbed. With fingers crossed for a continued clear day, I zoomed on for Meall Gorm, 949 metres, resting for the moment by the little slab stalking hut close to the summit, which was choked with snow.

Feeling hungry, I checked my meagre ration supplies. I had one Mars Bar and a handful of dry, mouldy cereal to last for the next two days, which I promptly ate to avoid any further mathematical complications! Skirting the snowy slopes of Sgurr Mor, I saw dozens of orange and yellow dots that turned out to be an Edinburgh school party in fluorescent waterproofs. Their leader explained they were heading for the loch tonight and that the weather report was for a high pressure area over the Highlands, guaranteeing fine weather.

Skipping for joy, I raced on to Munro no. 3, Beinn Liath Mhor Fannaich, just as the first of the snowflakes began to fall! It turned very cold. Winter was back with a vengeance. The fourth peak, Sgurr Mor, 1,110 metres, gave a grim battle.

A council of war was held at the summit: go on or turn back? Definitely on: it's just a freak storm. At the col of Carn na Criche, progress was reduced literally to a crawl. Snow stung my face. Thank goodness for my goggles. It was madness to continue.

A steep descent was made to the glen, where an angry Allt a'Choire Mhoir roared a frenzied charge towards the loch. I cursed my laziness yesterday in not attempting the three Munros I had been forced to leave out today. My ambitious plans were falling to pieces, and what about the school party? Surely they would be heading off the hill? They could be as much as an hour and a half ahead of me, so they wouldn't necessarily be in sight. The burns got wilder and wilder as I drew closer to Loch Fannich.

I was worried not to see any more of the school party. I was to learn later that they had experienced problems. One girl became terrified of the river conditions, and one of the boys took ill with colic after drinking too much burn water. They had forced their way to Fannich Lodge and phoned for a lift from their other group, based at a youth hostel near Inverness.

After 24 miles of walking and four Munros climbed, I settled down to a spartan meal of Angel Delight mixed with water and the last of the cereal.

Any ideas of rubbing your face in the dew the next morning, the First of May, would probably have resulted in frostbite. Breakfast consisted of one mug of black tea. There was no food left at all. It was very cold again, with the snow level down to 1,800 feet, and the wind roaring in defiance outside. Traversing the west end of the loch, a raging Abhainn a'Chadh'Bhuidhe threatened to cut me off. Fortunately, a sunken iron bridge was crossable with care. Walking along the south shore of the loch, I scanned the hillside opposite for any sign of the school party. However, smoke rising from the chimney of Fannich Lodge reassured me they must be all right.

It was a relief to reach the Land Rover track that runs alongside the hydro-electric pipeline through Strath Chrombuill. A little hut provided shelter for a brew, and I was amused to see the name of a long-distance walker attempting the Munros in 1982 written on the wall. I added my usual signature, a drawing of a bunny rabbit, next to some guy called Egon Ronay.

My rumbly tummy was beyond the stage of hunger, as the easy

northern slopes of Fionn Bheinn, 'the Pale Coloured Hill', 933 metres, were assaulted. Spindrift blowed a welcome from the summit. Memories came flooding back. This had been my first Munro, eleven years ago, climbed with Geoff Payman's 'Hill Squad' from the Glasgow Academy. I remember the excitement of finding fools' gold in the burns, and seeing a huge herd of deer, at least 150 strong, race off into the distance. Thankfully the same sights still thrill today.

The mountain's northern corrie, Toll Mor, is far more dramatic than the OS map would have you believe. It was good to stand on the summit of my 75th hill, 74 days out from home. To celebrate, I dug deep into the soaking pocket of my Gore-Tex jacket and found one single Rolo sweetie that had been floating around for a few days. It sounds revolting now, but at the time it was like finding treasure, as the taste was long savoured. With eight miles covered and another ten to go, it was a very hungry walker who arrived at the bunkhouse of the Kinlochewe Hotel.

CHAPTER 3

May 1985

Beinn Eighe to Slioch

—

Whirling through the Whitbread
Wilderness

—

Flowerdale to Torridon

—

Sanctuary in the Willowfields:
Applecross to Achnashellach

—

Attadale to Strathconan

—

Glen Strathfarrar

BEINN EIGHE TO SLIOCH, 2–6 MAY

Today felt like a holiday. The sun beamed on the pretty village of Kinlochewe. Civilisation certainly had its advantages, as the hotel's bunkhouse would be my base for a couple of days until Tom and Doreen visited again.

The village shop was an Aladdin's Cave, as I eyed with pleasure the endless shelves of fresh milk, fruit, cakes and other yummy goodies. The lady behind the counter looked at me strangely with a curious, questioning frown as if to suggest, 'Where have you just escaped from?' I pointed at the shelves, then myself, saying in an animal-like voice, 'Me hungry.' I then bought my first newspaper in weeks, the shop assistant cheekily remarking, 'To eat or to read, sir?'

The rocky crooked path opposite the farm of Anancaun spiralled upwards. Gone were the memories of the past six soaking, storm-lashed weeks and the worries of a tattered schedule ahead; before me lay two new mountains to climb. The track led through the heart of the Beinn Eighe Nature Reserve, the first of its kind established in Britain. It contains some of the country's oldest fossils, and is a safe home for pine martens, wild cats and golden eagles.

The track came to an end like a severed hosepipe, as do most tracks that enter the wild interior of Torridon, surrendering as they do to the lunar-like landscape and the maze of boulder-fields. A lot of huffing and puffing took me up the scree slopes of Meall a'Ghiubhais, 800 metres, to her summit plateau. There are two cairns here, the more southerly being the higher. The fine Torridon mountains filled the horizon. Sitting independently from their neighbours, few other peaks inspire the hillwalker's dreams and whet his appetite for the future as these do. The hill's proud slopes fall steeply to the high moorland of the interior, strewn with lochans and boulders, once a hide-out for wanted or banished men. To the south lay Ruadh-stac Beag, 896 metres, towering through the afternoon's mist like an evil fortress cast out

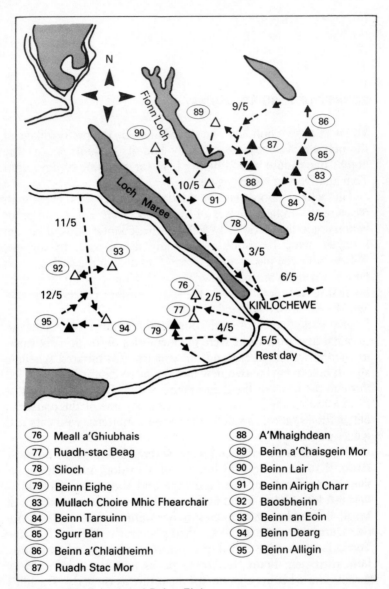

76	Meall a'Ghiubhais	88	A'Mhaighdean
77	Ruadh-stac Beag	89	Beinn a'Chaisgein Mor
78	Slioch	90	Beinn Lair
79	Beinn Eighe	91	Beinn Airigh Charr
83	Mullach Choire Mhic Fhearchair	92	Baosbheinn
84	Beinn Tarsuinn	93	Beinn an Eoin
85	Sgurr Ban	94	Beinn Dearg
86	Beinn a'Chlaidheimh	95	Beinn Alligin
87	Ruadh Stac Mor		

Map 14   Whitbread and Beinn Eighe

from the long Beinn Eighe ridge, which stretched like a giant grey tidal wave at its back. It was fun clambering on her southern ridge, over and round the huge boulders, some the size of lorries. This was the mountain's most sensible approach. Surprisingly, the summit was almost flat, and this, combined with her steep slopes, gave me the feeling of being on top of a multi-storey building.

What seemed like an inviting descent via a scree slope turned into a nightmare as the rocks became as big as footballs, making the going tediously slow. It was pleasant to descend the track towards Kinlochewe as a rosy sun sank at my back.

An early morning phone call was made to Tom about arrangements for the weekend. The telephone box brought back happy memories. In November 1978, during a walk from Glasgow to Cape Wrath, I had crawled in here one cold, wet night and started cooking a meal, while the wind howled outside and rain lashed the windows. Then came a knock at the door. A man wanted to use the phone. He phoned his girlfriend while I shivered outside. The conversation was amusing: 'Hello, darling. Oh, hold on a minute while I turn down this fella's stew!'

A fine track led along the northern shore of Loch Maree. The mass of driftwood and mangled trees bore witness to the recent wild weather. My track split off into Gleann Bianasdail, crossing the Abhainn an Fhasaigh, meaning 'the River of the Dwelling Place.' Sadly, it is devoid of any habitations now. High above lay Slioch, 980 metres, 'the Hill of the Spear', which sits so dramatically over Loch Maree. A faint track became more distinct as it led into her amphitheatre-like corrie. Snow still clung to her summit. At the cairn were Philip and his dog Pasha. He was a British civil engineer working in Nepal because he liked climbing mountains, and was on holiday here for the same reason. A hole appeared in the mist to reveal Loch Maree, one of Scotland's finest freshwater lochs. Her thirty islands were once strongholds and hiding places during the days when raiding Viking galleys ravaged the area, and later when the MacKenzies and MacRaes crossed swords with the MacLeods, driving them from their Gairloch lands. Along the northern shores of the loch there had been several ironworks and the surrounding forest had been denuded for their use. A razor-sharp ridge led on to Slioch's eastern top, Sgurr an Tuill Bhain. The wild hills of the Letterewe Forest beckoned to the north.

The morning mist still clung to the high tops of Beinn Eighe, 'the File Mountain'. A good track led up the side of the Allt a'Chuirn to join the long slopes from Coire Domhain to Creag Dubh, the most easterly point of the mountain's five-mile ridge. It was pure joy to get my hands on some rock again, as the shattered pinnacles of the Black Carls provided an enjoyable scramble with plenty of holds. Walkers-only may wish to leave out this, the most easterly section of the ridge.

Despite its long length, Beinn Eighe has only one Munro summit, and it lies on an offshoot ridge to the north: Ruadh-stac Mor, 1,010 metres. As usual, I arrived at the summit alone. However, within seconds, people arrived from almost every direction and I soon found myself with about twenty companions. This was the May Holiday weekend and a couple of popular Irishmen celebrated their climb by handing round a bottle of whisky.

Beinn Eighe's real treasure lies in her three northern-facing corries, in particular Coire Mhic Fhearchair. It's surely Scotland's finest corrie, its dark blue lochan overshadowed by the magnificent triple buttress, today laced in white. Back on the main ridge, a small boy pleaded with his father to take more photographs of a magnificent snowy Liathach to show his school pals. I finished my film as well, then enjoyed a fabulous glissade into Coire an Laoigh.

Before leaving the hotel that morning, I had asked which bedroom Tom and Doreen would be staying in. This, I was assured, would be Room 9. Wishing to surprise them, I barged open the door, shouted 'Yippee!', and threw my smelly balaclava in at a young couple I had never met before! A bark from Munro in the next door room confirmed my mistake.

I shared the one room with Tom, Doreen and Munro, as the hotel was full. With so much to do on rest days, I was up early next morning and, armed with maps and writing paper, walked innocently into the residents' lounge. Suddenly, all hell broke loose. Bells started ringing. I had set off the burglar alarm in the lounge, and an angry manager appeared at the door. Munro barked at him and upset the magazine table. I felt the manager was relieved we were leaving next day.

WHIRLING THROUGH THE WHITBREAD WILDERNESS, 6–10 MAY

Munro woke me up at 7.00 a.m. Being careful not to set off any alarms, I gently opened the hotel's front door and we stepped outside. Unfortunately a freak wind slammed the door shut behind us. Not daring to ring the bell, I sneaked round the back of the hotel and started throwing pebbles at Tom's window. It was the wrong room ... I found myself staring up at the man who was involved in the unfortunate balaclava-throwing incident the day before. He seemed to have lost his sense of humour ...!

Arrangements were made with Tom and Doreen to meet again in three weeks' time. Midday had them heading south to Glasgow, while my route took me east ... a fourteen-mile walk back to Loch Fannich. It was a pleasure to meet Ian Crosby there with a school party. We had met almost exactly a year before in the same area. In front of a roaring fire we enjoyed a great *ceilidh* as the youngsters were introduced to mountain life.

The bright morning sunshine beamed on the long grass of Sgurr nan Each, 923 metres, making it shine like golden hay. This was the first of the three Fannich Munros remaining to be climbed. It would be easy to be annoyed with myself for having to return to mountains that could perhaps have been climbed the week before with a bit more foresight. But then, this walk wasn't a hectic race: it was a year-long honeymoon, the climax to a lifelong love affair with the hills and wild places.

A hoodie crow cawed a welcome from the summit. A long wide ridge led on to Sgurr nan Clach Geala, 1,093 metres, while dramatic cliffs plunged towards a peaceful Allt a'Choire Mhoir, flowing gently down the glen: a contrast to last week's foaming cascade. Ptarmigan scattered in all directions as I sighted a strange, multi-coloured boulder that, on closer inspection, turned out to be a huge pile of rucksacks from another school party. The youngsters streamed from the summit of Meall a'Chrasgaidh, 934 metres, faces beaming with pleasure and excitement. Minutes later I had the summit to myself.

A few cheery songs passed the miles to the west end of Loch a'Bhraoin. Here it was pleasant to laze on the warm grass which only the week before had been ankle-deep in snow. A cuckoo serenaded me from its secret hiding place.

The following day was one that had been anticipated since the start of the walk, for this morning I would penetrate the inner sanctuary of the 'Whitbread Wilderness', so called after Colonel Whitbread, a previous owner. Here lies Scotland's wildest scenery, a lost world of stern crags and high-perched lochans so remote that two new Munros were found here as late as 1974.

The massive Mullach Coire Mhic Fhearchair, 1,019 metres, slowly increased in size as I inched my way nearer. Encumbered with a heavy pack, it took me four hours to reach the summit. To the south-east lay one of the mountain's two 'tops', Sgurr Dubh, whose narrow ridge is dramatically slashed by nature to form a chasm: easily enough got round in summer, but best avoided in winter months, unless one is equipped for climbing. Today's route resembled a helter-skelter ride, as I bombed down the scree, moving quickly with the heavy pack which had been left waiting at the previous cairn.

Ahead lay Beinn Tarsuinn, 936 metres, 'the Transverse' or 'Crossways Hill', a fitting name for this dramatic mountain. It's more reminiscent of the lands of the Incas, with a table-top plateau sternly cut like a Christmas cake. It was pleasant to share this remote summit with Gerry Wright, a charming Londoner, whose stories of visits to the Alps and Norway eased the pain of the long pull back up to Mullach Coire Mhic Fhearchair.

A welcome grassy patch allowed me to avoid the unpleasant rocks and boulders that covered the murderous incline of Sgurr Ban, 989 metres. This mountain is best known for the spectacular rocky slabs that shield her eastern slopes. With the mist closing in, Gerry left me for far-off Carnmore. He seemed as fresh as a daisy. Unlike me!

Beinn a'Chlaidheimh, 'the Hill of the Sword', is my favourite of the group. Far below, Loch na Sealga shimmered in the evening light, while tiny figures could be seen at the bothy below. The easiest descent is to follow the ridge north, then eastwards by gentle slopes towards Abhainn Loch an Nid. Memories of a more direct route to the north were confirmed by the gentle contours on the map. This turned out to be a nightmare. I was soon peering over crags and weaving down gullies. It was a slow business indeed, creeping down the mountain's northern crags.

The bothy was a hustle of activity in the morning. Members of a

Leicester mountaineering club were scattering in all directions. A German named Lutz was continuing his long trek north to Tongue. I was bound for three peaks in the very heart of the Whitbread Wilderness. The formidable rivers of Strath na Sealga and Gleann na Muice still required wading today. Many an adventure has been defeated by their intimidating flow.

The distinct track led up Gleann na Muice Beag to where the spooky mist covered the lochans that marked the top of the pass. A left turn led up to Fuar Loch Mor, the area's highest loch. A quick scurry on sandstone scree led to the crumbling summit of Ruadh Stac Mor, 918 metres, whose shattered face sits silently above the col. Here I found a small stone shelter, still covered in snow. Some idiots, who had mustered enough strength to bring in supplies, had left an empty bag of rubbish behind. If only they had seen the pathetic sight of a young deer with its hoof hopelessly trapped in a rusty tin can, or a dead goat with a bloated stomach after eating plastic bags ... perhaps then they would carry their rubbish to the nearest bin.

With my ice axe left behind, a tent pole was improvised for the ascent of the snowy slopes opposite, leading to the summit of Scotland's remotest Munro, A'Mhaighdean, 967 metres, 'the Maiden'. This is the place to have one last joke on your friends and insist your ashes are scattered here, or better still to have a wedding.

It is only fitting that our most secluded peak should reward its visitors with the most breathtaking views. Today's was cloaked in mist, but the memory of a previous visit one summer's evening, with the sun casting a rosy shadow over Scotland's wildest and finest scenery, will last a lifetime.

After returning to my rucksack for some food, it felt good to be zooming up the 'Big Forbidding Hill' or, in the Gaelic, Beinn a'Chaisgein Mor, 857 metres. If she were to be judged alone by her gentle, eastern slopes, the mountain would be relegated to lowly ranks of mediocrity. But a wrong step to the west could take you down one of the longest and most spectacular cliffs in the country, the famous Carnmore Crag.

After fifteen miles of walking, it was good to descend the cheerful track to the glen below. A curtain of rain tried unsuccess-fully to cover the breathtaking spectacle of white horses racing across the Dubh Loch, under the stern, precipitous shadow of Beinn Lair's magnificent 1,500-foot cliffs.

The causeway that separates Dubh Loch from Fionn Loch was almost submerged as a result of the wettest spring for twenty-five years. Today felt trouble free, as the mist sifted from the high tops. Colonel Whitbread had insisted that only ponies were to be used on the estate for load-carrying, hence the fine stalking tracks and welcome absence of Land Rover tracks.

From the Bealch Mheinnidh, gentle slopes led to the summit plateau of Beinn Lair, in contrast to her spectacular northern crags. The area should be avoided during the stalking season. Two young climbers, rumour has it, found this out to their cost. Halfway up Carnmore Crag, they looked down to see their tent being set alight by the estate's staff!

The view from the summit was superb. The islands on Loch Maree had an almost tropical appearance. Folklore tells us that a Norwegian prince returned to the islands, after a long expedition, to his beloved wife. She unwisely decided to test his love by pretending to be dead. Full of remorse, he fatally stabbed himself. This broke the silly lassie's heart and she committed suicide in the same manner.

A winding track led round the sharply pointed peak of Meall Mheinnidh to the sunblessed slopes of Beinn Airigh Charr, 791 metres. This 'Hill of the Rough Shieling' is a real gem. It offers fine views over the wild moorland to the north and the gentler western scenery, where a crannog, an ancient island dwelling, stood out on Loch Kernsary. The pretty village of Aultbea beamed in the distance. It was from here during the Second World War that convoys used to leave, bound for Russia, to run the gauntlet of German U-boats. North of the summit lies the great tower or Martha's Peak, in memory of a local heroine who fell to her death there while gathering her goats.

It was a long thirteen-mile walk from the summit to Kinlochewe, but the time passed quickly. A deer leapt gracefully over a six-foot fence at Letterewe, then a family of goats accompanied me for miles. My collie dog Munro has a healthy respect for these shaggy, smelly creatures. On the island of Jura the previous year, he gently sniffed a baby goat, only to get a vicious head-butt for his trouble. Daylight was slipping fast from the mountains as the twinkling lights of sleepy Kinlochewe were reached.

FLOWERDALE TO TORRIDON, 11–17 MAY

After the luxury of a cooked breakfast, I whizzed along the shores of Loch Maree on the bike. Unlike the cars racing past, I had time to enjoy the scenery. A hard pull led to Am Feur-Loch at the top of the pass between Loch Maree and Gairloch. Here was a fine hiding place for the bike. Five miles to the north, across the rough-hewn land of small, stony mountains, lies Loch Tollaidh, reputedly home of an ancient Macbeth fortress. The Birnam woods would have plenty of problems trekking here!

A fine rocky track led to Loch na h-Oidiche, which sounds as if it were named on Hogmanay, meaning 'Loch of the Night'. Gentle moorland led steeply to Baosbhein, 875 metres, 'the· Wizard's Hill'. One could easily imagine a spell had been cast on the area: the endless miles of boulder-fields and bogs stretch in all directions, stark and foreboding, but strangely friendly, too.

The kind sun baked down on her ancient slopes. The fine cliffs south-west of the summit have been branded unclimbable. The beauty and the stillness gave me a reverent respect for nature. A pair of eagles playfully dive-bombed each other, while a small speck on the horizon was identified as Clisham on Harris. Was it only seven weeks ago that I stood on her snowy summit?

To the south lay the Isle of Skye, for once clear, except Glen Brittle of course! It was here, after a drunken dinner, that a MacLeod war party sailed forth in a huge black galley, determined to win back their beautiful Gairloch lands from their enemies. They sailed into Loch Gairloch, hid behind the tiny island of Fraoch-eilean, and prepared for the attack. However, they were spotted. The fiery cross had been sent round to raise the clansmen, and hordes of MacKenzies and MacRaes waited in deadly ambush. They showered the trapped MacLeods with a merciless rain of arrows. Only two escaped to sail back to Skye.

Opposite lay this mountain's sister hill, Beinn an Eoin, 855 metres, 'Hill of the Birds'. With evening light fading, I scurried up her broken slopes and enjoyed the everlasting sight of the untamed wilderness of scattered lochans and endless rocks at peace with the fine spring evening.

It was a pleasure having the Ordnance Survey 1:25000 outdoor leisure map with me. Its intense detail seemed to outline every rock. Navigation in mist was no longer a problem: simply walk round a boulder and compare its shape with the countless thousands of others marked on the map.

Navigation was not left in doubt today, as the towering bulk of Beinn Dearg, 914 metres, filled the horizon. This 'Red Hill' seemed such an ordinary name for one of Scotland's most splendid peaks. At 2,998 feet high, its altitude has been checked and double-checked for inclusion in Munro's Tables. Ravenous Munroists, eager for a new peak, poured over her steep battlements in expectation of her promotion to the first division of 3,000-foot peaks. The hue and cry over, she now sits in the peace and quiet of the more modest Corbett tables.

Sneaking up on this wild hill from behind had its advantages, as several easy routes were spied from the An Coire Mor, and an enjoyable scramble was had along the summit ridge. I have never been an enthusiastic reader of guide books, but wish I had on this occasion. The inviting western slopes fell steeper and steeper, and the friendly burns marked on the map formed deep hostile gullies, as I weaved in and out of the ledges, with my knees grumbling over the way they were being treated.

Beinn Alligin, 'the Jewelled Mountain', 985 metres, was busy in contrast to my previous peak. It was good to follow the 'Horns' of Alligin, whose playful summit towers gave some easy and highly enjoyable scrambling. I caught up with Jock and Jim 'frae Keith' and our humorous banter eased the long pull to the top. At the summit we had to admit that, with the difference between Aberdeenshire and Glasgow dialect, we hadn't understood a word any of us had said!

We descended, passing the remarkable Eag Dhubh na h-Eigheachd, a wondrous black cleft that gashes its way down the craggy slopes and is not recommended for climbing or descending.

The gentle northern slopes led me down to the rock-strewn moorland, the start of a ten-mile walk back to the bike. Stopping for a couple of pints at the Kinlochewe Hotel was a bad idea, as afterwards I had difficulty in unlocking the bike's padlock. Stags serenaded me in my mad dash to get to Torridon Youth Hostel before it shut for the night.

In the morning tired legs were not enthusiastic to get out of bed, but, with the skies promising a dry day, they sprang into life. Cycling round the head of peaceful Loch Torridon, my eyes were pulled to the sight of a misty Beinn Damh, 902 metres, meaning 'Hill of the Stag'.

At the back of the Torridon Hotel a delightful track led through the fresh-smelling woodland. A thick carpet of fallen pine needles enabled me to walk quietly, increasing the possibility of a glimpse of a pine marten or wild cat.

A side track left the main path up towards the mountain's gentle northern ridge, under the watchful eye of Creag na h-Iolaire, 'the Eagle's Crag'. An alternative but longer route from the south, starting from Loch an Loin, rewards the walker with a close study of the mountain's famous 'stirrup mark'.

From the summit, two figures in orange cagoules could be seen following the path to Loch Damh under the stern shadow of the mountain's eastern-facing crags and gullies.

I had bought some apple tart and a can of lager to celebrate my 100th hill of the walk, and soon a mad cheering could be heard from the summit. Later I realised that a miscalculation had been made and I was still a little short of that number. But at least it gave me the opportunity to celebrate it again later!

In practice for this, I visited the Beinn Damh bar, situated handily at the foot of the mountain. The barman asked me if I had seen any motor-bikes on the mountain. Seeing my puzzled frown, he explained that every year, in preparation for the Fort William motor-bike trials, a couple of bikers visited from the south and took their brutes of machines up the mountains. They even ride down Liathach's great stone shoot, which I normally confess to walking down gingerly. I could see the newspaper headlines now: 'Long Distance Walker Knocked Down by Motor-Bikes on Slopes of Alligin'!

The strong morning winds rattled through Glen Torridon and reduced my cycling efforts to a snail-like pace. A car slowed down for a chat. Inside was Peter from Northern Ireland, a fellow patron of the pub at Kinlochewe. He was bound for Alligin and, on hearing my plans for climbing Liathach, 'the Grey One', he frowned, 'By jeepers, Craig, in this wind?'

These words of doubt echoed in my mind, as the rocky path led steeply into the jaw-like Coire Liath Mhor. Above lay the twin

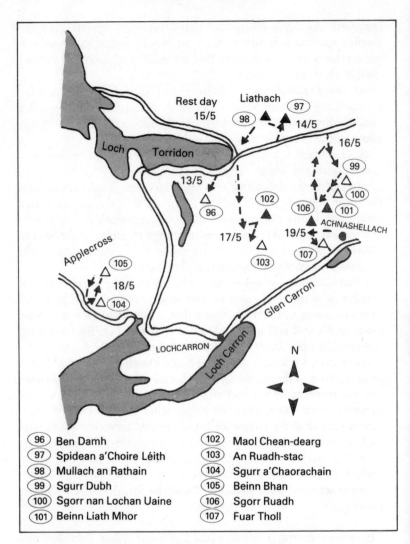

Map 15 Torridon and Applecross

mountain of Liathach, with its two Munro summits and the exciting pinnacle ridge between them. The wind blew me across the boulders to Spidean a'Choire Léith, 1,054 metres, 'the Peak of the Grey Corries'.

The summit was clear of snow, yet only a few days earlier a

party had been traversing the ridge in snow. One had fallen, lost his ice axe and was hurled down the slopes, hell-bent on a course of certain death, when he steered himself to smash into a boulder, breaking an ankle. The rock had saved his life, for it was precariously resting at the edge of a thousand-foot cliff.

An Englishman and his American girlfriend joined me as we huddled around the storm-blasted cairn. They explained they had been climbing in the Cairngorms that morning and got blasted here. I could well believe it. Bent double, I inspected the pinnacle ridge, normally a highly enjoyable scramble, but in today's conditions out of the question. We opted for the 'tourist route' round the south side of the mountain. This beautiful track wound its way round the sandstone ledges, making us feel like extras in an Indiana Jones movie, as the crags fell away into oblivion, inches from our feet.

Liathach wasn't giving up her second summit without a fight. Now on open ground, gale-force winds blew us violently off course as we inched our way painfully forwards. The lassie was knocked down in one blast, and her map case sailed off, bound for the Isle of Skye. It was with a great cheer that we reached the cairn of Mullach an Rathain. Fond memories of a fast and pleasant scree run down the great stone shoot were soon shattered. Years of heavy usage had reduced it to a steep, unpleasant escarpment, which enforced a tiring knee-jerking descent to the luxurious and friendly Torridon Youth Hostel. Here a schoolteacher was taking great delight in dissecting the regurgitated waste of a sea bird to a group of disgusted pupils.

After a peaceful rest day I awoke the following morning with batteries recharged, ready for any obstacle ... the first of which was to perform my morning duty of cleaning the gents' toilets!

The Ling Hut on the south side of Glen Torridon was an ideal place to hide the bike. The stalking track shown on the map as fizzling out in the moorland actually stretches, with the odd gap, most of the way to Bealach Ban.

Above, hidden in the clouds, was the first of three peaks planned for today. I avoided Sgurr Dubh's northern crags and climbed high into a misty moorland of lochans and tortured rocks resembling a scene from *The Hound of the Baskervilles*. At last I pulled on to Sgurr Dubh's bumpy summit (782 metres). Sadly,

these fine peaks are often left out, being overshadowed in popularity by their higher neighbours. I left the cairn singing happily,
blissfully unaware that the 100th peak of the walk had been
climbed. My route swung south-west towards Sgorr nan Lochain
Uaine, 873 metres 'the Peak of the Green Lochan' who was starting to peel off her misty veil. I was rewarded with a brief but
spectacular view of her beautiful turquoise lochans.

Mountain after mountain became visible on the horizon. Keeping to the east of the biggest lochan, a flank led up to the delightful two-mile-long summit ridge of Beinn Liath Mhor, 925 metres.
This 'Big Grey Hill' is exactly that, as Torridon sandstone mixes
with quartzite. Care should be taken to avoid the troublesome
rocks and crags to the south and south-west of the summit, especially in bad weather.

In a purposeful mood, a herd of deer diagonally crossed the
hillside opposite. Down in the glen a pair of eagles swooped
down on an intruding bird trying to muscle in on their territory.
Time after time the ace pilots fought their aggressive dog-fight,
till at last the intruder flew sulkily away, its great wings casting a
dark shadow in the fading evening light.

Grey mists clung to the summits, and the morning rain tumbled
from the skies, but it was a pleasure to be walking on one of the
country's finest paths. A soldier coming down the glen explained
he had been dropped off at Coulags in Glen Carron. He had
walked the seven miles by Bealach na Lice and been amazed at
the beauty and solitude. I passed a cairn in memory of the Roberts-
sons, which is puzzling, as it is far away from their homelands in
Atholl. Mystery surrounds much of the old place-names in the
Highlands, especially those in memory of the ancient Fingalian
heroes, which appear in almost every district. On the far side of
this pass the Clach nan Con-fionn was the rock where Fingal
tethered his hunting hounds.

The stalking track encircles Maol Chean-dearg, 933 metres,
'the Bald Red Head'. Seen from the north, this Munro appears as
a large dome guarded by unpleasant rocks and crags. From the
lochans at the top of the pass, I cut back on the summit across the
ankle-breaking rocks to today's cheerless summit.

An Ruadh-stac, 892 metres, 'the Red Peak', was a much more
forbidding prospect. The sight of her steep eastern ridge, water

pouring down the slippery polished slabs, brought a lump of fear to my throat. Confidence, however, grew as I climbed higher, creeping over the boulders and giving a wide, respectful berth to steep, misty emptiness either side of the ridge. My trusty compass led me to the huge cairn on the summit. The cold wet weather was sapping energy and concentration. This mountain gave me the creeps, and I followed the compass back to the ridge. Fifteen minutes later, I found myself facing another huge cairn: 'Oh, no!' I had followed the wrong arrow and walked round in a complete circle. If you think that's bad, my worst navigational mistake was leading a party in the Luss Hills up the wrong mountain! The most worrying thing about this marathon walk was that my support team really thought I was going to succeed.

It was good to be able to descend into a world of vision, if a very wet one. Back at the youth hostel, some Welsh climbers were reliving their day's adventures while climbing Liathach. They had been narrowly missed by a huge boulder that crashed down the mountain. I could well believe it. A few years earlier, I witnessed a massive boulder plummet off that mountain's northern crags and smash down the precipitous terracing to crash into the glen with a sickening roar that echoed for ages round the surrounding hills.

SANCTUARY IN THE WILLOWFIELDS: APPLECROSS TO ACHNASHELLACH, 18–20 MAY

My poor bike was beginning to show signs of strain. A buckle on the rear wheel seemed strangely compensated for by several broken spokes on the front. It rattled its way into Glen Shieldaig, as I turned my back on lovely Loch Torridon. To the right lay pretty Applecross. This fishtail-shaped peninsula was home to two Corbetts, and my blood raced at the thought of two new peaks to climb. My plan was to take full advantage of the public road that climbed over the peninsula by the Bealach na Ba, 'the Pass of the Cattle', taking me almost to the doorstep of the first mountain. Such dreams were soon eclipsed by the leg-punishing reality of cycling from sea level to the top of a 626-metre pass.

The gentle ridge leading to Sgurr a'Chaorachain, 792 metres, was tarnished only by the ugly transmitter station on its western top. But it was well compensated for by the sight of a golden eagle almost within touching distance, hovering in the wind above the crags overlooking the pass.

The A'Chioch, a massive rocky tower, rose like the long throat of a giant dinosaur from the mountain's northern spur. For this was no tame mountain, but the ultimate in untamed beauty. Two miles to the north was a warren of black boulders, some precariously positioned, left there since the Ice Age. Here lay the sleeping giant of Bheinn Bhan, 896 metres, meaning 'the White Hill'. Her seven spurs strain in all directions like the legs of a massive octopus. Mist prevented a full view, but occasional glimpses of their endless cliffs and pinnacles were exciting enough. The mountain has pulled some of the finest climbers to her remote corries: Chris Bonington, Tom Patey and Joe Brown among them. It is no doubt a favourite stamping ground for Martin Moran, who now runs an adventure centre in nearby Loch Carron.

While I was crossing Coire nan Cuileag the mist cleared to reveal the pretty Applecross village with the Island of Raasay beyond. St Mol Rubha established a church here in the year 671. It was a famous sanctuary, and many a man has reached the safety of its boundary stones with his enemies at his heels. Only once was the sanctuary invaded. An evil Viking longship crept stealthily into the bay. Over the sides poured the brightly clothed Norsemen, wielding their axes and clubs with great ferocity as they attacked the community with terrible brutality. The carnage over, the murderous Vikings set sail. Then justice was done, as their longship sank with all hands.

Cycling back down the pass was a pleasure, but demanded concentration. A dangerous side wind threatened to unseat me as the battered front wheel waggled unhelpfully about. Eleven gentle miles led me to Gerry's independent hostel at Achnashellach, meaning 'the Field of the Willows'. Gerry was away for a few days, but had left the place open. Guests took foods from his store, made a list of what was used and, on leaving, paid their dues to an old lady across the road. Such trust helps restore one's faith in human nature.

The track led through the woodland under the shadow of a misty Fuar Tholl, 907 metres, as squirrels scattered to their favourite trees. Achnashellach railway station was as peaceful as ever. On a previous walk the small waiting-room-cum-shelter gave me a good berth one night. A peaceful night's sleep was followed by embarrassment as I slept in. With the early morning train waiting, I threw all my kit into the train corridor, much to the amusement of some schoolgirls.

I chuckled at these memories of years before as the pine-needle-cushioned track broke free from the woodland and followed the River Lair, whose cascading waterfalls were revelling in the morning's soft rain. The fine stalking track split in three: mine climbing to the west under the impressive buttresses of Fuar Tholl, to end in a maze of lochans. It was here in 1870 that the Prince of Wales, soon to be Edward VII, was almost killed in a rockfall while enjoying the barbarity of a driven deer hunt. Careful navigation led to a drenched Sgorr Ruadh, 958 metres. It was a shame to be cheated of a view of this mountain's splendid western crags.

Recrossing the loch-strewn bealach, deer danced like ghosts in the mist. A series of false bumps led to the summit of Fuar Tholl. There is reputed to be a fine scree slope just west of the summit, but in today's poor visibility it was difficult to find any enthusiasm for leaping into the misty unknown.

At the bealach, the mist cleared to reveal a dark Loch Carron, with the little village of Strome in the distance. In 1602 the MacKenzies stormed the MacDonnels' ancient fortress of Strome Castle. In 1873 a crowd of 2,000 locals rioted against a boat unloading cargo on the sacred Sabbath day. Perhaps most interesting of all is the case of the Lochcarron-based SS *Ferret* which left the Clyde on a homeward journey, only to disappear. After great searching, she was presumed sunk without trace. Then quite by chance, she was found in Melbourne, Australia, renamed the *India*. The crew had planned the theft of the ship for years, and had even forged stamps and documents.

Down at Gerry's cheery cottage hostel, it was good to relax in front of a roaring fire with other mountain folk, whose adventures spanned the world. In pride of place, pinned to the wall, was a letter from a barman with an impressive CV, inquiring if there were any job vacancies available at the hostel!

The morning mist sifted from the trees of the Achnashellach Forest. Cycling up the steep forestry track with the heavy load

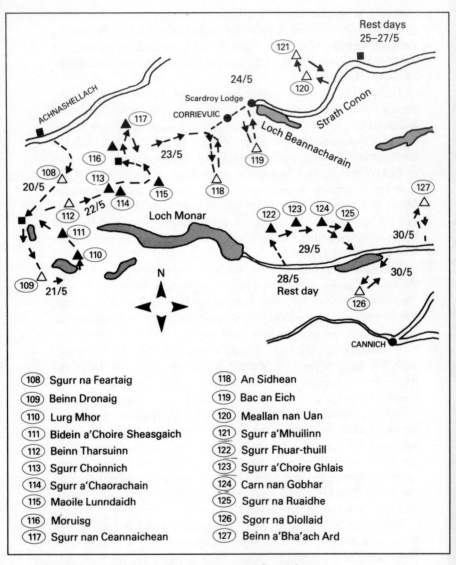

Map 16   Loch Monar, Strathconan and Strathfarrar

was hard work. Even harder was trying to avoid the minefield of puddles that barred the track leading south to Glenuaig Lodge.

After hiding the bike in some woodland, it was good to traverse west and the climb the easy slopes of Sgurr na Feartaig, 862 metres. A fine stalking track crosses its ridge, then splits in two, one heading west to Strathcarron, the other north to Achnashellach. The bridge opposite Lair is a wire nightmare. Memories of crossing with a heavy pack in November, with the River Carron in full spate, keep recurring every time I see a horror film. There is a fine bridge two miles up river.

At my back stretched some of the remotest mountain ranges in Scotland. From Loch Ness and Strath Bran to Glen Shiel lay 52 Munros and Corbetts, contained within 700 square miles of almost empty country. The enormity of the challenge of the walk forced me to take each day as it came and never look at the overall project.

Descending, I witnessed a strange phenomenon. Cold air filled the glens and hot air lay above the hills, trapping the mist and causing it to roll down the hillside, then disappear. The entire effect was of a continuous misty avalanche.

Friends Alastair and Simon visited the area a few weeks later and were entertained by a group of fishermen with huge carry-outs. The generous anglers insisted they join the party. Alastair, who doesn't drink, gave his ration to a very happy Simon.

ATTADALE TO STRATHCONON, 21–25 MAY

The kind sunshine unrolled like a golden carpet over the Attadale mountains. Ahead lay an old friend, Bendronaig Lodge, now a locked building. I arrived on its doorstep one cold November night soaked to the skin with a saturated sleeping bag, having cleverly fallen in the River Ling at Reidh Breac, nicknamed 'ready brek'. The door was unusually open, and never was I happier to find a couple of musty old blankets to keep me warm.

What a joy to follow the sunny stalking track round the end of Loch Calavie to climb the gentle green slopes on Beinn Dronaig, 797 metres. The sunshine and clear views made this one of the most pleasant hills of the walk. To the west lay the famous Mam Attadale pass. Here an invading force of 160 Redcoats were ambushed and defeated by a small group of MacKenzies.

It was a long pull up the slopes of Lurg Mhor. To the south lay an area of boggy moorland and glens, where General Monk was forced to abandon many of his pack ponies and their cargo, which had become hopelessly stuck in the mud. The Jacobite clansmen plundered what was left and found something called chocolate, which they presumed was a salve for putting on wounds. Lurg Mhor is a massive, remote peak and fairly tests the resolve of the most ardent Munro enthusiasts. But to stand on its remote summit at the west end of Loch Monar is to appreciate the glorious beauty of the Western Highlands.

Like a cat with two tails, I bombed on for a real gem of a mountain, Bidein a'Choire Sheasgaich, 945 metres, strangely meaning 'the Peak of the Corrie of the Milkless Cattle'. Luscious grass covers its rocky ridges culminating in a beautiful pointed summit, a gentle contrast to its more stern neighbours in Torridon. The cliff on the mountain's northern spur that descends to Bealach an Sgoltaidh appears intimidating. However, difficulties can be avoided by walking around the crag, or you can enjoy a scramble down a chimney close to the small lochan at the top.

The previous day's golden sunshine seemed like a dream as I pushed headlong into the rain plastering the bumpy ridge leading to Beinn Tharsuinn, 863 metres. It's a Corbett which is often climbed while Munro enthusiasts push on for the fine horseshoe of Munros at the west end of Loch Monar.

A rousing chorus of 'Ye Jacobites by Name' led me up the twin Munros, Sgurr Choinnich, 999 metres, and Sgurr a'Chaorachain, 1,053 metres. They share a spectacular corrie, which is the centrepiece of scenery for anyone climbing up the forestry track from Glen Carron.

The gentle ridge led me down to Lochan Gaineamhach, 'the Sandy Loch', and avoided the unpleasant scree on the north face of Sgurr a'Chaorachain's western ridge. Long slopes led up to a propellor-shaped Maoile Lunndaidh, 1,007 metres. Careful navigation was required in the thick mist to her rain-soaked cairn. The descent was cheered by meeting hillwalkers employed by British Rail. They, like myself, had cycled in to the locked building of Glenuaig Lodge, though they had enjoyed a competition to see who could fall off the most times. A small, toothless, bruised little man with thick glasses proudly introduced himself as the winner. And I thought I was nuts!

A strong wind rattled through the glen as I charged up the fine stalking track behind Glenuaig Lodge, which was under a thick cloak of drizzle and mist. Easy slopes led up to Moruisg, 928 metres, a gentle mountain, except for her interesting northern corrie that plummets to Coire Toll nam Bian. The wind buffeted me on my approach to Sgurr nan Ceannaichean, interestingly called 'the Pedlar's Peak'. Both these mountains are close to the Glen Carron road and, as a result, tend to suffer in being earmarked for murky days when the weather prevents more adventurous deeds. They deserve better.

I missed my four-legged trusty companion Munro. He would have liked this hill, with plenty of decomposing deer to roll around in. Sadly the need to cycle ruled him out most of the time. What did his doggy brain think of his master, seeing him only once a fortnight, smelling of the hills?

Back at the tent, I broke the news to my bicycle. No, it wasn't going down that nasty, pot-holed Land Rover track to Glen Carron. It was going east to Strathconon, eight miles of single-track, bicycle-hating paths. Cycling was impossible as pedals dug into rocks and earth. Then the left pedal came clean off! Like leading a stubborn mule, I carried and pulled my wrecked bicycle over boulders and through rivers, as the spokes twanged every five minutes. If anyone talks to me about the joys of cross-country cycling again ...

Camp was established at the junction of Allt an Amise. I fixed the pedal and did what I could with the broken spokes. A stalking track led south through waist-deep heather, bound for An Sidhean, 'the Fairy Hill', 814 metres. It was close in the ratings for the most remote Corbett. The heather got higher and thicker as the path got thinner. Thank heaven I didn't have my kilt on!

Leaving the cold, misty summit, I was surprised to see across the glen a flying-saucer-shaped tent pitched at Loch a'Chlaid-heimh, 'the Loch of the Sword'. After weeks of solitude in the hills this puzzled me. Then it twigged. This is the time of the 'Ultimate Challenge', when 250 hardy individuals walk coast to coast across Scotland, taking the advantage to explore some of her wildest parts. Remote bothies or bed-and-breakfast establishments that hardly get a visitor all year would enjoy a few days of frenzied activity. With the evening light fading I hurried down to my tiny nylon home, pitched a different shape every night. Tonight it was squarish.

The tent was packed up and I was walking, or rather pushing, by 5.30 a.m. Opposite the Creag na h-Iolaire, 'the Crag of the Eagles', I passed what was surely an 'Ultimate Challenger' tent, cruelly ringing my bicycle bell. I would love to have heard the breakfast conversation . . . Mile after mile I dragged my protesting bike, till at last we reached the bliss of the road at Corrievuic.

It was pouring with rain and low mist hung to the treeline. Somewhere up there was Bac an Eich, 849 metres, 'the Ridge of the Horses', the first of three Corbetts to be climbed this long day. The burn leading down to Corriefeol soon developed into a deep gorge. Halfway up I was surprised to find a telegraph pole on either side of the gorge with a single wire and pulley connecting them. No doubt these were put to good use during the stalking season, as this is a prime area. The summit gave no view and I felt a little cheated not being able to see into remote Glen Orrin.

Back down at the bike my stomach was beginning to trouble me. A bag of suspicious shrimp curry was responsible. With the rain pouring down, I took shelter under the bridge over the River Meig and boiled up some powdered milk, as the icy raindrops filtered through the planks and down my neck.

It was a joy to cycle or waggle down lovely Strathconon. I have never been to Canada, but I would imagine this is similar: fresh-smelling woodland, steep hills and lochs galore. I stopped near the Thomas Telford church by Strathanmore. I was starving and scoured in all my cycle bags for anything edible. Suddenly the cavalry arrived in the shape of an ancient bus, a travelling shop full of fresh milk and home baking. Bliss!

With my body refreshed, the steep slopes were soon below me as the summit cairn of Meallan nan Uan, 840 metres, 'the Little Hill of the Lambs', came into view. These gentle hills reminded me of the Braes of Balquhidder. Strangely they are tucked away from view, but give a good outlook themselves. From the top of Sgurr a'Mhuilinn, 879 metres, the moorland of Strathbran to the north rose steeply to the Fannichs and the Deargs, climbed only a few weeks before.

The ground around the Allt an t-Strathain Mhoir was very boggy. Lambs were everywhere, their spring-loaded legs recoiling for another leap across the hillside. After fifteen miles of walking, I wished I felt the same way.

It was great to be welcomed to the friendly East Lodge Hotel, and sink into a hot bath. Tom and Doreen would arrive tomorrow with Munro, my chaotic collie, sure to disturb the tranquil peace of the glen for ever.

GLEN STRATHFARRAR, 27–30 MAY

The 48-mile cycle ride from Strathconon to Glen Strathfarrar still left me with a tingle in my legs. The hectic rest days were anything but restful and were usually spent repairing my bike and planning the busy fortnight ahead. I awoke to a nightmare: wind roared down the glen and spindrift towered from fresh snow on the hills. I groaned and rolled over and had a proper rest day, sleeping for some seventeen hours.

My batteries fully recharged, I rose early. The private road to Loch Monar dam was deserted, save for a herd of deer who raced for the sanctuary of the woodland. What fear they have of men, as they squeezed through the trees, banging on fence posts as they went.

A grassy stalking track led up to Loch Toll a'Mhuic under the stern, rocky frowns of the bumpy southern ridge, steering for Loch Monar. Ahead lay the Strathfarrar 'gang of four'. This group of Munros is usually climbed in a rush, as climbers who have used the private road hurry back before its gates are closed for the evening. A pleasant, grassy ridge led to Sgurr Fhuar-thuill, 1,049 metres, 'the Peak of the Cold Hollow'. Lonely Glen Orrin lay to the north. The pioneering spirit raced through me with thoughts of how this glen could be used for a fresh approach on these hills next time.

Sgurr a'Choire Ghlais, 1,083 metres, is the highest of the group. Here the steep and sometimes savage beauty of the west ends, and the gentler hills of the east begin. I was soon skipping over Carn nan Gobhar and Sgurr na Ruaidhe, and enjoying a good brew-up in the corrie below. The burn gurgled down to Loch a'Mhullidh, whose island was a hiding place for Lord Lovat of Clan Fraser after the disastrous battle of Culloden. Imagine his feelings ... his proud clan defeated, his castle destroyed. The clan won a pardon, however, by raising over 1,800 men to fight in the American wars.

It was good to be back in Strathfarrar, for here the previous year the idea of the walk had begun while chatting to Simon Stewart from Dundee. Over a mug of tea and a sparking fire the seeds of the mad adventure had been sown.

Early morning sunshine beamed on the glen, and the air smelt of the bouquet of wild flowers. Gentle hills to the south of the glen rose to the rocky point of Sgurr na Diollaid, 818 metres. The pretty woodland at Cambussorray was reflected in the still black waters of Loch Beannacharan. There the romance ended as I tugged and pulled myself up the mountain, a jungle of heather barring the way. Far below me, a family were launching a boat in Loch a'Mhuillidh. A moment's lack of concentration had me tumbling down the slopes, losing about twenty precious heather-pulling feet. I came to the conclusion that this mountain would be better climbed from Glen Cannich, to the south.

The little rocky-peaked summit looked down into Strathglass, the long glen that stretches from Cannich to Beauly. After Culloden, the evil Major Lockhart prepared his troops to fire the glen. This order was not well received by his men, as some of them had relatives living there. The following morning, before the barbaric major could give the order, he was mysteriously shot dead by a sniper.

It was a pleasure riding my repaired bike for, with new wheels, it now went in a straight line! Further down the glen, the Glen Affric Hotel minibus blocked the road. It had a flat battery. I helped the driver push-start it. It juddered into life, then suddenly stopped at the foot of a steep hill, the engine shuddering weakly. The driver got out and said, 'Och, I didn't want to drive away without thanking you.' Luckily he got back in before the engine stalled.

A maze of Land Rover tracks had me confused on the lower slopes of Beinn a'Bha'ach Ard, 862 metres. At last, through the

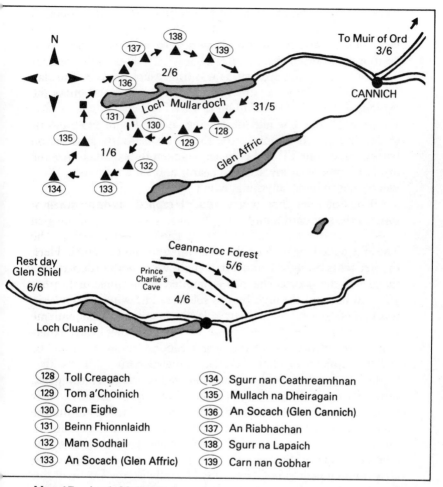

Map 17   Loch Mullardoch

(128) Toll Creagach		(134) Sgurr nan Ceathreamhnan
(129) Tom a'Choinich		(135) Mullach na Dheiragain
(130) Carn Eighe		(136) An Socach (Glen Cannich)
(131) Beinn Fhionnlaidh		(137) An Riabhachan
(132) Mam Sodhail		(138) Sgurr na Lapaich
(133) An Socach (Glen Affric)		(139) Carn nan Gobhar

muddle, I found the path leading up the Neaty Burn. It was very hot, and, out of the corner of my eye, I noticed a large brown branch just ahead, moving slightly. Then an adder coiled to life and slithered into the ferns with a heinous hiss, as my spine shuddered.

It was a delight to reach the summit as a welcome cooling breeze raked the cairn. This hill could be climbed as a pleasant horseshoe, combining today's route with the pleasant stalking track a mile to the east that drops gently to Inchmore. Miles of lonely empty moorland stretched to the north, in contrast to the view to the east, where traffic rushed to and fro a now very cosmopolitan Inverness.

In the cool of the evening, it was a pleasure to cycle south to Cannich. The lady at the Kerrera House bed-and-breakfast explained the house was full and, with a rather worried expression, added that I would be staying in her brand new luxury chalet. She proudly showed me the lavish cabin, with carpeted bathroom, colour TV and polished wooden floors. She looked at my filthy breeches, my scraggy beard, and said anxiously, 'You will try not to break anything, won't you?'

'Och, don't let that worry you,' I replied, as my rucksack toppled the standard lamp!

The bike pulled me high up the steep hill into Glen Cannich. Here the Redcoats brought Hanoverian civilisation, with orders to put the glen to the sword. The glen is haunted by the ghost of a three-year-old boy run through by the soldiers. The winding road led through pretty woodland to arrive at the massive looming hulk of the Loch Mullardoch dam. From here a three-day foray would take in twelve Munros surrounding the loch.

I was cursing my late start as I tangled with the incredible chest-deep heather in the woodland to the south of the dam. From Creag a'Bhaca a gentle but long ridge rose to Toll Creagach, 1,053 metres, 'the Rocky Hollow'. The big mountains beckoned to the west with the evening sunshine smiling kindly on the gentle slopes of Tom a'Choinich ahead. I was beginning to regret leaving the bike behind.

A tranquil lochan in Coire Mhic Fhearchair, 'the Corrie of the Farquharsons', was an ideal camp-site, with a swimming pool a few feet from the tent door. After a good meal, I day-dreamed. What valiant deed had Fionn and his mysterious warriors done to have this corrie named after them? Perhaps we will never know. The rosy sun sank slowly over the peaks of Glen Shiel and Glen Albyn. Could that really be Ben Nevis? Like a child determined not to sleep, I watched the panoramic view, my eyes slowly closing in the gentle darkness.

CHAPTER 4

June 1985

LOCH MULLARDOCH TO GLEN MORISTON AND PRINCE
CHARLIE'S CAVE, 1–5 JUNE

Today was the first of *miòs meadhoin an t-Sàmhraidh*, or just simply June. It was good to be up early. I have never lost the childish delight of walking in early morning sunshine. Other hill-walkers were rushing to pack their tents far below by Loch a' Choire Dhomhain.

The spine-like ridge rose gently to the summit of Carn Eighe, the highest mountain west of the Great Glen. Few indeed are the days in which the hills are so clear. With my early start, I was a happy clansman. To my back stretched lovely Glen Affric, whose lochs and woodlands are so like the forests of Canada that the BBC shot their TV series 'The Last of the Mohicans' there.

The ridge to the west had mouth-watering summits waiting, but a detour had to be made north to Beinn Fhionnlaidh, pronounced Benully. This involved a drop of over a thousand feet just to pat her remote cairn. The mountain overlooks Loch Mullardoch. The previous sweltering summer I had climbed down to her western end as darkness fell at the end of a long seventeen-hour day . . . to find the two stalking huts I had planned to sleep in had been burnt to the ground. Ferocious midges allowed only an hour's sleep till I could stand the torture no more, and got my earliest-ever start on the hills at 3 a.m.!

Andrew and Alan, from the Jacobite Mountaineering Club, gave me a welcoming cheer to the cairn of Mam Sodhail, 1,180 metres. Theirs was the tent I had spied earlier in the Choire Dhomain. This peak was used extensively by the Ordnance Survey during its preliminary mapping of the Highlands in the 1840s.

Leaving the sun-baked cairn of An Socach, 920 metres, it was good to cool hot feet in a small lochan. Before the war the landowners of this estate were very unfriendly to walkers, posting sentries on the hill tops and glens. Fortunately things have changed, and the only restrictions are the normal ones during the stalking season.

Ahead lay the big mouthful of Sgurr nan Ceathreamhnan, pronounced 'Kerranan'. She is the cornerstone of the fifteen-mile-long ridge stretching from the east end of Loch Mullardoch. Leaving my rucksack at the main summit, I enjoyed a playful scramble to her western top. To the north-west thundered the magnificent Falls of Glomach which pour with such strength into the chasm that leads down to Glen Elchaig. When the falls are in spate, one can see from miles away the misty spray towering above the spectacular cascade. Although a place of great beauty it is haunted by the chilling ghostly spectacle of a happy group of Highlanders and their families who were enjoying a walk there when they were suddenly attacked and murdered by an enemy clan.

A long ridge led me out to Mullach na Dheiragain, a remote peak that stretches northwards from the main ridge like a raised sword. For many this is a painful mountain, for it takes them further away from their base in Glen Affric. But, with my tent on board, home was where I fancied. An eighteen-mile day had given six Munro summits, the best tally of the walk so far. My camp by the Allt na Criche, 'the Burn of the Foray', had an almost alpine feel, as cattle watched me pitch my strangely shaped tent and enjoyed nibbling the guyropes.

Despite being away at seven, it was very warm close to the summit of An Socach, 1,069 metres (not to be confused with yesterday's mountain of the same name). It was good to stop for a brew-up. To the west, dancing in the sunlight, lay the mountains of Attadale and Torridon, climbed last week. I spied little An Cruachan, a small remote mountain to the north, seldom visited except for enthusiastic geologists who come to study her unusual rocks. Beyond lies lonely Loch Monar and Pait Lodge, one of Scotland's remotest inhabited lodges.

I have always been fortunate with the weather in my visits to these hills and today was no exception. The mist sifted off the narrow, grassy ridge of An Riabhachan, revealing multi-coloured spectres and full glories beaming on her northern slope. These wonderful tricks of light, occasionally seen on mountain tops in misty conditions, are among the many rewards. The ridge skirted the mountain's rough northern corrie, where a large herd of deer cooled off from the heat.

Sgurr na Lapaich, 1,150 metres, strangely meaning 'the Hill of the Bog', is the largest mountain of the group. Her many subsidiary tops are a test for the most ardent Munro enthusiast. The still air allowed the midges and flies to climb the 3,775 feet to the summit. The mountain's graceful shape stirs the heart, and, once climbed, will be always remembered. A young Fraser clansman, being sent to fight with Wolfe at Quebec, stole out of his barracks in Inverness, and rode to Strathfarrar for one last loving glimpse of the snowy slopes of Sgurr na Lapaich.

Carn nan Gobhar, 992 metres, 'the Hill of the Goats', was the last of the group. From the summit I looked down on a peaceful Loch Mullardoch and tranquil Glen Cannich beyond. This was the land of Clan Chisholm, whose devotion to the Stewarts ended bloodily on Culloden Moor. Undefeated, some of her clansmen continued a guerilla war, sweeping down on the unsuspecting Redcoat columns. The famous Chisholm stone can be seen on the north side of the loch close to the dam. It was there that the chieftain held his daily parliament.

My plans for a morning assault on some remote Corbetts in Glen Affric were scuppered when the bike developed a torn tyre and, for the only week of the journey, I was without a spare. The bike limped into Muir of Ord, where John, who runs the bike shop, supplied a replacement.

With the best part of the day over and a support team to meet in far-off Glen Shiel in three days, a quick replan was made. By cycling south to Glen Moriston I could have a quick stab at the Ceannacroc mountains and be handy for Glen Shiel.

Feeling lazy, I enjoyed breakfast in bed while the River Moriston flowed a few feet away under the shadow of 'the Craig of the Wolf' on the opposite bank. Rain started to spit as the bike wound its way west on the narrow road. To the left lay a cairn in memory of Roderick MacKenzie. After Culloden, Prince Charlie was in hiding in the mountains with the Redcoats' cordon growing tighter every day. Two soldiers chased and shot young Roderick who bore a remarkable resemblance to the prince. With his dying breath he shouted, 'You've shot your prince!' Believing Charlie dead, thousands of soldiers came down from the hills, allowing the prince to escape from their grasp.

The bike shuddered on the Land Rover track passing Cean-

nacroc Lodge. Kit was transferred from cycle panniers to rucksack while the midge clan rose in their ferocious thousands.
Ahead lay the Conbhairean group of three Munros, with Prince
Charlie's cave ideally situated in Coire Mheadhoin, nestling at
their feet.

The pot-holed track wound its way westwards beside the roaring River Doe, while stormclouds gathered on the mountains
ahead. There is a chilling local story of a barn full of hay that
stood in this glen, locked and undisturbed for many years. One
day an estate worker, caught out in a storm and unable to open
the door, jumped down into the hay through a skylight.
Unknown to him, the barn was infested with hundreds of adders
living in the warm hay. He was bitten to death.

Soon the crags of Coire Mheadhoin filled the horizon. Somewhere nestling among the mass of rocks lies Prince Charlie's
Cave. It is not clearly marked, and I was becoming exasperated
looking for it when I had a brainwave: use a cross-bearing. All
those hours of studying books on compass navigation would be
put to good use. I aimed my trusty compass at one hill and then
another on the opposite side of the glen, drawing a line from each
on the map. I watched expectantly as the lines drew nearer.
Where they crossed would give my position in relation to the
cave. Clever stuff! Alas, the map had an unhelpful soggy tear just
where the X marked the spot.

With the mist closing in on the corrie, I wandered through the
boulder-field and stumbled across a plaque fixed to a boulder at
the rear entrance to the cave. I lowered myself into the snug rocky
shelter. Prince Charlie stayed here for five days with his legendary
bodyguards, the Seven Men of Glen Moriston. These hardy guerilla fighters were disgusted with the Redcoats' barbarous murdering of wounded and prisoners after Culloden. The extermination
of innocent women and children in the Highland glens went on
for years after the battle. The seven resolved never to give up the
cause, and fought a bloody campaign against the Redcoats, many
of whom were lowland Scots who imagined the Seven Men of
Glen Moriston were many times their number. Each day one of
the seven men would make the long forty-mile round trip to Fort
Augustus to get food and, more importantly, find out the
Redcoats' movements.

My evening meal simmered as grey mist covered the corrie,

giving the famous cave an austere atmosphere. Prince Charlie's secret hide-out was safe for another night.

> No more we'll see such deeds again,
> Deserted is each Highland glen.
> And lonely cairns are o'er the men,
> Wha' fought and died for Charlie.

In the morning, a cold wind blew through the cavern. It was the 110th day of the walk. I peered out from my rocky lair on to a bleak scene. Icy rain lashed the corrie like a meteor storm, with normally trickling burns swelling to white torrents. I could find little enthusiasm for venturing on to the storm-battered tops, so I sadly splashed down the waterlogged glen, bound for Kintail.

At Shiel Bridge it was a pleasure to meet old friends Andy and Carol who had made the long trip north from Wolverhampton. Carol's mothering nature took pity on my shaggy, dishevelled appearance and repaired an obscene tear in my breeches. My 'no transport' rules applied to rest days too, so we left our bed-and-breakfast at Inverinate, bound for a bar supper in Dornie, three and a half miles to the west, Andy and Carol by car, with me following on my battered bike. The next day we enjoyed a visit to lovely Eilean Donan Castle, a rebuilt version of the ancient MacKenzie stronghold, whose turbulent history is a book in itself. Andy, a keen ornithologist, enjoyed his visit to the lonely River Glennan, a place once renowned for illicit whisky distilling.

OVER THE SEA TO SKYE, 7–14 JUNE

> If you are a delicate man,
> And of wetting your skin are shy,
> I'd have you know, before you go,
> You had better not think of Skye.
>
> Sheriff Alexander Nicolson

The Isle of Skye seems second choice for tourists visiting Scotland, Edinburgh in the far east taking precedence. But for the mountain enthusiast it is heaven. Apart from the famous Black

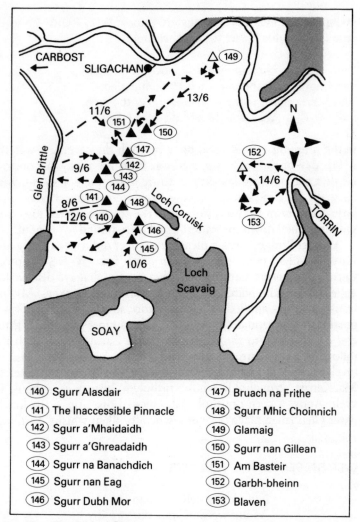

Map 18   The Isle of Skye

Cuillin, Skye, 'the winged isle', has many wild unspoilt mountains in her five wings or peninsulas to last a lifetime of visits ... from the sharp ridges of the Cuillins to the peaceful MacLeod's Tables, or the shapely Trotternish ridge. Whether rock-climber or beach-rambler, all will be left with everlasting happy memories of the 'Isle of Mist'.

Andy was annoyed that the short ferry crossing to Skye took just five minutes: hardly surprising, since I had promised him a five-hour luxury cruise with an opportunity to enjoy river gambling! They were heading for Portree, the island's capital, Carol seemingly under the impression that a metropolis of Debenham's and Marks and Spencer's lay waiting for her.

The main road to Portree wound its way to Loch Sligachan. Skye has over 600 miles of coastline, much of it covered with old paths ... an exciting challenge for any coastal walker. This part of the road is haunted by the ghost of a 1930s Austin motor car which drives at you with lights glaring. You can camp at Sligachanm or stay at the hotel and emulate old climbing heroes such as Norman Collie. Either way, it is a grand base which will leave you spoilt for choice of peaks to climb.

The road became narrower and narrower as the bike wheeled down a forested Glen Brittle, the road ending at the attractive grassy camp-site. The atmosphere was alive with freshness, as waves crashed on the beach, filling the air with the invigorating smell of salt. Andy and Carol arrived for some tea. Later, with darkness falling they hurried back to their bed-and-breakfast in Carbost. Their departure brought a tear to the eye as their cheerful yellow car disappeared over the last hump in the road.

I was awakened by another car, headlights shining on the tent. Alastair Conkie and Simon Strachan had arrived. They had kindly volunteered to come up and help me over the more difficult of the Cuillin peaks. The comic duo hadn't brought a tent, thinking they could squeeze into mine. Simon, a big lad, opted instead to sleep in his Mini Metro, Alastair tried squeezing in with me, but gave up and slept outside in his bivy bag, ignoring Simon's warnings to watch out for the binmen in the morning!

Any hopes of an idyllic day on the ridge were swept away with the morning wind that rattled the tent. The southern part of the Cuillin Ridge is the first barrier to face the Atlantic lows sweeping across the ocean. As a result, it has 300 wet days a year! So it was no surprise this morning to see sullen grey mist covering the ridge.

Our plans to attempt the eleven Munros that sit on the airy crest of the Cuillin Ridge were thwarted, as the threatening dark clouds above turned on the taps. The traverse of the ridge in a 'oner' requires some rock-climbing experience to get over one or two 'nasties', like the Thearlaich Dubh gap. However, walking and scrambling routes can be found up most of the peaks, if a bit of cunning is used.

We were soon weaving up the rocky slopes of Sgurr Sgumain, a top on the ridge leading to Sgurr Alasdair, highest of the Cuillin peaks. Some easy scrambling came to an end as a small crag, about fifteen feet high, blocked our way. Although short, it overhung slightly. We cheered as Alastair clawed his way to the top, then lowered the rope to his soggy fans. I huffed and puffed up the rock then suddenly – rip! – Carol's careful sewing of my breeches came apart, much to Simon's amusement as he was following behind.

Pushing on for Sgurr Alasdair's rocky summit, it was chilling to hear through the mist the sound of a party scree-running down the mountain's great stone shoot. Like the rumbling of a volcano the eerie sound scaled the invisible mist-shrouded cliffs inches from our feet.

We were soon bombing down the Great Stone Shoot. It is worth double-checking from Sgurr Alasdair's col that you are definitely descending north-west into Coire Lagan. For in the mist it can be confusing ... a similar looking, tempting screen slope falls gently to the south-east, then plummets over a sheer cliff! The Cuillins should not be feared, but always respected.

An hour later found us on the opposite side of the corrie, weaving up the rock-strewn slopes of Sgurr Dearg. Alastair raced ahead while I became totally disorientated and got lost. Half an hour later, we met a very cold Alastair at the cairn of Sgurr Dearg. This is not the summit, though no doubt many wish it was, for this mountain holds a savage surprise. Further down the slopes towered the Inaccessible Pinnacle. Sadly, for many, it is aptly named. I had forgotten how daunting it appeared, towering out of the mist, as a savage wind blasted the mountain. Despite my cheery jokes, a tingle of fear ran down my spine.

The Pinnacle is a huge, wedge-shaped rock, and the climber is given two options: either clawing his way up the short, steep eighteen-metre climb to the summit, or the easier option of climbing up the spine of the wedge. Although a 'Moderate' climb, it is incredibly exposed. Alastair led the way, with his two pupils following faithfully behind. Having three on the rope made it a slow climb. Waiting at the belays was a chilling business, as sleet

and gales strafed the mountain, increasing our difficulties tremendously. I decided rock-climbing was not for me. I will never forget
an instructor at Glen More Lodge shouting down a snowy gully:
'You! Tie a bowline there, quick!'

I replied, remembering my rope technique drill, 'The rabbit
comes out of the hole, round the tree ...'

Frozen hands struggled to grip the holds as, inch by inch, we
clawed our way up the rock. At last we stood cheerfully at the
summit, Simon and myself congratulating ourselves madly, while
Alastair looked as if he had just been out for a walk around the
block. With Scotland's most difficult mountain climbed, we were
soon joyfully abseiling down to the more sheltered scree below. I
tried emulating the SAS abseil technique of bouncing down the
face ... and got a squashed nose for my trouble!

Back down at the tent we celebrated with a half bottle of
sherry, then Alastair and Simon drove off for the pub at Carbost.
Much as I wanted to follow them, I hadn't the energy to cycle.

> Lovest thou mountains dwell,
> peaks to the clouds that soar,
> corrie and fell where eagles dwell
> and cataracts dash evermore.

> Sheriff Alexander Nicholson

Simon's face wrinkled in agony, every feature straining in pain, as
he pulled on his soaking cord trousers to the cheers of the youth
hostellers staring out of the steamed-up kitchen window of the
hostel. He followed us, walking bow-legged, up into Coire
a'Ghreadaidh, meaning – aptly for Simon – 'the Corrie of
Torture'.

Alastair rushed ahead. We caught up with him on the summit
of Sgurr Thuilm, where he was busy drying his socks. Ahead lay the
delights of the middle part of the narrow Cuillin Ridge. To our
backs, the jagged mountains fell to the gentle forest and moorland sloping to Loch Bracadale. In 1739 a ship called the *William*
sailed into this bay and, before any action could be taken, the
crew had landed and dragged a hundred women and children on
board to be sold as slaves to the American plantations.

Sgurr a'Mhadaidh, 'Peak of the Fox', 918 metres, loomed out

of the mist, and Alastair raced ahead to enjoy a good scramble.
Simon and I skirted round to the easier approach from An Dorus.
The previous autumn while descending from this col, I heard a
loud rumbling noise behind me. I turned round to see a boulder
the size of a Mini crashing down the gulley. I jumped to the side,
then groaned as the rock altered course heading straight for me.
New-found energy made me sprint across the scree, as the
boulder hurtled past. A few more bumps and thuds were heard,
then a last sickening crash echoed around the corrie as the
boulder finally came to rest.

We met up with Alastair on Sgurr a'Mhadaidh's incredible
narrow crest, then worked our way south, scrambling out of
the slag-heap-like col of An Dorus, then walking to Sgurr
a'Ghreadaidh, 973 metres. The ridge between here and Sgurr na
Banachdich appeared very narrow in the mist, and had us sitting
astride one roof-top part like a saddle. The ridge isn't difficult,
but can be avoided by keeping to the westward side of the ridge.
We weren't aware of this, though our route was certainly fun.

Sgurr na Banachdich means 'Small Pox Peak', from the varied
collection of boulders in her corrie. We descended by Bealach
Coire na Banachdich and worked to the south of the corrie by
way of a very wide grassy ledge that led down to a distinct path.
Hopping over a boulder, my breeches ripped again, much to my
friends' amusement. Back down in the glen, Alastair and Simon
quickly packed their kit and prepared to drive back to Glasgow
with the prospect of a working day tomorrow. Alastair left me
with a touching present: a needle and thread!

The path seemed deserted as it wound its way round the towering
mountains to Coir'a'Ghrunnda. Another track streaked out to a
point jutting into the Atlantic: Rubh'an Dunain, meaning 'Point
of the Fort'. It sits beside Loch na h-Airde, precariously wedged
between the two coastlines as they narrow, like both sides of a
sharpened pencil point dipping into the Atlantic.

My plan was to climb the two Munros at the southernmost
end of the Cuillin Ridge. Rock and scree led up to the rock-strewn
ridge which resembled a rattlesnake's tail. The southern tip is at
Gars-bheinn, 895 metres: alas, not a Corbett, as it does not have
152 metres of reascent on all sides. It's well worth visiting
anyway. It is from here that most attempts at climbing the ridge

in a 'oner' are made. After reaching the summit of Sgurr nan Eag, 924 metres, the ridge led me through a mass of boulders and zig-zagged up a series of ledges to the narrow summit of Sgurr Dubh Mor, 944 metres.

Richard and Dave were on top. These two English climbers had arrived on Skye and decided to acclimatise before venturing on to the misty exposed ridge. They had visited the famous Quirang, the beautiful towering pinnacles at Trotternish in the north of the island, and were narrowly missed by a sheep falling from the cliffs above. Somewhat shaken, they had returned to Glen Brittle camp-site and started climbing a small pinnacle near by. Halfway up, to their horror, the rock and vegetation started to crumble beneath their feet! A couple of scarves were tied hurriedly together to form a short rope to help them to safety. After this, they decided they would be safer on the ridge.

The mist was just clear of the tops. Far below, Loch Coruisk lay still and black, hemmed in by its mountainous guardians, silent in its rocky lair. Skye has so much to offer, and a walk round Loch Coruisk can be just as rewarding as a testing day on the Cuillins.

Down at the camp-site I surveyed my torn breeches, which were now beyond repair and threatened to fall apart. Squadrons of midges were biting furiously, so I moved house to the youth hostel, remembering to don nylon waterproof overtrousers for decency's sake.

There is a saying that if you can see Skye it's going to rain, and if you can't see Skye it's raining already ... The island was back to how I remembered it. Rain lashed the hostel windows and the mountains roared in despair as white foaming torrents gushed down to the swelling River Brittle. At least it made me feel better about wearing my waterproof trousers indoors.

The weather demanded the softest of options available. The bike aqua-slid up the glen and was hidden in the forest opposite Coire na Creiche, meaning 'Corrie of the Raid'. Here the MacLeods clashed in one of their countless bloody battles with the MacDonalds. The MacLeods had rashly entered the fray while their chieftain Rory Mor was away from the island. Lacking his leadership, they were defeated.

The path to Sligachan over the Bealach a'Mhaim had been turned overnight into a flowing burn as the rain continued its merciless downpour. A path led up through the Fionn Coire as the misty summit of Bruach na Frithe, 958 metres, loomed ahead ... one of the easiest hills in the Cuillins. The previous summer, while relaxing at the summit cairn, we welcomed a couple of girls to the top. They had become confused crossing the Bealach a'Mhaim and followed the track up the mountain, presuming it led to the top of the pass! They were surprised to find themselves on top of Bruach na Frithe.

The summit cairn was no place to relax today, as the savage wind and rain howled over the ridge. I kissed the cairn and ran. Down at the hostel, the drying room was packed with drenched clothes, while in the packed common room laughter drowned out the sound of the hissing kettles on the kitchen stoves.

The rocky path climbed high into Coire Lagan under the frowning shadow of The Cioch. This dramatic rock protrudes from the cliffs on the south side of the corrie. Its summit is rounded like an egg, its edge plummeting hundreds of feet to the corrie below. It was this dramatic scene that was chosen for a spectacular sword fight in the Sean Connery film *Highlander*. Two actors were dropped by helicopter to fight their spectacular duel, but in the process they dropped a sword which clattered to the corrie below. A replacement sword was obtained, and the fight renewed among some of Scotland's wildest and most exposed scenery. Soon the combatants were whisked away by the helicopter and Coire Lagan returned to her peaceful sleep.

In the afternoon a London climber, reaching for a difficult hold on one of the popular climbs up to The Cioch, was amazed to find a sword sticking out of a crack in the rock. He pulled it out like Excaliber and shouted to his pal, 'I've found Prince Charlie's sword!' They hurriedly abseiled down the climb and rushed to the telephone box in Glen Brittle to phone *The Times* in London, which printed a story next day.

At the head of the corrie sat Sgurr Mhic Choinnich, 948 metres, meaning 'MacKenzie's Peak', sitting like a giant wedge. The toilsome scree to the south of the corrie led up to the col. This is the easiest way to climb the mountain, although more adventurous alternatives exist. If traversing over Sgurr Thearlaich, the delights of Collie's Ledge can be enjoyed, or a rock climb up Kings Chimney.

The scramble along the ridge in today's clear weather was greatly enjoyed. Climbing over or round the short walls was just good fun as the track led to the airy summit ... However, on my first visit, it was a different matter. Icy rain and wind strafed the ridge, obscuring the easiest routes, while thick mist greatly exaggerated the difficulty and exposure. At one stage my knuckles were white with fear as I traversed a gentle sloping slab, thinking the mist at my feet must reveal a cliff ·plummeting hundreds of feet to the corrie below. Alastair had leaned over pretending to hold a microphone in his hand: 'Now tell me, Mr Caldwell, what are your thoughts on hillwalking in Scotland at this present moment in time?'

With my 148th hill climbed, it was joy to bomb down the scree slopes and cycle out of Glen Brittle for the last time. An idyllic camp-site lay waiting beside the old bridge at Sligachan.

It was a misty morning. A hurried breakfast was a necessity as the midges were in a hungry mood. Although Skye boasts twelve Munros, she has only two Corbetts which keep respectfully east of their larger brothers. One of these lay ahead of me: Glamaig, 775 metres, meaning 'Greedy Woman', highest of the Red Cuillin mountains, so called because of the red granite that covers these mountains. This group in comparison to the Black Cuillin opposite offers relatively easy walking in similarly stunning scenery. Although the Cuillins are superb the delights of Skye's gentler peaks and spectacular coastline should not be ignored.

An easy climb by Bealach na Sgairde led to the summit. Opposite, across Loch Sligachan, lay the Braes of Ben Lee. The story of the poor crofters' desperate battle against the clearances of the 1880s makes sad reading. The evil landlord, Lord MacDonald, enrolled the services of a particularly brutal Sheriff officer called Ivory and fifty policemen. After several sickening baton charges they defeated the women and children trying to defend the small bit of hillside which gave them such a meagre living.

Late morning found me on the opposite side of the glen approaching Sgurr nan Gillean, 965 metres, meaning 'the Peak of the Young Men'. The path led up through a misty Coire Riabhach. Ahead lay 'the tourist route', which is something of a joke although not difficult. It does involve some exciting and enjoyable scrambling. I heard a party through the mist climbing up the scree to my right, which confused me, as I was sure my route lay ahead. I followed them and found a cheery Anglo-American group of lab. technicians. It became obvious that we had turned off too early. A hopeful-looking gully looked as if it would join the tourist route without us having to lose height.

Unwittingly I had become a guide, as my new-found friends followed me up the rocky gully. A boulder dislodged and rolled downhill. No notice was taken of my shout, 'Below!' which means to climbers what 'Fore!' does to a golfer. A change of style was required: 'There's a bloody rock coming!' did the trick, as the group swiftly moved out of the way.

We clawed our way over a huge overhanging boulder that blocked the gully; nothing, it would appear, is easy on Skye. It was snowing by the time we reached the incredibly narrow summit, only a few feet wide, so we shook hands and sang 'Jingle Bells'.

Sgurr nan Gillean's west ridge would be an ideal approach to climb her sister peak, Am Basteir. However, for the walker, the way is blocked by 'the Gendarme', a large lump of rock resembling a policeman that has to be traversed. Although not difficult, it is very exposed and, if unroped, a slip would end your climbing days for good.

It was a happy group that climbed down the mountain, though I had still one peak to climb. The entrance to Coire a'Bhasteir has a 'Lost World' feel to it. Cairns mark the way across a large slabby hill overlooking a roaring gorge, through which flows the Allt Dearg Beag, under the stern shadow of the pinnacles of Sgurr nan Gillean. The toilsome scree led up to the rocky summit ridge. It felt more like peering over the edge of a volcano as Loch Coruisk simmered below. An Basteir, 935 metres, meaning possibly 'Executioner', gives a pleasant and exciting scramble, the crux being a nine-foot drop. The Cuillin Ridge was momentarily at peace. The mist sifted gently in and out of the rocky, sabre-toothed mountains stretching south to the sea. I had arrived a little scared of these very different mountains. We had fought and were now friends, as I blew them a goodnight kiss.

The tent was packed in record time as the piranha-like midges attacked in their thousands. A 23-mile cycle ride found them ready to pounce again at the head of Loch Slapin. A rough walk led up to Bealach na Beiste 'Pass of the Monster'. I hoped I didn't meet it in my dishevelled state ... I wondered who would get the bigger fright! I turned my back on the picturesque little peak of Belig and stormed up the rocky slopes of Garbh-bheinn, 806 metres. It's the highest of the island's two Corbetts: with Blaven, 928 metres, it shares the wild Strathaird group of mountains. Prince Charlie climbed through these hills after sneaking off the Isle of Raasay. I wonder what he thought of their dramatic cliffs and tortured rocks that compete so much with the beauty of the Black Cuillin opposite.

Across Glen Sligachan lies Harta Corrie, scene of a particularly vicious battle between the MacLeods and MacDonalds. Some university geologists, recently surveying the corrie, were woken in the middle of the night by the sight and sound of dozens of ghostly clansmen running up the hillside.

The ridge south to Blaven was dominated by the spectacular sight of the rocky tower of Clach Glas, rising like a miniature Eiger. This part of the ridge is particularly awkward and should be left to experienced climbers with a rope. A scree gully led down to a rough Choire a'Caise to join the path in Coire Uaigneich. Tired legs pulled me up the zig-zagging track to arrive on the roof-top of Skye. Blaven, 928 metres, was the last of my fourteen peaks on the island. The summit was deserted, and the only sound was the hushing of the wind and the cackled call of a hoodie crow, while waves crashed on Camasunary beach. Far across Glen Sligachan twinkled Loch Coruisk and, soaring above her, the lofty, jagged Cuillin Ridge lay sullen and black under threatening clouds. The Good Lord fair excelled Himself when he made the Cuillins. With a long cycle ride ahead I turned to go, but was drawn back to the cairn for one last look and to salute the 'Isle of Mist'.

Broadford seemed the ideal place for a celebration bar supper. After I had ordered my meal, the barman, taking me for a tramp, looked me up and down, enquiring: 'Have you the money to pay for this meal?'

RHUM PEAKS, 15–17 JUNE

The cheery ferry left Armadale and arrived in a bustling Mallaig.

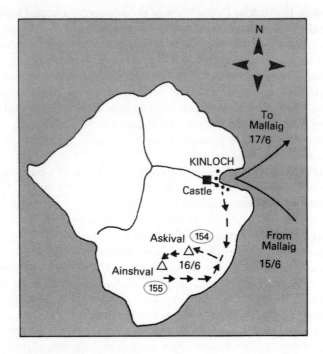

Map 19   The Isle of Rhum

This busy fishing town is supposed to resemble closely Port Stanley in the Falkland Islands. I rested on a seat at the foot of the main street. A small bespectacled Japanese tourist with a huge camera sat beside me. I had plastered up my fingers, but my ripped breeches were worse than ever. I turned to the tourist and offered him my newspaper, which he politely declined. With a fearful look in his eyes, he ran off.

A familiar red car came down the hill and Tom and Angus jumped out. Tom handed me a new pair of breeches, and soon we were piling on the *Loch Mor* ferry, bound for the island of Rhum. Rhum to me is very special. Fond childhood memories of visiting my aunt, who was for a time schoolteacher on the island, came flooding back when we sailed into Loch Kinloch. Most of the island's thirty-five inhabitants work for the Nature Conservancy in their dedicated study of the red deer. So that their work is not disturbed, it is necessary to write to the Chief Warden at White

House, Isle of Rhum, for permission to visit. However, this is not usually a problem, although access to certain sensitive areas may be restricted.

The island boasted a small Post Office shop, which has since sadly closed. Proudly displayed in the front window was a large poster warning that the television detector van would in the area soon! We had rented a cottage for the weekend, and since we had increased the population of the island by 10 percent, the locals decided to have a *ceilidh*. Some geology students arrived to join in the fun, as we twirled the night away to the delights of the 'Highland Fling' and 'Strip the Willow'. My own efforts added chaos to the proceedings as Angus cheekily shouted, 'It's a good job you've got your new breeches on!'

Tom woke us with a mug of tea at 6.30 a.m. Kinloch was still fast asleep as Angus and I took the fine path that leads round the island's spectacular south-eastern coastline. We spotted the ruins of the village Port nan Caranean, abandoned in the 1860s. Rhum has two Corbetts, Ainshval and Askival, the latter being the highest mountain on the island. Height, however, counts for little here, and smaller mountains can prove to be just as exciting as their larger neighbours. We skirted the southern end of Loch Coire nan Grunnd, and climbed high on to a plateau, then up a rocky gully that came out practically at the summit of Askival, 812 metres, 'Hill of the Ash Trees'. The Nature Conservancy workers had painted each rock with a number in an elaborate geological study of the gully.

The view from the summit was superb, as the Isle of Eigg and the unfortunately named Isle of Muck danced in the sunlight. Beyond, stretching like an arm into the Atlantic, was the Ardnamurchan peninsula. The history of the island of Eigg makes sad reading. In early times Saint Donman and over fifty followers were murdered here by pirates. In 1577 another horrific massacre took place when a war party of MacLeods landed on the island and lit a fire at the front of a cave in which 395 MacDonalds were hiding. All of them died.

We skirted round the side of Trallval, which the Norse named 'Hill of the Trolls'. The little men they imagined living in the mountain proved to be Manx Shearwater birds, which arrive in their hundreds in the evening and disappear, cackling loudly, down a maze of rabbit burrows. Climbing on the scree up Ainshval's slopes was hard work, but well worth it. As we sat by its cairn the whole island was laid out like a relief map at our feet. Although well populated with deer, the island is famous for its wild ponies, supposedly related to some which swam ashore from one of the many shipwrecks of the Armada.

The island was owned for many years by the Bullough family, who built a beautiful Edwardian mock castle at Kinloch and filled it with incredible antiques, gathered on their world-wide travels. Guests would enjoy a hard day's shooting in the hills, then return to the castle to be treated with the utmost luxury. Wet clothes were taken away to be dried for the morning, and brandy was served while the guests relaxed in hot, scented baths, before sitting down to a beautifully prepared dinner.

We descended to wild Glen Dibidil and met up with Tom. Unlike the Bulloughs, we had no fancy picnic and made do with a brew-up and some crumbling compo biscuits, before following the twisting path back to Kinloch.

Sadly, in the morning we had to pack up to catch the ferry back to the mainland, but had some time to look around the castle before boarding the *Loch Mor*. A couple of winters ago Tom and I were leaving Rum, when the warden gave us a Christmas tree to be delivered to the school on the treeless island of Canna. It was dark by the time the *Loch Mor* sailed into the island's narrow jawlike harbour. We handed our Christmas tree to a Highlander on the pier and helped unload some other light cargo. The captain looked down from the bridge and shouted, 'You're doing a fine job, boys', to which Tom replied, 'Aye, we're thinking of signing on, Captain'. A lovely Highland voice came out of the darkness, 'Have you made enquiries about the pay?'

We joined the captain for some tea on the long voyage back to the mainland. I asked how he knew whether it was safe to take the boat out in the morning; did he listen to the shipping forecast? 'Och, no,' he replied. 'I look out the window and, if I see the seagulls sitting on the end of the pier leaning into the wind with their wings folded, I don't take the boat out that day.'

LOCH TREIG TO RANNOCH MOOR, 18–24 JUNE

The following day found me cycling east, away from the rugged mountains of the western seaboard to the more gentle summits of the Grampian Mountains. My route had to adjust to the complications of the stalking season which would start in earnest in six weeks' time. A 72-mile cycle ride led me to the head of Loch Treig in Glen Spean, and the comfort of Nancy Smith's hostel at Fersit.

I felt sad the next day to be leaving such a friendly hostel, but the timetable could be a slave-driver at times. I said farewell to Nancy and also Alan and Clark from the East Kilbride Mountaineering Club. Today I would climb the hills that they traversed yesterday. A pleasant path led west to Strath Ossian. Some friends were to venture along it this coming winter, the leader assuring his pal that he had heard a warm and dry bothy lay only a couple of miles ahead. 'The bothy' turned out to be a ruin full of snow! This resulted in some interesting conversation and a cold night's sleep huddled against an open wall.

The northern ridge of Stob Coire Sgriodain, 976 metres, was the first of today's three Munros to be climbed high opposite Loch Treig, meaning 'Loch of Desolation'. In the days before the road along Glen Spean and the railway along its shore, it was a remote place indeed. Many a wanted man hid in a cave along its shore. The MacDonalds once had a fortress on an island to the north of the loch, which they held against the Campbells. As a result of the dam, it is now under water.

When leaving the summit I almost stood on some ptarmigan chicks, so well were they camouflaged. Easy slopes led on to Chno Dearg, meaning 'Red Nut', 1,047 metres. How different were these gentle hills, with their wide ridges, from those of the Cuillins of Skye! Today was what a Highlander would call a soft day, as mist clung to the summit and gentle rain filled the glens. I met up with a cheery Manchester walker who explained that his wife allows him two weeks on the hills every year. He loved the peace and quiet, and any problems he had when he left seemed insignificant when he returned.

Beinn na Lap was teeming with deer. It is a gentle Munro and one that can be climbed between trains at Corrour station. I stared down on Loch Ossian, jet black, surrounded by luscious green forest. This oasis in the wilderness boasts a railway station

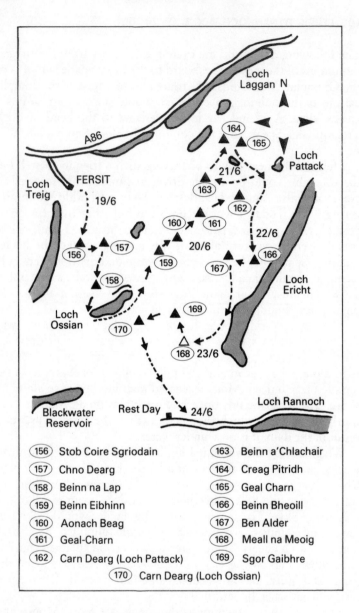

Map 20   Loch Treig to Rannoch Moor

and a youth hostel. Thoughts of a warm meal and a roaring fire at
the hostel had me rushing downhill. Alas, it was full. However, a
lean-to open stable opposite provided a good shelter. A soldier
called Nick arrived to join me. He explained he had experienced
insects all over the world, in steaming jungles and parched
deserts, but had never come across anything as bad as the Scottish
midge. We were both glad to see the threatening storm burst into
heavy rain which kept the wee devils at bay.

'Oh, goody, here comes breakfast,' said Nick as a giant beetle
scurried across the floor. His smile dropped when I offered him
some of my dehydrated food. We packed up as a host of midges
gathered strength outside the door. Nick was bound for Glencoe
across lonely Rannoch Moor.

A heron slowly glided across Loch Ossian as I worked my way
along its shore. Soon I was climbing the long flank of Beinn
Eibhinn, 1,100 metres, the first of four Munros that stretch east
towards Loch Pattack and give a fine high-level walk through the
heart of the Grampian Mountains.

The ridge skirted her dramatic amphitheatre and pulled up to
Aonach Beag, 1,114 metres. Below lay the lonely glen of An
Lairig. For years the Ordnance Survey omitted to mark the
distinct path that travels most of the glen's length. Snow still
clung to the Coire na Coichille that lies to the north of Geal-
Charn, 1,132 metres, unnamed on the map, yet the highest peak
of the group. I took great care on the descent of the steep craggy
ridge between Loch Coire Cheap and Loch an Sgoir, whose dark
waters are sheltered by the narrow Lancet Edge, seen so well from
the glen below.

A rousing chorus of 'The Gallowa' Hills' led me up to the last
of the group, Carn Dearg, 1,034 metres. It was good to see the
welcoming sight of Culra bothy below: perhaps not one of Scotland's most beautiful huts, but this is more than compensated for
by her stunning position under the dramatic shadow of Ben Alder
and Lancet Edge. Intensive work was carried out recently on its
asbestos roof. I was furious to see that some moron had ripped up
part of a sleeping platform for the fire. Sadly, this place tends to
suffer from vandalism. On one occasion a policeman and a traffic
warden made the long journey here to make probably the
remotest arrest of their careers.

The table in the main room was laden with food. The visitors' book explained the mystery. The son of the owner of the estate had invited his pals from university for a weekend at his 'shooting lodge'. Their dreams of staying at a Victorian mansion were soon dashed when they arrived at the bothy, complete with suitcases containing their dinner suits. After a weary trek across the boggy moorland, they made a quick retreat back to a hotel in Dalwhinnie.

The wind and rain hurried me down the glen. In a day-dream, I missed the stalking path that leads to Loch a'Bhealaich Leambain, the centre of today's peaks. But whistling happily, I followed the distinct path down An Lairig, unmarked on my map. It was not until the familiar sight of a ruined shieling appeared that I realised I had followed the wrong glen, leading away from the hills I had planned to climb. No wonder this walk was taking so long! To make matters worse, I had made the same mistake on my last visit!

All was not lost, however, as a way was spotted up the southern slopes of Beinn a'Chlachair, 1,087 metres 'Stonemason's Hill'. This dog-leg-shaped mountain boasts a deep rocky corrie which, no doubt, once supplied the rocks for the Macpherson shielings in the glen below. A fine stalking track led to the col of Creag Pitridh, 924 metres, where a young Aberdeen trio appeared out the mist. They warned that the downdraught of wind on the summit was incredible. 'And I lost my bunnet,' moaned one of the lads. They explained that they were sleeping under a bridge near Lochan na h'Earba, so if I found it maybe I could return it to them.

The lads were true to their word about the wind. A wailing sound was heard well before reaching the summit, and the wind blasted like an explosion on the top. Crawling was the only effective mode of travel. A red blur moved, trapped against a boulder: it was the lad's 'bunnet'. With the wind at my back lightning ascent was made of Geal Charn, 1,049 metres. I met the Aberdeen trio again and young Willie was delighted to receive his 'bunnet' back.

The bothy was now empty, so I was set to enjoy an early night's sleep. But just before midnight, the door opened and in marched twenty-four strangers, complete with an accordion playing 'Dancing in Kyle'. They were here to celebrate the climbing of a friend's last Munro ... best of all reasons to have a *ceilidh*. The bothy rocked to the strains of 'The Portree Kid' and 'Wild Rover'. So much for my early night.

I was up at six, stepping over sleeping bodies as I packed my kit and made the tea. Then I sneaked out of the bothy, after arranging to meet the rest of the crowd for a champagne celebration on top of Ben Alder at 1 p.m. It was a miserable day to celebrate a last Munro, as the rain pelted down. A waterlogged path climbed to Loch a'Bhealaich Bheithe, its dark waters nestling under the stern crags of Ben Alder. These wild mountains proved too much for Cromwell's 'Ironsides' when they tried to penetrate the mountainous domain of the Clan Macpherson.

I left the heavy rucksack at the top of the pass and climbed unladen up and over the rain-lashed bumps of Beinn Bheoil, with the grey mist obscuring the view of pretty Loch Ericht. Ben Alder wins the prize for being not only the highest but also the most spectacular peak in the area. Its table-top plateau and rugged western crags are instantly identified from many miles away. The scene at the cold, misty summit was enough to warm the coldest of hearts, as the group from the bothy danced a reel round the cairn. Rick played happily on his accordion, oblivious to the rain falling in torrents.

White burns led down from the pass. Suddenly, I walked below the cloak of mist covering the mountains. Before me lay the reputedly haunted Ben Alder Cottage bothy, a cheery puff coming from the chimney, the smoke drifting gently over the lovely wooded bay. Near by were the large boulders that were once the basis of Cluny's Cage, a well-camouflaged man-made shelter that Bonnie Prince Charlie stayed in before escaping to France. Peter and Brodie gave me a welcoming brew at the bothy. As always, I was touched by the warmth and generosity of fellow hillwalkers.

I was up at five and away by six: even the bothy mouse was asleep. Outside, a pleasant hazy mist drifted over Loch Ericht, and the sweet smell of pine lingered in the forest. At the bridge over the river known as Cam Chriochan, I left the track and was soon floundering in a rough bogland. Ahead, through the thick mist, lay a recently promoted Corbett, Meall na Meoig of Ben

Pharlagain. The summit seemed a mass of hillocks, and navigation became a nightmare. Only after walking around the Lochain Meoigeach several times did I find the correct top.

Deer scattered as I pushed on for Sgorn Gaibhre, one of two Munros that sit on the wide, pleasant ridge to the south of Loch Ossian. A huge herd of deer were grazing in Coire Eigheach. The mist cleared on the summit of Carn Dearg. Lonely Rannoch Moor stretched out like a crumpled carpet. Mention its name and people think of cars abandoned in snowdrifts and deadly bogs. In the old days, it was known as 'the Thoroughfare of The Thieves', where robbers and exiled men lived. Robert the Bruce led an 8,000-man army across the moor, weaving in and out of the tortured lunar landscape of bog, boulder and loch. Search in Lochan a'Chlaidheimh and you will find a two-handed sword thrown there by the Chief of Atholl as a gesture of peace, which ended years of feuding with the Camerons.

Tom and Doreen were waiting at the Moor of Rannoch Hotel. What a pleasure to enjoy a hot bath and a good meal! The following morning would bring a day of rest and packing for the fortnight ahead.

GLEN LYON (THE CROOKED GLEN OF THE STONES), 25–30 JUNE

Tom and Doreen kindly dropped off my heavy cycle luggage at the foot of Glen Lyon. The bike went like a rocket without the encumbering weight on its 28-mile journey from the hotel. I enjoyed cycling up a familiar glen, stopping for a breather opposite MacGregor's Leap, named after a clansman who made a superhuman leap across a gorge to escape from his enemies, the Campbells.

Early morning the next day found me sneaking up the side of the old Campbell fortress of Carnbane Castle. It has remained a ruin since the night that a raiding party of Camerons swooped down the hillside with flaming torches and set it alight. Farther up the hillside, a wood was busy with wildlife. A roe deer chewed happily in the long grass, rabbits sat on their haunches washing their faces with their paws. Red squirrels, so rare since the invasion of the grey type, chased each other, leaping from branch to branch.

A steep pull led up to a mist-covered Creag Mhor, the first of four Munros that make up the Carn Mairg group, so easily accessible to Scotland's heavily populated central belt. The hills were deserted and only a cold wind welcomed me to the summit of Carn Mairg, the highest of the group. Gurgling burns fell to Glen Sassunn. Imagine the feelings of the English army, assisted by the MacDougalls, marching down this glen intent on capturing Robert the Bruce and annihilating his tattered little army. Then suddenly, out of the mist came a flood of Robertsons with shouts of, 'A Bruce!' echoing round the glen, their avalanche of Highland steel sending their enemies home to think again.

My Gore-Tex waterproofs were well tested on Meall Garbh, 968 metres, as a vicious rainstorm attacked the summit with the ferocity of a fireman's hose. At last the cone-like summit of Carn Gorm, 1,029 metres, was reached. Whether on foot or by ski, this group of gentle peaks is always a pleasure to visit. Stuck out from the rest of the group lay a Corbett, Beinn Dearg, pronounced 'jerrack', 830 metres. Its slopes fell steeply to Camusvrachan, where you will find a flat stone named Bodach Chraig Fhiannaidh. A young eager recruit had to be able to lift this boulder before joining the ranks of Fionn's ancient army.

After a long day it was good to relax in my tiny tent. The midges were on the war-path. I resorted to chemical warfare, but managed only to get a drop of the stinging insect repellent in my eyes.

It was a delight to cycle up Glen Lyon, the gentle woodland and luscious pastures sparkling in the morning sunlight. This was the stronghold of the ancient Fingalian hero, King Fionn, who built twelve forts in the glen, garrisoned by 9,000 warriors. The road split in two, my route veering off towards Loch an Daimh. A hill fox raced ahead as I climbed gently to Cam Chreag, 860 metres, meaning 'Crooked Crag'. A train blew its whistle as it chugged along the railway that crosses Rannoch Moor on its long journey to Fort William. My eyes gazed across its lonely expanse, the rugged peaks of Glen Coe jutting out of the horizon like shark fins from the sea. Prior to the railway being built in the 1890s a party of seven surveyors got hopelessly lost on the mist-covered moor. They were rescued only just in time by shepherds. Many a poor Irish navvy trying to reach his work at the Blackwater

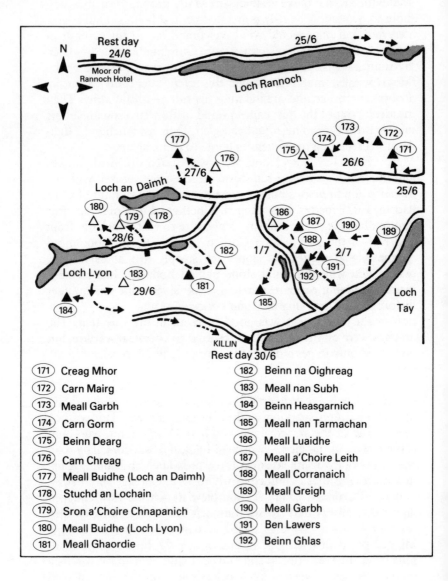

171 Creag Mhor
172 Carn Mairg
173 Meall Garbh
174 Carn Gorm
175 Beinn Dearg
176 Cam Chreag
177 Meall Buidhe (Loch an Daimh)
178 Stuchd an Lochain
179 Sron a'Choire Chnapanich
180 Meall Buidhe (Loch Lyon)
181 Meall Ghaordie

182 Beinn na Oighreag
183 Meall nan Subh
184 Beinn Heasgarnich
185 Meall nan Tarmachan
186 Meall Luaidhe
187 Meall a'Choire Leith
188 Meall Corranaich
189 Meall Greigh
190 Meall Garbh
191 Ben Lawers
192 Beinn Ghlas

Map 21   Breadalbane, including Glen Lyon

Reservoir, where a dam was being built, wasn't so lucky, and succumbed to the blizzards and other dangers of Europe's wildest moor.

A few cheery songs led me across Coire Odhar, bound for the gentle banana-shaped ridge of Meall Buidhe, 923 metres, a favourite mountain and one that can give an easy afternoon walk. Soon I was cycling to Loch Lyon at the head of the glen. A sign advertising bed and breakfast was too good to resist, with a chilling wind coming down the glen. Peter Conway and his son made me very welcome. Their visitors' book seemed to be full of Ultimate Challengers on their annual trans-Scotland migration each May. One party complained of the heatwave, the next year another lamented over the blizzard-like conditions they had been forced to endure. Peter complained at breakfast that his lambs had suffered terribly this spring due to the cold, and he thought the Ice Age was coming back.

At the head of the glen are the remains of several of Fionn's castles. They were built like brochs with only one entrance, a formidable fortification. Fionn lived in the days before history; his 10,000-man army was huge, considering the sparse population of the country at the time. The truth of the legends of his army and what fearsome enemy the castles were built to keep at bay we may never know. All that is left are the mountains and corries, the glens and rivers named in his honour.

For anyone travelling up the glen it is the bulk of Stuchd an Lochain, 958 metres, that fills the view. It was good to stand on her summit again as the wind funnelled up her northern corrie. Mad Colin Campbell, a former chieftain of his glen, took great delight one day in climbing up this mountain with his men and chasing a herd of goats over a cliff. The poor shepherd almost followed the same fate, but escaped just in time.

Sron a'Choire Chnapanich, 837 metres, was a newly discovered Corbett. With the resurveying of the Highlands for the new metric maps, several mountains were 'found', and retired Munro and Corbett climbers were soon searching for their old boots. I had hoped to find another new peak to bring the walk's total to 500 mountains, but failed dismally.

I almost stepped on a young deer calf as it sat in perfect camouflage, not moving a muscle. Springy turf had me bouncing towards Meall Buidhe, 907 metres, and I wondered how many people had visited her lonely summit this year. A fine path led along the north shore of Loch Lyon, which was dammed just after the war. A local man took seven years to build the four-mile-long track.

Back at Dalchoirlich, Peter cooked me a fine meal. He was going to Glen Dochart to a *ceilidh* but it was too far for me to cycle. I settled down with Lochay, their favourite collie, to watch my first TV in weeks. By curious coincidence, the programme was the film 'The Mad Death', which had been filmed in Glen Lyon.

The farm's cockerel was a splendid alarm clock. I needed an early start as a long day lay ahead. It says much for Highland hospitality that, despite Peter's late night at the *ceilidh*, he insisted on getting up and making me a full breakfast. Between Glen Lyon and Glen Lochay to the south lies a huge ridge of gentle, bulky mountains. I would combine two easy days into one long one today, and climb the four mountains that barred my way to Killin.

Stronuich Reservoir was now far below, looking a tiny puddle as I climbed high on the gentle slopes north of Allt Laoghain. With the exciting buzz of an early start, I sprinted up the cone-like summit to the top. Meall Ghaordie, 1,039 metres, is a favourite hill, at its best in autumn colours. It's a mountain one can climb in a summer's evening, or devote a whole day to, exploring her treasures like the Caisteal Samhraidh, meaning 'Summer Castle', a rock on her southern slopes.

Two miles to the east lies Beinn nan Oighreag, 909 metres. From the summit I was treated to a last view of Glen Lyon. It was here that the Roman Governor Pontius Pilate was born. This caused a few laughs centuries later, when a tourist approached the local minister asking where his house was. The minister replied that he didn't recognise the name from his congregation, but to be sure and try in Killin ...

A steep cycle ride took me to the top of the private hydro road between Glen Lyon and Lochay. A quick jaunt took in Meall nan Subh, 804 metres, 'Hill of the Raspberry', whose summit was a maze of hillocks. Its wet bogs broke in my spare boots which had been resoled by the cobbler. Energy was being saved, however, for Beinn Heasgarnich, 1,076 metres. This little-visited Munro rises from the moorland like a sleeping giant. On a previous visit I was treated to the sight of a spectacular mini-avalanche, as melting snow rolled off a crag on the opposite side of the corrie. She is often climbed in an energetic horseshoe route with neighbouring Munro Creag Mhor from the head of Glen Lochay.

It was a tired but happy hillwalker who cycled down the glen as rabbits scattered in every direction. The bike glided into Killin, where a cheery welcome was waiting at the youth hostel. In the doorway I overheard two Glasgow cyclists talking.

'Hey, Jim, did ye read in the papers, there's some nutcase cycling around Scotland, trying to climb every mountain over 2,500 feet in a non-stop, self-propelled journey *and* he's a Partick Thistle supporter?'

His pal replied, 'Och, that explains it!'

It seemed my efforts were getting recognition at last, as I prepared to enjoy a rest day in Killin.

CHAPTER 5

July 1985

The hills of Breadalbane

—

Crianlarich and Glen Falloch

—

Ben Lui and the hills of Strath Fillan

—

In and around the Black Mount

—

Cruel is the snow that sweeps Glen Coe

—

Morvern

THE HILLS OF BREADALBANE, 1–3 JULY

The morning papers were moaning about the weather, with a headline reading: 'Why is the weather being so bad this year?' It had been the coldest spring for twenty-five years, followed by a bitter May and June. One weatherman blamed the series of Icelandic lows crossing the Atlantic. Another commented that, as the spiders were spinning big webs, we were assured of a dry summer. I wondered what Alexander Buchan, the famous Scottish meteorologist, would think of that theory? Little did I know that our troubles with bad weather were not coming to a close, for ahead lay the wettest and coldest summer since 1897. Raging burns and flooded rivers were to make my journey a real 'drookit' struggle, more enjoyable to look back on than to experience at the time.

The bike creaked its way up the twisting road that crosses from Loch Tay to Bridge of Balgie in Glen Lyon. It passes the Ben Lawers visitors' centre, run by the National Trust, well worth a visit for details of local alpine flowers and wildlife.

A cairn marked the top of the pass, a perfect starting point for the neighbouring hills. A faint track led up the long bumpy ridge to a misty Meall nan Tarmachan, 1,043 metres, meaning 'Hill of the Ptarmigans'. Today's approach was a pleasant stroll but it scarcely does justice to such an interesting mountain, whose real delights exist further west. Tarmachan ridge weaves its narrow way over the rocky hills to end at Creag na Caillich, overlooking Glen Lochay. Imagine the sight in 1746, when the proud MacGregor clansmen came down this glen after the disaster at Culloden. They reached Killin and, with pipes playing, marched three times around the Campbell castle of Finlarig, before returning to their own glens.

It is always a delight to find something undiscovered on a mountain. I stumbled across an unmarked cave hidden in the mountain's steep northern corrie, no doubt once a spartan home for an outlawed clansman. I was soon on the opposite side of the pass, bombing over Meall Luaidhe, probably the easiest Corbett of them all if climbed from the high altitude of the roadside. However, a more energetic climb from Glen Lyon would be much more rewarding. To the east, across the Gleann Da Eig, 'Glen of the Two Eggs', lay Meall a'Choire Leith, most northerly of the Lawers group of six Munros, which give a pleasant romp along her seven-mile ridge. Meall Corranaich, 1,069 metres, was the second Munro, sitting high above Lochan na Lairige. Although navigation wasn't difficult in the mist, as usual it slowed my progress painfully. At last the trusty compass led me down from the misty world. The hostel had been invaded by cyclists, and their exciting conversation told of their adventures stretching to the four corners of the world.

Ben Lawers lay hidden under a cloak of mist, Loch Tay still and quiet. The northern end of the loch, however, often experiences subterranean impulses, making the water froth and foam. Deer were grazing by the Lawers burn, which flows from the impressive Lochan nan Cat, the inner sanctuary of the Lawers range. The most easterly Munro of the group is Meall Greigh, 1,001 metres, meaning 'Hill of the Horse Studs'. Its summit was deserted as rain pelted through the misty veil. A gentle walk led on to Meall Garbh, 1,116 metres. This group of mountains is a botanical paradise: different flowers in various stages of growth are seen as you climb higher. How lucky we are to have free access to such pleasures!

The rocky An Stuc made the going tough in the wild weather as strong winds howled up the crags above Lochan nan Cat and mocked man's puny effort at mountain travel. At last the summit of Ben Lawers appeared out of the mist. Alan and Dave welcomed me to the top and asked if I would sign their form. I wondered if I had won a prize: maybe a luxury holiday in the sun! In my mind, the case was already packed. Then they explained they were doing a study for the National Trust on path erosion and usage of the mountain. The poor souls had been sitting by the soaking cairn all day and I was their second, and probably last, customer. At an altitude of 3,984 feet, Lawers is just 16 feet short of joining the 4,000-foot club of Scottish peaks. In 1878 Malcolm Ferguson from Glasgow insisted on building a 20-foot cairn on top to take the summit into the 4,000 foot league. Thankfully, the wild Highland winters have reduced it to the more modest size we find today.

It was good to reach the chilly summit of Beinn Ghlas. Only a couple of rocks marked the top, but there was little doubt of my position as the slopes fell steeply to the glen below. Nonchalantly I descended without a proper bearing, and was soon paying for my mistake by traversing awkward ground to walk down to Loch Tay. Back at the hostel, I asked Jim, the friendly warden, if anything unusual had happened in the area. His face lit up; a favourite story was obviously in the offing. He explained that to the south of Loch Tay rise the rough Strath Earn hills. Through these wild lands the eccentric chieftain of the MacNabs led his men to attack a band of robbers living on an island on Loch Earn. This was mad enough in savage mid-winter weather, but he insisted the men carry with them their own boat! For five rough miles the clansmen hauled their heavy load until they were overcome by a blizzard and were forced to sleep out in the freezing cold in nothing but their kilts. In the morning they decided to continue the foray without the boat, the remnants of which were still to be seen up to a few years ago.

As I was cycling out of Killin, a group of Glasgow cyclists whizzed by on their sleek machines. They seemed amazed at the sight of my heavily loaded bike. Bulky items like sleeping bags and spare clothes, although not heavy, soon had the bicycle's panniers bulging. A minibus raced by, spraying water in all directions from the soaking road. The rain poured down relentlessly, filling the bulging River Dochart to bursting point.

I tried to imagine the feelings of Robert the Bruce, pushing like me along the Glen Dochart, fleeing from defeat at the battle of Methven. He had only a few hundred men and camp followers when suddenly both ends of the glen were blocked by the enemy. The hills on either side of the glen exploded with the blowing of horns and the echo of thousands of ferocious voices. Flooding down the hillside, like today's white burns, poured hordes of MacDougalls and MacNabs, sworn enemies of Bruce. Only by forming a tight wedge with the remnants of his cavalry was Bruce able to force his way through the enemy host. He left many friends – and his jewelled brooch – in the hands of his foes, who tried to pull him from his horse.

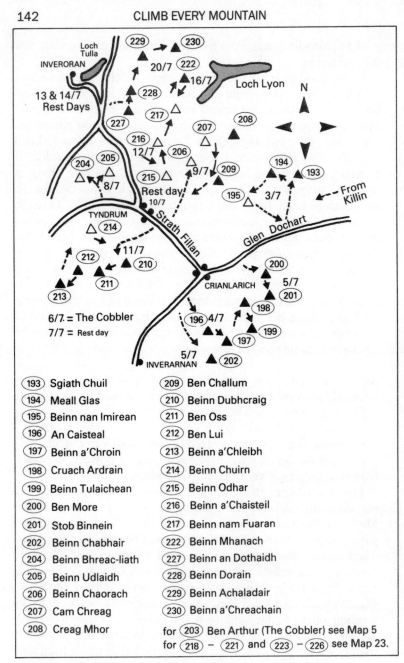

Map 22   Glen Falloch and Strath Fillan

The farm at Auchessan soon disappeared in the mist as I floundered through the boggy moorland. Somewhere ahead lay three mountains, rising like islands from a heathery sea. The rocky summit of Sgiath Chuil, 935 metres high, consists of two tops, the most southerly being the higher. But according to my Ordnance Survey 1st Series map, the northerly top has an extra contour, so you had better visit both before they change their minds! I climbed low enough to get a brief glimpse of Glen Lochay before sweeping up on to the whalebone-shaped Munro, Meall Glas, 960 metres. Rain hammered the mist-covered ridge. How different the story had been a few years earlier when, in the early light of a perfect June morning, the hills danced in the morning sunshine.

The soaking hillside led me to a remote pass overlooking the sad, ruined village at the head of Glen Lochay, tucked away from view under the shoulder of Meall Glas. Her only visitors now are stray hillwalkers and buzzards hunting over the ruins where children used to play. Beinn nan Imirean, 844 metres, meaning 'Hill of the Ridge', is a lonely Corbett and, like the rest of today's hills, most enjoyably climbed from green Glen Lochay to the north. Climbing down out of the mist, I surprised a fox running across the hillside below me. I barked twice at it and it stopped and looked downhill. I barked again. It turned around and sprinted off.

Crianlarich Youth Hostel had been converted into a five-star palace. There are some who abhor the bright new hostels, with their small dormitories and television lounge, saying they lack the friendly atmosphere of the smaller, basic hostels, but while sympathising with their argument I must say it was a pleasant change not to have to queue for the shower.

CRIANLARICH AND GLEN FALLOCH, 4-7 JULY

The morning train pulled into Crianlarich station, and out popped a familiar figure, Alan Comrie. It was a delight to have company for a day. Alan's entertaining stories of adventures in the Alps shortened the walk on to the northern ridge of An Caisteal. A trusty compass guided us over the knolls that led to the summit, the highest of three rugged, popular Munros that give newcomers to the hills a taste of what lies ahead. It seemed strange to be on what for me are local hills. My mid-April climb of the most northerly peak of the walk, Beinn Spionnaidh, seemed light years ago.

We worked our way south through the thick mist to Beinn a'Chroin. Tired of walking, we gave our hands some exercise scrambling up an easy crag. Beinn a'Chroin means 'Hill of Danger': no doubt it earned healthy respect in days of old. Alan confessed to being hill-daft, but tended to concentrate these days on the hills of the Southern Highlands. He had climbed Ben Lomond twenty-five times last year; at the age of sixty his fitness was comparable to a hillman half his age.

Alan had the evening train to catch to Glasgow. I followed him to the head of Coire Earb, then sprang off to climb Cruach Ardrain, 1,046 metres, the higher of the two peaks that stretch from Crianlarich to Inverlochlarig Farm. The mist was now clearing from the tops and a pleasant walk led south to Beinn Tulaichean, a pretty mountain overlooking the Braes of Balquhidder, a happy green fertile glen where the sun always seems to shine: a fine homeland for the famous Clan MacGregor. The clan became outlawed after the battle of Glen Fruin when they annihilated a Colquhoun army four times their size, losing only one man to the Lowlanders' two hundred. Unjustifiably, a price was put on the clansmen's heads, their children sent south to be educated, their women branded. With almost every sword against them, the clan seemed to face extinction. Amazingly they did not. Forced to live in caves and hide-outs in the wild, misty corries, they slowly gathered their strength and earned themselves a new name, 'The Children of the Mist', venturing down from their mountain stronghold on moonlit nights to fight back at their enemies with terrible vengeance.

> The moon's on the lake, and the mist's on the brae
> And the clan has a name, that is nameless by day.
> Then gather, gather, gather, Grigalach,
> While there's leaves in the forest, and foam on the river,
> MacGregor despite them shall flourish for ever!
>
> Sir Walter Scott

Word was obviously getting around about the new hostel: it was bursting at the seams. I grabbed a telephone to wish my young nephew a happy birthday and got the usual 'goo goo goo' response! July the fourth was the end of the two Buchan cold spells in the summer months, so I slept well, with dreams of endless sunny days. Epic walks would be done and my battered schedule speedily caught up with.

The hour of 7.00 a.m. found me cooking breakfast. To say a storm raged outside was an understatement: the rain thrashed the windows with the force of a water cannon. Fellow hostellers made their plans for the day, one comedian producing a drawing of an Ark. 'So much for the spiders spinning big webs,' commented the warden as I stepped out into the torrents.

A soaking Benmore Farm was soon miniature in size as I raced up the steep slopes of Ben More, 1,174 metres, meaning simply 'Big Hill'. It's a long and brutal climb from this route, but in today's weather there was little scenery to admire. Although an easy hill in summer, in winter it is a more serious undertaking. Many a walker has died simply slipping over her crags.

On the summit little could be seen of the wreckage of a passenger plane that tragically smashed into the top of the mountain in the early 1970s, killing the captain and crew. I huddled down in the hollow below the trig point to celebrate my 200th mountain by singing 'The Summer Time Has Come'. A rocky descent led down to the bealach. It is disheartening to lose about 1,000 feet of height and to see Ben More's twin, Stob Binnein, towering to almost the same height opposite. By the time its storm-lashed summit was reached, I was soaked. Even the incredible qualities of Berghaus Gore-Tex waterproofs have their limitations. Being 100 per cent waterproof was one thing, submergible was another. Back down in Crianlarich, I enjoyed a mug of tea in the Ben More café and walked out, leaving a huge puddle around my table, much to the waitress's disgust.

Some miserable-looking hitch-hikers stood by a road sign. I cycled past, shouting the popular tourist slogan, 'Scotland's for me', as the chilling rain ran up my sleeve. The bike slithered down Glen Falloch, where at Derrydaroch I joined a muddy West Highland Way, the long-distance path from Glasgow to Fort William. A couple of drenched 'wayers' toddled past, arguing as they went.

'These waterproofs aren't Taiwan rubbish, you know, they're the best there is; made in Formosa, they are'! I should have been locked up for even thinking of climbing another hill in this atrocious weather. But if climbing Beinn Chabhair, 931 metres, would give me a total rest day on Sunday, it was worth struggling for. Tired legs pulled me up Glen Chuilinn as the river somersaulted down the glen in a demented frenzy, the trees growing from her banks clinging on with every inch of their soaking roots.

The boulder-strewn bealach soon disappeared from view as I pulled my way on to the mountain's confusing bumpy summit ridge. At the cairn I was delighted to find a soaking mash of peanuts and raisins in my jacket pocket which gave me enough energy to walk down the glen. A bedraggled group of deer watched me go by as they sheltered in the hillside. It was 9.30 p.m. before I peeled off my soaking waterproofs and sat by the hostel fireside, steam rising from my damp clothes. Beside me was a huge boiling teapot. Never did I think when I planned this walk that an inflatable canoe would be an essential part of the equipment!

Early morning found me cycling back down Glen Falloch on a perfectionist's mission. When climbing The Cobbler in Arrochar this March, ice foiled my attempt at taking the one exposed step on the ledge leading to the top of the giant boulder, the mountain's true summit. While cursing my cowardice, I knew a slip could have been fatal. This mountain boasts at least one tragic example.

It was a relief to leave my heavy cycle luggage with Mary at the friendly Inverarnan Drovers Inn, command HQ of the MacGregor clan. Unladen, the bike whizzed down to Arrochar, and I was soon following the pleasant track leading up from the roadside, weaving its way through the steep woodland. The Allt a' Bhalachain was still in a turbulent mood after the previous day's torrents. The pleasant winding track led up the mountain under the shadow of the cliffs, where the famous climbers of the 1930s learnt their skills. An easy scramble led up to the true summit, although a rope would perhaps be comforting for those without a head for heights, as they make the one exposed step on to the top of the rocky tower.

I had lunch with a sad Glasgow climber, who moaned that he was getting married at Christmas and was trying to climb as many hills as possible before the happy day. Without wishing to disrupt his plans of matrimonial bliss, I gently pointed out that it didn't sound the most perfect of matches. A platoon of cheery soldiers were coming uphill with their heavy radios. They asked if there was a café on top. I replied there was, but they wouldn't be allowed in with their boots on.

Back down in the glen, the bike was soon sprinting over the narrow isthmus between Arrochar and Loch Lomond, where raiding Vikings once used logs to haul their longships between the lochs. Arriving at Inverarnan felt like coming home: the roaring fires at each end of the bar, a cheery welcome and a warming dram. The support team were already there and Munro barked a special welcome. By coincidence, a pipe band was returning from a Highland Games and came in playing, the sound of 'The Black Bear' echoing around the room and making the glasses rattle. This got the evening off to a grand start, and soon we were soon enjoying a fine *ceilidh*. With Angus Cameron on his tambourine and Alasdair's and Elspeth's gentle voices, the bar was soon rocking to folk-song classics. So much so that the owner, Duncan MacGregor, brought in his wee Highland pony to join in the fun.

BEN LUI AND THE HILLS OF STRATH FILLAN, 8–12 JULY

Batteries were recharged after a peaceful rest day, and my battered bike cranked its way up Glen Falloch for the last time. The tourist season was in full swing as caravans wove their way up the soaking roads. The relentless rain pelted down on a strange giant wigwam pitched in Strath Fillan. The tourist trap of Tyndrum had sprung to life, with coffee bars and shops in full swing. Wedged in the triangle of roads between Glen Lochy and Glen Orchy lay two superb Corbetts, whose northern, denture-shaped corries offer fine climbing.

It was good to climb clear of the forest above Arinabea, reach the open hillside and climb up to the lip of the amphitheatre-like Coire Ghamhnain, 'Corrie of the Stirk' (one-year-old calf). Gentle slopes led up through a dense cloak of mist to Beinn Bhreac-Liath, 803 metres, meaning 'Speckle Grey Hill'. The glens echoed with the roaring of the burns feeding the turbulent River Orchy below. Like a pendulum, I swung across to Beinn Udlaidh, pronounced 'oodly', meaning 'Dark Gloomy Hill'. However uncheerful its name it is a spectacular mountain, best seen from Glen Orchy. In the heat of a summer's day a choice of paddling pools lie along the summit ridge. I climbed down, avoiding Creag nan Cuaran, 'the Crag of the Sandals', to a busy world below the clouds.

Back at the hostel, it was good to relax and study again my soaking maps, which would lead me to far-off Morvern on the distant western seaboard before the month was out.

My bike followed a busload of tourists, who were seemingly unimpressed by the scenery of Strath Fillan as the rain obscured the view from their windows. The Glen got its name from Saint Fillan, who had a priory here. A grey wall snaked its way up the glen's eastern slopes, over the undulating hillside which hides the high peaks beyond. I left my bike under the railway viaduct which, like a giant archway, led into Gleann a'Chlachain.

Grassy slopes led up Beinn Chaorach, 818 metres, while pathetic ruined shielings could be seen in the glen below. Dozens of white blurs appeared out of the mist, the sheep being too cold and wet to run away. I was surprised to find a tiny windmill powering an even smaller electric fence, its two strands only inches off the ground.

The next Corbett, Cam Chreag, 884 metres, was a more interesting mountain, its summit guarded by gentle crags. My helter-skelter route followed the district boundary to Creag Mhor, 1,032 metres, towering above Glen Lochay. Here dramatic Coire-cheathaich was living up to her name, 'Corrie of the Mist'. A place of great beauty, it inspired local bard Duncan Ban MacIntyre to write:

> The Misty Corrie of the hinds vagrant,
> The darling corrie of the freshest land,
> The stags and the hinds at morn in Maytide,
> Are early on grassy plains uprist,
> Red herds of them on every brae-side,
> Round the rough corrie named of the mist.

Climbing back over Cam Chreag, I was soon ascending the long, mist-covered rocky slopes leading to a pyramid-like Ben Challum, 1,022 metres. Someone had left a wodden cross in the cairn.

Ben Challum is something of a forgotten mountain, climbed only by those who must, in their dedicated tour of the Munros. It lies hidden behind the high moorland that slopes to Strath Fillan. It was well into the evening by the time I was down in the glen. The hostel was full and I planned to camp, but could get up little enthusiasm in the continuous downpour. Mrs Rea welcomed me to her guesthouse, and sat me down by a roaring fire with a pot of tea and scones and jam, as the wind and rain banged against the window. Heaven!

The bike made slow progress cycling north to Tyndrum as heavy rain crashed down from the heavens. The prospect of the Ben Lui group of peaks did not fill me with much enthusiasm. A rest day was the only answer. While enjoying a coffee in the Inver Hotel, I read my first newspaper in weeks. My horoscope said, 'It may take you a long time to get started today as you will feel weary and tired. However, energy will soon be on the upsurge and you will be able to make up for lost time.' Adventurer Tom MacLean had just returned from his six-week occupation of Rockall, 250 miles off St Kilda. Before leaving, he had painted a Union Jack on top.

Like a retreating army, a group of West Highland Wayers limped past the window, soaking waterproofs reflected in the light. Their grim set faces had eyes only for the road ahead, while their capes trailed behind them.

The storm had not passed overnight. The Land Rover track leading to Cononish farm was streaming with water, while the river roared down the glen close to bursting point. Ahead, shrouded in mist, lay Beinn Laoigh, pronounced Lui, and her three neighbouring Munros. Arguably the finest mountains in the Southern Highlands, their great bulk is squeezed in between Strath Fillan and Glen Lochay. Lead used to be mined in the area, and now they are seriously mining for gold. Local legend tells us that the wild mountains are inhabited by a 'Urisg', a monster, half-goat half-human, with shaggy hair, long teeth and claws.

It was a relief to find the bridge over the River Cononish still standing and so allow the ascent of Beinn Dubhchraig and Ben Oss. It is these two peaks and their deep Coire Garbh that fill your view when driving up the shore of Loch Lomond. The merciless rain hammered down, but out of the gloom and despair came a strange pleasure. 'Going to climb you, Going to climb you,' was the shout, while I floundered up the rain-lashed slopes of Ben Lui, its cairn beautifully exposed, sitting at the head of Central Gully – a classic winter climb.

To the south-west lay poor old Beinn a'Chleibh, stuck out from the rest of the group, demanding a lengthy detour. Nobody seems to have a good word for her, which is a pity, for on a clear day you are treated to a splendid view of Cruachan to the west and the wild empty moorland which stretches south to Loch Fyne. That land of wild little mountains and rushing burns was once home to hundreds of MacNaughtons. Now only the deer and the eagles dwell there. My route painfully skirted the steep western slopes of Ben Lui. Cars could be seen hurrying down Glen Lochay, while my snail-like pace led on to Beinn Chuirn, 880 metres, a delightful Corbett overlooking Tyndrum, whose steep Coire na Saobhaidhe, 'Corrie of the Monster', to some extent challenges the splendour of Ben Lui.

I climbed down to the glen, cursing the weather. Then a huge roaring sound stopped me in my tracks. Down Ben Lui's magnificent Coire Gaothach came a thousand jet-white burns, roaring to a deafening pitch and making the mountains seem alive. Dripping from head to foot, I smiled with pleasure. Here is the Scotland the tourists will never see, 'land of the mountain and the flood'.

In the morning, my clothes were still soaking after yesterday's onslaught. I looked in desperation at the black, seething waters of Allt Coralan, which prevented any further progress. Feet were soon trudging up the soaking grass of Beinn Odhar, 901 metres, first of the three Corbetts that line the east side of Auch Gleann. It is this fine hill which dominates the view when driving north from Crianlarich. The slopes stretched past Coire Luaidh, 'the Corrie of the Loved One', to the top. Legs felt like lead today as I seemed to have caught some sort of bug. It was painful to have to lose almost 500 metres of height. The burns roared through the mist as today's downpour added to their spate condition.

A gentle ridge led up Beinn a'Chaisteil, 883 metres, as if nature had expended all her energy making the dramatic black cliffs that fall precipitously to Auch Gleann far below. The grassy slopes of Beinn nam Fuaran were the last effort of the day. In my tired state it had taken ages to traverse the three mountains, and although Beinn Mhanach beckoned across the glen my legs refused to co-operate. I avoided the foaming Allt Coralan by nipping over the railway viaduct, and rescued my bike from a resting place that had become a large puddle.

The rain slashed Loch Tulla like machine-gun fire as the bike wound its weary way the last few miles to the Inveroran Hotel. Amazingly, despite the heavy rain, my clothes were merely damp. I squeezed into the hotel's friendly little bar. After I had eaten a warming meal, Liz, the barmaid, produced a guitar. With thoughts of rain-ravaged mountains far away, Scottish and Australian voices joined for a beautiful rendering of 'Always Argyll'.

The sun came out in the morning, but my legs had no energy at all. Tom and Doreen arrived, and we started the first of what was to be a two-day task of replanning routes and checking gear. On Sunday the rest of the support team arrived, took one look at my pale appearance and decided I needed a brisk walk!

IN AND AROUND THE BLACK MOUNT, 15–21 JULY

It was just getting light when the familiar sound of rain hammering on the roof woke me up. The foaming Abhainn Shira squeezed its way under Victoria Bridge, its roaring only bettered by the cheerful bark of the collies at Forest Lodge. One mile along Glen Kinglass lies the tiny Glasgow University club hut known as Clashgour. It looked about the size of the average bus shelter, though it boasts a second floor and is reputed to sleep twelve in comfort: no doubt with two up the chimney!

The path led along the side of the river. Unfortunately in places it is starting to fall into the water as the river digs further into its sandy banks. At Loch Dochard the peaceful silence was shattered by the roaring of engines as a couple of fighter jets raced overhead. I was soon weaving between the slabby rocks on the shoulder of Beinn nan Aighenan, 960 metres, meaning 'Hill of the Hinds'. The burns that fall to Glen Kinglass bore deep into the mountain, forming great ravines, as a young Dutchman the summer before found out to his peril. Having fallen into a gully,

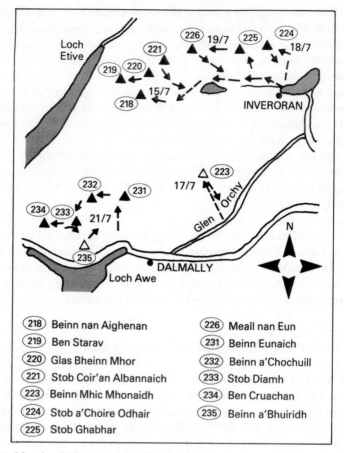

Map 23   Loch Awe and the Black Mount

he lay trapped for days with a broken leg until a sudden rainstorm washed him further downstream ... fortunately within shouting distance of Glen Kinglass lodges, whose keepers came to his rescue.

A delightful narrow ridge led to Ben Starav, queen of the five wild mountains that make up her group. It is this peak that looks so spectacular when seen from Glen Etive. Most walkers climb from that pretty glen, using the fine path leading up the side of Allt nam Meirleach, 'the Thieves Burn', to enjoy a fine horseshoe route of the group.

The mist revealed an inky view of the fiord-like Loch Etive. It was here that MacDougall of Lorn anchored his great fleet of galleys while his men were defeated by Robert the Bruce at the Pass of Brander. The wind and rain were refusing to let up as I squelched my way over Glas Bheinn Mhor, 993 metres, to the impressive Stob Coir'an Albannaich, 1,044 metres, 'Peak of the Corrie of the Scotsmen'. This delightful peak boasts a cone-like summit which fills your view when walking up Glen Kinglass from Loch Tulla.

At the Col of Meall Tarsuinn, I conceded defeat. Another Munro, Meall nan Eun, lay only a mile away, but my bug was sapping energy. It was a relief to climb down from the storm-ravaged summits. Crossing even the most minor of burns was a problem. With pockets full of water and soaking boots, I wove my way through the maze of lochans west of Loch Dochard to reach the bliss of the path, and a long squelchy walk to Loch Tulla. After fifteen hours of walking, I collapsed into bed without a meal, hoping to shake off the malaise which seemed to have overtaken me.

Loch Tulla was still and quiet the following morning as the mist shrouded her calm waters. The Forestry Commission have fenced off an area of woodland along the roadside, which contains one of the last remnants of the Caledonian pine forest that once covered the glens as far as Loch Maree in Wester Ross. Now the barren wilderness where they once grew is referred to as 'deer forest'. If only the people of old could have seen warning signs by the roadside: 'That which burns never returns'.

The bike free-wheeled into Auch Gleann for a second visit. The Allt Coralean was as inhospitable as ever. The Auch Viaduct allowed a dry crossing while ears listened carefully for a train. George Roger, ex-president of the Scottish Mountaineering Club, and his dog were tragically knocked down and killed by a train on the same viaduct a few years earlier in terrible weather. A Land Rover track now thrusts up Auch Gleann, frustratingly weaving in and out of the river. Ahead lay the twin-topped summit of Beinn Mhanach, 954 metres. The rain poured down on the grassy slopes and it was a relief to shelter in the lee of the cairn.

To the north in Glen Cailliche lies Tigh nam Bodach, 'the House of the Old Man'. This ruined shieling contains five dumbbell-shaped heavy water stones. They were known as 'the old woman and her family' and were considered very lucky. When the shielings were prepared for the summer migration of folk to the glen, her little house would be rethatched to assure good weather and healthy cattle. When the chilling autumn winds blew up the glen and it was time to come down from the mountains, the thatching would be removed and her walls sealed to keep the winter weather out. This tradition continued for centuries.

With the fierce weather continuing, I could find little enthusiasm for venturing on to the other Munros, to Beinn Achaladair to the west. Down in the glen I crossed Allt Coralaen, a normally peaceful burn, but today it tugged violently at my legs. It was a great relief to reach the other bank. Douglas and Lorna at the Inveroran Hotel didn't have a bunkhouse, but had arranged to give me, at a reduced rate, a staff room, which was ideal. I was delighted to meet Libby Whittome in the bar. Libby has a pony-trekking centre with a difference. She takes small parties on friendly forays into the hills, moving from one bothy to another. Her small party had left Glen Creran on a seventy-mile round trip by Loch Etive and Glen Kinglass and back home via Glencoe, giving her lucky guests a highly enjoyable and memorable journey.

After breakfast, Libby and her posse rode off for Glencoe, while my bike trundled down Glen Orchy. It had been raining all night and the hills were streaked with white burns. The River Orchy, an awesome sight at the best of times, was somersaulting down the glen, carrying a fallen tree with it. A bridge led across the torrent, and the bike strained on the steep cycle-ride up the forestry road leading to the mouth of Allt Broighleachan. A faint track wove through the mist-covered forest. The trusty compass led me free from the jungle of trees to some ruined summer shielings, Airigh Chailleach. Above, through the endless grey fog, lay Beinn Mhic Mhonaidh, 793 metres, a little-climbed Corbett overlooking Glen Strae. In the early days of the Scottish Mountaineering Club they used to meet at Inveroran Hotel, and this hill was a favourite climb for them.

A huge herd of deer raced ahead. The summit had a massive cairn, but again I was cheated of a view, which was a shame, for in clear weather the hill would give a superb scene of the Black

Mount. It was in Glen Strae that a party of raiding MacDougalls returned from a succcessful foray with a herd of Rannoch cattle. To their horror they realised an avenging group of clansmen were on their tails. The MacDougalls sent their precious cattle ahead with some men while the others charged and routed their enemies. In triumph they marched down the glen with their enemies' banners flying. However, when their comrades with the cattle saw their enemies' flags in the distance they thought they had been defeated, hamstrung the cattle and fled.

It was a relief to find my way through the mist-covered trees to the little glade where the bike lay. That was when the fun began. Bicycles don't perform very well on Land Rover tracks, especially when wet, as the brakes fail to grip. The cycle down the steep hill to Glen Orchy became an unstoppable helter-skelter ride. The bike hurtled through the burns and jumped over dips like a show jumper. It was exhilarating, but a fall would have led to a hospital bed.

On the way to Inveroran I met Tom and Doreen, who came up to join me for dinner. They brought news from the Glasgow Weather Centre that the bad weather would continue till the end of September.

There are some days that are destined to go wrong. Still feeling the effects of the energy-sapping tummy-bug, I decided to keep the momentum of the walk going, if only by having easy days, rather than rest up and stagnate. I stepped out into the torrential rain. A crow flying overhead dropped a white bombshell with great precision on my balaclava. Things could scarcely get worse.

Stob a'Choire Odhair, 943 metres, stands like a cornerstone of the Black Mount peaks. Cast out from their endless ridges, she has a unique, gentle appearance and gives an easy day from the road end at Forest Lodge, especially if the fine stalking track leading into Coire Toaig is used. I was soon wending my way through the rocks in Coire Creagach, meaning 'Corrie of the Cliffs', the going slow in my tired condition. Mist and rain welcomed me to the rocky bump of Beinn Toaig. This little peak is often mistaken for the Munro behind. With water squelching from pockets and boots, I climbed the gentle, tan-coloured slopes that led up to the summit cairn.

Stob a'Choire Odhair was my 224th peak, and she treated me

to a brief glimpse of the fine Coireach a'Ba, 'Corrie of the Cattle'. This well-sheltered corrie, lying in the shadow of rocky Black Mount peaks, was an ideal base for the Rannoch clansmen to graze their stolen cattle, with a safe escape, if required, through the mountain stronghold at their backs. What had been a morning's walk was enough for my drained energy reserves. So, with rain tumbling down, I slunk off to the hotel, where it was a pleasure to meet a Swiss family who entertained the hotel guests with their mountain songs, explaining to everyone they had come from Bridge of Orgy!

The atrocious weather and my temporary illness had made a mockery of my plans to sweep through the Black Mount. Two mountains lay unclimbed, shrouded in mist above Glen Kinglass. The road leading to Forest Lodge was one of the major cattle drove roads in the country. The hardy drovers would drive their cattle about fifteen miles a day, the men sleeping out in their tartan plaids in all weathers. This made them a hardy breed. Without the cattle to slow their pace, these men would think little of walking fifty miles a day. Lord Breadalbane objected to them passing his new Forest Lodge and went to court to change the route of the ancient drove road. Happily, he lost the case.

The Land Rover track led through a young forestry plantation to Clashgour Farm which, in the harsh winters of yester-year, would sometimes be blocked off with snow from winter to spring. A long pull led up the side of the cauldron-like Coire na Muic to Stob Ghabhar, 1,087 metres, meaning 'Goat Peak'. It is this fine mountain that draws your eyes like a magnet to appreciate her long ridges and craggy corries when driving on the main road to Glen Coe. Her northern cliffs fall to Coirein Lochan. A more splendid place for a high camp in breathtaking scenery is hard to imagine. The rain poured down, backed with a chilling wind, as the ridge curved westwards to a jewel of a peak, Meall nan Eun, 928 metres, meaning 'Hill of the Birds'. When seen from Loch Dochard she looks just like a volcano after an eruption, with lava flowing down her eastern slopes. It was a happy walker who made his way back to Loch Tulla, despite his waterlogged boots and stern clouds above promising the same tomorrow.

A large Alsatian dog watched me walk past the mountain rescue post at Bridge of Orchy, his big eyes glowering as if to say, 'I will be up to get you later!' The path shot up Coire an Dothaidh, her black crags appearing gloomily from the mist. The slopes were empty and peaceful today, but in 1469 the corrie echoed with battle cries as the Stewarts of Appin were defeated in their fierce, close-run battle with the Campbells and their allies, leaving hundreds of dead on the hillside.

A long ridge led south to Beinn Dorain, 1,076 metres, meaning 'Hill of the Otter'. This fine mountain is seen at its best when driving north from Tyndrum, where she rises above Auch Gleann like an Alpine peak. Her beauty compelled Duncan Ban MacIntyre to write:

> Praise o'er mountains every one
> To Ben Dorain be,
> All I've seen beneath the sun,
> Methought fairest she.

Her sister peak, Beinn an Dothaidh, although less dramatic, gives a superb view of Rannoch and the Black Mount. She has two summit cairns, the smaller, easterly one being the higher.

The soft rain added to the already full burns as I pushed on over the lip of Corrie Daingean, meaning 'the Strong Corrie', to Beinn Achaladair. This is the middle peak of the three mountains, rising like a tidal wave above Rannoch Moor.

Suddenly the rain stopped and the cold wind blew the mist away as the summit of Beinn a'Chreachain drew closer. This is the remotest Munro of the group, sitting between Loch Lyon and Rannoch Moor. Many a clan's cattle-raiding foray crossed over her shoulder. A certain honour existed among the cattle thieves, or Caterans. They would never steal *all* an enemies' cattle if it was likely they would face starvation as a result. The MacDonalds of Keppoch and Glencoe showed no such restraint. In October 1690 they plundered Glen Lyon, herding in front of them hundreds of cattle, nearly a thousand sheep and as many stolen household items as they could carry.

The wood at Crannach is a relic of the Caledonian pine forest that once covered the moor. The railway track allowed a quick, if uncomfortable, route back to Bridge of Orchy. The station master told me that in the previous blistering hot summer he had managed a swim in Loch Tulla between trains. No such enthusiasm could he find this cold year: he would have to break the ice!

It was 5 a.m. when I left Loch Tulla. A herd of deer jerked into action, surprised at the sight of an early-morning cyclist. The bike sped through lovely Glen Orchy, her trees swaying in the wind, to arrive twenty miles farther on at Loch Awe, the longest loch in Scotland. Standing at her head lie the ruins of the Campbell stronghold of Kilchurn Castle. Here the evil Campbells, with the favour of the king's friendship, introduced new legislation to oust the MacGregors from their homelands in Glen Strae and Glen Lyon. Above the loch towers mighty Ben Cruachan, whose corrie is now home to a huge reservoir feeding the second largest hydro-power station in the world. My route was to sneak around her back, first visiting a couple of favourite peaks overlooking Glen Kinglass.

Easy slopes led up Beinn Eunaich, 989 metres. This fine Munro overlooks Glen Kinglass, a peaceful inner sanctuary in the heart of Lorn. The mist started to clear on her sister peak, Beinn a'Chochuill. From there a painful descent led across the Lairig Noe to join the main Cruachan ridge. Stob Diamh is classed as a separate Munro, her sharp summit giving a fine view down the island-dotted Loch Awe, a canoeist's dreamland. On the lower slopes of Cruachan lies the narrow Pass of Brander, separating Loch Awe from Loch Etive. It was here in 1308 that Robert the Bruce pretended to play into the MacDougalls' ambush, marching his men through the pass as their enemies hurled boulders upon them. But it was the MacDougalls who were trapped, as down from the misty mountains streamed the other half of Bruce's army. Fifteen hundred clansmen crashed like a torrent of steel into the backs of the unsuspecting MacDougalls, hurling them down the mountain.

An easy scramble led on to Cruachan's summit ridge, my 234th peak. A young Fifer was on top, his third day out on a week-long holiday. He pointed excitedly to the Isles of Mull and Jura, rising clear and bright from the ocean, while at our back dark Loch Etive pierced the wild mountains of Lorn like a dark sword. It seemed so strange to be able to enjoy a summit view and not have it covered in mist. I scurried back along the ridge bordering the giant sink-like Coire Cruachan for one final pull up the scree slopes of Beinn a'Bhuiridh, 896 metres, the splendid Corbett overlooking Loch Awe. Hamish Brown, on his non-stop trek over the Munros in 1974, enjoyed a high camp here on his second night out. A wise choice: what bliss to wake to a view of the group of green islands like a necklace round the graceful neck of Loch Awe!

It was midnight by the time the familiar sight of Inveroran Hotel was reached. A honeymoon couple were just finishing a bottle of champagne and kindly gave me some. Today's weather had allowed me to pull off a long day: 40 miles of cycling, 16 miles of walking and five peaks crammed into a nineteen-hour day. Whew!

CRUEL IS THE SNOW THAT SWEEPS GLENCOE, 22-29 JULY

It was sad to be leaving Inveroran; it had been a cosy base. The cold rain pelted down on my bike as it made slow progress on its journey to west Scotland's most dramatic glen. The friendly Clachaig Inn at Glencoe, run by Peter and Eileen Daynes, was an ideal rendezvous to meet Angus and Carol. Angus had good news. Alasdair Brown, from the support team, had successfully recorded a song dedicated to the walk called 'The Hills and Glens So Peaceful', with all proceeds going to our charity, Erskine Hospital. It was later to be played on local radio stations and on STV. We settled into cheery Glencoe Youth Hostel, but our plans for climbing the Aonach Eagach ridge were scuppered by the weather so I cycled on for a rest day in Fort William, meeting Angus and Carol there. This was my first big town in four months!

At 7.30 a.m. a deadly silence came over the hostellers in the Glencoe Youth Hostel as Dot, the warden's wife, switched on the radio for the weather report: 'Occasional showers in the west'; boos and hisses echoed around the kitchen. I donned my waterproof armour suit and stepped out into the Scottish monsoon. The road hugged the shores of Loch Leven, which thrusts into this mountainous land like a Norwegian fiord. It is a quiet road now, a relic from the days before the Ballachulish Bridge, when tourists in their cars would weave like a giant centipede round the loch rather than queue for the ferry.

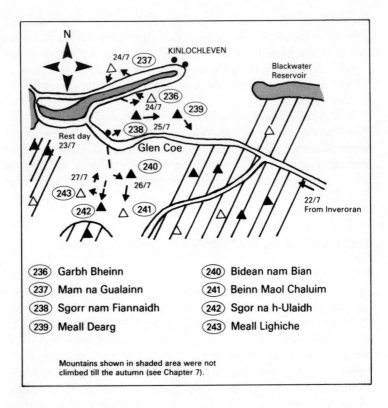

N

24/7 (237) KINLOCHLEVEN

Blackwater
Reservoir

(236)
24/7 (239)

Rest day
23/7 (238) 25/7

Glen Coe

(240)

27/7 26/7

(243)

(242) (241)

22/7
From Inveroran

(236) Garbh Bheinn
(237) Mam na Gualainn
(238) Sgorr nam Fiannaidh
(239) Meall Dearg

(240) Bidean nam Bian
(241) Beinn Maol Chaluim
(242) Sgor na h-Ulaidh
(243) Meall Lighiche

Mountains shown in shaded area were not
climbed till the autumn (see Chapter 7).

Map 24   Glen Coe

Legs felt heavy today as they pulled me up the long western
ridge that leads to Garbh Bheinn, 867 metres. This 'Rough Hill' is
a fine Corbett, her wild northern slopes reflected in the loch
below. But, like most Corbetts, her summit is dearly won. A
strenuous climb from sea level, she is no peaceful afternoon stroll.
Wind and rain hammered the mountain, but through the mist I
sighted a rewarding view of the magnificent sawblade-like ridge
of Aonach Eagach overlooking Glencoe: tomorrow's hills. On the
opposite side of the loch lay another muscle-testing Corbett.
Being without a hang-glider, the only approach was to lose all my
precious hard-fought height, cycle round the loch and start the
game again. A squad of soldiers were canoeing on the loch. I felt
like asking them for a loan of a kayak as the rain tumbled down

the slopes of Mam na Gualainn, 796 metres, 'the Pass of the Shoulder'.

The route up from the roadside was punishing, the ground getting steeper and steeper the further I climbed. However, a handy stalking track leads up from Callert House and climbs over the peak's western shoulder to join the West Highland Way in Larighmor. The summit was icy cold, as it was now well into the evening. My late start and weak state had made today's hills tediously slow. Halfway down, the lights of Kinlochleven shimmered through the veil of mist and rain. As I cycled round the lochside the downpour grew heavier and the rain ricocheted off the road as the sky cracked with lightning. A rumbling like a great volcano echoed through the glens. It was like cycling through a flooded river, but it continued for miles and miles. Loch Leven erupted in the storm, the water splashing as if a million tons of pebbles had been thrown into her stormy waters. At last the bike turned into the car park of the Glencoe Youth Hostel. It was 10.30 p.m.

Despite a thundery forecast I woke to a clear day, and boots were soon pounding up the path that zig-zags by the Clachaig Gully, whose steep slopes give a tortuous descent. Above lay two Munros whose names most people will probably forget after climbing them. But what will never be forgotten is the Aonach Eagach, 'the Notched Ridge', a delight of rocky walls and pinnacles, the most spectacular ridge on the Scottish mainland. Sgorr nam Fiannaidh is called 'the Peak of Fionn's Warriors', and is named in their honour. Although history has forgotten, the mountains still remember the day the Vikings came. A host of longships sailed into Loch Leven in an attempt to seize the lands of the legendary King Fionn. For days the clash of swords and axes echoed around the glen till the Viking ruler fell, and the Norsemen fled.

A gentle walk led on to Stob Coire Leith like a show-jumper slowly gathering strength before a jump. Now the fun begins. For two miles the narrow ridge clambers up gullies and over pinnacles. A sheep track avoids one area of difficulty, otherwise you are committed to continue or go back. In summer those who enjoy a scramble will have a whale of a time, but the ridge is not for those suffering from vertigo. In winter it becomes a serious undertaking, and the sight of headtorches bobbing down to Clachaig is a common sight. I was about to shinny down a gully when a head appeared at my feet. Stephen climbed up on to the top of the knoll, his collie dog grinning from his rucksack. He couldn't cope with that bit, explained Stephen, as the relieved dog struggled free.

All difficulties on the mountains are increased by poor weather. The ridge is one to enjoy in good weather, so it can be appreciated at its best. The crampon-scratched rocks led on to the steep, weaving track leading to the easterly Meall Dearg, meaning 'the Red Hill': disappointing for such a dramatic peak. The path zig-zagged its way steeply up Am Bodach and on to Sron Gharbh, where a gentle path leads down by the side of the gurgling Allt-na-Reigh to Glencoe. An old drover's track saved me from walking along the busy road. Cars and caravans raced by too fast to take in some of Scotland's finest mountain scenery. Towering above the glen rose the magnificent cliffs of the Three Sisters. The most westerly, Aonach Dubh, is home to Ossian's Cave, legendary hiding place for Fingalian heroes. There was once a visitors' book for those adventurous enough to scale the heights.

Down at the friendly Clachaig Hotel, Peter served me a much-needed pint. Stephen asked me to look after his collie while he hitched up the road to get his car. Despite my petting the dog and giving him titbits, he could only whine until his master returned. Then he leapt around the bar, the worried frowns disappeared from his face, eyes bright and mouth laughing: the touching devotion of man's best friend.

Next morning the shepherds in Fionn Ghleann were grabbing a few dry moments to shear their sheep. They would have to be quick, for within an hour another low pressure system swept across the Atlantic, blanketing the glen with mist and rain. I wondered how many MacDonalds fled up this glen that bitter cold night in February 1692. The MacDonalds of Glencoe, with most of the Highland clans, had signed an oath of allegiance to King William. So their Chieftain MacIan saw no danger when Robert Campbell arrived with 120 Redcoats, asking if they could be billeted in the glen, there being no room at Fort William, and promising them safety. Although the clan were short of food they treated their old enemies with the greatest hospitality and entertained them for twelve days. Then one bitter cold night, the soldiers turned on their hosts, murdering them in their beds. The soldiers, reluctant to obey their heinous orders, killed only about thirty-eight people; the blizzards accounted for at least the same again as the clan fled into the mountains. The Highlands were stunned. Hospitality was sacred. How guests could turn on their generous hosts was beyond belief. It became known that the original plan had been on a grander scale, and had included the extermination of the Camerons of Loch Eil and MacDonnels of Glen Garry. This was cancelled only at the last moment for lack of troops. The atrocity fuelled the fires for three further Jacobite rebellions.

> They came in the night while our men were asleep,
> This band of Argyll, through snow soft and deep
> Like murdering foxes among helpless sheep
> They slaughtered the house of MacDonald.
>
> J. McLean

The rain crashed down just as I gained the southern ridge of Bidean nam Bian, 1,150 metres. As her name suggests, she certainly is a 'Peak of the Mountains': few others compete in beauty or drama. This is a mountain to be enjoyed and treated with respect, for her tame, grassy northern spurs all end overlooking precipitous crags. Most people climb her by the track leaving Achnambeithach, leading up into Coire nam Beith. Of all her wild corries my favourite is Coire Gabhail, 'the Corrie of the Spoil', where the MacDonalds would hide their stolen cattle. From the roadside at Glencoe, close to the meeting of three waters, a well-trodden path leads over a massive rockfall which hides the treasure behind. Then, suddenly, all is revealed: ahead lies the lost valley, a green, flat glen with luscious short grass, tame in a rough world of beauty.

A mist-covered slippery scree slope led up to the unfriendly world above, as wind and rain sprayed the summit cairn. On my descent, I spied a cairn promising an easier route. It led into a vile scree-filled gully that plummeted straight over a crag. It was an eerie feeling, desperately trying to get uphill as the mountain moved at your feet, rocks slipping over the misty drop. After a good deal of messing about I crossed an exposed rocky spur and found my ascent route, promising myself not to be so stupid again.

By gentle contrast, Beinn Maol Chaluim, 904 metres, was a grassy ramble. She is a forgotten little mountain, hidden by Bidean's massive bulk. But what is hidden away is often good, and her narrow Bealach Fhionnghail, hemmed in by cliffs, is well worth exploring.

Back down at the hostel, Dot complained she had taken advantage of an offer for suntan oil and had boxes of the stuff. I helpfully suggested, 'Och, take the labels off and sell it as midge-repellent. They'll never know the difference!'

We had been treated to a spectacular lightning storm which illuminated the glen the night before. In the morning, the carnage of broken branches was strewn across the roads. It was bucketing with rain as I followed the turbulent Allt na Muidhe. Today's two peaks should have been climbed with yesterday's group, but the atrocious weather was making a mockery of my plans. Sgor na h-Ulaidh, 994 metres, is 'Peak of the Treasure'. It is a remote Munro, four miles from any road, and thus seldom visited by motor-bound man. Slipping round the foot of her northern crags led me to Meall Lighiche, 772 metres, a newly promoted Corbett, whose boomerang-shaped ridge looks down on lovely Glen Creran, a glen renowned for its ancient healing wells.

With the rain battering at my back, I returned to the hostel. Tom and Doreen arrived and we spent two days replanning the routes ahead. My chief worry was the stalking season, starting in earnest in a fortnight. My route was designed to avoid sensitive areas, but my source of information, a book called *Access* (see introduction), was hopelessly inaccurate. The new SMC guide books provide up-to-date information on stalking restrictions.

MORVERN, 30–31 JULY

It was good to feel the sea breezes on the short ferry crossing of Loch Linnhe. Crossing the Great Glen once more was significant, even if a few peaks remained in Glen Etive for climbs in the autumn. The landing-craft-type ferry was packed. I well remember crossing with Libby Whittome, with her five anxious ponies

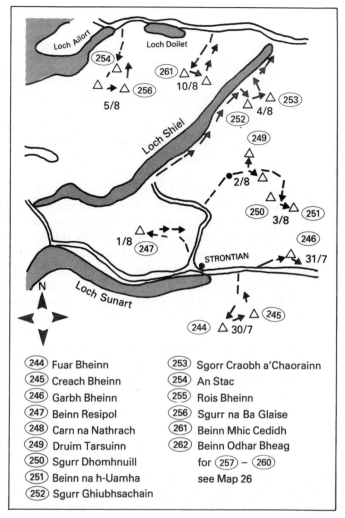

Map 25   Morvern, Ardgour and Moidart

threatening to kick out at the expensive cars surrounding them. They didn't have tickets for ponies so charged us for bicycles instead!

Once the cars had whizzed past on the other side, Morvern returned to her normal, sleepy state. Glen Tarbert provided a handy, if midgy, camp. With the soggy woodland behind, I was glad to be free of ankle-tugging heather. The sun shone on the tranquil slopes of Fuar Bheinn, 765 metres. She is the most southerly in this Corbett kingdom of Morvern, Ardgour and Moidart, home for sixteen Corbetts – empty, wild hills, free of the crowds chasing the Munro game. From the summit, the view down Loch Linnhe was superb, every indentation on her craggy slopes overlooking Glen Galmadale had been enthusiastically named on the map. Loch a'Choire glinted below, a perfect natural harbour and one much appreciated by the Vikings, who are reputed to have made a strong base there till thrown out by the Lord of the Isles.

Her sister mountain is Creach Bheinn, 853 metres, 'Mountain of Spoil': no doubt connected with the forgotten story behind the Allt na Crieche, meaning 'Stream of the Raid'. For this was the land of Clan MacLean, noted warriors and cattle thieves. On top were several bivouac shelters, and what a view the lucky users would wake to in the morning: the mountains of Lorn and Lochaber, and Islay, Mull and Jura – a grand sight while cooking breakfast. After Culloden, HMS *Termor* and *Princess Anne* sailed down this coastline in a show of force, blasting eighteen villages afire with their cannons.

The bliss of a sunny day turned to a peaceful night and a meal *al fresco*. It was almost as if crossing the Great Glen had transported me to a new world, leaving the cloudy wet one behind.

The familiar mist and rain returned with the morning, as did the midges. Above lay Garbh Bheinn, 885 metres, meaning 'Rough Hill', which is a bit of an understatement to describe the Western Highland's wildest Corbett. While climbers rave over her Great and Pinnacle Ridge east of the summit, and the walker can approach from the south, all will find it good. The mist was very low as the compass guided me to the two lochans close to Meall a'Chuilinn. The climb up the mountain's eastern ridge felt like clambering up a giant rocky leg to the surprisingly flat and peaceful summit plateau, a placid oasis in a mountain of forbidding crags and rocky towers. It was disappointing to have been cheated of a view, for to the north lay Ardgour, realm of uninhabited small mountains, stretching to Glenfinnan.

After a brew-up at the tent, it was packed up and repitched in Strontian. This modern village felt more like an English hamlet, with a village green and shops. Some holiday-makers were busy chasing the travelling bank, which was seemingly geared up for deposits and not withdrawals, and trying its best to avoid them. A nature trail leads up to the old mine shafts by the Strontian River, which is well worth a visit.

After dinner, a strong breeze kept the midges at bay and gave me a chance to write up my diary. It was five and a half months since I'd left home, with 246 hills climbed. I had become quite used to my nomadic existence. To get one good clear month while the days were still long would make all the difference. While respecting the weather forecasters' high standard of meterological science, all I wanted to know was: 'Are you gonna give us a break?'

CHAPTER 6

August 1985

Sunart

—

Ardgour

—

Moidart and Glenfinnan

—

South Loch Eil and Gleann Dubh Lighe

—

Loch Arkaig

—

Glen Dessary

—

Glen Kingie

—

Loch Nevis

—

Knoydart

—

Barrisdale

SUNART, 1 AUGUST

Strontian village was still fast asleep. Only a collie dog barked as my battered bike clanked its way out of town on the road to Polloch. Beinn Resipol was today's challenge. She is best climbed from Ariundle, and from there it's a three-hour climb up a long grassy ridge to the summit. It was a delight to follow the old path leading to the disused mines on the eastern shoulder of the mountain. I had long looked forward to climbing this magical little mountain, one of Scotland's finest Corbetts. The well-trodden miners' path, as it wound up the mountain-side, gave a spring to the heels. Alas, it does not go near the top, so I was soon taking a bearing and disappearing into the mist. It was great to be exploring a new mountain. Resipol's slopes had suffered badly from this summer's torrential downpour. Small burns had gouged huge gashes and scarred her slopes. The summit was further than it looked, as bump after bump appeared through the mist. Each one looked higher than the last, till finally the top was reached. Far below lay Loch Sunart. For years, Somerled, Lord of the Isles, had fought a daring guerilla war in the area against numerically superior Vikings, eventually driving them out.

Close to the cold misty summit a ghostly tap-tapping on the rocks was heard. The 'ghost' turned out to be Chris, a geologist, who had been working away with his hammer all summer, exploring the hillside: a wise choice, for the area is rich in minerals. Chris said that west of the summit lay no higher mountain till you crossed the Atlantic, that ocean being only slightly wetter than Resipol's summit that day.

Soon I was down in the glen and cycling the long steep pull over to Loch Doilet. The old mines near Bellsgrove Lodge are active again and providing welcome work locally. With a heavy load on the bike it was an incredibly steep pull. Perspiration mixed with dust from the lorries completed the torture. At Kinlochan the route took the forestry track up the north side of Glen Hurich, bicycle tyres digging into the soft forestry road surface which led through soaking young trees to Resourie, a delightful bothy in the heart of the Ardgour mountains.

ARDGOUR, 2–4 AUGUST

Next morning, the mist was right down to the woodland as I headed west on the path to Lochann Dubh. Great pools of water lay everywhere. A tiny burn had become a raging torrent and was split crazily. It had found a dozen ways to reach the foaming, roaring River Hurich, crashing down the glen on its destructive course. From the lochan the route took the northern slopes of Carn na Nathrach. This wild little Corbett lies in the centre of the Ardgour Mountains, a forgotten corner of Scotland's wilds. The rain pelted down relentlessly and the mist shrouded the mountains, giving them a wild, menacing look. Winding my way in and out of the small crags, the summit was finally reached.

Because of the rain, I decided not to continue on the long journey east to climb the other two Corbetts, Sgurr Dhomhnuill and Beinn na h-Uamha. Gambling on a better day tomorrow, I descended to the lochan, heading up through the mist to the top of Druim Tarsuinn.

It was blowing a gale ... surely I was the only visitor to the summit in weeks. The sound of white burns roaring echoed across the glen, a frightening, strange beauty that any visitor to Scotland's wilderness must experience. I descended steeply by the Coire ant-Searraich, 'the Corrie of the Colt', and was soon down in the glen. Near here recently a party of young hillwalkers bumped into a Scot who was dragging a sledge laden with his gear and a crate of whisky. It was mid-July!

Another rainy morning. The River Hurich was doing somersaults as it crashed down the glen. The soaking path west crossed one foaming burn after another. The burn coming down the Gleann na Cloiche Sgoilte was in spate. Halfway across, with the water tugging at my feet, I was wishing I was somewhere else. 'Relax,' I told myself, 'it's just mind over matter. The river doesn't mind and you don't matter!' This burn had turned into a foaming river that any white-water canoeist would have revelled in.

The route lay up the northern ridge of Sgurr Dhomhnuill. At

888 metres, this is the highest mountain in the district. It is very remote and seldom visited, which is sad, for it's a fine peak, with impressive crags on the northern slopes. Why do so few people visit this wild outpost of Ardgour? The mountain could be climbed on day trips, the hills reached by the long glens to the east.

Two hours later I was standing on the misty summit, trusty compass in hand. I crossed Gleann Mhic Phail, scrambling in and out of an amazingly steep ravine, then pushed on to Beinn na h-Uamha, 'Hill of the Caves'. Having battled to the top in awful weather, believing it to be my 250th hill, I discovered that in fact I was ahead of that figure by this stage. My knees were trembling with excitement. After five and a half months on the hills, I was halfway there, with only 248 hills to go! This knowledge helped keep me going as I fought against gale-force winds. Hillock after hillock appeared out of the mist, each slightly higher than the next.

Beinn na h-Uamha was not going to give up her crown without a battle: the wind bowled me over several times, forcing me to crawl to reach the summit. There I gave three cheers, thinking that the second half could hardly be much worse. This was the land of the warlike Clan MacLean. When surrounded by Cromwell's army at Inverkeithing in 1651, they refused to surrender. To shouts of, 'A man for Hector!' (MacLean), they died fighting at the chieftain's feet. The rain didn't let up as I squelched along the track back to the bothy, whistling 'Singing in the Rain'.

The next day's two mountains lay only eight miles to the north, but were too awkward to get at from my base in Glen Hurich. It was necessary to cycle twenty miles on Land Rover tracks up the shore of Loch Shiel. The scenery was great, especially over the wild hills of Moidart to the west. Near the south end of Loch Shiel lies Eilean Shona and Castle Dorlinn, fortress of Clan Ranald and site of their famous victory over hoards of invading Campbells.

Today's route lay up the Coire Ghiubhsachain, then steeply to the summit ridge of Sgorr Craobh a'Chaorainn, 'the Peak of the Rowan Tree'. The summit is a steep knoll, giving an enjoyable scramble from the south side. A strong wind brought in a heavy rainstorm, soaking everything in seconds. The wind buffeted the jewel-like lochan at the col, as I hastened up Sgurr Ghiubhsachain (849 metres), 'the Peak of the Little Pinewood', which still holds true on its western slopes. She is a beautiful mountain, with wild crags stretching west and north, offering scrambling possibilities. I descended down the northern ridge, weaving in and out of the small crags. The way wasn't always obvious, and you could be left scratching your head in confusion. The mist blew in and out like a curtain at a peep-show. Here was the majesty of the Scottish Highlands, wave after wave of mountains stretching in all directions. It was late by the time I got down, and the midges were out in force. You spend most of the midge months longing for winter, and most cold winters longing for summer. Climbers are a funny breed.

MOIDART AND GLENFINNAN, 5–10 AUGUST

I cycled west early through Glenfinnan, stopping at Lochailort to stock up with chocolate bars. To the south, through a thin veil of soft rain and thick mist, lay the Rois Bheinn group of three Corbetts. For once, they were close together and would be challenge enough in today's foul weather. The tiny Glenshian Lodge Hotel looked as if it had stepped right out of *Brigadoon*. A path strides out over Tom Odhar, then disappears. A steep, two-and-a-half-hour climb through wild grass took me to the mist-shrouded top of An Stac. Translation from Gaelic to English can be very helpful in determining the roughness of the terrain. This hill, for example, is exactly what is described by its Gaelic name, 'the Steep Rocky Hill'.

From the lochan in Coire na Cnamha, I pressed up a gully to the king of the group, Rois Bheinn. A Corbett is defined as a mountain over 2,500 feet high, with a minimum reascent of 500 feet on all sides. So it's a rare thing indeed to get three Corbetts so close together. Warm memories of another misty visit to Rois Bheinn filled my mind, this time on pony with Libby Whittome on one of her wild mountain pony treks. Today the mist sifted in and out, with an occasional glimpse of a view. Ardnamurchan stretched out like an arm across the Atlantic. This was the home of the MacIan clan. Life was hard on the peninsula, so the clan turned to piracy for a living, terrorising the west coast of Scotland in search of plunder.

The magical little peak of Ben Hiant on the peninsula stood out on the horizon. Here the Clearances continued as late as 1853. To the north, across the wild Ardnish peninsula, lies Loch Nan Uamh, 'Loch of the Caves'. Here Prince Charlie landed to raise the clans in August 1745.

I hurried down to Bealach an Fhiona and up the wonderful peak of Sgurr na Ba Glaise, 'Peak of the Grey Cow', whose gentle, south-facing slopes belie its wild northern crags and eastern ridge to An t-Slat-bheinn. The delights of the narrow Druim Fiaclach Ridge is well named, 'the Jagged Backbone'. The hills all round are wild and majestic, yet none reach the magic 3,000-foot mark of the Munros. Many are far superior and wilder mountains than their larger brothers.

With a chilling mist around, I headed down the Coire a'Bhuiridh — where a hawk scoured the glen for dinner — to Inverailort, first passing through the ruins of the old second World War Commando base. It was getting dark as I cycled back towards the tent at Glenfinnan, stopping at the Lodge Hotel for a pint. There I over-heard two American tourists talking:

'Say, Elmer, wasn't that a swell monument we saw today of Bonnie Prince Charlie?'

'Sure was, Wilma. Didn't he marry Princess Di?'

After a support team visit and a couple of planning/rest days, I awoke to a grey and threatening morning. Following the Land Rover track — an ugly scar on the landscape, partly washed away by the rain — I headed north-west up the glen, soon branching off to head up the steep slopes of Stob Coire nan Cearc. The mist cleared a little. Ahead lay a figure on the slopes above, two collies whining and pawing at an apparently lifeless body. As I reached for my first-aid kit ... the 'body' sat up and said, 'Fine morning!' The shepherd had simply nodded off.

Streap, the first of today's mountains, lay before me. At 909 metres it is reputed to have the steepest grassy slopes in Britain. Streap, translated, means scrambling or climbing, though the best scrambling here lies on Stob Coire na Cearc, at the head of Gleann Dubh Lighe.

Streap has two summits, the higher being the westerly one,

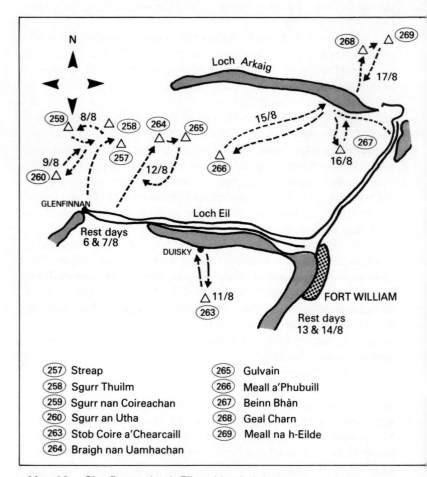

Map 26   Glenfinnan, Loch Eil and Loch Arkaig

with a narrow ridge leading to the top. On the way I chatted to a couple of shepherds, who pointed out the big cairn on Streap's southern slopes, a huge boulder-field, once a haven for wolves. Now foxes have taken over, and a fox, once established on the cairn, is very difficult to flush out.

On top of Streap, my gaze was fixed to the north and west, for here lie the Knoydart Mountains, the Rough Bounds. It's a beautiful wilderness. Hopefully, the weather would be kind, as the area contains twenty of the wildest mountains Scotland can offer.

There's a quick descent from the summit of Streap, going right down to the glen to the west ... though you would need a parachute! A steep pull up the Druim Coire a'Bheithe brought me to the top of Sgurr Thuilm, 963 metres, as ptarmigan clattered away from their rocky hiding places. To the north lay Glen Pean and a ruin. It was here that Prince Charles fled from the field of Culloden, leaving his wounded to be murdered by the Redcoats. By the end of his wanderings, Charlie was an accomplished hill man. For five months he went from cave to cave, protected by the Highlanders, Jacobites or not. The reward on his head was £30,000 — an immense fortune then. But no price could ever be put on Highland loyalty.

A line of rusty fence posts marked the way as I headed west over the Beinn Gharbh, towards Sgurr nan Coireachan, 'the Peak of the Corries'. Today's east–west route is the best way to complete the horseshoe. Mist blocked the view, but in clear weather one is treated to a spectacular view of Knoydart's glories. Many fine deep corries lie to the north and west, wild sanctuaries for the deer. There was now a strong wind, and the mist cleared enough to give a view down into the dark loch in Glen Pean, known as the Priest's Loch.

Though a path is shown going round the north side of this loch (Lochan Leum an t-Sagairt), it does not exist. It is best to keep to the south side of the loch. Priest's Loch got its name from a priest who, surrounded by soldiers, was hiding on its woody shores. The loch was several hundred yards wide, and the priest jumped in and escaped. To this day, Glen Pean is haunted by the ghost of a pursuing Redcoat.

It was a steep climb to the top of 'the Peak of the Corries'. After kissing the trig point, I headed down its south-east ridge, the Sgurr a'Choire Riabhaich, 'Peak of the Grey Corrie'.

Back down in the glen, I met some friends and had a good evening, with humour and songs flowing before a roaring fire.

Bound for a wild little mountain (Sgurr an Utha), I headed west bright and early, following a Land Rover track some of the way up the Allt a'Chaol-ghlinne. At 796 metres, it is seldom climbed. Its northern slopes were full of interesting little crags, providing plenty of scrambling. A steep climb led to the top of this rain-drenched Corbett. The view was its chief pleasure when the rain stopped, revealing the wild, empty lands around Loch Beoraid lying to the west. An eagle flew overhead to complete the scene. The beauty of the Highlands, wild and untamable! This was my 260th hill.

With an early morning start, I cycled down the misty glen under the famous Glenfinnan viaduct and west towards Loch Eil. Two gems of mountains, both Corbetts, still needed to be climbed in Moidart. With the midges biting, I headed up the wild, rough glen into the Coire Buidhe, the best ascent route for the two wild hills of Beinn Mhic Cedidh and Beinn Odhar Bheag. It took ages, as hassle grass hampered progress. It is best described as like grass that a herd of elephants have run through, leaving huge deep footprints in their wake.

On top of the Bealach a'choire Bhuidhe, I gazed longingly at the lonely, misty hills to the south. Seldom visited, there are no Munros here; instead the smaller, wild mountains sitting proud and majestic, a forgotten corner of Scotland's mountain domain. A steep pull led up the long slopes to the summit of Beinn Mhic Cedidh. On the mountain's northern slopes lies the grave of a Redcoat deserter, believed to have died of exposure to the elements. The mist cleared enough to give a glimpse west to the beautiful wild Druim Fiaclach ridge.

It was heartbreaking to lose so much height going down to the col before climbing the long western slopes of Beinn Odhar Bheag. Its smaller sister hill to the north, Beinn Odhar Mhor, is some 41 feet lower. She boasts an interesting ridge, with great views down Loch Shiel. After struggling back through the hassle grass, it was a relief to be able to walk along the tracks of the West Highland railway line. During the Second World War, British spies were trained here in the art of jumping on and off trains, helped by the train's slow progress and the abundance of tunnels. Today, such an event would surely be sponsored by the Scottish Tourist Board!

SOUTH LOCH EIL AND GLEANN DUBH LIGHE, 11–12 AUGUST

Next morning looked grey and threatening which, by 1985 standards, was a good day. I cycled along the south shore of Loch Eil. At Duisky, it was hard work climbing through the barren moorlands, as heather tugged at your feet, a breeze just failing to keep the midges at bay. A seemingly endless climb led to the top of Stob Coire a'Chearcaill, whose fine eastern corrie faces Fort William. A lonely Corbett cast out by her neighbours, she was my last mountain in Ardgour to be climbed. All sixteen Corbetts south of the Mallaig–Fort William road had now been conquered. A large pocket of the planning map would be shaded in with great pleasure next time I met the support team.

Canoes and sailing boats were out on the loch, no doubt from the Locheil Centre opposite, which has a reputation for getting things done. They once contacted British Rail, offering to build their own station by the centre. BR had no objection, so the station was soon built. Loch Eil was the scene of a furiously fought battle at Achdalieu, where the Camerons routed a large force of Cromwell's army.

After a midge-infested camp, I pushed on next day up Gleann Dubh Lighe, 'Glen of the Black Grave', before climbing on to the long ridge leading to Braigh nan Uamhachan, 'Hostage of the Caverns'. The mist was kept on the move by the strong wind at my back. Ptarmigan scattered in all directions. Then on to Gulvain, 987 metres. The glen below was the perfect example of a glaciated valley as it wound its way north. Gulvain is a fairly remote mountain, demanding a lot of leg power from any direction. Like many solitary Munros she is, I suspect, thrown in as an afterthought on a wet day. She deserves far better, for those who climb her on a clear day will be treated to one of the finest viewpoints in the Western Highlands.

It was 6.00 p.m. before the summit was reached. Watch you don't go wrong on this hill, for the actual summit is marked on the Ordnance Survey Landranger Series Sheet no. 41, not the trig point at 961 metres marked on Sheet no. 40. My gaze fell longingly on Meall a'Phubuill, a remote Corbett near by, by there was no time to climb it, so I descended reluctantly to Gleann Fionnlighe. At the house marked Wauchan — an OS misprint for

Uamhachan — the route took me west over to Gleann Dubh Lighe as darkness fell. I had climbed all the hills south of here — 265 was the current tally. There was no sunset, but the light grey shadows looked majestic all the same. A stag stood on a boulder in the gloaming.

LOCH ARKAIG, 15–18 AUGUST

> I hear the pibroch sounding, sounding,
> Deep o'er the mountains and the glen.
> While light-springing footsteps are trampling the heath,
> 'Tis the march of the Cameron men.

After a short visit to Fort William I headed north to Loch Arkaig. The route was by the old road up the west banks of the Caledonian Canal, then a ride past Achnacarry, seat of the Cameron Clan. A very rough Land Rover track led west along the foot of Loch Arkaig. The bike groaned and clanked its way over the rough track up Glen Mallie.

I climbed through the mist to gain the broad east ridge of Meall a'Phubuill which, oddly enough, means 'Hill of the Tent' or 'Pavilion'. This remote Corbett does not give up her summit easily: she is a long way from any roads. But those who make the effort will be treated to the sight of huge herds of deer which frequent the area. It was misty and windy on top, but another remote and lonely Corbett had fallen.

All the peaks to the west and south had now been climbed, but soon the stalking season would be in full swing. I hated to bother stalkers, who are keeping one of the Highlands' last industries alive. In a full year they ask but two months to have the mountains to themselves. I headed back down the glen, cycling on the steep, rough track like a show-jumper out of control. We raced down hills, crashing over rough rocks and through swelling burns. Passing a bridge across the River Mallie, I spotted some smoke rising from the woodland on the southern shore of the river. How could there possibly be a fire with all this wet weather? It turned out to be two couples on a twenty-four-hour survival exercise. I wished them luck in their makeshift bivouac and hurried off to my nice warm tent.

It was a wet, blowy morning, as the route headed up through the wild forestry to gain the northern slopes of Beinn Bhan. It was hard going in the rough woodland. I came across a Scots Pine with three straight branches growing from the trunk, like a cactus in a Hollywood movie.

It was a relief to get through this jungle of forestry on to some open ground. Anyone considering climbing this mountain should take any route other than the one I was following today — unless he's in training for a jungle expedition! It had been sixteen days since last experiencing a clear day on the hills, and still the rain and mist blocked my view today. This 'Fair' mountain (bhan means fair) commands a prominent position in the glen, with its amphitheatre-like corrie facing south, dropping steeply to Glen Loy.

It was wild and windy on top, but at least it gave a view right up Loch Lochy and the Great Glen. Opposite lay Kilmonivaig and High Bridge, where the first shots of the '45 rebellion were fired. Another corner of the walk had been turned. Here was peace and quiet, while down in the glens sailing boats on the loch struggled against the elements, and traffic rushed along the roads like speed-mad beetles. I took some photographs before toiling through the unpleasant woodland, a mixture of fallen trees and new ones. Dreams of endless brews and pleasant company at the fireside kept me going.

Starting off early, I cycled back along the Land Rover track towards Achnacarry, giving the rim of my buckled rear wheel a terrible bump. I stopped at the phone box in Achnacarry and arranged to meet the support team on Sunday. Behind stood the house of Achnacarry, the basic training centre for the Commandos in the Second World War. Over 25,000 British and Allied men passed through the gates in their quest to win the coveted 'green beret'. The training was very tough. They lived off the land in the surrounding hills; many stone bivouacs seen today are visible remnants of that time. The Commandos soon became a legend, striking terror into the hearts of the enemy. Their tough training in the hills must have given them a strong feeling for Scotland. When they stormed the beaches on D-Day, it was to the blood-curdling Highland battle cry, 'Caberfeidh Ya Bass!', meaning 'Antlers, you bastards!' As can be expected, the men were a wild bunch. Some of their humorous antics included ensuring that their well-groomed mascot — a white horse — was totally drunk for their passing-out parade, while the RSM was barricaded in his office!

Alexander MacDonald, the stalker, gave me his permission to climb two Corbetts; Geal Charn (White Cairn) and Meall na h-Eilde, so I cycled to Achnasaul, passing the rusty old field gun, a trophy brought home to the Cameron family after the First World War. The farm of Achnasaul looked like a model as I climbed high on the stalking track, bound for the heathery slopes of Geal Charn. Today felt like a holiday: I could actually see the hill I was climbing and, for once, it was warm. Amazing how a little sunshine restores morale! To the west lay the Mile Dorcha, or 'Dark Mile', so-called because of the woodland shading the road. To the south of Achnacarry, the Mackintoshes fought a clan battle in which bows and arrows were used for the last time.

The summit was quiet and peaceful today, as I sat by the cairn and ate some chocolate. I looked to the west by the wild hills of Knoydart and blew them a kiss. If only the weather could stay like this for a while I should, with luck, win through.

My route crossed over Meall coire nan Saobhaidh, 'the Hill of the Corrie of the Den of the Fox', to push on to the summit of the second Corbett, Meall na h-Eilde. On the way down, I disturbed a herd of over 200 deer. I hated to scare them, but this was the stalking season, and they weren't taking any chances. A six-hour round trip, and the two Corbetts that stand guardians between Loch Arkaig and Glen Garry had been climbed. I camped near Achnasaul — with the midges for company! Tomorrow would take me into the Rough Bounds of Knoydart, an area that I knew quite well and, as a bonus, I would have the company of Munro, the world's daftest collie!

After breakfast in the tent (and a mad dash to beat the midges), I packed my gear in record time. It was good to leave them behind and cycle west along the shoreline road of Loch Arkaig. Near by, an officer in Cumberland's army was shot by mistake when Cameron of Clunes mistook him for a brutal Redcoat officer whose horse he had borrowed that day.

The bike clattered its way along the road. A herring gull flew languidly down the loch. Ahead lay the Glen Garry lands of

Knoydart, great towering hills disappearing into the mist, home of the eagle, wild cat and pine marten. Arriving at the head of the loch a bit ahead of schedule, I explained to John Morrison (the local stalker) that I was on a long-distance walk and that weather problems had held me back. Would it be possible, I asked, to climb some hills in his area when he wasn't planning to stalk on them?

'Since you're doing it for charity,' he replied, 'you can have a free hand on my hills.'

At the west end of Loch Arkaig I waited about ten minutes ... then a familiar red car appeared, with a black dog barking from the rear window. Tom's radio-cassette was blaring out the new Erskine song, 'The Hills and Glens so Peaceful'. Tom and Doreen laid a tablecloth on the bonnet of the car and produced a feast of cold meats, salad, rolls, cakes and red wine. Quite a treat after my dehydrated diet! Munro made the usual fuss. Then we walked over to A'Chuil bothy across the boggy glen. They helped me over with a lot of stores, as I was going to be in the area for the best part of a week. They had even bought cans of dogfood for Munro, some real food for me, and a quantity of beer and whisky. What a tremendous morale-booster.

GLEN DESSARY, 19–20 AUGUST

The cheery bothy grew smaller as man and dog wound their way up Sgurr Cos na Breachd Laoidh, the first of today's four mountains. Munro raced ahead like a coiled-up spring released. Mist floated in and rain pelted the long, grassy ridge leading to the summit. Wild mountains deserve the wildest weather — who would change that?

Legend has it that at the western end of Loch Arkaig is buried Prince Charlie's treasure chest and 15,000 French gold coins. Munro looked happy, though wet. As we sat by the cairn he unhelpfully shook himself, soaking me even more. We aqua-slid down to the col and climbed to join the long ridge that guards the south side of Loch Quoich. This stretches for eight miles and includes five mountains, three of which I hoped to climb today. We skipped over An Eag, Munro trotting happily at heel. The pull up Sgurr nan Coireachan (953 metres) looked wild and

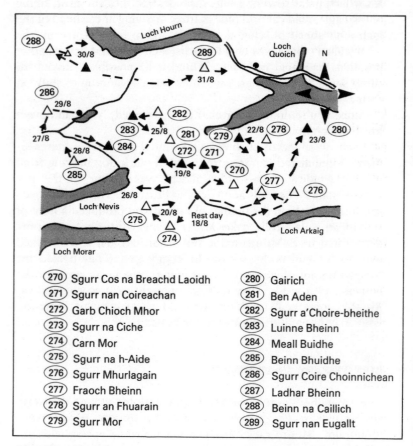

Map 27   Knoydart

270	Sgurr Cos na Breachd Laoidh	280	Gairich
271	Sgurr nan Coireachan	281	Ben Aden
272	Garb Chioch Mhor	282	Sgurr a'Choire-bheithe
273	Sgurr na Ciche	283	Luinne Bheinn
274	Carn Mor	284	Meall Buidhe
275	Sgurr na h-Aide	285	Beinn Bhuidhe
276	Sgurr Mhurlagain	286	Sgurr Coire Choinnichean
277	Fraoch Bheinn	287	Ladhar Bheinn
278	Sgurr an Fhuarain	288	Beinn na Caillich
279	Sgurr Mor	289	Sgurr nan Eugallt

impregnable in the mist; but on closer inspection it was easy. The ridge leading west was superb. A wall follows the crest of the ridge, a remnant of the days when estates with wealthy owners and cheap labour could easily afford elaborate boundaries. The most popular way to gain access to the Sgurr na Ciche range is by Glen Dessary. The grandest way is from the west by the estate boat which, on occasion, visits the head of Loch Nevis — though the times are fickle.

Munro led on, and we enjoyed a scramble over the easy Garbh Chioch wall. Munro beat me to the top. Garb Chioch Mhor was recently added to Munro's tables, and its wild form deserves to be granted entry to the magic list. A track of sorts led up the rugged, steep slopes to the summit of Sgurr na Ciche.

One trig point lay on its side, a victim of the weather, while a new one stood in its former position. This terrific hill looks superb from any angle; from Ben Nevis she appears to tower above the mountains around. The summit was no place to linger. Our descent took us back to the Feadan na Ciche, 'the Pass of the Whistling', which was living up to its name. To the north of the path lies the Coire nan Gall, which Prince Charlie traversed 'while skulking in the Hielands'. The Coire na Ciche is a deer sanctuary in wild weather; it has an impregnable look about it.

Avoiding the steep cliffs of Druim nan Uadhag, we squelched east to return to the bothy. Hamish Brown, in his first-ever continuous walk over the Munros, had a wild time in the glen below us, the Mam na Cloich Airde. In mid-June, a warm day suddenly turned freezing cold, with snow down to 2,000 feet. He felt he was suffering from exposure and made an emergency camp. It was the lowest ebb of his trip. Today dog and master had experienced much kinder weather as they pushed happily along the track after a successful day in the hills. Some recent days had been frustrating, when a full day had to be devoted to cycling and climbing a Corbett tucked away up some forgotten glen. So it was good to get a reasonable bag of summits in rotten weather. It must have been Munro's leadership.

You might think it odd that despite experiencing the wettest summer since 1897, I was neither down nor depressed. This was entirely due to an excellent support team and the tremendous comradeship of fellow hillwalkers and other lovers of wild places.

A brighter morning. Munro and I eagerly bounded up the forestry-ditched slopes behind the bothy. Geologists had recently been staying there and had surveyed the hill. Carn Mor is a massive Corbett whose gentle ridge starts at Strathan. Eight miles later, among rocks and crags, it falls steeply to Loch Morar in the west, Europe's deepest loch. It's reputed to be the home of a monster similar to the one in Loch Ness.

Munro was soon soaked after climbing through the west grass. We struggled to cross a deer fence, then pushed on over easy ground to reach the misty summit of Carn Mor, one and a half hours after leaving A'Chuil. With the mist swirling around, we nervously picked our way down the steep, craggy slopes to the lovely jewel of a lochain, Eanaiche, with its delightful sandy beach. No need to get down early 'before the Jerries' here!

After a feast of Galaxy bars and jelly for encouragement, we climbed the steep, forbidding slopes of Sgurr na h-Aide, 'Peak of the Hat'. It is sometimes confused with Sgurr na Ciche — they look familiar from Glen Dessary. She is my favourite Corbett, a magical little mountain, wild and rugged as any Scottish peak. Munro bounded enthusiastically up the hill, and soon we were in a maze of wee crags. At one stage, it was almost vertical. As Munro's paws clawed at thin air, he fell back and I caught him — it was like something out of a Tom and Jerry cartoon. Finally, he charged back up the crag and barked at me from the top. Near a small lochan at the top, we pushed on up the final ridge. Wild mist and rain clung to the rocky slopes as, triumphantly, we arrived at the top and shook paws!

By common consent, we decided to find an easier way down, heading further east and finding just as wild a descent, then crossed into the forestry kingdom of Glen Dessary, cursing the ditches. After ages, we eventually found a forestry track that took us back near the bothy.

GLEN KINGIE, 21–23 AUGUST

It was raining again as we left, eating chocolate for encouragement. At Strathan we took the indistinct path over Glen Kingie in the middle of the pass. Leaving the pack behind, we headed up Sgurr Mhurlagain, (879 metres), taking the long, easy ridge. She is one of three Corbetts standing between Glen Kingie and Glen Dessary, each with 1,500 feet of climbing between them. Sgurr Mhurlagain's gentle slopes to the south belie its wild, northern corrie, but the mist and rain prevented any view from the top.

Back down in the glen, we sheltered next to a boulder to get a short respite from the weather. Through this pass, the children from the House of Kinbreak used to walk to school at Strathan, a nine-mile round trip across featureless terrain. Despite darkness or bad weather, they were never late. Munro gave a shake, spraying water everywhere. This is better than lying in front of a fire at home, isn't it, Munro? No comment! We pushed on up the steep, rocky slopes of Fraoch Bheinn (858 metres), which provided some fun. Despite the busy bothy, I was yet to meet someone on the hills. Perhaps they had more sense and were all going through the glens. This isolated small mountain is a wee cracker, sitting proudly independent among its higher neighbours. It was wild and blowy on top.

Suddenly I realised that I had made a very stupid mistake. Next day my plan was to be in Glen Kingie to climb hills to the north, but my gear was back at A'Chuil bothy. There was nothing for it but to trek back. There were a couple of mini-buses and some eighteen Germans lying around, unenthusiastically looking at big packs in the pouring rain. They were heading for Sourlies bothy at the head of Loch Nevis, which they eventually reached about 1 a.m.

It was late morning by the time that everything was packed. At 8.30 I headed east along the Land Rover track, cursing my stupidity yesterday. As we headed north into Glen Kingie, the rain poured down relentlessly, continuing as we descended to the glen. Glen Kingie appeared out of the mist like Utopia among the wilds. These were the 'disputed' lands, where the Camerons and Macintoshes battled for over 350 years over ownership.

We headed west up the glen, and climbed the easy slopes to Sgurr an Fhuarain, a Corbett of particular beauty: its wild northern slopes falling to Loch Quoich. From here, an eight-mile walk west takes you over four Munros to Sgurr na Ciche at the head of Loch Nevis. It was a treat to catch a glimpse of the hill that mist had obscured on Monday. The path and the lodge house have long disappeared under the waters of the now-dammed loch. Then on for Sgurr Mor at 1,003 metres. From the summit cairn I gazed down into the magnificent Coire Buidhe, whose stalking track strides distinctly downhill, only to disappear into the loch: another victim of the dam.

A grisly find was made not so long ago at the loch's remote west end — a skeleton in a sleeping bag. Perhaps some lonely soul went off to make peace and rest forever in the Rough Bounds.

Back down at the tent, Munro tucked into appetising dog food, whilst I opted for dehydrated Beef Bourgoignon, and wondered who was getting the best of the deal!

It had been a wild night, and by morning the burns were back to their foaming whiteness. Out of all the years I could pick to climb the Munros and Corbetts, I had to choose the year with the worst wet weather this century. With a cry of 'Ard-choille Grigalach!' — the battle cry of the MacGregors — we were off. We had difficulty crossing the burn near the tent. Munro jumped on a boulder, slipped and hurt his back. I rushed to comfort him, but he seemed all right and licked my hand. We crossed the burn — Munro in my arms — and headed down to the River Kingie, finding the widest, shallowest part. Munro, as trained, went against the current beside me. I held on to his collar as we struggled across.

Taking the path on the other side of the river, we headed north towards Loch Quoich. It was a wet, wild day, when sensible folk stayed at home. The stalking track wound its way up the steep slopes of Gairich, (919 metres). The mist and the wet wind blew in our faces, yet we were happy away from the rat-race. All we had was a daily battle, which suited any Scot! For a moment, I thought seriously about my country. The clans are gone, but the wilderness remains. Now it is under threat from acid rain and pollution. If industrialists think we will sit back and see our heritage destroyed, they can think again!

I whistled 'The Summer Time Has Come', as a bedraggled Munro scooted ahead in the mist. The wind and rain blew over the wide plateau, pushing us towards the summit. Gairich, 'Hill of the Yelling', was living up to its name today. My pockets were full of water, the compass was held in an icy hand, and a cold wind made your ears throb — it was exhilarating! At the top, we celebrated my 280th hill. Another remote mountain range had been won.

The burns were in full spate as we crossed back over to Glen Dessary, singing happily in defiance of the wind and rain. At A'Chuil bothy I met my father Tom, who thrust a welcome dram into my hand. Jim and Val, a charming couple from Liverpool, invited us into their holiday house at upper Glen Dessary. After a hot bath and a good meal, the white roaring burns outside seemed far away. It was typical of the generosity of the people I met throughout this long journey that they would invite two strangers and a wet dog into their house and entertain them royally.

LOCH NEVIS, 24–25 AUGUST

We said goodbye to Jim and Val, whose kindness had surpassed even Highland hospitality. Tom drove off with a very sleepy Munro. When he got home, he slept for three days! I headed west over the Mam na Cloich Airdre. The wind was blowing hard, with a penetrating, driving force that soaked everything. The pack was very heavy, so I took it off and got some sort of shelter behind a boulder as the rain lashed down. Around me the well-worn track was empty, and I suddenly felt very lonely. Will this awful weather ever ease up? Head-down against the rain, I pushed towards Sourlies bothy. It was great to meet support team members Graham and Julie.

When they had arrived the night before, sixteen of our German friends had been in residence. Somehow, they all squeezed in to the tiny refuge. We all laughed at the thought, and looked forward to a quiet, roomy night ... when a head popped round the door and said, 'Hello, chaps. I'm Scoutmaster of Weston-Super-Mare troop, and there's twenty-six of us ...' We squeezed in as many as we could; the rest were forced to camp outside. It was the wettest night of the year and their tents flooded. In the morning the hut was full of half-drowned Scouts and saturated sleeping bags. However they were a hardy bunch, and nothing was going to stop them enjoying themselves as they laughed and joked and wrung out their sleeping bags.

Heading off early with Graham and Julie, the weather looked reasonable — at least it had stopped raining. We wound our way north towards Camusrory, now used as a shooting lodge, and once the base for Tony Montgomery's Adventure Centre. Graham and Julie headed for Meall Buidhe, while I went up Glen Carnoch, bound for one of the remotest and wildest Corbetts: Ben Aden (pronounced Etchaken). I climbed the west side of this incredibly lonely hill; few Munros give as tough a climb. Only the previous year (1984), a rescue team had found a climber dead on the hill. He had fallen over a crag.

A grand view lay behind, straight down Loch Nevis, where Tom McLean has his outdoor centre at Ardintigh. The Ministry of Defence tried to buy this wild area for a military training base, but fortunately a public outcry stopped their plans. The summit just failed to give a view, but it was great not to have wind and rain hammering down on you.

After picking my way down the wild northern slopes, in and out of the crags and huge boulders, I arrived at the Lochan nam Breac, 'Loch of the Trout'. It was here, one spring a few years ago, that I hid a food cache with a week's food. Stupidly, I had put it in several polythene bags and hidden it among some boulders. When I returned in July I found that foxes and mice had scoffed the lot.

A delightful stalking track wound its way up to the top of Gleann Unndalain. Leaving the track, my route took me up the wild slopes of Sgurr a'Choire-bheithe (913 metres), sitting proudly among her neighbours to the west. This peak runs neck and neck with Beinn Dearg in Torridon for being the highest Corbett. It was through these hills that Prince Charlie traversed one night, slipped off a ledge and nearly fell to his death. He managed to wrap his legs round a tree, and his guides rescued him.

The weather had cleared on top, and it was great to sit by the cairn on a summer's evening and enjoy the views. To the north lay Gleann Cosaidh, again Prince Charlie country. Time was getting on — I had forgotten it was now near the end of August, and it would be dark by 9.30, so I pushed on for Luinne Bheinn, which has the obvious nickname, 'Loony Bin'. I ran breathlessly up the slopes, stopping only to take in the breathtaking views over to Meall Bhuidhe, as the sun started sinking slowly into the west. Then I hurried down to Corrie na Gaoithean, wishing I had time to push on to Meall Buidhe, but darkness was not so far away. Skirting over some steep slabs, I then crossed the hussocky hassle, or elephant grass — nature's minefield!

It was dark by the time I reached the bothy. Graham and Julie produced a welcome brew. Cheery voices filled the bothy later, till sleep could be delayed no longer.

KNOYDART, 26–28 AUGUST

Some modern-day prophet had forecast the world would end today, 26 August. Waking up, I certainly wondered about the possibility. It had been the wettest night of the year, according to the radio. The rain was coming down in torrents, adding to the already foaming white burns.

All our bold plans for the hills were scuppered, as the burns roared down the mountainside. We decided to evacuate to Inverie. Leaving Graham and Julie to join us later, I teamed up with two English lads. The noise of our squeaking, soaking boots was deafened by the sound of the crashing burns echoing around us. Cautiously we approached the roaring River Carnoch which was in full flow. In dry weather you can cross it without getting your legs wet. It's a long river — six miles of it — from Lochan nam Breac, with over thirty burns feeding it. So in wet weather it soon becomes a wide and deep impassable current. Now there is a bridge across the river, in memory of a couple who drowned trying to cross in January 1980. Today it was quite impassable. You could hear the rocks tumbling in the water, which raged down the glen like the Ride of the Valkyries. Some lovers of wild places had objected to the bridge being built, suggesting it took away from the real wilderness experience, but we were glad of it today. Even then, we had to wade to reach the bridge, as the river had burst its banks. Soaked, we pushed on for the old ruins of Carnoch, all that remains of a small village that used to boast a shinty team at the turn of the century.

As a young greenhorn on my first visit to the wilds, I took such useless items as a tape recorder with a large selection of cassettes. However my two companions today, Boris and Steve, were even more organised. Boris had a huge rucksack, containing such essentials as an army webbing system of ammunition pouches, a cassette tape recorder, a huge machete-type jungle knife with a removable handle full of hooks, compasses and rabbit snares. In the pockets of his camouflage jacket were concealed a catapult and 5 lbs of lead shot ammunition. Steve had a big pack too, sensibly carrying a snorkel and mask! Unfortunately neither had found room to pack a set of waterproofs, which they sorely missed as we walked through the heavy rain.

Small burns had turned into raging torrents, over which with difficulty we threw our packs, then waded across, arms linked, to prevent being swept away. The rain hammered down relentlessly as we squelched our way down the waterlogged track that had turned into a burn. The waters roared down the hillside to join the brilliant white Allt Gleann Meadail. This was a real Knoydart wash-out. The path crossed over a bridge near the bottom of the glen. The river crashed round the base of the bridge, only a couple of inches from sweeping over its top. Like drowned rats we descended into tiny Inverie. It is reached by boat or a 25-mile walk over mountain tracks from a lonely road end ... there is no other access. But the friendly village folk took pity on our bedraggled state and put us up in the estate hostel. Hot showers, a bed, table and chairs, electricity — what luxury!

Graham and Julie were bound for the mainland, while I chatted to the stalker. He had just finished stalking on the two mountains — Beinn Bhuidhe and Meall Buidhe; we had waded down the pass between them yesterday. To have attempted them then would have been crazy. But this morning it had not been raining for fourteen hours and, amazingly, the rivers had returned to near normal. Passing An t-Uiriollach, 'the Precipice', I climbed through the boulders to the misty summit of Meall Buidhe. She was a three-hour climb from Inverie and I was disappointed not to be able to see her wild, northern slopes, a jungle of crags and boulders. It was cold on top, yet I had warm memories of this mountain, when I had climbed it in a heatwave and sunbathed on top. But there was little sunbathing done in the summer of 1985, the year of the Scottish monsoon.

The ridge to the north to Luinne Bheinn is particularly wild and typical of these Rough Bounds. I skirted in and out of the crags to reach the path below. It was incredible to be able to cross the Allt Gleann Meadail: only the previous day you wouldn't have been able to put one foot into its white, foaming fury.

Beinn Bhuidhe is a wild Corbett. Its steep rocky slopes gave way to grass, as along its bumpy ridge I pushed on to the summit. What a superb view! A white fishing boat glimmered in the shiny waters of Loch Nevis which licked around the slopes of the mountain. Inverie lay to the west, the shielings looking peaceful in the summer glow — a short respite of good weather, no doubt, before the next onslaught.

To the north lay Loch Hourn, 'the Loch of Hell', reputed to be the home of the 'wild beast of Barrisdale'. A crofter once described it as a huge, three-legged beast with gigantic wings, which he saw flying towards him across the hills of Knoydart. My route followed a wild gully down to the Glean Meadail below. In such a wild place you often believed you could be treading on ground that no human being had ever set foot on. Knoydart's mountains are wild and untamable. They are best visited by hill-walkers who have earned a basic apprenticeship in less remote hills. Then the full pleasure of climbing in the Rough Bounds can be enjoyed from a camp in a lonely glen with a lochan of your own for washing in.

BARRISDALE, 29–31 AUGUST

During a morning phone call I learnt that *The Climber and Rambler* had carried a piece on my walk, so people were at last taking notice. This would help the charity-raising section of the support team. Today was to be an easy day. I walked through the lovely woodland at the back of Inverie and started up the easy slopes of Sgurr Coire Choinnichean (796 metres). The sun was shining. It had not been possible to climb this hill yesterday because of stalking. The whale-backed hill had several bumpy knolls on her summit ridge, but from the top a magnificent view could be seen across today's flat peaceful sea, to the Small Isles and Rum. Was it over two and a half months since I had visited those islands' rugged peaks?

Deer grazed happily in the huge corries at the south side of tomorrow's peaks, Ladhar Bheinn and Beinn na Caillich. The old ruined shieling of Folach, 'the Place of Concealment' is well named, sitting as it does in the lonely, wild hills of Gleann na Guiserein. The poor MacDonnel clansmen who lived in these lands suffered terribly during the Clearances.

More recently, in 1948, the crofters tried to fight back. Seven men (the Seven Men of Knoydart) seized some land from Lord Brocket and prepared drains for crofting, but the law ruled against them. Today, the Knoydart estates seem destined to be sold in small fragments to settlers from abroad who covet a piece of Europe's loveliest wilderness. This may not be such a bad thing if they mean to work the land. The Knoydart may yet have a busy school with the sound of laughing children. Others are more sceptical. Inverie is really an oasis among the wild, rugged grandeur of the Western Highlands.

An excellent track led over the steep Mam Barrisdale pass.

Down below Barrisdale, where one family lives, is a small clump of fir trees — all that is left of a once great forest. Old dams still remain along the River Barrisdale, a reminder of the days when the river was used to float logs to Loch Hourn. At the time of the '45, a terrible raging fire swept from Achnacarry, destroying everything in its path, till it reached the rivers of Barrisdale, thirty miles away.

There's a mountain hut at Barrisdale, which the estate kindly leaves open outside the stalking season at a modest charge of about £1.00 a night.

I was awakened in the morning by the sound of stalking ponies banging their heads against the door. They seem to prosper on the weird assortment of rations fed to them by climbers. Fears about the wet weather today were well grounded, as a roaring, southerly wind whistled round the bothy. I walked along the path that leads into the Coire Dhorrcail, bound for Knoydart's jewel, Ladhar Bheinn. She's a beautiful, massive mountain — a steep climb from sea level — boasting over twelve miles of ridge-walking.

I took the ridge heading west to Stob a'Coire Odhair, a wild top with a narrow ridge leading to the summit of Ladhar Bheinn, (1,020 metres). The wild cliffs of Coire Dhorrcail appeared briefly out of the mist. A couple of hoodie crows swooped at a buzzard hunting in the corrie below. Ladhar Bheinn, pronounced Larven, means 'the Forked Mountain'. It's a huge, wild peak that deserves slow exploration — her ridges and corries are well worth while. The summit was a wild, windy place today. Huddling in the lee of the cairn, I had a bite to eat. What a contrast to my last visit, the previous June. When on the top we had stripped to the waist, as the Western Isles gleamed like diamonds in the glistening sea to the west. This is one of my favourite mountains — a real gem and the most westerly Munro. Ladhar Bheinn can be climbed in a long day from Kinloch Hourn, a fourteen-mile trip to Barrisdale alone; or it is sometimes possible to arrange a boat trip to take you over from Arnisdale. There is a magnetic variation on Ladhar Bheinn's north flank that can cause confusion in the mist.

My next hill was Beinn na Caillich, 'the Hill of the Old Woman' or 'Witch'. She had certainly cast her spell on me today — the wind and rain hammered the mountain mercilessly.

Cautiously I climbed down some very steep ground, trusting in my compass, as trained. My bearing took me to a small lochan which, in the mist, seemed the wildest, most remote place I had ever visited. It was a head-down struggle along the wide, bumpy, rocky ridge, the wind roaring in defiance over the Belach a'Choire Odhair. A startled fox tried to run for cover, but gave up fighting the wind and raced frantically down to Loch Hourn.

Thankfully the ridge was not exposed, for I was repeatedly pushed over by the incredibly strong wind: it blew me more than twelve feet to one side. Shouting defiantly 'Ard-choille Grigalach!' I charged down against the wind — only to be pushed over flat on my face. I thought seriously of putting rocks in my packs to prevent lift-off! In the mist, I walked round one lochan to check that it was the right one, and took a bearing. It seemed to take hours to battle through the mass of lochans to the north of Beinn na Caillich. But the adrenalin was flowing and, in a strange way, I was enjoying my predicament. Most hillwalkers would agree that, if you ever have to die, it's best to do so with this wild feeling in your heart.

It was a relief to get some shelter from the wind when climbing Beinn na Caillich, a wild and remote Corbett. Extreme care was taken on her bouldery slopes — what a place to come a cropper! Savagely, I kicked the cairn and vowed never to return in weather like this.

With the wind now at my back, I rocketed across the misty, loch-strewn plateau, descending from the grey, misty veil to Loch Hourn and the inhabited cottage of Li. The fight to get back before dark had been won. Relaxed now, and glad to be off the hill, my cheeks glowed with the excitement of the day. Soon the cheery sight of Barrisdale could be seen. The previous occupant of the cottage used to own a Tiger Moth and regularly flew round the glens, returning to his mountain home like an eagle to her eyrie.

The last day of August. They were going to start stalking in Barrisdale on Monday, so I had just made it by the skin of my teeth. The mist was low and it was raining. My route lay up Glen Barrisdale, the ruins of Barrisdale House slowly disappearing as the path wound up the glen.

It was here that Colla Ben, who led the Knoydart MacDonnels

with great valour in the '45, lived. Glen Barrisdale took a bend on its wild course to Loch Quoich. This was the place to take a bearing for the col of Sgurr nan Eugalt. Compass in hand, I disappeared into the misty mountain-side, weaving in and out of the steep, grassy slopes, strewn with boulders. Unhelpfully, my nose started to bleed, owing to a cold. It just would not stop. I lay down on a slab of rock, blood pouring out quite uncontrollably: I was beginning to think that I had developed haemophilia. The rain poured down my face as I coughed and spluttered. At last the bleeding stopped and I found some water to wash (no shortage of that!). An overflowing lochan was the ideal place to take a bearing.

The rain pelted the summit ridge of Sgurr nan Eugallt which, at 894 metres, just fails to make it into the Munros list. This mountain stands guard over Glen Barrisdale and Kinloch Hourn. From the summit, a pleasant, narrow, north-east ridge descends to a stalking track, leading down to Coire-shubh in Glen Quoich. It felt strange to have tarmacadam under my feet.

As I headed east towards Loch Quoich, it stopped raining — what a relief to take waterproofs off for a change. Two buzzards stalked the wild glen as nature came to life. The glen echoed cheerily to the sounds of 'The Portree Kid' and 'Lads Among Heather'.

It had been six and a half months since I had left home. Almost 300 mountains had been climbed in the most appalling conditions anyone could imagine. Tomorrow — the First of September — would be a long day, so I relaxed for half an hour in my tent, trying to read a soaked paperback about the Ghurkas. It had been floating in the bottom of my rucksack for several days and it was long overdue at the library!

CHAPTER 7

September 1985

Loch Quoich and Tomdoun

—

Farewell to MacKenzie, High Chief of Kintail

—

A deep raid in Lochaber: Ben Nevis, the Grey Corries
and the Mamores

—

Glen Etive

LOCH QUOICH AND TOMDOUN, 1-3 SEPTEMBER

Loch Quoich has always fascinated me, like a remote sea in a forgotten world of mountainous peaks. It was a favourite hunting ground for the Royal Family, but the memories of those days at the Quoich shooting lodge sank beneath the waves when the loch was dammed. Last century an army deserter, rather than serve overseas, escaped with his family to an island on the loch, where they lived a hermit's existence.

Three Munros cast a shadow over the loch's northern shore. Glen Quoich has forced a narrow gap between them like a breached castle wall, only to be firmly stopped by the rocky bastion of the south Cluanie Ridge behind. A fine stalking track gave an easy approach to Sgurr a' Mhaoraich, 1,027 metres, 'Peak of the Shellfish'. It is her rocky bulk that blocks the winter sunlight from Kinloch Hourn, turning it to darkness at 3 p.m. on a winter's afternoon.

Too many people wish to race through their Munros, reaching the summit by the easiest or shortest route. The temptation here is to climb this mountain, descend to the roadside and assault her neighbouring peaks. But, in doing so, one will have missed out half the mountain, for to continue on over the narrow Am Bathaich will leave you with everlasting memories. Such pleasures were not possible for me, as a support team meeting the following morning dictated that the shortest route be taken to today's summits.

The area is well blessed with stalking tracks, and a fine one ran up the shoulder of Gleouraich. Close to the summit I caught up on an elderly gentleman from Glasgow. After exchanging pleasantries I bombed over the boulder-strewn summit and saw to my surprise, standing at the cairn, a large, bearded, familiar figure in a Marks and Spencer anorak: Simon Strachan, last seen on Skye in June. Our meeting was purely by chance. His welcome was choice: 'Oh, hello, Craig: have you fixed your breeches yet?' He and his friend Ron Waddel started explaining that, at the

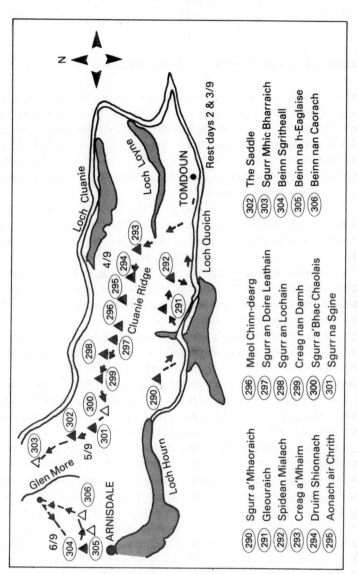

Map 28   Loch Quoich, Cluanie Ridge and Arnisdale

290 Sgurr a'Mhaoraich
291 Gleouraich
292 Spidean Mialach
293 Creag a'Mhaim
294 Druim Shionnach
295 Aonach air Chrith

296 Maol Chinn-dearg
297 Sgurr an Doire Leathain
298 Sgurr an Lochain
299 Creag nan Damh
300 Sgurr a'Bhac Chaolais
301 Sgurr na Sgine

302 The Saddle
303 Sgurr Mhic Bharraich
304 Beinn Sgritheall
305 Beinn na h-Eaglaise
306 Beinn nan Caorach

roadside, they had met a strange man, at which I interrupted, 'Och, aye, he's coming up behind — that's my father!'

The laws of access are thankfully strong in Scotland, dating back to the days of cattle droving. The only restrictions are during the stalking season, when you will find little or no constraint in National Trust and Nature Reserve areas, the Cuillin Ridge on Skye, or the Galloway Hills. Elsewhere is best avoided. My sympathy lies with the stalkers, struggling to keep alive what in many estates is their only source of income. They ask only to have their mountains free from mid-August to mid-October, and if politely contacted will usually be obliging. I know of only one exception: an infamous landowner who is rumoured to shoot in the direction of walkers trespassing during the stalking season. There is a story that the same bullying man, out with his stalkers, once came across a lone climber. The landowner, taking his jacket off, told him he was going to get a good thrashing. The climber, outnumbered, decided attack was the best means of defence, lashed out with a fine upper-cut, and made off.

Reluctantly Simon and party descended to the glen. It was strange to wave goodbye. A few feet into the mist found me totally alone as if on a deserted mountain. My route skirted the northern rock-climbing corries to Spidean Mialach, 996 metres, 'Peak of the Wild Animals'. It was 8 p.m. before the roadside was reached. Ahead lay a long ten-mile walk east along Glen Garry to the Tomdoun Hotel. Nursing the first blister of the walk, I arrived exhausted after fifteen hours of activity over three mountains and 24 miles of walking. The hotel was full and I was shown to a dark, musty outhouse with a rickety bed, which to me was as good as any luxury suite at a posh London hotel.

Tom and Doreen arrived and a hectic couple of days were spent in the friendly surroundings of the Tomdoun Hotel. On the last night it was good to meet the friendly lads from Garry-gualach, a very special outdoor centre on the remote southern shore of Loch Garry.

In the early morning light my friend Munro stood in the doorway, complete with bone, as I shouldered my heavy pack and stepped out into the soft rain. Sheep were being gathered today, so my walk would not be causing any great harm to stalking. A track led through the East Glenquoich Forest and across the often trouble-

some River Loyne. It was a tremendous feeling to climb up on the
Creag a'Mhaim, the most easterly summit of the South Glen Shiel
Ridge. Along its twenty-mile ridge lay nine Munros and two
Corbetts, a hillwalker's dreamland.

The SMC guide book advises that the traverse of the ridge is
best done with two cars, which Hamish Brown points out in his
book, *Hamish's Mountain Walk*, must be awful hard on the
suspension!

Cars could be seen hurtling down Glen Shiel too fast to
appreciate the scenery, while the only movement on the ridge was
Munro's black tail bobbing in the distance. He has incredible
hearing, although often deaf to shouts and whistles. A rustling
sweet paper could be heard from half a mile away and he would
charge back, starvation written all over his face.

From Druim Shionnach the gentle ridge led over Aonach air
Chrith, the third Munro in one and a half hours. What a difference from those so bitterly won in Knoydart! The threatening
mist came and went and eventually stayed by the time we reached
the summit of Aonach air Chrith, 1,021 metres, meaning
'Trembling Hill.' The further west we went characteristically the
mountains got rougher. With two further Munros under our belts
we were soon following the bumpy ridge to Sgurr an Lochain,
'Peak of the Lochan', named after the loch in its corrie; strangely,
this is the only one to be found along the ridge's rough northern
slopes.

The morning of clear weather was obviously all we were going
to get as a familiar drizzle engulfed the summit. I nearly led
Munro off the wrong spur of Creag nan Damh, 918 metres, his
puzzled frown making me check my compass. Out of the mist
loomed a short rocky wall. Munro was already on top and playfully pawed my head as I clambered up the easy steps. A gale was
blowing over Bealach Dubh Leac, the pass between Glen Shiel
and Glen Quoich. A wall topped with iron posts was a great place
for securing guy ropes. I laid out my tiny nylon home, wondering
if it would last the storm. Munro lay inquisitively as if to say,
'That's nice; where are *you* sleeping?' With the tent up I laid out
my sleeping bag inside and went to fetch water, only to return to
find a soaking Munro sleeping quite happily on it. He wolfed
down his Mince Morsels in seconds, then took a keen interest in my
cooking. Prince Charlie crossed this pass. I wonder what he would

have thought of my dehydrated food; perhaps he would find a new use for it, like loading it in his cannons and using it as grape shot.

Munro had snored all night long so we were up early. While breakfast was cooking I explained the day's route to Munro, who thoughtfully chewed on a Mars Bar wrapper. With our high camp we had only 135 metres to climb to our first peak, Sgurr a'Bhac Chaolais, 885 metres, first of the ridge's two Corbetts. Adrenalin was now flowing as what I though was my 300th peak loomed out of the mist, Sgurr na Sgine, 945 metres, meaning 'Peak of the Knife'. Her eastern crags are more menacing than the map would have you believe, but a wall leads to her easy southern slopes. Singing 'one to go, one to go, one to go,' we pushed on for what was actually my 301st summit. It started snowing, the first of the bitter winter to come.

Dog and master enjoyed a celebratory lump of fruit cake on top, while snowflakes flurried around the cairn. From Bealach Coire Mhalagain we pushed on for The Saddle, 1010 metres, by climbing on to the last easy stage of the Forcan Ridge. This superb narrow ridge of airy crests and pinnacles gives an exciting scramble, although those who are strictly walkers only may wish to avoid it. On top were two surveyors, one of whom I had met in Strathconon in May. They kindly shared a can of Guinness with me, before descending to Glen Shiel. Munro had raced off and met another collie coming along the ridge. His owner was a delightful Englishman who beamed with enthusiasm at the beauty of Highland scenery.

The grassy pointed ridge curved round the steep slopes of Coire Uaine and would descend gently to the shores of Loch Duich, but is stopped from doing so by the rocky Corbett, Sgurr Mhic Bharraich. Seen from the height of the ridge, she appeared like a small knoll, her bulk increasing as we drew closer. It was among her rocky crags that the raiding Camerons cunningly hid their stolen cattle right under the noses of their previous owners, the MacKenzies of Kintail. While the MacKenzies searched high and low for the robbers, they never dreamed of searching a hill so close to their homeland.

Munro did not seem impressed by the misty summit and left his own mark on the cairn. Down in the glen we followed the fine track leading into Glen More and the cheering sight of a nearby bothy.

The morning started ominously as we stepped out into a sleet storm with Munro racing ahead. A faint track was found leading towards Coire Dubh. Stretched out in front of us like a giant clamshell lay five peaks. All are superb but only the middle three are over 2,500 feet. It was Beinn Sgritheall, 974 metres, which drew us like a magnet; her north-eastern ridge rose narrowly and overlooked the sparkling lochan in Coire Min. Munro, however, was more interested in rolling gleefully about on the decomposing remains of a deer.

Try and keep this peak for a clear day as her views of Loch Hourn and the Inner Hebrides are superb. To the north-west lies Glenelg, where there is an alternative crossing to the Isle of Skye. The narrow Kyle Rhea is so confined that a Norse princess once put a huge chain across it and charged a toll for anyone wishing to cross the straits. The whole peninsula is full of exciting things to see: a Celtic broch, ruined Bernera Barracks, and at Sandaig the ruins of Camusfearna from Gavin Maxwell's immortal *Ring of Bright Water*: too much to squeeze into one rest day.

From Bealach Arnasdail a line of old iron fence posts shot up Beinn na h-Eaglaise, 804 metres, meaning 'the Hill of the Church'. The slopes got steeper and steeper, but the intrepid fence posts clung to the side of the hill. We were treated to a bird's eye view of Loch Hourn and the many peaks of Ladhar Bheinn beaming opposite. Druim na Bo, 'the Ridge of the Cattle', led us on to Beinn nan Caorach, 773 metres. This 'Hill of the Rowan Berries' seemed a calm and peaceful contrast to her more stirring neighbours. To the west lies pretty Glen Arnisdale, where the modern world clashes with the old in thoughtless brutality. Here lies a long line of electricity pylons bringing welcome power at scenery's expense. There they stood, a long column of thoughtless grey giants hissing in the rain.

Back at the bothy was John Lynch from London, enjoying a welcome break. We chatted at great length about the hills while Munro snored anti-socially in the corner. The bothy danced in the flickering candlelight as we lay in our sleeping bags on the floor. John explained he was a motor-bike express rider in London. The money was good but you could expect to land in hospital every six months as a victim of the hectic traffic. He lay back against a candle and a puff of smoke appeared at his back ... his sleeping bag had caught fire. Quickly I grabbed the bottom of the bag and hauled him out unceremoniously. We were both unburnt and only the bag suffered slightly. 'Better than an electric blanket,' joked John, before dropping off to sleep.

Mid-morning the following day found me on the south side of Loch Duich with Tom and Doreen as we reorganised the next stage.

FAREWELL TO MACKENZIE, HIGH CHIEF OF KINTAIL, 9–15 SEPTEMBER

A phone call had ensured that today's hills would be free from stalking. I cycled around the edge of Loch Duich; ahead, on a little hill, lay a war memorial erected by the Macraes for those lost in the First World War. Scotland has paid a heavy price for her world-wide reputation for producing brave and fierce soldiers. The smallest of hamlets have memorials with long lists of the dead; whole families were wiped out. Despite having less than 10 per cent of Great Britain's population, she lost 140,000 men, almost 20 per cent of Britain's losses in the so-called 'Great War' of 1914–18.

From Dornie, Loch Long resembles a short bay, but it took five twisting miles to reach its head. It must have been an exciting spectacle when St Fillan, son of the chieftain of Kintail, was buried here, carried up the narrow loch by a huge longship. The road became rougher as it curved into Glen Elchaig. A grey fog of spray hung above the roaring torrents of the Falls of Glomach. Such beauty has sadness too, for the falls are reputed to be haunted by the ghost of a lady who committed suicide in the area. There is a path that climbs up the side of the falls, but care should be taken as it is now breaking up in places.

At the head of the glen I donned boots while the midges got their last vicious bites in before the autumn frosts put them to sleep till next summer. Two Corbetts lay at the head of the glen. The rain fell from the heavens as the fine stalking track led under the crags of Leac na Nighinn, meaning probably 'Slab of the Lassies'. Another track branched off, leading some of the way to the plateau summit of Faochaig, 868 metres, 'the Whirlpool'. After I had left the prominent bump that marks the summit, the torrential rain stopped and gave me a dry, if mist-obscured climb

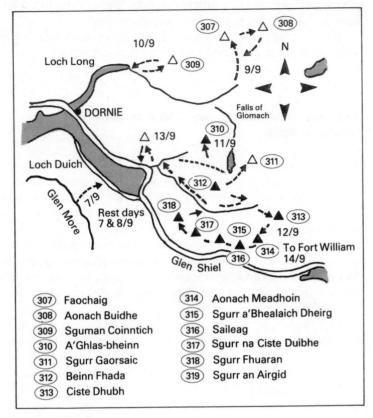

Map 29   Kintail

(307)	Faochaig	
(308)	Aonach Buidhe	
(309)	Sguman Coinntich	
(310)	A'Ghlas-bheinn	
(311)	Sgurr Gaorsaic	
(312)	Beinn Fhada	
(313)	Ciste Dhubh	
(314)	Aonach Meadhoin	
(315)	Sgurr a'Bhealaich Dheirg	
(316)	Saileag	
(317)	Sgurr na Ciste Duibhe	
(318)	Sgurr Fhuaran	
(319)	Sgurr an Airgid	

up her sister peak, Aonach Buidhe, meaning simply 'Yellow Hill' after the hay-coloured slopes. These two hills had given an easy walk, but it was cycling to reach them that had sapped my strength. Darkness was falling as I saw the familiar lights of Ratagan Youth Hostel after a 50-mile round trip.

Morning found me repeating the long journey to Glen Elchaig as one more Corbett remained unclimbed. At Eilean Donan Castle tourists were busy clicking their cameras at this pretty restored fortress, originally built to keep at bay the Vikings who had settled on Skye. It became a MacKenzie stronghold till destroyed

Tent and bicycle in Glen Fyne, Argyll (Above)

Looking east from Beinn an Oir, Isle of Jura, the island's only Corbett (below)

View west from the summit of Clisham on the isle of Harris, the most
westerly Corbett (Above)
Liathach seen from Beinn Eighe. Two of Torridon's most
spectacular Munros (below)

Tourist track around south-eastern slopes of Liathach (Above)
Loch Coruisk from the Cuillin Ridge, Isle of Skye (Below)

Craig on the summit of Sgurr an Utha, a remote Corbett in Morar Loch. Beoraid in the background

Unusual pine tree with three trunks on the northern slopes of Beinn Bhan, Lochaber

Spidean Mialach from Glen Loyne (Above)
Ciste Dhubh (a Munro) taken from Am Bathach (a Corbett), both
in the mountain stronghold of Kintail (Below)

Icicles in Glen Clova (Above)
January snow covers a landrover track along the shore of Loch Garry (Below)

Creag MacRanaich in winter white

Ben Lomond, the final peak, taken from Beinn A' Choin, the last
Corbett

Craig on the summit of Beinn Alligin (985 metres). The steep slopes of
Beinn Dearg (914 metres) lie in the background

The final summit, Ben Lomond. From left to right: Craig Caldwell,
Allan Comrie, Julie Watson and Graham Moss *(Alan Thomson)*

by English frigates at the time of the Jacobite rising of 1719. I looked across Loch Duich, stormy in today's wind and rain, and wondered at the stamina of Duncan Macallister, who used to think nothing of swimming across the mile-wide loch to visit his girlfriend on the other side.

At the head of Loch Long towered the craggy slopes of Sguman Coinntich, 879 metres, 'Peak of the Moss'. A stalking track led through the pleasant woodland at the back of Killilan into Choire Mhoir, giving a welcome easy approach to the summit.

Sguman Coinntich boasts an approach by paths on all her four sides. The mountain was once the centre for illegal whisky distilling, and many visits were made by the Excisemen. On one occasion they turned a cottage inside out looking for whisky and couldn't find any trace. They never thought to disturb a lassie who was sitting down, her long dress covering a keg of whisky. Legs were tired after yesterday's strenuous efforts and it was good to relax at the top of my 309th mountain. In the 1880s the glen was rented by a wealthy American who was solely interested in shooting deer. His gamekeeper became annoyed, for some strange reason, that a MacRae of Kintail was keeping an abandoned lamb at his cottage as a family pet. The American took the family to court over the affair, as sheep were supposed to be forbidden to graze on land reserved for deer. Mr MacRae lost the case at the court in Dingwall. Then the powerful Earl of MacKenzie took the side of the MacRaes and the matter went to the Court of Session in Edinburgh. Here 'The Pet Lamb case' became headlines. The public were overjoyed when justice was done and the MacKenzies triumphed. The MacRae children kept their pet lamb and the American's lease was not allowed to be renewed.

It was sad to cycle down the pretty shore of Loch Long for the last time. Hopes of climbing another peak that evening faded as darkness approached, and a puncture knocked them well out of sight. With the bike's dynamo buzzing it was nice to arrive again at the friendly Ratagan hostel

The last few days had felt like a holiday, climbing from the hostel's cosy base. Now I packed my rucksack for a three-day foray to climb ten of Kintail's most breathtaking peaks. The path up mossy Gleann Choinneachain had an alpine feel to it, especially when the mist-covered, jaw-like Bealach an Sgairne (or Chisholm's Pass) was reached, its crags closing like a sprung gin trap. Despite its appearance, an easy scramble led north of the pass towards A'Ghlas-bheinn, 918 metres. With mist reducing visibility to a few feet, fingers were soon clinging to heather and rock as my easy route became a bit too steep for comfort. Then one last pull and I was on a gentle ridge leading to the summit. A'Ghlas-bheinn is a mountain that deserves a day to itself, perhaps with a visit to the Falls of Glomach on the way home. Sitting apart from her congested neighbours she has some beautiful views; warm memories of fresh snow glistening on the Glen Affric peaks made up for today's gloomy veil of secrecy.

Down at the bealach I had lunch with a group from the Combined Services mountain training centre at Ballachulish. This cheery group had a hungry collie which, they assured me, was actually a Royal Marine taking part in a covert operation. Their officer explained he had managed to learn to bark all right but hated eating dog food. Before he could say 'Rover' I had opened my pack and gleefully handed him a packet of my dehydrated food: 'Try him on that tonight! He will learn to love dog food if *that's* the alternative.'

The massive bulk of Sgurr nan Ceathreamhnan filled the view. I had climbed this splendid Munro in early June. Perched like a window-box on her slopes lay the rounded Corbett summit of Sgurr Gaorsaic. This little mountain would be bliss to climb on a warm summer's day, with the swimming-pool lochan yards from the summit. The lochan must be fed by an underground spring, and strangely does not seem to have any burn leading away from it. Although in a popular climbing area, this hill is little climbed. Even if today's view was obscured I was happy, for there is something strange about the Scottish hills that gets into your blood and never lets go. To leave work on a Friday night, with worries and hassles alive in your mind, for a weekend in the hills, transforms you into a different person on Monday morning ... one who has a deeper understanding of the more important values of life.

With evening light fading the race was on to climb the mountain opposite, Beinn Fhada. This peak's name is a classic Gaelic tongue-twister, for 'Fhada' is pronounced 'Attow.' Sadly, only a small number of people speak Gaelic today. However, most Scots do hold an advantage over others, adding the odd gravelly sounding 'Ach' or drum-rolling 'Sgurr' in the right place, which is at least convincing if not necessarily accurate. Beinn Fhada means 'Long Hill', a somewhat inadequate name for one of Kintail's finest peaks. Her five-mile-long ridge, overlooking Loch Duich, starts rocky and narrow to end gracefully in Glen Affric. A pleasant ridge led right up to the summit; the same route was to give our group a superb winter route fifteen months later. Gentle rain sprayed the ridge as I hurried down to Fionn Gleann, darkness casting its shadow over the green giants of Kintail.

Cattle were grazing on the slopes of Ciste Dhubh. This mountain is the tail of the eleven-mile ridge that stretches west above Glen Shiel. Although the ridge has ten mountains, only six make it to Munro status. The most westerly peaks are known as the Five Sisters, and where I was climbing in the east is known as the Five Brothers. Ciste Dhubh means 'Black Chest'. In poor weather her dark corries are a formidable sight. Once a clansman running from the Redcoats raced into an awesome black cleft in the mountain with a torrential burn roaring through it. He came out soon enough, preferring to face the Redcoats' guns than his sinister hide-out.

Mist and rain swept over the mountain as my track followed a pleasantly narrow crest. I debated whether to include Am Bathach, an outlying Corbett, which lay temptingly close. However, shrinking daylight hours were a problem and I fortunately left it out. A long pull led up to Aonach Meadhoin, 1,003 metres, which is unmarked on the map, although her smaller top, Sgurr an Fhuarail, is. The Ordnance Surveyors are not such dedicated Munro enthusiasts as to name every summit, nor does the existence of a triangulation point confirm the highest point.

A cawing raven welcomed me to Sgurr a'Bhealaich Dheirg, 1,031 metres, while cars like beetles could be heard through the mist hurrying down Glen Sheil. From here on, the ridge is National Trust property, as are Beinn Fhada and the Falls of Glomach, a gift from the generous mountaineer Percy Unna who also gave them Glen Coe. A gentle dip led on to Munro number four, Saileag, 959 metres, meaning 'Little Heel'. The going became rougher, the wind and rain scorning my efforts as the ridge led to Sgurr na Ciste Duibhe. The peak was deserted today. It was a popular place on 10 June 1719, for almost 1,200 Highlanders retreated up the mountain after the battle of Glen Shiel. Here a 1,500-man Highland army, supported by 300 Spaniards, was defeated by General Wightman's well-equipped 1,200 troops. Brave Highland hearts, swords and shields were no match against rifles and mortars.

My legs were getting tired now as the rocky knoll of Sgurr na Carnach was crossed and the final pull began up the towering peak of Sgurr Fhuaran, at 1,068 metres the highest of the range. It is this peak that gives such a picture-postcard view when seen from Loch Duich. A knee-jerking descent led to Gleann Lichd as darkness began to fall. I was glad I had decided to leave out that outlying Corbett earlier in the day. This was to be climbed in November with one last fleeting raid west, when the hills would be free of stalking restrictions.

The local residents have a name for the thick veil of heavy rain that often covers Kintail. They call it 'the Clunaie Curtain', and it was drawn fast this morning. The burns had been topped up with the rain of the last few days and were now in full spate. On either side of the glen the mountains spewed forth their white torrents, charging down the hillside to meet a frothy River Croe. The glen itself was like a wind tunnel, causing falling burns to spiral upwards like a smoking chimney. Gleann Lichd has an eerie atmosphere: indeed, the locals believed the glen was inhabited by a monster. Such mysteries exist to this day, scoffed at by visitors until they are shown the dismembered remains of a sheep or deer with claw and fang marks too deep to be the work of any animal native to the British Isles. Years earlier a man called Murdoch MacRae disappeared while taking part in a big hunt in the glen. The men searched high and low for fifteen days until they found his body. But they could not tell how he had died, and the story is listed among Scotland's greatest unsolved mysteries.

One more mountain required to be climbed in Kintail: Sgurr an Airgid, 841 metres, meaning 'the Silver Peak'. What I hoped was going to be an easy climb turned out to be a struggle against the worsening weather. The stalking track shown on the map was overgrown and of little help in reaching the mountain's wind-blasted col. The strong wind blew me this way and that, and I wondered about the madness of this game as height was slowly gained, bump by misty bump. It was a pleasure to reach the summit, although no shelter from the ice-cutting wind could be found there. Further downhill I dived into my rucksack and gobbled the last of my rations. The empty moorland between here and Glen Elchaig was once populated but now lies deserted, left to the deer and the eagle. With no major peaks to climb it is a forgotten place, which is sad, for some fine paths cross her rough lands of forgotten rocky mountains. This was the land of the hardy MacLennans, who won fame among British troops in the eighteenth century for sleeping out in the snow with only a wet plaid wrapped round them to keep the Arctic winds at bay.

The descent was frustrating, as I missed the overgrown track and was soon floundering in thick bracken. With the bike loaded and the thought of a warm bed at the Clunaie Inn to spur me on, I was soon cycling up Glen Shiel. It had turned into a real 'hooley'! The wind roared down the glen and icy sleet stung my face. It was a relief to reach the cheery lights of the inn.

I wolfed down breakfast, shivering at the sight of the wild weather outside. A young couple looked out in dismay, their plans of catching the ferry from Skye to Harris ruined by the storms. Wind and rain hammered the window, sheep huddled round rocks, and an animal feed-bag took off like Concorde down the glen. It was over 40 miles to Fort William, where I had arranged to meet Tom and Doreen for one last visit before they went on holiday. Although a short distance, it was a gruelling journey riding the heavily loaded bike against the gale-force winds. A phone call ahead allowed the luxury of a rendezvous with Tom to pick up the luggage, to enable me to cycle unladen.

Fort William is a busy tourist town but one you grow to like. The West End Hotel is the friendliest and most comfortable hotel I know. It had been a handy stopover on many a long trip, where Mrs Chisholm would keep food parcels and spare clothes for me. Sadly I arrived to hear the news that poor old James, the well-loved friendly waiter, had passed away; everybody had a kind word for him. While tucked up in my warm bed I thought of the hardy members of university mountaineering clubs who, when in Fort William, sleep in a car park underneath a supermarket.

A DEEP RAID IN LOCHABER: BEN NEVIS, THE GREY CORRIES AND THE MAMORES, 16–21 SEPTEMBER

After a couple a days reorganising I arranged to meet Tom and Doreen in Aviemore in three weeks' time. Aviemore — just think of that: the Cairngorms, what a milestone to reach! After an early breakfast, I pushed the bike out into the familiar downpour. It had now rained for a hundred days in Lochaber, said to be the worst weather since 1897. Tourists hid in shop alleyways with rain bouncing off the pavement, while I cycled out of town whistling 'The Haughs of Cromdale'. The warden at Glen Nevis Youth Hostel kindly let me put my bike in his bike shed, for it would not be needed for the next five days. In that time a deep foray would be made over Ben Nevis and the Grey Corries, the hills of Loch Treig and the Mamores: a grand U-shaped journey, 70 miles of walking over 24 peaks. If only it would stop raining!

High above, covered in a dark grey blanket of mist and rain, lay Ben Nevis, at 1,344 metres Britain's highest mountain. A few hundred feet higher and she would have a permanent glacier, as the average summit temperature is just under freezing, a fact forgotten by the swarms of tourists who flock up her track in shorts and tee shirts. It was a long pull with a heavy pack up the soaking path. As a publicity stunt a Model T Ford was twice driven up the zig-zagging track. Other extroverts have followed, walking to the top carrying pianos and pushing wheelbarrows.

Today there was no one — just me, the wind and the rain. The tourist track scarcely does justice to this massive mountain. From this route she appears a tedious hulk. Her Jekyll and Hyde character is seen in her northern-facing Corrie Leis. For here the mountain has been chewed by the Ice Age, leaving a series of vertical cliffs rocketing to the flat-topped summit. Here great deeds are done on the snow filled-gullies, some of which are so difficult they require perfect weather conditions for a successful assault.

On the summit, the ruins of the old observatory looked drowned with the effects of this summer's deluge. It was founded in 1883, and for twenty-one years the scientists gathered information with their complicated instruments, replicas of which are still in use today by modern meteorologists. The observatory staff had to endure terrible weather conditions from ferocious

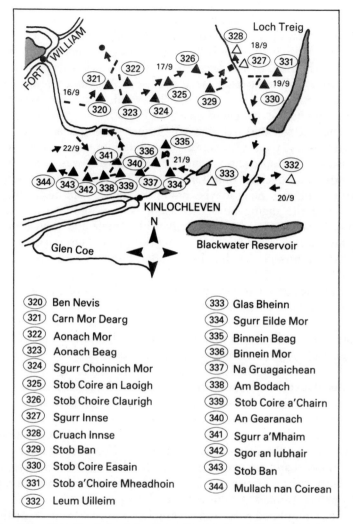

Map 30   Ben Nevis and the Grey Corries, Loch Treig and the Mamores

blizzards to 150 m.p.h. winds; many a journey outside had to be made with the party roped together. However they also had a lot of fun adapting sledges with sails and even carving a table tennis table from thick frozen snow on the summit.

A careful compass-bearing was taken at the bitterly cold summit, the trusty needle leading me south-east to the Carn Dearg Arête, the name given to the knife-edge ridge that leads on to Carn Mor Dearg. This is the way for the experienced walker to enjoy 'The Ben' by the long narrow ridge which sweeps around the edge of the spectacular Coire Leis. A couple of drookit-looking Americans were on top, 'Hi, ye all' being the strangest greeting I have experienced on a Scottish hill.

The rocky ridge led east to Bealach Giubhsachan. It was evening now, the torrential rain had gone into overdrive and the pass had developed into a wind tunnel. The day was over — the weather had decided that. On the map I spied a building at the bottom of the glen, maybe an open stable. Optimistically, I followed the raging burn. At last it was in sight — a lovely wooden workman's hut, no doubt with a table and chair inside. What luxury! I couldn't wait to get out of the high velocity rain whistling through the glen. Just another hundred yards then ... it was locked!

I pitched my tent on the only available bit of dry ground, ripping my overtrousers in the process. I settled down, cosy in my nylon home, while the elements battled outside. A miniature bottle of whisky was a fine companion as I enjoyed the last few pages of Douglas Reeman's *The First to Land*.

I was awakened by the sound of wind shaking the tent: it was raining yet again! Something would have to be done about my waterproof overtrousers. Soaking breeches have a tendency to cut away at the inside leg, making it raw and painful. Improvisation was found in the shape of a black plastic rubbish bag, worn like a kilt underneath the overtrousers. I hoped I didn't meet anyone, with the refuse collection slogan sticking out of the top of my trousers, reading 'Put rubbish firmly in its place'!

The determined wind and rain buffeted my route up the gentle northern slopes of Aonach Mor as the glen echoed to the sound of 'My old man's a dustman, he wears a dustman's hat ...' Aonach Mor's eggshell-like summit was layered like a water biscuit made of crumbling sandstone. Her northern slopes would soon be covered in pylons and tows for the new ski centre, which will no doubt create the same rubble-ravished ecological disasters as their counterparts elsewhere. It brings cheers of delight from

Scotland's skiers and work-starved Lochaber, while conservationists break down in tears. The real loser is the mountain and its
wildlife.

It stopped raining by the time I reached her twin summit,
Aonach Beag. Although the name means 'Little Hill', she is
actually higher than her sister peak. When the hills were named
they were done so from the glens; often you will find a little and a
big hill named the wrong way round, as Hamish Brown points
out in his book, *Climbing the Corbetts*. Mountains were
christened at a time when to travel out of your clan lands was an
adventure indeed. There was little communication between the
people to see if their simple mountain names were being repeated
elsewhere, hence our multitude of Ben Mores, Geal Charns and
Deargs.

The ridge fell steeply east as I pushed on for Sgurr Choinnich
Mor. This is the first of the four peaks known as 'the Grey
Corries'; the grey rocks covering their slopes can trick the eye into
thinking it's snow when seen from a distance. The ridge had a
few deep gashes which reminded me of the fissures on Ben
Donich near Arrochar. The hills were taking on a more gentle
east-of-Scotland appearance as the ridge led on the Stob Coire an
Laoigh, 1,115 metres, 'Peak of the Corrie of the Calf'. To the
north among the Leanachan Forest lies a dismantled tramway
which gives handy access to the ridge's gentle northern slopes.

Two figures were standing on the cairn of Sgurr Choinnich Mor,
the Munro I had just left. Half an hour later I noticed one was still
there. Afterwards I was to learn they had accidentally toppled one
of their rucksacks and it had fallen to the corrie below. At Stob
Choire Claurigh, 1,177 metres, the ridge takes a sharp left turn to
descend to Glen Spean. Like the Mamores opposite the Grey
Corries have one more Munro which sticks out inconveniently
from the main ridge. This peak, Stob Ban, was a temptation.
However, with daylight fading, I decided to leave it for the
morning.

At Larig Leacach bothy I found Val, a charming English lass.
She had forgotten her spoon and was eating porridge with her
hands! She had walked through Glen Nevis and was waiting for
her two friends, whom I had seen on the ridge. Their two headtorches were spotted, their lights floating down the hillside. They
had forgotten their spoons, too.

The Lairig Leacach was quiet today, but in days of old it was a busy route for hardy drovers taking their cattle to the trysts at Drymen or Crieff. Two Corbetts stood across the glen; when seen from the high Grey Corries they looked like a couple of small bumps. They were to be an easy climb, for the track in the glen floor rose to almost 500 metres. This made it possible to start, already three-quarters of the way up the mountain.

From the dip between the two peaks I enjoyed an easy scramble up Sgurr Innse, 808 metres, meaning 'the Peak of the Meadows'. Although it was just a rough walk to the summit, when I got there it felt like standing on the tip of a sharpened pencil. The mountain's crags and scree offer good scrambling potential, falling away steeply to the glen below.

Cruach Innse, her sister peak, was a gentle climb in comparison. The mist lifted to reveal a damp Glen Spean to the north. Directly across the glen, above Roy Bridge, lies a flat-topped hill called Maol Ruadh. There, in the summer of 1688, was fought one of the last clan feuds, the two warring clans battling over the age-old problem: the disputed ownership of land. The MacDonnels took up a defensive position on this knoll, while over 1,000 Mackintoshes swarmed up the slopes. Bullets whistled across the hillside and the glen filled with gunsmoke and the smell of powder. The battle had reached a stalemate when, suddenly, a MacDonnel half-wit attacked madly with a huge club. This turned the tide of the battle and the Mackintoshes were routed.

After a brew-up at the bothy, it took a bit of willpower to step out into the mist and rain and bomb up the western spur of Stob Ban, the outlying peak I had missed out yesterday evening. Unlike the Grey Corries she is not covered in quartzite but in schist, a grey rock. It was on this peak in the twilight of a March evening that Martin Moran looked sadly across Glen Nevis at the sight of his last two Munro peaks, which the next day would mark the end of his winter assault on the Munros. I wondered how I would feel when my final hill was in view for the first time; I dared think my ambitious plans had some chance of success.

The small and uncomfortable bothy had been invaded by a swarm of youngsters from Locheil Outward Bound. It was all very friendly though, as we squeezed into the little bothy, jokes and laughter filling the room. Scratched on the door were the names of many previous visitors, dating back to the turn of the century.

Between Lairig Leacach and Loch Trieg lie two pointed peaks, known as the Easains. They are in the usual situation of being in wild uninhabited country, but handily placed between two railway stations, so one can get off the morning train at Tulloch, climb over the hills and catch the train home from Corrour. Mechanisation has its advantages.

A gurgling burn led almost to the summit of scree-covered Stob Coire Easain meaning 'the Peak of the Corrie of the Little Waterfall'. She is the higher of the two Munros. My route pendulumed over to Stob a'Choire Mheadhoin before swinging back again to Easains' rocky summit. There are two paths that lead down the Allt na Lairige towards Loch Trieg. On the east back it is boggy and indistinct while on the west it is firm, well defined and dry. I was on the east bank.

The track wove delightfully to a very full Loch Trieg. At Creaguaineach abandoned sheep pens were well under water. If I hurried I could climb one more peak before it was dark. However, by the time I reached the top of Gleann Iolairean, darkness was already starting to fall on the high tops.

A tired body was reluctant to move as the wind and rain slashed Loch Chiarain. But with the exciting prospect of two new hills to climb, it jerked into life. It was bliss to be walking without my encumbering heavy pack. I was soon in a grey world of mist, working by compass over the shoulder of Beinn a'Bhric towards a fine Corbett, Leum Uilleim, 908 metres, meaning 'William's Leap', reputedly named in honour of Scottish hero William Wallace, who lived in Rannoch for a while with his allies. The summit has several rocky bivouac shelters, which gave a brief refuge from the biting wind. Mist obscured a view of Rannoch Moor, although I could hear a train rumbling along the track that crosses its empty waste.

It is Coire a'Bhric Beag that seems so enticing when seen as the train chugs into Corrour station. A good track leads on to the peak's northern spur, where a fine horseshoe route of the mountain can be enjoyed. To the south lies the Blackwater Reservoir, where Lancaster bombers in the Second World War practised dropping Barnes Wallis's ingenious bouncing bomb, which was so effective in destroying the Mohne and Eder dams in occupied Europe.

The corner had been turned on this long foray into the wilds of Rannoch as I followed the fine stalking track that weaves like a bicycle chain to Loch Eilde Mor. Below me lay the Blackwater Reservoir Dam. Many thousands of Irish navvies worked on its construction. Sadly, many died in the course of its being built, most falling victim to exposure while caught out in blizzards, returning over the Devil's Staircase track after a good drink at the Kings House Hotel in Glencoe.

With the wind and rain strengthening, I hurried over my 333rd hill, Glas Bheinn, 789 metres, a Corbett whose gentle western slopes led down to a boisterous Loch Eilde Mor. A snowstorm came and went, while foaming waves crashed on the shore. I was delighted to find a corrugated iron shelter with an earth floor; my rucksack shone in its soaking state. As always, my sleeping bag had been wrapped in several poly bags and was dry. It felt very cold. I had three mugs of tea to warm me up as the stew simmered. The corrugated iron framework whined and clattered in the wind. I wondered what my chances would be on the Mamore Ridge tomorrow, as I took my soaking boots inside the bag to prevent them freezing.

It was a cold morning. A splattering of snow greeted me from the mist-covered mountains. I was away early, determined to make the best of the day. Although some tempting stalking tracks crossed the shoulder of the first peak, they involved a lengthy detour. So a frontal assault up the scree of Sgurr Eilde Mor seemed the best approach. Resting by the misty snow-splattered summit, I gazed west in the hope that the grey cloak of darkness which seemed to be my constant companion would lift for this special day. For ahead lay ten more Mamore peaks, over eighteen miles of varied ridge-walking, with broad ridges and narrow ones leading to offshoot peaks overlooking Glen Nevis. It is an unashamed peak-baggers' paradise.

Like the Grey Corries opposite, the eastern end of this ridge has an outlying peak. I was glad to have climbed the reclusive Sgurr Eilde Mor while still feeling fresh. By taking advantage of the fine stalking track that skips over Coire a'Bhinnein, I was soon weaving up the boulders and scree to another independent hill, Binnein Beag, 940 metres. From her rounded, rocky summit you are normally treated to a splendid view of Glen Nevis, the

famous 'Road to the Isles.' This spectacular through route comes
to a climax when walking west, as the path narrows to weave its
way above the river's steep craggy slopes to join the main road in
the glen.

My compass guided me south through the grey mist that licked
the lower slopes of Binnein Mor, 1,128 metres, the highest of the
Mamores. I climbed, fully expecting the summit to be thick with
snow and was surprised that it wasn't. My morale rose with the
barometer, as the mist started to clear. Soggy boots led on to Na
Gruagaichean, meaning 'the Maidens.' It was strange to see Loch
Leven below, stretching out to the Atlantic and last seen in storm-
lashed July. September had been only slightly better. What a year
to pick to attempt this walk! But in other ways I counted my
blessings: lack of injuries, good health, friendly companions and
an efficient and dedicated support team.

A handy series of stalking tracks ensnare the middle section of
the ridge, giving easy access from Glen Nevis or Lairig Mor to
the south. The continuous tour of the Grey Corries and the
Mamore ridges has produced some superhuman performances.
Philip Tranter raced over the nineteen peaks, involving 40 miles
of running, in 24 hours; this record was slashed in June 1983 by
Martin Hudson in 13 hours 54 minutes.

With the rain coming in I donned my waterproof trousers and
dustbin bag liner, much to the amusement of an Edinburgh party
walking by. It was becoming obvious, slowed down by my heavy
pack, that I wasn't going to complete the full ridge by tonight ...
and I had left my route card with the warden at the hostel advising that I would be back that evening. I pushed on for Am
Bodach, then skipped back to Stob Coire a'Chairn. It was good to
get some hands on rock again as the narrow ridge led north to An
Gearanach, which in summer conditions is in no way difficult
and gives an enjoyable and exciting scramble as the track weaves
over the slender rocky spine.

Descending, I was confused to see a fine stalking track far
across the hillside, then realised that lack of concentration had
made me miss its erratic right-hand turn that avoids the craggy
northern slopes.

The locked mountain hut at Steall is in a beautiful position in
this wild part of the glen, with the tremendous Steall waterfall
crashing down the crags. When frozen it is reputed to give a

spectacular ice climb. Even such well-frequented areas have their unexplained mysteries. Some friends in Aberdeenshire swear they saw a large black animal resembling a panther race up by the side of the falls and disappear. But this is a glen of mysteries, for a mile further downstream lies Uamh Shomhairle, or MacSorley's Cave. Legend has it that this is the home of Fionn's warriors and that they still live in the cave, sleeping, awaiting the day someone finds their huge hunting horn and blows it three times to bring them to life. It was a pleasure to arrive at the cheery hostel. I was surprised to meet Gordon, the warden of Crianlarich Youth Hostel, in the kitchen. He was doing what he liked doing best with his spare time: hostelling!

The bike's buckled rear wheel forced the cycle to wobble up the glen, while my broken toe-clip tapped against the road's surface. The popular crags at Polldubh loomed into sight. Here the road crosses over a stone bridge, while the bulging River Nevis flows underneath. Youngsters from the local Outward Bound Centre revel in their training by jumping off the bridge into the cold waters, clutching an airbed. A sight well worth seeing is the Nevis raft race held every year, when a strange assortment of home-made craft float down river, often with hilarious results.

When travelling up the glen, it's the towering heights of Sgurr a'Mhaim that fill the view, her quartzite-covered summit resembling snow. She is the everyday view for a local recluse who camps in the glen and is known simply as 'Tent Man'. From the summit I followed the Devil's Ridge, the dramatic name of the delightful knife ridge joining the peak to the main ridge, one of the most enjoyable ridge walks outside the Isle of Skye.

Yet another Munro, Sgor an Iubhair, 'the Peak of the Yew', welcomed me to the seemingly endless spine of the Mamore ridge. Far below lay Lairige Moire. The right of way in this glen was supposedly nearly forfeited through lack of use. Now it receives thousands of visitors every year as a result of the West Highland Way, the 96-mile path from Fort William to Glasgow. I wonder how many 'wayers' plodding up the track with the thought of a bus home and a pint at Fort William climb up on to the Mamore Ridge to end their journey in style.

I was soon stumbling up to the summit to Stob Ban, 999 metres, meaning 'Light-Coloured Peak'. Unusually for the Highlands, the mountains at the western end of the ridge now take on a tamer appearance, as quartzite gives way to red granite underfoot. Narrow ridges are left behind as the red 'motorway lanes' lead on to Mullach nan Coirean, 939 metres. A handy windbreak led through the forest down to Glen Nevis.

The friendly nature of youth hostels is at times remarkable. While trying to write some postcards I got absorbed in a fascinating chat with an American who had spent six weeks in the wilds of Brooks National Park in Alaska, his only companions being bears and the serenading of timber wolves to send him to sleep.

GLEN ETIVE, 24–28 SEPTEMBER

During the previous day's restful cycle ride to Glencoe I had bought a new pair of overtrousers and now felt respectable again. It seemed strange to wake up in the huge bunkhouse of the Kings House Hotel. It could sleep twenty-four people and had a huge dining area, but it lay empty and I had it all to myself. It had rained heavily overnight and was continuing with renewed enthusiasm. It took some willpower to leave the cosy bunkhouse and cycle down Glen Etive as water sprayed from the bike's tyres. To my left, shrouded in mist, lay the craggy slopes of Sron na Creise. But access to that rough hillside was firmly barred by the foaming River Etive

I spied a bucket bridge: these contraptions are popular in the area and great fun to use. They consist of a wooden box whose wheels are mounted on to two thick cables of wire. You simply jump in, push off and haul yourself up the other side with the aid of a rope. Unfortunately this one was padlocked. I tried crossing on the wire cables themselves but they were too far apart to be of any use. Frustrated, I raced the bike back to the hotel and stormed up the road leading to White Corries, the west of Scotland's only ski tow. The route was hardly scenic, walking under the maze of wire cables as the seats rocked in the wind.

Above lay Meall a'Bhuiridh, the popular Munro overlooking Rannoch Moor. Bhuiridh means 'bellowing', referring to the roaring of the stags. It was a relief to climb on to her northern shoulder, the thick mist hiding the unsightly oil-stinking machinery. From the summit the ridge dips, then gives a pleasant scramble

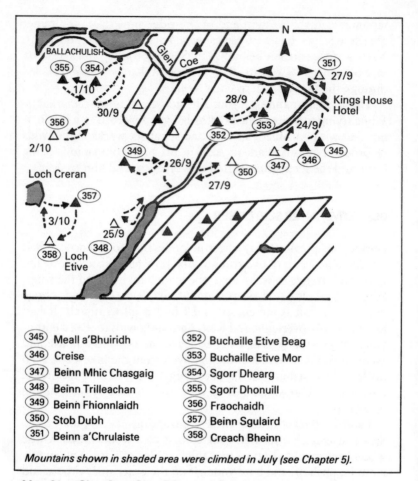

(345) Meall a'Bhuiridh

345 Meall a'Bhuiridh	352 Buchaille Etive Beag
346 Creise	353 Buchaille Etive Mor
347 Beinn Mhic Chasgaig	354 Sgorr Dhearg
348 Beinn Trilleachan	355 Sgorr Dhonuill
349 Beinn Fhionnlaidh	356 Fraochaidh
350 Stob Dubh	357 Beinn Sgulaird
351 Beinn a'Chrulaiste	358 Creach Bheinn

Mountains shown in shaded area were climbed in July (see Chapter 5).

Map 31   Glen Coe, Glen Etive and Creran

up on to Creise, 1,100 metres. Creise means Grease, which probably refers to the slippery rock-covered slopes of this mountain. It was good to lie in the shelter of the cairn as the icy wind
howled over the summit. Creise is part of the fine ridge that gives
fourteen miles of superb ridge-walking, stretching from here to
Starav, overlooking Loch Etive.

Strangely, the wild stormy conditions that day were almost
almost exactly the same as on my last visit, the previous November. I tingled with excitement as the wind blew me about on the

descent to the col. Ahead lay the grassy slopes of Beinn Mhic Chasgaig, 862 metres. This overlooked little mountain lies hidden at the bottom of the map. Stalking tracks lick round her western slopes to come to a halt in the wilds of Coire Laoghan and Coire Ghiubhasan, a delightful corner of the Black Mount.

The River Etive had fallen a little, enough to allow a safe crossing, although halfway across doubts filled my mind as the black waters tugged at my legs. A refreshing pint was waiting at the friendly climbers' bar of the Kings House Hotel.

Five peaks lay still unconquered in Glen Etive, four of which I knew would clash with stalking interests. I made a phone call to Alex Hunter, the stalker at Dalness, who was very helpful and said I could climb Stob Dubh next day. He was surprised at the amount of interest in this peak these days; obviously the Corbett game was growing in popularity.

In the early light of morning, I whizzed down Glen Etive. Close to the hunting lodge at Dalness a smart figure in tweeds leapt out of some bushes and stood in the middle of the road. He held his hand out like a policeman, which he wouldn't have done had he known about the faulty state of my brakes. The bike screeched to a halt, assisted by my boots dragging along the tarmacadam. It was Alex Hunter, the stalker. He politely asked if I wouldn't mind missing out Stob Dubh today, as the wind had changed and they were going to shoot there after all. He suggested Trilleachan at the end of the glen, which was free of stalking on its eastern side. I was touched by his genuine concern not to ruin my day's walking.

The night before he had been involved in a rescue. A party had climbed into 'the Lost Valley' at Glencoe, mistaking that reclusive cul-de-sac for the Lairigh Eilde, which joins Glencoe with Glen Etive. They were confused when they found a mountain barring their way, but, undeterred, climbed over the shoulder of Bidean nam Bian to descend in darkness down the craggy slopes towards Dalness. They became stuck at the edge of the precipitous waterfall known as the Dalness Chasm and sensibly prepared to stay there till dawn. However, Alex's keen eyes had noticed their torches and climbed up to bring them down to safety.

Pretty Glen Etive is the greenest glen I know. Here the children would walk for miles to school carrying with them a peat for the school fire. Sadly the glen suffered terribly from an outbreak of tuberculosis at the turn of the century.

I was conned into thinking Beinn Trilleachan would be an easy quick climb. But its 840-metre rise from sea level gave me the best part of a full day's effort. She is famous among rock climbers for her Trilleachan slabs. This 'Hill of the Sandpipers' was well shrouded in mist as the rocky slopes led me up over Meall nan Gobbar, 'the Hill of the Goats', to climb on to her bumpy ridge. The summit was no place to linger in the biting wind.

A promising-looking gully led down the side of the Etive slabs. A raven cawed from its mountain home. I cawed back and we kept up this nonsensical conversation for a few minutes till the mist cleared to reveal a passenger boat sailing up the fiord-like loch across the waters. I could hear the muffled sound of a guide describing the scenery through his loudspeaker. I wanted to hide from this intrusion into my mountain homeland.

The path along the lochside led back to the road, weaving in and out of the ageing woodland. There are several rocky plat-forms built along the shoreline though their purpose escapes me. Glen Etive was the homeland of the beautiful Pictish Princess Deirdre, who lived here in the first century and the glen is full of unsolved mysteries and legends.

It was a long fourteen-mile cycle back up the glen to the hotel, I spied Alex Hunter coming down to the house of Alltchaorunn with a dead stag on each of his two ponies. This, of course, was a sad sight; but unfortunately the deer must be culled, otherwise the whole herd will face starvation. Memories of a spring walk along the west coast of Jura with the hillsides littered with dead deer confirmed my thoughts.

Early morning found me whizzing down the now familiar road. Mist hung low to the floor of the glen. At Invercharnan I took the bike up the steep forestry tracks, the tyres digging into the soft wet ground. About 800 feet up I said a cheery hello to a couple of men working on their Land Rover. There was no reply. They just stood and stared at this ghostly apparition of a cyclist who lurched by, disappearing into the mist.

My map was not as detailed as the new Ordnance Survey Landranger Series, and it was puzzling to come across some tree-less moorland. My compass told me I was way off course ... how embarrassing having to use a compass to find a roadside mountain! By following the outer edge of the forest I eventually came back on course and hoped I would be able to to find my bike again.

Above, somewhere, lay the twin-topped Munro, Beinn Fhionnlaidh. She is a remote mountain, with approach made difficult by the forestry on Etive side and Glen Creran. I had permission to be on the hill, but a loud gun bang towards Glenure told me that stalking was in full swing in that area. The summit ridge led over an easy scramble to the top. Alan Wilson, a vet from Glasgow University, was on top rushing round the last of his Munros before the new term started.

Another long cycle led up the glen to the bliss of a hot shower and a good meal at the bunkhouse.

The morning rain had returned the glen's burns to their normal foaming whiteness, as my poor rusty bike wobbled down Glen Etive for the last time. Past the deer farm at Invercharnan I branched off for the riverside. Here a fine bucket bridge shot me across the water. It was great fun and I repeated the performance three times. Above Glencietlein House rise the steep slopes of Stob Dubh; this Corbett was my last mountain to be climbed in the glen. She is little-climbed, living up to her sister peak's name, Beinn Ceitlein, 'Hill of Concealment' or 'Hiding'. To her west lie a confusing mixture of remote corries and glens that somehow make their way to Glen Kinglass.

A mile further down Glen Etive lies the cottage called Coileitir. This was home to Charlie Cattanach and his wife. Charlie, who sadly died in 1985, was a great friend of the many walkers who passed his door. Visitors would be ushered in and fed on bread and jam, while his wife introduced them to her many cats. His favourite story was that of a couple of German lads who arrived one night in a poor state; one had new boots that were crippling him. They camped outside and it poured with rain. Overnight the river rose and carried the offending boots away to Loch Etive.

After another joyful crossing on the bucket bridge, I started cycling up the glen. North of Dalness I met Alex Hunter in his Land Rover. He stopped and we had a grand chat. He was very interested in my journey, and especially my bike.

'Have you never had any trouble with it?' he asked.

'No, just the odd buckled wheel and about a dozen punctures,' I replied.

He wished me good luck and drove off. I must have cycled twenty yards up the glen before my rear brake fell off. Turning round, I fell into a ditch, breaking the rear light.

The day was not over yet. Abandoning the bike at the bunkhouse I stormed up the slopes of Beinn a'Chrulaiste, the fine Corbett that rises behind the Kings House Hotel. The race was on to the reach the top before dark. She is the highest of the wavering line of hills that rises from the barren moorland of Rannoch Moor, which along with Loch Laidon and the Blackwater Reservoir help to cheer the weary scene of peat hags and boggy pools. The mist cleared at the top and I rested by the cairn looking over an unforgettable panorama as the wild beauty of Glencoe came to life. The magnificent buttress of Buachaille Etive Mor and the pointed peaks of the Bidean nam Bian hills, which had lain hidden for weeks, grumbling under their misty veil, came to life. A darkness crept in. I crossed my fingers in the hope that the view would be the same in the morning.

Any visitor to Glen Coe cannot fail to be impressed by the sight of Buachaille Etive Mor, 'the Big Shepherd of Etive.' It drew like a magnet. Today it was clear … the sun even shone; a miracle! This was the Glasgow September weekend and parties were already hurrying to the hills. The Lairig Gartain drives a wedge between Buachaille Etive Mor and her neighbour, Buachaille Etive Beag, known affectionately as the Wee Buchaille. Its scree slopes were the usual one step up, three down affair. Her summit, Stob Dubh, is the familiar pyramid shape that fills the view when looking up Glen Etive. While dots of people could be seen on nearby Bidean nam Bian, I swung back over the empty Lairigh Gartain and on to the long bumpy ridge that dipped and climbed to the Big Buachaille's summit, Stob Dearg. A party had just arrived on top after climbing its curved ridge, the exciting scramble up the mountain's spectacular buttress. It felt strange after weeks of solitude to be surrounded by so many people on the hills. Afternoon walkers were coming up the rocky Coire na Tulaich.

Suddenly I heard a familiar voice call my name. It was Graham and Julie from Glasgow. They had decided to spend their holiday weekend trying to find me. With my father on holiday they had had difficulties tracing me. However, *The Climber and Rambler* magazine had details of my route and they had figured correctly my position. By chance, several other friends had arranged to stay in a chalet at the Clachaig Inn at Glencoe so we were assured a fine *ceilidh*.

The English proprietors of the inn, Peter and Eileen Daynes, took our cause for Erksine Hospital under their wing and raised over £1,000 for our deserving charity. After a mouth-watering full breakfast I was tempted to relax in the company of friends and recharge batteries while the sun shone: a decision I would later have cause to regret.

The following day I awoke to a deluge of rain that crashed down from the heavens. Tents that were pitched in the calm of a beautiful autumn evening now lay surrounded by a moat of water. At Ballachulish I followed the soaking Gleann an Fhiodh path as a warning rumble of thunder roared in the distance.

I was beginning to feel weak and sick again, similar to the mystery bug that laid me low in July. Ahead lay Fraochaidh, 879 metres, meaning 'Heathery Hill.' Its lower slopes bristle with forestry like a hedgehog. The rain had turned on to maximum flow as I climbed on to the mountain's long north-western ridge. Two miles from the summit lightning flashed across the glen. Bitterly disappointed, I turned back ... the risks of becoming a black charred fencepost were too great.

Problems always seem to happen in threes. Retrieving the bike from its hiding place, I cycled down the track leading to the village. Suddenly — twang! — the front brake went. Unconcerned, I pressed the back, then remembered it had fallen off in Glen Etive! The bike gathered speed as a shut gate loomed ahead. Only one thing for it: abandon ship! I forced the bike off the track so that it ran uphill, where it reduced speed before throwing me off.

The front brake was fixed in the comfortable bike shed at Glencoe Youth Hostel as the rain smashed tauntingly on the roof. My day of living dangerously was over.

CHAPTER 8

October 1985

Appin

—

The High Cairngorms

—

The Eastern Cairngorms

—

Corrieyairack and Glen Roy

—

Easy days in the Spey Valley

APPIN, 1–3 OCTOBER

It had now rained continuously for a hundred days in Ballachulish, and this morning was no different. A small, damp dog
whimpered outside a cottage door. I tried to read a soaking wet
newspaper. A dustbin rolled down the rain-drenched streets. The
track up Gleann an Fhiodh was even more like a bog than it had
been the day before. The river was a roaring torrent of white,
foaming water. Others had had trouble with this river. In 1913 a
party crossing from Loch Etive to Glencoe came down through
this glen and found the remnants of a bridge, consisting only of
one log with nails sticking up. It had been raining non-stop for
seventy-two hours. A young bachelor in the party was sent across
first. I know the feeling well . . .

Above in the mist lay the twin-peaked mountain of Beinn
a'Bheithir (pronounced Vair), 'Hill of the Thunderbolt.' She's a
fine mountain, whose two Munro summits sit high overlooking
Loch Levan. I had long looked forward to climbing this beautiful
peak again. The rough grass soon gave way to the bouldery slopes
for which this mountain is renowned. The green forest laps
around her slopes like a petticoat. Four miles and three hours
later, the misty cairn of Sgorr Dhearg was reached. Though mist
obscured the view, warm memories remained of seeing this
mountain from the shores of Loch Levan: here her huge amphitheatre corrie can be best enjoyed.

A path wound through the rocks skirting the corrie to rise to
a'Bheithir's other Munro, Sgorr Dhonuill, 'Donald's Peak.' It was
named in memory of the massacred MacDonalds of Glencoe
who, in a blizzard, fled from the murdering Campbells to the
safety of Glen Duror.

My feet tugged and twisted at the granite boulders, as they
slipped a little further downhill. At the top the corrie soon echoed
to the cheers of my 355th mountain. It was across Loch Leven at
Callert that almost the entire population died of the plague when
a Swedish ship carrying the disease anchored there some 200
years ago.

The six-mile plod back to Ballachulish was full of thoughts of the future. With only three more mountains to climb in Appin, I would soon be leaving for Aviemore and the Cairngorms. That meant a new mountain range, new adventures and, hopefully, better weather. The wettest summer since 1897 had just washed through the Highlands, the raging burns clawing through the glens like a new Ice Age.

In the morning the rains continued to lash the window panes of Glencoe Youth Hostel. Soon the bike was aqua-sliding down to Ballachulish where I found the path up Gleann an Fhiodh was in the same submerged state as yesterday. Six long miles away, hidden in the mist and rain, was the summit of Fraochaidh, 'the Place of Heather.' Monday's atrocious weather and lightning storms had forced me to retreat — there would be none of that nonsense today.

My body was going at half-speed. Something was wrong.... probably, I thought, just a physical barrier. Fraochaidh is easily climbed from Glen Creran, a 26-mile cycle ride away. She is a lonely Corbett, and one you should have to yourself. A helpful line of fence posts led to the summit. The Coire Dubh has been well named, as today's inky black skies cast a gloomy shadow over the mountain.

The strain of the walk was now beginning to tell. The mind was blurred. Only the legs pounded on like a machine, back over the four small hillocks that led from the summit to the top of the pass.

Torrential rain thundered down as dawn raised its cheerless head. It took a long three hours to cycle the 26 miles to Glen Creran: the performance of a weak and drained body was having its effect. The remote and trackless mountains between Glen Etive and Glen Creran contain three Munros and four Corbetts. All were climbed except Beinn Sgulaird, 932 metres, and Creach Bheinn, 810 metres. A stalking track was of help up the impressive slopes of Sgulaird. Some stags roared through the mist.

In my weak state it was a slow three-hour climb to the top. After traversing the S-shaped ridge, it was a relief to rest by the cairn. The mist cleared enough to show Trilleachan, looking tame from this angle. What a wonderful, wild peninsula this is, with the fiord-like Loch Etive and Loch Creran encircling the mountains like a lobster's claw. Only one mountain stood between me and my planned cycle ride to the Cairngorms: Creach Bheinn, 'Mountain of Spoil.' It looked miles away and it was tempting, in my weak state, to leave it out.

It would have to be climbed quickly if I was to reach the summit before dark. The rocky ridge slowed progress, but at last the grassy hillocks of the bealach were reached. The adrenalin flowed as speed was increased to a fast jog up the steep slopes of Creach Bheinn. Every second seemed to count, and the wet, springy moss underfoot was a help ... as was the MacGregors' shout of 'Ard-choille Grigalach!' to ensure the west was won that day. A fierce sleet storm welcomed me to the summit. A check at the map revealed another top further west — it had better be visited, even though the sleet and freezing wind slammed against my face.

Progress was slow, head-down in the wind with all the resistance of a sheet of cardboard in a hurricane. However, I finally reached the top in triumph as the dark clouds of day became those of night.

The long, three-hour cycle back to Glencoe was soon under way to the familiar hum of the bike's dynamo. The moon came out and stunningly lit up the island fortress of Castle Stalcaire, stronghold of the Stewarts of Appin. In 1468 the Stewarts and their allies won a ferocious battle here against the MacDougalls and Campbells. Hundreds died on both sides.

Tired legs strained at the pedals. I had not felt like eating all day. Sleepy eyes peered through the darkness, counting each milestone, till I reached Kentallen, and the realisation that I was nearly home filled me with relief.

The bed in Glencoe was bliss, but I would only pick at the cooked breakfast that Mrs Macdonald put before me. The wind and rain hammered against the window, and my mind groaned at the thought of another long day. The heavily laden bike was slowed down further by the strong northerly headwind. At Spean Bridge, 22 miles later, I felt all in. Unbelievably, I was dehydrated. Who would have thought that possible in the year of the Scottish monsoon? It was 35 miles east by Loch Laggan to Newtonmore, but it might as well have been 350. The sleet and rain lashed down and the wind howled. My body was numb to sense and feeling, and only one thought ran through my mind: to get to Newtonmore and rest up. Every fifteen minutes or so, I stopped the bike and lay exhausted, aching all over and vomiting as the sleet lashed down on me.

At Laggan, less than ten miles from my target of Newtonmore, I 'hit the wall': reached a stage of total exhaustion. I lay in a large puddle, my mind and body yearning for sleep. But that could be fatal. Cars went by, tooting their horns. Near by stood a war memorial, with its long list of dead. I thought of all the ex-service-men at Erskine Hospital, and I knew that the hospital would close without donations. My struggle was nothing compared with theirs. Self-pity gave way to anger. With a fist raised at the spitting sleet, I vowed, 'I'm not going to be beaten by you!' My mind concentrated on counting each rotation of the pedals as the milestones went by. At last, the twinkling lights of Newtonmore appeared in the distance. There I staggered into a bed-and-breakfast, and slept the sleep of the exhausted.

Leaving my heavy cycle luggage at Newtonmore, I cycled weakly towards Aviemore to meet the support team. This was the lowest point of the walk. It felt strange to be in a busy urban atmosphere again. Six long days were to pass before I felt well enough to resume my journey.

THE HIGH CAIRNGORMS, 11–14 OCTOBER

The heavy pack strained my shoulders, but it was grand to feel the dusty trail of the Lairig Ghru underfoot. This pass is one of the most ancient and famous through routes in Scotland, gouging through the heart of the Cairngorm mountains. There stands a large boulder called the Clach nan Taillear, placed in memory of three tailors who died while trying to travel through the pass in a blizzard. At the top of the rock-strewn pass, one felt swallowed up by the high, misty ramparts of the steep, surrounding mountains.

My plan this week was to climb eighteen peaks — fifteen Munros and three Corbetts, leaving Sgor Gaoith and Mullach a'Blair at the far west end of 'The Gorms' till later. It was a great morale-booster to be in a new area, though I still felt unwell. If

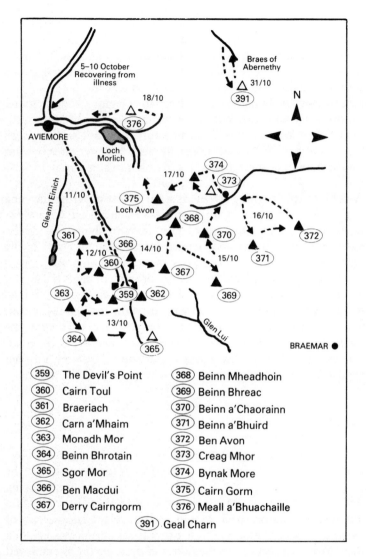

Map 32   The Cairngorms

only the weather would be kind! My body felt weak and
dehydrated.

The Cairngorms are high mountains, but look mild and tame
compared with the rugged peaks of the west. When the Cairn-

gorms are angry in a wintry mood however, there are none deadlier. The few purpose-built shelters in the Cairngorms are small and can easily become overcrowded. They are home for one of Scotland's most famous characters, Bothy John, living on a meagre pension and the kindness of people he meets.

Crossing the bogland to Corrour after legions of walkers had tramped across it this wet summer was like something out of a First World War battlefield. Surprisingly, the dark and tiny bothy was empty. One would normally feel hungry after walking fourteen miles in seven hours, yet I couldn't eat a thing.

A cold, crispy morning dawned, a hard frost covering the rocky path that weaves its way up the Coire Odhar. I shall never forget that morning. After months of rain, the sun shone! The golden light crept up behind and danced on the slabby crags of The Devil's Point. This wild wee peak makes up for its inferiority in height by its rugged splendour, so prominent from Glen Dee, where the mountain seems to block off the entire glen. What a feeling! Deer could be seen grazing far below in Glen Geusachan. The sun glistened over the gentle, rock-strewn plateau leading to the summit cairn. It had taken less than an hour to reach the top. The mist sifted gently, unveiling a clear and magical world. There is nowhere else on earth that I would rather have been that day.

> May your heart keep true to the peaks above,
> May your feet be sure on the hills you love,
> May the summer mist and the winter storm,
> Never hide your path to the High Cairngorms.
> Seton Gordon

Like a cat with two tails I stormed off for Cairn Toul, 1,291 metres, the sharper peak of the group. Two Glasgow climbers were on top, grinning with pleasure at the day's weather. They had wisely camped near the Wells of Dee on the Braeriach the previous night. In the unaccustomed clearness it was good to look down into Coire an t-Saighdeir, 'the Soldier's Corrie,' and the Lairig Ghru below. Edward I led his army through this pass ... as did Graham of Montrose, who recruited a tiny army of High-landers and Ulstermen. These tough hill men were born to a life of raiding and ambushing. Against terrible odds they crushed the huge Covenanting army, recruited by the Campbells, in six victorious battles.

From the top of Sgorr an Lochan Uaine, or 'Angel's Peak,' it was fantastic to see the huge An Garbh Choire, the rims of which are shaped like a giant B. A few years ago, a piece of piping was found here, believed to have fallen from the fuselage of a German Zeppelin airship, which mysteriously flew over the Cairngorms in 1916. The weather had been too good too soon, and mist shrouded my approach to Braeriach, Scotland's third highest mountain, far less often visited than Nevis and Macdui. Below the summit lay the Coire Brochain, 'Corrie of the Porridge.' Distances are more easily covered over the mountains in eastern Scotland. Three peaks had been climbed, yet it felt like an afternoon's walk.

It was a marvellous surprise to meet support-team member Simon Strachan at Clach nan Taillear 'the Tailors' Stone.' He had left home in Uddingston, near Glasgow at 4 a.m., driven over a hundred miles to Braemar, and walked the seven miles to Corrour bothy — to miss me by half and hour! How glad I was that he had correctly anticipated my planned route! Soon the smell of tomato soup simmering on his stove lingered in the air like nectar.

On Cain a'Mhaim, the familiar sight of mist covered the long, gentle ridge leading to this easy Munro. On the top we said goodbye, and Simon started his long journey home. It would be January before we would meet again. Being ill and alone in the mountains is depressing, and Simon's visit was a boost to my morale. Besides, back at the bothy he had left a small bottle of whisky!

The morning mist still clung to the bothy. My route followed a faint track round the bottom of the southern crags of The Devil's Point for Glen Geusachan. The glens were still roaring with the sound of stags challenging each other. The rutting season was under way. Suddenly, through the murky mist in front of me, I heard the terrifying roar of an angry stag. Then another stag appeared behind me. Caught in the crossfire! I remained motionless while the stags roared at each other. Eventually they took off with one last roar and the scuffle of hooves.

Only tree stumps remain in this wild, trackless glen. The river had suffered terribly during this year's monsoon. Parts of old trees lay strewn along the flooded banks like debris after an avalanche. It was slow progress through grass and thick heather. After an hour and a half of this it was a relief to start climbing to easier ground. Opposite lay Coire Cath nam Fiann, 'Corrie of the Battle of the Fianns.' It is sad that the history of Fionn and his wild warriors is lost in time, for most mountains and glens mention their names in some way.

It was windy, but starting to clear on the steep slopes of Monadh Mor. Loch na Stuirteag lay to the north, well known as a nesting place for seagulls. It is one of the highest nesting grounds in Britain — 2,800-odd feet and well over forty miles from the sea. The mist cleared on the summit of Monadh Mor, called unimaginatively 'Big Hill.' Together with Bheinn Bhrotain, it forms the southern part of the Cairntoul plateau. The kind sun glowed, but the cold wind warned of winter's approach. A path led through the rocky boulder-strewn slopes towards Beinn Bhrotain, 'Hill of the Mastiff.' Twenty miles to the south, as the crow flies, lies the A9, with not a road or habitation in between. Such is the scale of the Scottish wilds.

To the south lay Carn Cloich-mhuilinn, 942 metres, now a top, but at one stage reckoned to be a separate mountain. It was one of the two Munros that Sir Hugh Munro himself failed to climb before dying of tuberculosis. The other was the Inaccessible Pinnacle of Skye. Whenever Sir Hugh was there, the weather seemed to be atrocious — sounds like Skye!

With sunlight at my back, it was an easy matter climbing to the summit of Sgor Mor, 813 metres, one of the Cairngorms' three Corbetts. This little peak lies between Glen Dee and Glen Lui. Though small compared with her neighbours, she gives fine views, and was once used as a viewpoint for robbers spying on their future victims. Not a soul was about as the autumn skies faded and a red glow covered the mountains before sinking silently into darkness.

Ben Macdui, 'Macduff's Mountain', lay well hidden in her misty mantle. It was a long two-hour climb by 'the Tailor's' Burn' to the plateau. Such a fine mountain deserves a more dramatic ascent. The route by Sron Riach, at the head of Glen Luibeg is highly recommended: it takes you close to the wilds of Coire Sputan Dearg and the colourful waters of Lochan Uaine. The gentle mist clung to my thermal jacket as I followed the well-cairned path that leads from Loch Etchachan over the rock-strewn plateau to the summit.

Near here are remnants of bivvy shelters built by Commandos during the Second World War. In the nineteenth century Ben Macdui was believed to be the highest mountain in Britain, till it was found that Ben Nevis was 50 feet higher. A plan by the Earl of Fife in 1819 to build a pyramid on top, containing a burial vault was, fortunately, dropped. In 1940 an RAF plane crashed near the summit — a monument still marks the place.

Ben Macdui (Beinn MacDuibh) is famous for Am Fear Liath Mor, 'the Big Grey Man,' who is said to haunt the summit. In certain conditions, your own shadow is cast much larger than normal, giving the impression that you're being followed by a giant. I have never experienced anything out of the ordinary myself, though Norman Collie, a famous scientist and mountaineer, fled from the summit in terror, and in the 1940s an Aberdeen mountaineer emptied the contents of his Army revolver into some frightening misty shape. Oddly, one figure has been seen with parties of two or three, giving only one shadow. However, none of the locals seem willing to talk about it.

Ptarmigan scattered everywhere, seeking hiding places in the boulder-field that leads to the summit of Derry Cairngorm. She's a little-visited peak, which is a shame, for there are few finer, giving views into the Lairig an Laoigh. The mist was sinking into the glens, leaving the summits standing out like the jewels of a crown.

It felt strange to disappear from the sunny world into the mist again. Loch Etchachan was the launching pad for Beinn Mheadhoin, 'the Middle Hill,' my favourite Cairngorm peak. Its steep slopes rise to a gentle plateau, with a series of rocky tors giving a gentle scramble to the summit. I felt wonderful sitting above a sea of mist and catching the occasional glimpse of wild Loch Avon. This spectacular loch, with the Shelter Stone Crag silhouetted in the loch's turquoise waters, rivals even the wild grandeur of Loch Coruish in Skye.

To visit the loch and stay at the tiny natural shelter of the Shelter Stone is to enjoy the real wilderness experience of the area. Members of the legendary tough Glasgow Club — the Creag Dubh — used to sleep here at New Year, their only cover an old Army blanket.

With the darkness of evening creeping in, it was time to descend to the Hutchison Memorial Hut. Three mountains, involving over 1,000 metres of climbing and some eleven miles of walking with a heavy pack, did little for my appetite. After a light meal my stomach was upset — the effects of eight months of dehydrated food.

THE EASTERN CAIRNGORMS, 15–18 OCTOBER

Today, 15 October, marked the eight-month anniversary of setting off on the walk. I had now climbed 368 mountains, but the wettest summer since 1897 had put me almost a month behind my original ambitious plans. September had been my peak month, with sixty-four mountains climbed. The dedication of the support team kept up my morale. A fortnightly visit, at least, kept me in touch, and there was no time to be homesick.

The mist lay low in Glen Derry, and the roar of a stag's challenge echoed from the Coire an Lochan Uaine. The gurgling Glas Allt Mor led me on to Craig Derry for the first of today's Munros, Beinn Bhreac. This twin-topped hill lies to the south-west of the huge plateau that stretches for ten miles to go beyond mighty Beinn a'Bhuird and Ben Avon. A trail of cairns marked the way to Beinn a'Chaorainn, three miles to the north, crossing the springy, peaty morass of the Moine Bhealaidh. My body felt weak and ill, but I was cheered as the mist cleared above the Coire nan Clach, revealing the twenty-mile-long Glen Avon and her soft, rolling hills. Far below lay the black waters of the River Avon. It was here that the beautiful wife of Fionn (that warrior hero again) was swept away and drowned. Here also a party of Redcoats were swept to their deaths.

The Fords of Avon refuge is a small but useful hut in a potentially wild and inhospitable area. It is a three-man shelter, cocooned inside a cairn. Well I recall a freezing March night spent there, teeth chattering, curled inside a cheap Woolworth's sleeping bag, meant for summer use.

A hard frost that night gave way to a beautiful morning with brilliant sunshine. One and a half miles of walking down Glen Avon took me to the bridge that crosses the River Avon. A track hidden under thick heather wove its way on to a lovely gentle sloping ridge towards the Spion rocks. How fantastic it was to feel warm sunshine glowing on a tired face as I headed up the long, long slopes to the summit of Beinn a'Bhuird, 1,196 metres. The perfect weather made for easy going, though the effects of stomach problems were making themselves felt, and several times I had to force myself to be sick. Lack of fibre was having its effect on my system. Mheadoin's summit tors looked magnificent, with the mist lapping like an endless white sea around her lower slopes.

The northern slopes of Beinn a'Bhuird become thick with snow in the winter, and are reputed to be ideal for snow-holing. The summit cairn sits above the wild eastern-facing Coire nan Clach. My route followed a faint track three miles to the east. The sun glinted on the rocky tors of Ben Avon, appearing like warts on the summit. The highest tor is called Leabaidh an Daimh Bhuide, 'Bed of the Yellow Stag,' and an easy scramble takes you to the top. My descent by the Slochd Mor took me through one of the wildest glens in Scotland — it's a fine setting for a mystery! Several years ago, a man's body was found near here. He was dressed in a top-quality Saville Row pin-striped suit, and wore silk socks and black patent-leather shoes. On the rocks above him lay his shaving kit, neatly resting on a boulder. To this day no one knows who he was.

A hard frost overnight promised another fine day. From the summit of Creag Mhor, 895 metres, I was treated to a spectacular view: only the highest peaks pierced the sea of grey mist that filled the glens. Bynack More is another mountain renowned for its rocky tors, some of them offering interesting climbs. The springy moss of the summit of A'Choinneach felt like a trampoline underfoot, while Loch Avon's turquoise waters glistened in the sunshine.

Working by compass through the mist to the summit of Cairn Gorm, my week of sunny solitude was rudely shattered by the sight of dozens of figures round the cairn. The main path down resembled a staircase to an underground station, with its taped-off areas and steps. The wolf inside me howled at man's plastic intervention on one of Scotland's most famous mountains. An alternative, but slightly longer way down was clear. The well there is named after the Marquis of Huntly, following his rout of the Campbells at the battle of Glen Livet.

My dreams of a good meal and a hot shower at Loch Morlich Youth Hostel were ruined as it was closed for a fortnight's holiday. With no food or fuel left, I walked in sombre mood to a nearby bothy. Two friendly climbers, George Larvey and John Bisland, welcomed me in and laid on a splendid meal. Such is the generosity of hill folk.

> Hielan man show me the way
> We will o'er the hills this day
> To view the Haughs of Cromdale.

It was a glorious morning. The Abernethy Forest spread out like a thick green carpet as I climbed up the well-defined path to the summit of Meall a'Bhuachaille. This picturesque Corbett is well worth a visit for its views of Loch Morlich and the Cairngorms. It was great to relax at the top. The whale-backed shape of the Hill of Cromdale glinted to the north-west, site of the famous Jacobite defeat in 1690.

The track wound its way down to Glen More, the sweet smell of pine lingering in the air. The eight-mile walk from the glen to Aviemore was pleasant, content as I was in the knowledge that the Cairngorms were secure. The weekend was occupied with a welcome visit from the support team.

CORRIEYAIRACK AND GLEN ROY, 21–25 OCTOBER

After a 36-mile cycle ride, it was bliss to snuggle down in a warm sleeping bag. Outside the tent, the stars shone over the eastern slopes of the Corrieyairack Pass. It had been a cold night, and ice coated the puddles on the old military road which crosses the pass. It was built by General Wade in 1735. Ironically, among the first to use it were Prince Charlie and his Jacobite army. A bridge lay in a ruinous state, the rocks numbered by conservation enthusiasts planning to repair it. The erection of electric pylons has given the pass a stale feeling, for as the pylons hum over you, you sense little of the remoteness of the area. It was an easy climb to the summit of Corrieyairack Hill, 896 metres. To the north, Glen Tarf bent into wooded seclusion, while Loch Ness lay still in the

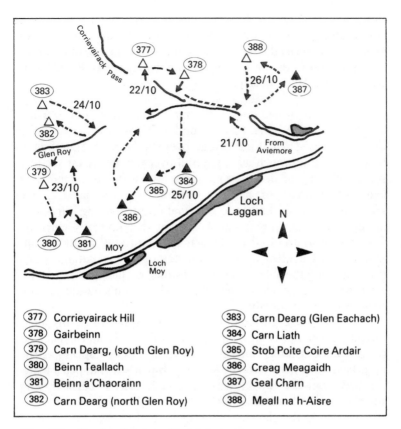

Map 33   Corrieyairack and Loch Laggan

morning sunlight. Only a handful of peaks — left during the stalking season — remained unclimbed west of there.

A hill fox got the fright of his life on my approach to Gairbeinn, strangely also 896 metres high. He raced off to the north — a wise choice, for he could run forty miles before finding a road or house, such is the expanse of the Monadhliath Mountains. Steep slopes took me to Melgarve. A delightful path led west to Glen Roy, and my route was cheered by the sight of the biggest herd of deer that I have ever seen. Like a huge army of cavalry, it crossed the glen in search of fresh grazing.

The day had given sixteen miles of walking, so it was a relief to arrive at Luibchonnel, a cottage maintained by the Mountain

Bothy Association. It had an upstairs loft, which was very comfortable. I had a good meal and enjoyed a quarter bottle of Scotch, which friends had given me for my twenty-sixth birthday on 29 October. In the interests of lightweight travelling, I was persuaded to drink it early.

My watch was turned back one hour to fool myself into starting early: it read 8.45 when I left. Bound for Glen Roy, I crossed the now badly eroded natural bridge over the burn of Agie. Somebody had left a branch as a handrail over the narrowest section. Beautifully curved and formed rocks lay far below in the river bed, which years of nature's torrents had produced. Some Highlanders of old had little imagination for naming hills hereabouts. There are three Carn Deargs at the head of Glen Roy. Carn Dearg south of Glen Roy was the first to fall to my vibram soles today. Glen Roy lay far below, famous for its parallel roads running along the side of the glen, formed by falling water-levels after the Ice Age. Folklore held them to be Fionn's hunting roads, built by his giant warriors.

Loch Sguadaig glittered in the autumn sunshine, my next mountain, the newly promoted Munro Beinn Teallach reflected in its waters. It looks tame from the road in Glen Spean, as the moorland rolls gently to the summit. But it's a fine peak when climbed from the north, with its rough eastern corrie falling steeply to the Allt a'Chaorainn.

I welcomed the clear weather again, as I pushed up the long slopes to Beinn a'Chaorainn. A magical blue lochan, nestling among the crags, sent its gushing burn down into the heart of the Core na h-Uamha (Corrie of the Cave). In 1/46, in the final days of Prince Charlie's flight, he crossed these very hills, no doubt keeping a watchful eye for Redcoats in the glens below.

There were not enough daylight hours for me to push on for Creag Meagaidh — the glen below beckoned. A mass of burns poured from the hillside to flow into the Uisge nam Fichead, well-named 'the Burn of the Twenty Tributaries.' It had been a long seventeen-mile day, and darkness had fallen by the time the bothy came in sight.

My diary entry the next morning was: 'Carn Dearg and Carn Dearg opposite Carn Dearg' — rather confusing! A faint stalking track headed up the side of the Allt Chonnal. In thick mist, intense concentration was required to navigate over the feature-less terrain. Two hours took me to the top of Carn Dearg (north Glen Roy).

Back in January 1645, in blizzard conditions, Montrose abandoned an entrapped position at Fort Augustus. He led his men on a legendary forty-mile night march over the shoulder of this mountain ... to fall on the unsuspecting Campbells at Inverlochy at dawn. The Highlanders lost three men, the Campbells 1,500.

I crossed their route at the top of Glen Eachach (the Glen of Horses), for yet another Carn Dearg. If monotonous thoughts crossed my mind, they were soon dashed when nearing the summit. The mist cleared, and I was treated to the spectacular sight of deer boxing each other. They stood on their hind legs with front hooves flailing, as if practising on a punch-bag. A stalking pony greeted me back at the bothy, and soon developed a taste for compo biscuits! It was dark by the time the tent was pitched.

The stars shone brightly on the river Spey, yet did little to guide me on my early-morning assault on the Creag Meagaidh group. Three Munros lay ahead. The eyes of startled deer lit up in the gleam of my headtorch. A weak, grey light heralded the dawn, while high above in the mist and rain I worked by compass to the summit of Carn Liath. When Martin Moran climbed this group, he had for company some of Britain's top mountaineers and adventurers: Chris Bonington, Hamish Brown and the Crane brothers. Today, I was alone on the hills in the mist and rain.

At Stob Poite Coire Ardair you could sense the steep drops to the Coire Ardair, even if the mist obscured your view. The corrie offers some of the best winter climbing in Scotland. Based in the middle of the country, it avoids the worst weather of the east and west coasts.

Creag Meagaidh is a mountain demanding the greatest respect. For many years she carried the name 'Killer Mountain'. Her ridges marked on the OS map resemble a terrible storm on a weather chart. Accurate navigation was needed to lead off the summit plateau along the narrow ridge to the summit.

It had been a seventeen-mile day. On the long walk back to the tent my head was full of plans for the future. After climbing the remaining mountains in the Monadhliaths and the scattering of Munros and Corbetts around Aviemore, I would make one last foray west. The aim would be to take on the rest of the hills that were abandoned during the stalking season, now thankfully over.

EASY DAYS IN THE SPEY VALLEY 26–31 OCTOBER

It was a cold morning as I cycled through the mist south of Garva Bridge. The road was covered in white frost, and feet froze with the cold. It was a relief to remove the trainers and give my toes a good rub. A stalking track led up to the easy slopes of Geal Charn, and birds twittered happily overhead. It felt like spring and I wished it was ... it seemed to have been forever winter until I arrived in the Cairngorms.

Geal Charn is the most westerly of the Monadhlaith group of Munros, and to climb it today, along with Meall na h-Aisre made sense. Geal Charn sticks out a long way, six miles from the nearest other Monadliath Munro. At 3,036 feet, she may look uninteresting from the roadside, but hers are hidden treasures. She has some fine crags that fall steeply to the Lochan a'Choire and the Piper's Burn.

The Monadhlaith Mountains are terrific for skiing — the high moorland extends for miles in all directions before hitting any form of road. The good weather made me think of other plans, other walks. I was glad it was clear, crossing the featureless terrain to the Dubh Lochan and following a fence post to Meall na h-Aisre, 862 metres. To the north lay some of the most barren parts of Britain. Those wild moors, lochans and quagmires must hold many secrets lost in time.

The view from the trig point was superb. With light failing, my route down followed the gentle Leathad Gaothach (Blowy Slope) to Garva Bridge. At Newtonmore I treated myself to a bed-and-breakfast and prepared for a dawn assault on the hills.

It was pitch black, the only noise being the humming of the dynamo up the steep hill to Pitmain Lodge. As dawn slowly broke a light covering of snow speckled the hills above. A Land Rover track led over the shoulder of Carn an Fhreiceadain (the Cairn of

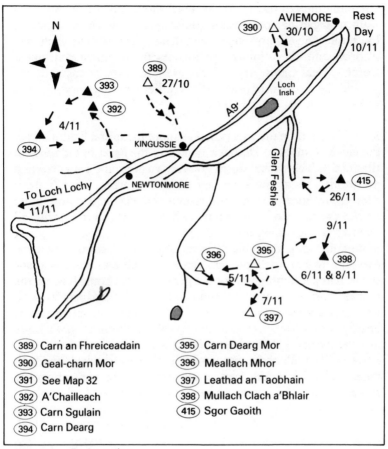

Map 34   Badenoch

the Guard), leaving the snowdrifts of the track behind. With compass in hand, I was soon celebrating my 389th hill.

Back down in Kingussie, some golfers were teeing off for their first game — such is the joy of getting up early. Then it was on to Aviemore and a meeting with old friends, Andy and Carol.

I couldn't have had a better birthday present. Isabel Fraser of Grampian TV explained they wanted to do some filming for 'North Tonight', the Grampian news programme. I was terrified! They filmed me walking along the beach at Loch Morlich — it was a beautiful day — and cycling along Glen More road, with countless retakes owing to the bike's squeaky brakes. Still, the walk was getting some useful publicity for our charity, Erskine Hospital. The support team would be pleased! The next day Andrew and Carol joined me for Aviemore's most convenient Corbett, Geal Charn Mor. In the evening, dark clouds gathered around the Cairngorm peaks: the weather was deteriorating once again.

Snow flickered on the streets of Aviemore as, at first light, I cycled the eighteen miles to Dorback Lodge, in the heart of the braes of Abernethy. The winter storm got very violent, and I was starting to wonder about the sanity of today's venture. Thankfully, I persevered. Snow covered the ruined shielings and grouse butts on the slopes of today's remote Corbett, Geal Charn ... they all seem to be Geal Charn in this area. I have never seen so many mountain hares, their heads stretching out of snowy burrows, ears straining at my approach. Freezing wind and a sharp snow-storm hampered progress up the gentle slopes. Some fence posts marked part of the way, as spindrift towered round me. It was a relief to stand on the summit, my face well sheltered by my frozen beard.

October had been a short month, with only three weeks fully effective. But 38 more mountains had been climbed and 237 miles walked. After the wettest summer in living memory, would the fast-approaching winter be kind?

CHAPTER 9

November 1985

A cold wolf in Badenoch

———

A last foray west: Loch Lochy and Glen Cluanie

———

Monadhliath Corbetts

———

Sgor Gaoith and the Arctic siege of Aviemore

A COLD WOLF IN BADENOCH, 1–10 NOVEMBER

My body still ached from the effects of my mystery bug; and a 26-mile cycle ride to a cold and windswept Dalwhinnie left me feeling sick and exhausted. I made a retreat to a guesthouse in Newtonmore. It was a bitter start to the month, the only consolation being the foul weather. After two days in bed I felt a little better. Hopefully a long day on the hills would sort out the virus once and for all.

Behind the town of Newtonmore the hills dip slightly into Glen Banchor, then rise to form the tidal wave of the Monadhliath Mountains. The range used to boast five Munro summits but when *Munro's Tables*, the bible of the game, was reprinted in 1981, two of those summits were wiped clear. Not that this made today's route any easier as they would all have to be visited anyway.

The Land Rover track leading up the side of the bubbling Allt a'Chaorainn came to a sudden stop and I wove up the heathery slopes of A'Chailleach, 'the Old Woman.' One dark October night I messed around on this hillside trying to find the little hut marked on the map. After an hour I gave up and bivied out — fortunately it was a dry night. In the morning I woke to see the shed fifty yards away!

Cailleach is famous in Celtic mythology as a one-eyed witch who reigns over the winter months, her temper causing the winter storms. A sigh of relief would go through the glens when at Candlemass (25 March) she would be ousted from her icy throne and replaced by a tamer personality. Often however she would make an unwelcome reappearance, turning the Highlands white with her periodic burst of anger until the summer arrived.

A gentle dip led on to Carn Sgulain, 'the Hill of the Basket.' From here you will see why the Monadhliath means 'the Grey Moors.' Hemmed in between Loch Ness and the A9 lies a vast region of high moorland ... over 250 square miles of forgotten country, unvisited save by a wandering gangrel or stalker. The mist and sleet cleared to allow me a brief glimpse of this empty and silent land, speckled white in snow. The stories of the people who lived there are long forgotten, save for the slightest hint given away by place names on the map, such as the Carn Coire na Creiche, 'the Hill of the Corrie of the Spoil' or 'Raid.'

The fence posts that mark the district boundary made route-finding easy as a bellowing mass of mist enveloped the mountain. They led towards the finest of this group, Carn Dearg, her narrow ridge sticking out from the rather monotonous moorland like an accusing finger. Her best looks lie hidden in her Coire nan Laogh where Loch Dubh nestles, sheltered in a perfectly shaped corrie. Today's sleet and rain had topped up the mountain burns to their usual brilliant white as the path led down to Glen Banchor.

At 6.30 a.m. it was inky black as the door of the guesthouse closed behind me. A cold wind rattled through the town as I wound my way north on my bike to Kingussie, a town whose attempted pronunciation has caused more giggles than Partick Thistle's cup record — the g in Kingussie is silent. The town is famous for its shinty team and the impressive Ruthven Barracks, built on an intimidating defensive mound. The original castle in 1574 withstood a siege against 10,000 attacking Highlanders.

This part of the Spey Valley is prone to flooding and had experienced more than its share this wet year of the Scottish monsoon. A bridge passed over the foaming River Tromie as it rushed to join the Spey. At last dawn began to break as I cycled into Glen Feshie, her woodlands smelling sweetly in the damp-ness of morning. Beyond Glen Feshie Lodge the track deter-iorated and the bike was soon abandoned in favour of Shanks' pony. A snowy wintry blast was my companion as I left the shelter of some high woodland and pushed up to the summit of Carn Dearg Mor, 857 metres. This hill lies in the heart of a forgotten corner of Scotland's mountains, where the vast lands of Atholl and Badenoch merge in the narrow Gaick Pass. Although the Munro game has made the three Munros east of the A9 at Dalwhinnie popular, few climbers bother to venture further east and explore the lonely and beautiful land of the Gaick.

The snow was now drifting on the track as it led west towards Meallach Mhor, an enthusiastically named Corbett meaning 'Big Lump.' One eye studied the stormy skies, while the other surveyed the spindrift towering from the mountain. It was a head-down struggle to push up on to her rounded summit. I was glad of my goggles as the icy wind sent snowflakes hurtling across the hillside. It seemed a bit unfair. These hills should have given an easy day out, starting from a glen already 1,000 feet up. Instead it had been a tiring struggle.

A nearby bothy was unusually deserted save for Janet from the West Midlands, a keen gangrel who was busy studying her notes for a seamanship certificate. I wondered if this year's weather had contributed to her taking up this new sport. We relaxed in front of a roaring fire, sitting on some well-made log seats, and finished off the last of my whisky ration.

The next day was bitterly cold, with driving wind and snow showers; the hills unfortunately were out of the question. The day was spent replenishing the bothy's fuel supply with fallen timber washed downstream by the River Feshie. In the evening two outdoor centre groups arrived. Its members were great fun and we enjoyed a grand sing-song in this popular bothy. Cameron McNeish, a well-known Scottish writer, arrived one night and was embarrassed to interrupt a young couple holding hands in front of the roaring fire and looking lovingly into each other's eyes. Feeling guilty at disturbing this lovers' nest, he was tempted to go outside and sleep in the snow!

Fresh snow slowed the pace on the Land Rover track that wove towards the empty lands of Badenoch. This land was once under the firm grip of Alexander Stewart, whose warring activities earned himself the title 'Wolf of Badenoch.' Present day wolves can be seen at the animal park near Kincraig, which is well worth a visit.

The track had been disappearing frequently under snowdrifts and now sank into a white snowy sea. Ahead lay Leathad an Taobhain, strangely meaning 'Slope of the Rafters.' This Corbett sits above the Minigaig Pass, highest point of the 28-mile long path that leads from Blair Atholl to Kingussie. On early eighteenth-century maps it was the only path shown leading north to the wild Highlands, where thieves and caterans lurked. This mountain is fourth highest of the Corbetts. At 912 metres, she is slightly lower than her remoter neighbour, Beinn Bhreac. It had been my plan to continue east to that lonely summit, but between us lay four miles of high moorland, the remotest corner of Europe. In the worsening weather there just would not be enough daylight hours to reach her much before dark. I would try again tomorrow. Through these same wastes Macbeth once led his Highland army on his way south to fight near Dunkeld.

Down in Glen Feshie I gazed at the memorial stone at Carnachuin. It was built in memory of the Special Mountain Warfare Units that trained here in the Second World War. They became expert skiers and learned to live off the land. Years were spent developing their mountain craft in readiness for the plan to invade Europe through Norway. When this plan was abandoned their first action was at Walchern in Holland — below sea level!

It had been a cold night, and wintry blasts slowed my progress up Glen Feshie. A vicious snowstorm forced me to stop at the foot of Sron na Ban-righ, 'the Queens Nose.' It was clear my plans to reach Beinn Bhreac and her two Munro neighbours, Carn an Fhidhleir and An Sgarsoch, were out of the question: the persistent snowstorms, backed by a strong wind, told me what the conditions would be like on the mountains. I returned to the bothy as the elements raged outside. A candle was put at the window to guide any night stragglers. It worked! At 1 a.m. a big group from Aberdeen University arrived.

If that day had been wild, the next was worse. However, the fact that there were more people about gave me greater confidence. Two more Munros lay unconquered on the western fringe of the Cairngorm National Nature Reserve. Near at hand, almost above the bothy, lay a very snowy Mullach Clach a'Bhlair. This hill lies at the less interesting southern edge of the massive plateau west of the Lairig Ghru. An interesting route from Glen Feshie is by the footpath leading to Creag na Gaibhre, then on to her south-western shoulder by Druim na Bo to the top.

My plan was to try to climb this hill and Sgor Gaoith, the fine peak which lies further north on the western edge of the plateau, whose crags stand like battlements above Gleann Einich. The cliffs rise for hundreds of feet around the narrow spur that marks the summit, peering out over the airy drop like a man on a springboard.

I told myself that the weather could only improve, as an icy blast hit me on the bothy doorstep. An unsightly Land Rover track led up Coire Chaoil. Halfway up, it was obvious the elements were waging winter warfare on the summits as snow pelted down the corrie like a rain of arrows. On the plateau visibility was abysmal. My beard froze, my face stung with the cold, and I had difficulty breathing in the near white-out conditions. Slowly the compass led me nearer and nearer to the top as the wind pushed me off balance. At last the snowy pyramid of a cairn appeared inches from my face.

The other Munro, Sgor Gaoith, lay four miles to the north across the high plateau. It offered no cover whatsoever, facing right into the teeth of the storm. It would have been suicide to have attempted to reach it. After the disappointments of the week it was a cruel blow, for every peak missed out now would have to be fitted into my tattered route later on in the journey, adding diversions to an already stretched schedule.

There was little peace in Glen Feshie either as the bike struggled through snowstorms to reach Aviemore. I walked into the reception of the Cairngorm Hotel, where the support team had made their HQ, and despite having rubbed the snow off my clothes and bags, it still seemed to be falling everywhere. The town itself had turned instantly white and for a few minutes the other side of the street was blocked from view. Tom handed me a welcoming dram and a pint of lager. Rarely had a drink tasted so good.

A LAST FORAY WEST: LOCH LOCHY AND GLEN CLUANIE, 11–20 NOVEMBER

After a rest day on 10 November I cycled the 50 miles to Roy Bridge in Lochaber. Several hills in the west, out of bounds during the stalking season, were now free to climb; in addition so were a few hills left out during my last visit at the end of the rain-lashed summer.

Above Spean Bridge stands the impressive Commando memorial, the stone figures of three tough Commandos studying the hillside.

We may feel sure that nothing of which we have any knowledge or record has ever been done by mortal men which surpasses the splendour and daring of their feats of arms. Truly may we say of them, When will their glory fade.

> Winston Churchill, 21 May 1948, at Westminster

The next morning I took the minor road that rises steeply into Glen Gloy from Glenfintaig Lodge. The bike slipped on the gravel at the roadside as my legs strained to pull it up an incredibly tight bend. The glen was once an ice-dammed lake, her ancient shore-lines forming parallel roads along her hillsides, exactly as in her neighbour, Glen Roy. In olden days the Highlanders believed the extraordinary motorway-sized lanes circling the hillside were actually Fionn's hunting paths. Sitting prominently over the glen rises a shapely Corbett called Beinn Iaruinn, meaning 'Iron Hill.' A detour was made to visit the interesting cave above Glen Fintaig before pulling up on a snowy ridge called Beith Og, meaning 'Young Birch,' which swung round to the summit.

To the west lay tomorrow's challenge, the Loch Lochy hills, with dark grey clouds inches above their summits. At my feet

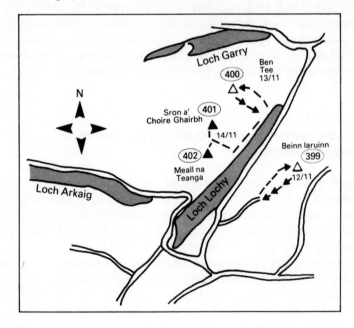

Map 35   Loch Lochy

rocky Coire nan Euan fell to a Glen Roy whose parallel roads resembled a model railway layout peeping through the snow.

With darkness falling the bike was soon whizzing along the shore of Loch Lochy. Lorna and Margaret welcomed me to the friendly Corriegour Lodge Hotel. Lorna apologised for the perfumed smell of the bedroom explaining that a male model had stayed the night before. I assured her that the smell of my socks would more than compensate for the scented aroma. Her big friendly dog Cruachan was under strict orders not to enter the dining room. In protest he stood in the doorway getting in everybody's way, paws millimetres from the forbidden carpet.

As I was cycling round the head of Loch Lochy I ran into Garth, whom I had met one evening near here in August. He and some pals were sleeping out rough in a lean-to bivouac made out of branches. Garth explained that they had decided to have a survival exercise and sleep rough for twenty-four hours with no food except what they could forage from the hillside. In the morning the two girls who were with them, and their dog, deserted to a nearby bothy where some German friends gave them breakfast, much to the lads' annoyance.

The steep slopes behind Laggan locks gave way to rough moorland rising to Ben Tee, 901 metres, meaning 'the Fairy Hillock.' This prominent hill rises from the Glen Garry moorland; the new OS map for the area shows off her steep western contours particularly well. She can be climbed in her own right or, as a part of a longer day, over the two Munros to the south-west, Sron a'Choire Ghairbh and Meall na Teanga. Despite her beauty few people visit her summit; except, that is, for the remarkable Richard Wood, who uses the mountain as a training ground for expeditions in foreign lands. Friends joined him for his 500th ascent of the mountain, and perhaps wished they had stayed at home as they battled through blizzards to reach the top. It was so cold on the summit the champagne they had brought for the celebration had frozen solid. By strange coincidence I was celebrating too, for this was my 400th peak. It felt strange to reach this milestone of the journey. There was no great feeling of ecstasy — I was just one stage nearer ending the most enjoyable experience of my life.

On the moorland of Ben Tee's eastern slopes flows the Allt

Cruinneachaidh, meaning 'the Burn of the Gathering.' It was here one hot summer day in 1544 that the MacDonald warriors of Clan Ranald assembled. At their chieftain's signal, they charged down the hillside on an invading column of 300 Frasers. What followed was a bitter struggle with both sides wielding their fearsome two-handed swords. Because of the blazing summer heat many of the Highlanders stripped to the waist; thus the fray earned its name Blar nan Leine, 'the Battle of the Shirts.' It is believed only five Fraser clansmen escaped back to their own lands.

I was still feeling weak with my mystery bug and decided to have an easy day and not venture on for Ben Tee's neighbouring Munros. One theory was that my condition was caused by a diet deficiency. The support team had given me some orange powders designed to restore the body's supply of roughage. They worked. Only later did I find out that they had been given them by a gynaecologist! They seemed to help my singing, too.

Loch Lochy lay like a sheet of glass in the morning light. Reflected in the still waters were the white snow-laced summits of her two Munros, Meall na Teanga and Sron a'Choire Ghairbh, the highest of the ridge that dips along her northern shore from Ben Tee to the dark woodland of Achnacarry.

I pedalled the bike along the forestry track leading through the South Laggan Forest. Above the ruin of Glas-dhoire rises Cam Bhealach, 'the Crooked Pass.' The path that once led up through the woodland had a gentle carpet of pine needles, allowing silent footsteps to catch a glimpse of an unaware wild cat or pine martin. The path handily zig-zags towards the summit of Sron a'Choire Ghairbh, 935 metres. Local climber Richard Wood had erected an information box close to the summit. It included details of the planned construction on the mountain of an ELF system. This extremely low-frequency contraption would be built to track enemy submarines. It would involve the construction of a series of poles twenty-five feet high, stretching for twelve miles, obliterating the scenery and chasing rare wildlife from one of their last hide-outs. Whitehall may go ahead but she will have to put down an armed rebellion by Scottish conservationists first.

I recrossed the crooked pass, up the grass – then scree – slopes to Meall na Teanga, meaning 'Hill of the Tongue,' whose summit is only inches above the neighbouring bumps that form this attractive mountain. To the west lay the ruined house of Feddon in Gleann Cia-aig, once used by the Commandos training at Achnacarry for night attacks. The same glen treated me to a wash-out of a camp one autumn night as heavy rain lashed the Invergarry mountains. I woke in the morning and found myself in a huge puddle of water.

Darkness was falling by the time I was cycling back along the forestry road to the end of the loch. Suddenly the bike skidded violently — a puncture, the fifteenth of the journey so far. The tool kit was out in a jiffy. Then disaster struck: the dumbbell spanner used for unlocking the wheel nuts cracked in two, making it useless. I pushed the crippled bike to the lights of Kilfinnan Farm, where the farmer was busily loading sheep into a huge float. I felt guilty disturbing him, but in friendly fashion he showed me to his workshed where all types of spanners were to hand. Soon the bike was mobile again. I shouted a thank-you to the farmer as he stood among the sea of bleating sheep.

In the early light of morning I cycled along the Great Glen north towards Invergarry. The glen's chain of lochs was believed to have been used as a transport system by the Vikings, rolling their long-ships on wooden logs between the lochs. The present day Caledonian Canal was built in 1822 but found to be too shallow. It was eventually completed in 1847 at a cost of £1 million.

The road climbed out of Glen Garry to drive above Loch Loyne. The view west from here is superb, as the mountains of Knoydart are seen from an exciting angle.

An even finer viewpoint is Meall Dubh, meaning 'Black Hill,' the forlorn Corbett that rises from the little-visited Beinneun Deer Forest. I climbed into Coire nam Brach, interestingly meaning 'Corrie of the Bear.' Mist hung to the summit as I foundered through the soft snow, accidentally stepping into snow-covered burns. One mile from the summit lies the Clach Criche, a march stone that marked the boundary between the Grants of Glen Moriston and the MacDonells of Glen Garry. To the west lay the Ceannacroc mountains of Glen Cluanie, the last bastion of hills unclimbed in the west. I was soon cycling under their massive slopes to arrive at the friendly Clunanie Inn, which was to be home for a couple of nights.

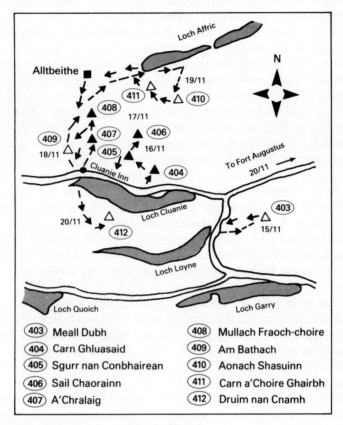

Map 36   Ceannacroc and Loch Cluanie

It was just light when I left the inn and started cycling back along
the shores of Loch Cluanie. It seemed a long time since June,
when the weather had spoilt my previous attempt at the Ceannacroc mountains while based at Prince Charlie's Cave in Coire
Mheadhoin. The cave was the mountain hide-out of the famous
Seven Men of Glenmoriston, Jacobite guerrilla fighters. This
brave band fought back against 'The Butcher', the Duke of
Cumberland, and his troops who were burning the Highlands
and starving the population by stealing their cattle. One of their
many actions took place at the spot where I left the bike on the
slopes of Creag Lundie. Here they attacked a large Redcoat

column with such ferocity that the troops fled, leaving the life-saving cattle with the Highlanders.

A stalking track led uphill but soon disappeared under a blanket of snow. The summit plateau of Carn Ghluasaid, 957 metres, has some fine crags overlooking Coire Sgreumh. On a previous visit I was treated to a bird's eye view of a shepherd expertly using his dogs to search the mountain's rough corries for stray sheep. Snow showers had been coming in with increasing regularity. I climbed towards Sgurr nan Conbhairean; from here ominous clouds could be seen developing in the west. A mad dash was made to reach Munro number three, Sail Chaorainn, before climbing down the gentle ridge skirting Coire Lair.

At the Cluanie Inn it was a pleasure to bump into Alison Rankin, who had been with the accordion party on the rainswept summit of Ben Alder in June. Throughout the journey I was surprised and pleased at how often I met people whom I had met previously during the walk. She joyfully explained that she had been made redundant from her Edinburgh job and was going to walk and ski as long as her money lasted.

It was an unexpected bonus having Alison's company as she joined me on the long slopes of A'Chralaig. This is the first of the two Munros running parallel to An Caorrann Mor, a glen the Ice Age moulded to perfection and which joins Glen Affric with Glen Cluanie. Talking of the Ice Age, if the autumn stayed this cold the skiing season would be off to a bumper start. Some climbers were recently climbing a winter gully in the Cairngorms. As the leader belayed his partner, a ski mountaineer casually walked past unroped, his skis in his rucksack. Fifteen minutes later the climbers had just finished a belay that had the rope crossing the gully when — swish — the skier hurtled down the climb, unaware of how lucky he had been!

In today's fine winter conditions, the ridge north formed a perfect knife-edge. Finding our path blocked by a small wall we winkled our way round by shinning up some steep ground overlooking Coire Odhar. Towards the summit of Mullach Fraoch-choire, Alison was having quite an introduction to her first Munro! The Glen Affric hills were showing off their new white coats, the peace disturbed only by the roar of a couple of fighter jets flying through the glen. A high speed bum-slide took us quickly to the glen below before returning to the merry atmosphere of the Cluanie Inn.

In the morning my rucksack was hurriedly packed for a two-day foray to seek out some secluded Corbetts. Above the Cluanie Inn rises the Corbett, Am Bathach, meaning 'the Byre' or 'Cow House.' An easy climb soon led on to her narrow grassy summit. This small mountain has a fine viewpoint and gives a memorable approach to her higher neighbours. An overnight thaw had left the snowy hillsides streaked like a zebra, the sharp ridge of Ciste Dhubh looking particularly stunning.

My mad catch-up route continued by weaving down to An Caorann Mor, as a huge herd of deer ran for cover on the other side of the corrie. Continuing under the shadow of Ciste Dhubh's steep eastern slopes I pushed on for Glen Affric, stumbling over the wreckage of an RAF plane, over the northern flank of Mullach Fraoch-choire. Near by lies the remote Glen Affric Youth Hostel. Although it is normally open only from mid-June to 1 October, the Scottish Youth Hostel Association kindly leave the place unlocked throughout the year. The ground close to the croft of Athnamulloch was badly flooded. It was here in 1721 that a government force unfairly tried to collect rent from the MacKenzies, taking advantage of that clan chieftain's enforced exile in Europe. The troops were beaten back with heavy losses.

The Land Rover track became less scenic as it led on through the regiments of trees to White Cottage, a bothy which I understand has now been converted by the owners into a holiday home. A welcoming puff of smoke came from the chimney. Inside I met a pleasant Lochaber couple whose psychopathic Alsatian dog would appear from his bad behaviour to have ambitions to star in 'The Hound of the Baskervilles'. At regular intervals he pinned me to the wall, and I eventually retreated to the other room, leaving the potential canine star counting the bones of today's victims!

The morning sunlight danced on the pine trees, which for a second made me think I was back in the Cairngorms. Mind you, with my navigation, anything's possible! A path led south following the Allt Garbh meaning 'Rough Burn.' A hundred yards along this track and I was in a new world. A ruined bridge lay across the burn and birds chattered from the treetops. The path left the woodland and carved its way through the waist-high heather, leading to the hidden Choire Garbh, home to two remote Corbetts.

A brew-up at Loch an Sguid gave me the energy to climb up the easy slopes of Aonach Shasuinn, 'Englishman's Hill'. The name possibly relates to the skirmish at nearby Athnamulloch. A stag's head in the Cluanie Inn is marked as having been shot on this mountain. The rock-covered summit gave spectacular views stretching as far south as Lochaber, all its peaks glistening in their winter white coats. A thin veil of smoke crossed the corrie as a man, no doubt from Affric Lodge, set alight the old grass in the glen.

Carn a'Choire Ghairbh, 863 metres, is 'the Cairn of the Rough Corrie,' a rather over-dramatic description for this peaceful part of the Affric Forest. Her western slopes fell steeply to Gleann na Ciche. On the six-mile walk to Glen Affric Youth Hostel, I must have sung every song I knew as the deer roared in protest across the glen. On approaching the hostel's familiar blue-painted door, I noticed a sheep's skull above it and wondered if Fang the psycho-Alsatian had been here! The place was deserted. It was a bitterly cold night so after a quick meal I was soon snug in my warm sleeping bag.

A morning walk led me back to the Cluanie Inn, where I was surprised to find the bar full of Scottish football supporters from the Isle of Skye, who were travelling down to Glasgow to see Scotland play Australia. If only Partick Thistle had this sort of support; they normally phone their supporters to see if they're coming to the game!

Only one more mountain remained unclimbed west of the Great Glen and it was without doubt the easiest one. The road leading south from the hotel was once the main route to the Isles, but with the damming of Loch Loyne it sank beneath the waves. Hemmed in by the moats of Lochs Cluanie and Loyne rises Druim nan Cnamh, 789 metres. It was a pleasure to cycle up the empty road and bound up her gentle moorland slopes. To the east was the strange sight of the old road disappearing into the dark waters of Loch Loyne, then rising out at the other side.

While the hill's southern slopes could be more interesting, this is more than compensated for by her northern crags, falling to the remote, trackless southern shore of Loch Cluanie. Rain sprayed the summit as dark clouds hung to the higher mountains. The hills braced themselves for another onslaught of rain which would draw the Cluanie Curtain across the glen. I blew a farewell kiss to the wild mountains of the west before skipping down to the roadside. A chugging Land Rover was coming along the road. I waved cheerily, but my smile disappeared when the vehicle came to a halt and the driver's window was rolled down. A grumpy old man leaned out, saying angrily 'All that way for nothing,' and drove off. It may have been nothing to him but the gentle climb that led to my last mountain west of the Great Glen had given me great pleasure. I wondered when that old man had last stood on the top of Druim na Cnamh admiring the views and counting his blessings.

It was dark by the time I reached the Cluanie Inn. With the bike's dynamo humming I started the long 28-mile cycle ride to Fort Augustus, the centre point of the Great Glen.

MONADHLIATH CORBETTS, 21–23 NOVEMBER

Click! The bike's panniers were fastened to the bike and I slipped out of town. It was exciting to be cycling on what was for me a new road, even if it did pull uphill steeply. A muddy Land Rover track led up Glen Doe towards the snowy slopes of Carn a'Chuilinn, meaning 'Cairn of the Holly.' This wild Corbett rises from the wilds of the Monadhliath, the forgotten land of count-less lochans and sometimes nameless mountains.

Heather and grass changed to rocky slabs as I climbed on to her summit, wondering if I was her only visitor this year. A freez-ing wind blew over the mountain, causing the snow to race across the maze of frozen lochans lying east of the summit. I wouldn't have blinked twice if I had seen a polar bear cross her vastness. This is no place to get lost. One can only admire the tenacity of the Ordnance Surveyors who studied in detail the empty lands of 'the Grey Moors'.

Descending, I caught a glimpse of Fort Augustus; it was here that the notorious Duke of Cumberland had his base. While he and his troops lived in luxury, the Highlands starved. Any man or

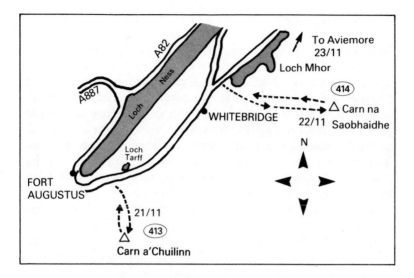

Map 37   Monadhliath

woman taking pity on the walking skeletons who came pleading
for food was flogged. There is still a great deal of bitterness in
Scotland regarding the activities of this evil man and unfeeling
barbarians like him who cleared the glens.

It started to snow as I cycled north towards Whitebridge. It
was bitterly cold and I had to put on all my clothes and snow
goggles — not a pretty sight. To the west lies Loch Ness, home
perhaps of the greatest mystery in the world, the Loch Ness
Monster. Many people scoff at the thought that a sea monster
could have survived the Ice Age living in this deep loch. It is
certainly a remarkable coincidence that Loch Ness runs along the
Highland fault line and could easily have a system of underground caverns, perhaps leading to Loch Morar, the deepest loch
in Europe, where a similar monster has been sighted.

The falling snow made it very difficult to see, and the sight of a
four-wheel drive vehicle ahead struggling on the slopes of the
next hill was hardly encouraging. At last I arrived at Loch Mhor
and despondently looked around for a place to camp, when I
stumbled across a sign advertising bed and breakfast. Gordon
and Shirley welcomed me into their cosy house and gave me

dinner in front of a roaring fire while the snow gathered on the window ledge outside.

West of Loch Mhor lies a real test for the most ardent Corbett enthusiast, Carn na Saobhaidhe, 'the Cairn of the Foxes Den.' What a secret lair it is, rising out of the barren landscape of forsaken Monadhliath. Although Land Rover tracks strain to reach her, all fall short and approach from any angle is going to give a full day's outing. I followed the track up the side of the strangely named River E. Sika deer were grazing across the glen, signalling to each other with their high-pitched squeals. It was the first time I had ever seen these miniature deer. Mist soon shrouded the path and snowflakes were falling by the time I reached the ruin, marked on the map, where three burns joined to form the river. Ahead lay two and a half miles of featureless moorland. With visibility down to a few feet the compass-bearing was double-checked. I have never seen contour lines so wide on a mountain's slopes; with the poor visibility and a howling wind it hardly felt as if I was climbing at all. Close to the top the weather turned really nasty as snow and sleet pelted the summit, stinging my face. I was beginning to think I had missed the summit when I stumbled over the cairn.

The Monadhliath Mountains are, to some, a vast range of monotonous moorland, and certainly they lack many fine pointed peaks and crags. However, out of that monotony comes a strange beauty, an appreciation of the remoteness. There are several unnamed hills and lochans, perhaps because hardly anyone has been there before to name them. If anybody wanted to 'disappear', the Monadhliath is the place to do it.

It was still snowing by the time I reached the bike. Another puncture ended my plans of cycling on to Aviemore, so a further pleasant evening was spent instead with Shirley and Gordon.

The morning radio reported the roads through Inverness-shire's high passes blocked with snow: winter was obviously coming early. But nothing was going to stop me reaching Aviemore. The bike led me through Strath Nairn which was bleak and cold that grey morning. Near here lies the haunted Loch Duntelchaig, where the chilling sight of two ghostly cavalry armies facing up to each other can sometimes be seen at dawn.

It seemed strange to join the A9 dual carriageway after the quiet roads of the last few days. With a triumphant cheer I arrived at Aviemore to find the support team waiting at the Balavoulin Hotel. A couple of days were spent replanning the next stage up to Christmas. Fortunately, for once I was not taunted with good weather during this break from the hills.

SGOR GAOITH AND THE ARCTIC SIEGE OF AVIEMORE, 26–30 NOVEMBER

Only one hill lay unclimbed on the western boundary of the Cairngorms: Sgor Gaoith. This peak had already beaten my attempt earlier in the month from Glen Feshie, when blinding blizzards on the plateau had made progress impossible. Now it was another cold morning as the snow-covered road led south past pretty Loch an Eilean to Feshiebridge.

I was soon donning boots and walking through the snow-covered fir trees into Coire na Cloiche. The air was still as the snowflakes fell silently. The mist was very low and the compass guided me up from the corrie above 900 metres. Then the weather turned ugly with an Arctic wind that froze my beard and made my Gore-Tex jacket feel as if it were made from stiff card-board. The icy wind howled over the summit, reducing visibility to a few feet, as the slopes climbed gently to the exposed cairn perched on the cliffs overlooking Coire na Caillich.

Sgor Gaoith is one of the finest of the Cairngorm peaks. She is seen at her best by walking up Glean Einich, where her wild corrie can be admired. On the end of her northern ridge lies the Argyll Stone, in memory of the Duke of Argyll's defeat at the battle of Glen Livet.

The summit was no place to linger as I carefully climbed down from the mist, practically bumping into a fox in the corrie, who must have expected the hill to be deserted in today's foul weather. The going was slow with the snow thigh-deep in places, until I broke through the barrier of mist and returned to a world of visibility.

The bike was making an awful racket as I cycled back to Aviemore, where an offending rusty chain was replaced.

It had snowed heavily overnight and my road east to Dufftown was blocked, leaving me marooned in Aviemore. This was followed by an Arctic freeze-up with temperatures below minus 18 at night. Even during the day it was impossible to cycle any distance in the sub-zero temperatures. This frustrating delay continued until the end of November, so I made the best of an enforced break and recharged my batteries. One delight was cycling to the swish Coylumbridge Hotel, where I would leave my rusty bike among the Mercedes and Porsches and go in for a swim lunch. This promotional idea allowed non-residents into the hotel to enjoy their terrific swimming pool, jacuzzi and sauna. Then at 1.00 p.m. one could retire to the dining-room and enjoy a carvery lunch, all for only £5.00: a fiver well spent.

CHAPTER 10

December 1985

The Whisky Country

—

Among Royalty's hills: Braemar and Balmoral

—

Glen Ey and the Forest of Mar

—

Glen Shee to Pitlochry

—

Arctic Dalwhinnie

THE WHISKY COUNTRY, 1-5 DECEMBER

A low-pressure area had come in overnight; for once I was glad to see rain falling as I started the 40-mile cycle trip up Strathspey to Dufftown. Snowdrifts narrowed the width of the road, making cycling unpleasant as lorries squeezed past. At Charleston of Aberlour the street was rutted with hard-packed ice, causing the bike to jerk and slide.

Dufftown lies in the heart of the whisky country. 'Rome was built on seven hills, Dufftown on her seven stills,' the saying goes. In the evening some locals tried to persuade me to stay on next day to have a look around the famous Glen Fiddich distillery. I was concerned, however, that if they let me into that gateway to heaven I might never wish to leave.

At 8.00 a.m. it was inky black as the bike struggled up the hill heading into Glen Rinnes. My twisting, turning journey would never be as far north again. The easy slopes of Ben Rinnes reminded me of the first hill of the walk, Broad Law in the Borders, climbed almost ten months ago. Ben Rinnes is the most northerly peak east of the Great Glen. She is renowned for a large population of mountain hares, which every March chase and box each other across the hillside in their eccentric mating ritual. The mountain was used as a source of peat to fire the many whisky stills in the area, illegal or otherwise.

Mist shrouded the summit and failed to give a view of the fertile lands of Moray, once the stronghold of the famous King Macbeth, whose valiant deeds and battles, so misconstrued by Shakespeare, fill the country with legends of a largely forgotten time. In the glen below, a column of Land Rovers came to a screeching halt, and a mass of tweed-dressed stormtroopers leapt out, their shotguns pointing towards the slopes of Meikle Conval opposite, where already the rabbits were placing white flags in front of their burrows!

Across the glen lies Corryhabbie Hill, 781 metres, a muddy track leading to her lower slopes from Ellivreid. Molehill-strewn

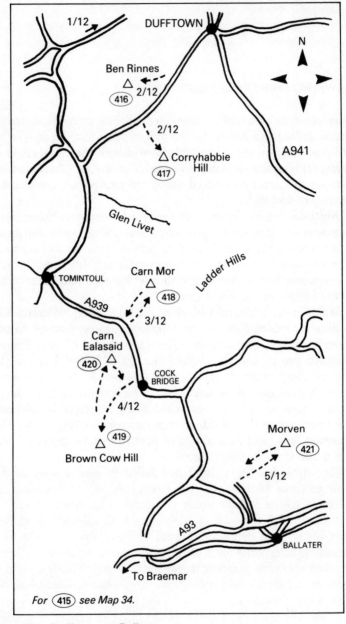

Map 38 Dufftown to Ballater

grass soon took the place of snow-streaked heather as I climbed higher towards my 417th hill. The mountain is the highest point on the ridge on the southern side of Glen Rinnes; unfortunately a Land Rover track leads most of the way along its length. The mountain is probably most interesting climbed from Glen Suie, where a visit to Elf House Cave makes a pleasant diversion. The anglicised names given to the area's gentle hills were in sharp contrast to the tongue-twisting Gaelic describing the wild sharp mountains of the west.

A triangulation point marks the summit. The mountain was an important base for the surveyors of the last century. To the south-east, across Glen Suie, lies Cooks Cairn. Sadly she had become the most recent Corbett to be demoted from 'The Tables', as she does not have 500 feet of reascent on her southern ridge. If it were not for this strict rule there would be many more Corbetts than the 222 currently listed.

Darkness had closed on these 'whisky hills' by the time I was mounted on the bike and cycling the twelve miles to Tomintoul, a village reputedly made famous by its fierce winter weather. Its snow ploughs had had plenty of work to do while I was stuck in Aviemore. However, the recent warm front had beaten the snow-line well up the mountain, although I suspected that the old witch Cailleach, the goddess of winter, was simply catching her breath.

I woke to a stormy morning. A roaring wind raced through the streets, sending a couple of upturned dustbins rolling out of town. I engaged the bike's lowest gear and, head-down against the gale-force winds, crawled southwards. Ahead lay the infamous Lecht Pass which, in the days before her popular ski centre, was often blocked with snow from September to May. The road was like a wind tunnel as my frustratingly slow pace led me inch by inch to the top of the 635-metre pass.

A short sharp slope led easily on to the moorland summit of the Ladder Hills, famous for its freebooters' whisky trail, the Ladder Path. A district boundary fence forced its way across the almost flat ridge, ploughing through a line of slushy pools to arrive at Carn Mor, 804 metres, meaning simply 'the Big Cairn.' She is the highest peak of the large region of small hills and moorland stretching to far-off Strathbogie. To the north lies Glen Livet, a peaceful and prosperous glen famous for its whisky. In

1592 the tranquillity was broken by the sound of clashing swords and whinnying of horses as the Duke of Argyll, with 5,000 Campbells, was defeated by Huntly's Gordons and their allies.

Rain lashed the ridge on my way down to the bike. Gale-force winds were raging through the pass, forcing me to push the two-wheeled brute to the summit. Cycling down to Cock Bridge was exciting, as an 80 m.p.h. gale threw me off the bike. The gusts were so strong that my trusty steed rolled over twice, her firmly fixed panniers ripped off and sent bouncing across the moor. After gathering the bags in the howling wind, it was an exhausting business trying to reattach them to the bike, and no sooner was it loaded up than another savage gale tore off the panniers once again. This was enough to test the patience of Robert the Bruce's favourite spider. I thought more problems were to follow for, with the bike reloaded, progress could be made only by lifting the frame a little off the ground and pushing it forward while maintaining a press-up position. Any advance was painfully slow as the bike was shoved only a few feet before I would collapse on top of it, gasping for breath, with bodyweight keeping all the bags in place. It took over an hour to travel a quarter of a mile. At last we lost height and the wind eased. What a relief to arrive at Cock Bridge where Ron and Kathleen welcomed me to the friendly Allargue Hotel. They gleefully displayed a collection of recent photographs which showed how wild and desolate their winters are, with cars buried under fifteen feet of snow and drifts up to the chimney stacks.

Overnight gales had cleared the skies of their ugly black clouds as Strathdon awoke to a cool crisp morning. The bike clattered past the whitewashed walls of Corgarff Castle, which was burnt to the ground in 1571 by the Gordons who left twenty-seven Forbes trapped inside. Whisky-smugglers gave it a wide berth in the nineteenth century when Redcoats were garrisoned there to control their activities.

Further up the glen sparkled the pretty lochan at Inchmore, which soon resembled a tiny pool as I climbed up the mist-covered slopes of Brown Cow Hill, a mountain which, despite her tame-sounding name, had its location near some of the wildest and remotest parts of the Cairngorms. At the summit I started crawling across the snow to get a close-up photograph of some mountain hares when suddenly on the horizon appeared a stag, the sun shining through the mist to form a gleaming halo around his antlers. Hearing the click of my camera the proud beast raised its head, barked a warning and danced off into the mist. The snap did not come out, but the memory will always remain. The mist cleared to reveal a glimpse of Lochnagar, one of the many pleasures still to come when Braemar was reached.

Afternoon found me climbing on the opposite side of the glen, up through the pleasant woodland to Carn Ealasaid: a far more pleasant approach than the tempting option to pounce on this 'Elizabeth's peak' from the roadside of the Lecht Pass. At the top I was treated to a fine view to the west of the maze of deep glens that gouge their way through this empty and little-visited part of the Cairngorms, giving the happy 'gangrel' an inexhaustible variety of through routes. Happy plans for future walks filled my mind as I climbed down to the warm atmosphere of the hotel bar.

It was a pleasure in the morning to cycle along Caulfield's old military road leading south to Glen Cairn. It was still and damp with a light wind, causing leaves to rustle along the verge. A few days earlier Strathdon had been gripped by Arctic weather, and locals were concerned to see a dogged cyclist push on through a blizzard towards Ballater. They hoped he made it!

Across the River Gairn I could see the house of Lary, the start of today's climb. Alas, it was to take another half-hour to reach that point, by the time the bike had trundled the five miles to Bridge of Gairn and up the river's east bank. The mist was hanging low above the lonely track that led to Morven Lodge. A faint path led me across the moorland, while somewhere above rose Morven, 871 metres, meaning simply 'Big Hill'. This Corbett lies a little out of place in a large bastion of moorland among the rich farmlands of Aberdeenshire. This agricultural treasure was bitterly fought over as dozens of battlefields and countless castles and hill forts can bear witness.

Morven is one of those pleasant hills that has several tracks leading to her foot from the moorland of her southern slopes, or through the interesting looking Tornashean Forest, whose rocky features appear like blisters on the map. An old well provided an anchor point to take a bearing to the damp, mist-cloaked summit. To the south-east lies Culblean Hill overlooking the barren Muir of Dinnet. Perhaps a similar veil of grey mist clung to her slopes back on that day in 1335 when the tiny Scottish army waited on the hillside, eagerly listening for the order from their leader, Sir Andrew de Moray, which was to send them charging down the mountain to trap the 3,000-strong English army on the boggy shores of Loch Kinord below.

Snow fell on the summit and the flakes followed me all the way down the glen. I arrived in Ballater, happy that the great psychological barrier of the whisky hills had been breached. It was to be a fortunate night for me as I was invited to join the weekly meeting of the Braemar Mountain Rescue Team, a selfless group of dedicated people who were to be of great help in the difficult days ahead. After a generous whip-round for Erskine Hospital, the team exercised their vocal talents and, led by Ernie Rattray and Struan Donald, the bar soon shook to the sound of 'The Bonnie Lass of Fyvie'.

AMONG ROYALTY'S HILLS: BRAEMAR AND BALMORAL, 6–12 DECEMBER

It was a cold morning as I donned two pairs of gloves before wheeling the bike out of town. Ernie Rattray had been out before me with his grit lorry, which was very considerate of him! The road twisted and turned through the green woodland of Deeside until the sight of Balmoral Castle filled the view. Here every year the Royal Family enjoy a couple of months' respite from their strenuous duties. The estate is well run, with its own shop and distillery! Now that is organisation for you!

Pine cones lay strewn across the track that led through the woodland to Glen Gelder. I was cheated of a view of the superb cliffs of Lochnagar as the mist clung to the track and snowflakes fell; the weather demanded the softest of options to be taken. Sitting at the east end of the wild grandeur of Lochnagar lies the three-topped Corbett called Conachcraig. The track crossing its shoulder gave a direct if unscenic approach to her rocky summit. Snow was falling horizontally on top, ruling out any possibility for pushing on to Lochnagar.

South of the summit lies Glen Muick. In 1863 Queen Victoria's coach overturned here but she was rescued by her personal

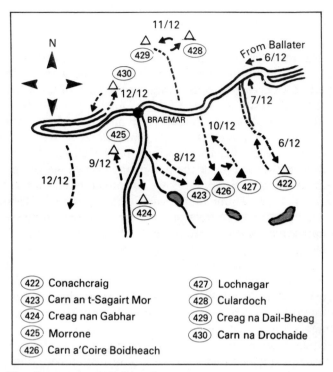

Map 39   Braemar and Balmoral

attendant and piper, John Brown. This loyal servant was twice to save her life when he tackled would-be assassins. Queen Victoria's passion for Scotland and her people did much to heal the wounds of the rebellions and the Clearances and her enthusiasm started a flood of Victorian tourists that blossomed into the thriving industry of today.

A snowstorm harassed me all the way down the glen. It was a freezing cold night as I snuggled into my sleeping bag hoping for better weather in the morning, while outside the snow continued to thrash the glen.

I listened intently to BBC Scotland's morning forecast. 'Heavy snow and strong winds especially on high ground' is what they said, and, on opening the tent flap, a flurry of snow blew in to reveal a white moving world outside. With my plans again in tatters, I retreated to Balmoral. The snow was down to the roadside as the bike worked its way west towards Braemar, the chain freezing in the Arctic weather.

I woke to a wintry morning in Braemar. It seemed the worst summer in living memory had turned into the worst winter. A bitterly cold cycle led to the bridge at the start of Glen Callater. Here I had arranged to meet Struan Donald and Bill Ross from the Braemaer Mountain Rescue Team and these cheery companions made me forget that my timetable was weeks behind schedule as we walked up a wintry Glen Callater. Some shepherds were amused to see the tyre marks of my bike going along the road and then disappear down towards the river where I had hidden it. Throughout the journey I had a constant fetish for concealing my bike in trees or under bracken, which now seems so stupid, but some city habits die hard!

The glen was once an important drove route, now known as Jock's Road, leading to Glen Clova. From a frozen Loch Callater a track led up the side of Creag an Loch towards Carn an t-Sagairt Mor. At 1,047 metres she is the smallest of the three Munros of the Lochnagar group rising about Braemar, Humorous banter compensated for the wintry weather as we waded through thick snow on the mountain's western slopes.

Struan explained that while they have been involved in many heartbreaking rescues, some do occasionally have happier endings. Earlier that spring 'the team' were called out to rescue an Irish climber who was believed to be climbing nearby Glas Maol overlooking Glen Shee. In the middle of the night, with head-torches gleaming, the rescuers set off for the summit. It was early May and there was now snow only on the top of the mountain, which they reached just as dawn broke. They spotted a survival bag huddled among the snow, and they raced over to check the Irishman for exposure.

He said, 'I'm glad to see you, boys. It seems I did the right thing digging in here last night.'

To which Straun replied, 'Well, yes, if you're lost on the hill that's probably the best thing to do.'

Dawn started to break as the Irishman pointed to Glen Shee. 'Tell me, boys, now what's that road down there?'

The team gave him a hot drink and replied: 'That's the A93, the Perth–Braemar road.'

'By jeebers,' said the Irishman, 'I was down there last night.' This brought an angry response from the rescue team. The Irishman continued: 'Oh yes, but I remembered my training at the Killarney Outdoor Centre – that if you get lost on the mountains you must dig into the snow. Being the springtime I had to climb all the way to the top before I could get snow deep enough to dig in!'

The biting wind and snow prevented us attempting any more summits, so we beat a retreat back down the glen. At Braemar, Struan and Bill introduced me to Lui Murray, head of the rescue team, who willingly showed me around his impressive headquarters, an efficient command centre which has helped save so many lives. In pride of place was their new Snowcat vehicle. In addition to its go-anywhere capabilities it boasted an incredible array of winches and searchlights. Lui explained the main advantage was that the Snowcat would be able to get the team quickly to their destination and provide a warm command centre close to the rescue spot. It was heartening to be given an insight into the professional and dedicated work done by Britain's mountain rescue teams.

A bitterly cold night had given the welcome dividend of a clear sky. Frustratingly, I had to wait in the village till 9.00 a.m. when the post office opened, so I could post home my camera which had developed a fault. A rushed phone call was made to a reporter from the *Evening Express* in Aberdeen; poor man, the pips from the hungry coinbox seemed to interrupt his every question.

At last I was on my bike like a coiled spring suddenly released, shooting out of town with eyes carefully watching the snow and ice on the road. A northerly breeze blew me four miles down Glen Clunie. The sun smiled kindly as boots and gaiters were donned, and a quick pull led on to the boomerang-shaped ridge of Creag nan Gabhar, 834 metres, meaning 'Goats' Crag', named after the feral goats that lived on the mountain until about twenty years ago. This easily climbed Corbett sits above the old military road leading into Glen Shee, her little Western crag looking down the long Glen Baddoch towards the distant peaks of Glas Tulaichean and Carn an Righ.

She can be easily climbed from her long gentle northern ridge or from the path leading from the roadside to Bealach Buidhe. From her multi-cairned summit I caught a glimpse of the fine corrie at the head of Glen Callater, crags shining in their glistening winter whites.

A fine bum-slide took me most of the way to the roadside, where the bike clattered along to the foot of another easy Corbett, Morrone, 859 metres, meaning 'the Big Nose.' The Land Rover track that leads to the top was under snow and of little help as I zig-zagged up the hillside. A far more attractive approach is by the footpath leading up from Braemar. Two men were carrying out some maintenance work to the small transmitter station on the summit, built to assist the mountain rescue team. Over a welcoming mug of tea (at last I had found a mountain with a café on top!) they explained they often worked on the mountain but, despite its multitude of tracks and tame appearance, it had given them a few scares. One night, while driving down the mountain in their old Snowcat vehicle, they got caught in such a bad blizzard that they drove off the wrong side of the mountain and became totally confused when the expected roadside failed to appear. It was several hours before they made it safely home.

Far below, Braemar was bustling with activity. Here lie the ruins of Kindrochit Castle. In medieval times it was garrisoned by Scottish troops, but incredibly it was destroyed by the very people it had been built to protect. Word had broken out in the village that some of the garrison were dying of the dreaded plague. This caused such panic among the local inhabitants that they formed themselves into a small force and dragged cannons all the way from Atholl. After blocking off all means of escape from the fortress they bombarded it to a pulp, mercilessly killing all the troops inside.

The stars sparkled across the night sky as the snow-covered road welcomed me back into Braemar, with only 73 hills left to climb.

It was still dark as I cycled out of the village the following morning and frost sparkled on the walls of Braemar Castle. The fortress is reputed to be haunted by the sound of swords clashing on its stone staircase.

Three miles later at Ballochbuie Bridge I met Struan Donald

from the rescue team, who was to be my friendly companion for the day. We wove our way along the pine-needle-cushioned tracks of the Ballochbuie Forest, the largest block of woodland in the Highlands. Straun disclosed that during the summer months you are quite likely to bump into a member of the Royal Family out for a stroll. He added that every year he looks forward to attending the Ghillies' Ball, a dance held at Balmoral for the estate staff and friends. It is an occasion enjoyed immensely by all, with the Queen Mother usually last to leave the floor.

The track now followed the snow-covered Feindallacher Burn which disappeared among the snowy moorland rising to Carn a'Choire Bhoidheach, 1,118 metres, meaning 'Hill of the Beautiful Corrie.' This romantic name goes to show that even the clansmen of old had an appreciation of their mountain homeland. Her northern-facing Corrie nan Eun stole the show as we skirted its precipitous crags and looked down on the frozen ice rink of Loch nan Eun, 300 metres below.

The freezing wind froze our Gore-Tex jackets, making them feel like cardboard, as we pushed on to Deeside's most beautiful peak, Lochnagar, whose beauty inspired Lord Byron to write:

Brave Caledonia, dear are thy mountains,
Round their white summits the elements war.
Though cataracts roar 'stead of sweet flowing fountains,
I sigh for the valley of dark Lochnagar.

Perched between two superb corries, she is the type of pointed peak a child would draw of a mountain, a perfect mountain offering gentle walking and varied climbing on her corries' north-facing cliffs. We rested at the summit while the mist cleared to reveal an endless sea of mountains stretching to the south, reminding me sadly that every step taken now was a step nearer home. We chewed on some hard frozen chocolate which tasted like concrete, while Struan told me that every year, on Midsummer's Night, a migration of people make the long climb to the mountain's summit to see the sun rise. However, this wet summer the weather had been so bad that police were posted at the start of every popular route of ascent, turning folk back.

Ptarmigan scattered as we climbed down the mountain's northern ridge. The boulders here had collected pools of deep snow which we floundered through, sometimes up to our chests. This was a more serious problem for Struan who was a good deal smaller than myself; fortunately he was wearing a brightly coloured balaclava!

Struan recalled that, earlier that year, the rescue team had been leaving the popular Cairnwell car park in Glen Shee, laden with planks and building materials to repair a fishing hut they maintain. An American tourist asked where they were going, to which they replied they were just safety-conscious mountaineers who always took their hut with them! Non-plussed, the tourist pointed to Struan, struggling behind with a big piece of wood. 'Who's the little fella at the end?'

'Oh, he's our mascot,' the team cruelly replied.

Back in Braemar we both enjoyed a celebratory pint. What a tremendous help the cheery members of Braemar Mountain Rescue Team had been in restoring my flagging morale at a crucial stage of the walk.

In the morning the twinkling lights of Braemar were left behind as the bike's lights showed up the icy road ahead. I took the estate road leading to Invercauld House. It was unsalted and thick with snow. I must have fallen off half a dozen times before resorting to Shanks' pony.

A track led north through the fresh-smelling woodland, which was once such a popular route with cattle drovers coming from Tomintoul. Ahead lay two remote Corbetts. My body buzzed with the excitement of two new peaks to climb. A posse of mountain hares ran for cover in their burrows, leaving their loop-the-loop tracks over the snow-buried path. The route up Cular-doch, 900 metres, was hard going as gale-force winds sent biting snowstorms to sting my face. Leaning over at an incredible angle was the only method possible by which to reach the dome-like summit. Lonely Glen Feardar lay to the south. It is a pretty glen, once well populated, but, as a result of the Clearances, stone rings are all that remind us of her bygone inhabitants.

Crossing back across the Bealach Dearg, I was surprised to see the hillside move. An avalanche? No, a herd of snow-covered deer came to life and raced off to the sanctuary of empty Glen Gairn. The twin-topped summit of Carn Liath resembled a giant figure of eight, the snow moulded by the Arctic blasts. The north-westerly of the two knolls, Creag an Dail-Bheag, is the higher, but it seemed to take ages to cross the half-mile tundra-like plateau. With the deafening wind raging, a hurried bearing led down to calmer shelter on the banks of the gurgling little green burn of Glas Allt Beag.

A pleasant path wove through the dark trees of the Invercauld Forest at Alltdourie. I could see across the river Dee to Braemar Castle, overlooked by the wooded hill of Creag Choinnich, which reminded me of a cat's back when angry, hunched and ready to pounce. Perhaps John Farquharson, the local hero known as 'the Black Colonel,' thought the same, for in the seventeenth century, with a handful of men, he opened fire on 150 government dragoons camped near the castle. They fled in disarray, thinking they had been attacked by a large army.

A thaw had helped cycling conditions considerably as I made my way back to the gleaming lights of Braemar.

The next day, owing to an overnight thaw, the snowline had retreated up the hillside. Hungry deer were low in the glen as the bike led me westward towards the pretty Linn of Dee. Unfortunately my route was not taking me as far as that bubbling little gorge, for the bike swung over the Victoria suspension bridge towards Mar Lodge. Another gorge, far less frequently visited but just as beautiful, is the Linn of Quoich. Here I disturbed some squirrels who rushed off to their drey, hidden among the trees. What a view they must have of the flowing River Quoich, under the dramatic shadow of the tree-covered Creag Bhalg!

Leaving my furry friends watching from their treehouse, I pushed on up the rocky heathery slopes of Carn na Drochaidhe, 818 metres, 'the Hill of the Bridge.' This was the last unclimbed mountain north of the River Dee. The mighty whitewashed summits of Ben Avon and Beinn a'Bhuird dominated the northern view. I was tempted to forget my schedule and reclimb these high hills, but sanity returned as I gazed westwards to where the long glens of Feshie and Tilt meet the Lairig Ghru, famous through-routes used by man since Stone Age times. The green woodland of Glen Quoich licks her way round this mountain and offers a pleasant return journey to base.

Black storm-clouds heralded a warning that the peaceful

morning was almost over, and by the time I reached the bike the rain had started to fall. But the day was scarcely half over, for at Inverey I took the long Land Rover track that shoots south on its five-mile journey along Glen Ey to the ruined Altanour Lodge ... on the doorstep of tomorrow's three remote Munros. It was in this glen that the famous Black Colonel hid at a place known to this day as 'the Colonel's Bed,' where he was visited every day by his girlfriend Fair Annie. A good piece of organisation, I'd say!

The weather had changed dramatically, as it so easily does in the Highlands. The glen had turned into a wind tunnel with sleet and rain hurtling through it at a ferocious speed. The only traffic was a Land Rover which screeched to a halt, the two dead hinds in the back evidence that their stalker had been up early that morning too. After a pleasant chat he said, 'Now tell me, I'm dying to know, how you city fellas get any enjoyment out in this sort of weather?'

I replied, 'You have to take the rough with the smooth, but a day on the hills, whatever the weather, is always preferable to a day in the rat-race of a busy pollution-filled city.'

The kindly stalker handed me a tasty sandwich, saying, 'Your need is greater than mine, laddie,' adding, 'And you're going to camp in this?' as a particularly nasty wind rocked the soaking vehicle. In an explosion of smoke the Land Rover chugged into life and as it headed down the glen, I saw the stalker's arm raised in a friendly farewell salute. As I stood there with the rain already swelling the full burns I had serious doubts about my sanity.

It was dark by the time I reached the ruined lodge called Altanour, the wind so strong I had to crouch to perform the simplest of tasks. Most of the trees surrounding the ruin had fallen in previous gales, small encouragement for the few that still creaked threateningly overhead. For the more fierce winter weather I had been lent a new tent, the Winter Gear Gemini Tent, which was made from breathable Gore-Tex. It was single skin – a dome-shaped shelter with a tunnel-type entrance. I pitched this man-made igloo, a little concerned about its baptism by Highland weather, but I needn't have worried for it stood as steady as a rock. What a pleasure to coorie down in my warm sleeping bag and cook a meal, while outside the gales whipped the glen.

GLEN EY AND THE FOREST OF MAR, 13–18 DECEMBER

Overnight storms had given way to a calm morning and my head-torch guided me through the fallen jungle of trees in the early light. The dappled burn of Alltan Odhar led me uphill towards Carn Bhac, 920 metres, 'Hill of the Peatbanks.' Dawn gently raised gracefully her winter head. Forests of moving deer antlers could be seen through the gloaming, while out of their snowholes white hares peered suspiciously. Carn Bhac is the most northerly of the group of five pleasantly remote mountains lying in the empty lands between Glen Tilt and Glen Shee. Empty, that is, except for Fealar Lodge, said to be Britain's highest inhabited dwelling, thirteen miles away from the nearest road, and home to the friendly Lean family.

Scree slopes led on the S-shaped ridge of Beinn Iutharn (pronounced 'yoo-hurn') Mhor, 1,045 metres, meaning 'the Big Mountain of Hell'. Fortunately she was in a tranquil mood today as little Lochan Uaine smiled below me. With mist closing in I worked my way east towards An Socach, 938 metres, 'the Hill of the Projecting Place'. This is a mountain where you can enjoy peace and solitude in sharp contrast to the Cairnwell, two miles to the east, which in the winter months is jam-packed with thousands of skiers.

The atmosphere of the ruined lodge of Altanour was peaceful today compared to its inhospitable welcome the night before. I packed the tent and loaded the bike for the return journey to Braemar. The five miles of Land Rover track were covered in an hour before darkness fell and shortly afterwards the welcoming lights of Braemar came into view.

I must have looked a strange sight to motorists as I cycled my heavily laden bike up Glen Clunie for the last time, one hand holding the handlebars while the other grasped the small transistor radio kept for weather reports. Blaring out was Radio Scotland's programme 'Leisure Trail', wishing me luck for the last 65 mountains. It was the start of a steady pull of publicity that was to reach a climax at the end of the walk.

A path led through the knee-deep heather, climbing steadily towards Carn an Tuirc, the most northerly mountain of the Glas Maol group of four Munros, rising above the glen like a moun-

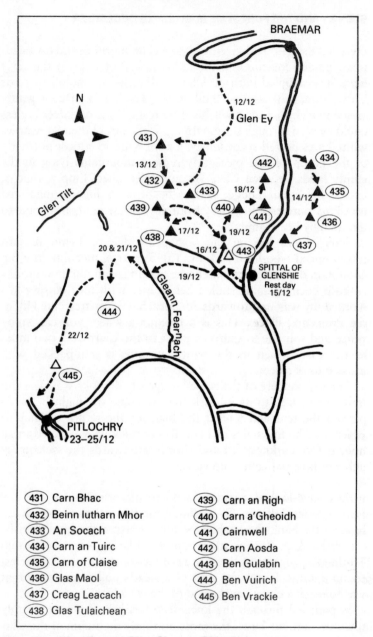

431 Carn Bhac
432 Beinn Iutharn Mhor
433 An Socach
434 Carn an Tuirc
435 Carn of Claise
436 Glas Maol
437 Creag Leacach
438 Glas Tulaichean
439 Carn an Righ
440 Carn a'Gheoidh
441 Cairnwell
442 Carn Aosda
443 Ben Gulabin
444 Ben Vuirich
445 Ben Vrackie

Map 40   Glen Ey and Glen Shee to Pitlochry

tainous wave filling the view to the east. It was a wet blowy morning as I left the misty glen below and, head-down against the wind, pushed on for this 'Hill of the Boar.' The wind buffeted me as the gentle slopes of Cairn of Claise, 'the Hill of the Hollow', came into sight. She is the second highest of the group that fill the Caenlochan Forest, the name given to the massive plateau that stretches east to join The Mount. Given a good weekend the ambitious Munroist can polish off fourteen Munros between here and Glen Muick.

The mist cleared to reveal cars hurrying over the ancient pass below. A few years ago over 2,000 skiers got trapped at the car park at the foot of Cairnwell. Deadly blizzards had blocked retreats down the glen, and they huddled into the café and any outhouses they could find, while helicopters evacuated those most in need of assistance. The pass was blocked for days, the scene reminiscent of a disaster movie, with abandoned cars and buses everywhere.

The remnant of an old fence led on to the highest summit, Glas Maol. An abandoned sweater lay frozen to the cairn. The ridge narrowed as it led on towards Creag Leacach, the most southerly and smallest of the four Munros. A gale-force wind roared over the ridge, forcing me several times against the stone wall that acts as a spine along its length. Suddenly I had a brainwave — get on the other side of the wall! More comfortable now in the lee of the wind, it wasn't long before the summit cairn was reached.

The wind made me feel like an unequipped hang-glider as I drifted down to the A93, trying to sing 'Rafferty's Motor Car,' as darkness fell on the mountains around. A long four-mile walk led back to the bicycle through the Cairnwell pass, before turning 180 degrees and retracing my steps through the pass to wheel into the car park of the Spittal of Glenshee Hotel. Here the dream of a hot bath and a warming dram in front of a roaring log fire became a reality.

The support team arrived in the morning and, although we were soon deeply involved in the work of replanning the next stage up to Christmas, among us was a real sense of excitement. I really believed now that the walk stood a good chance of being success-fully completed. As the hotel owners didn't allow dogs in the hotel, a miserable Munro was left in the car until we sneaked him in at night through a fire escape door.

Graham Moss arrived next day, kindly volunteering to keep me company for the last few days leading up to Christmas. We walked west into Glen Taitneach, meaning 'the Happy or Pleasant Glen.' We had planned to camp but were delighted to find a derelict shed. The door was warped and stiff to open, but after much shoving the door screeched ajar like the entrance to a Pharaoh's tomb, and we surveyed our new home. It had a rusty bed, a ricketty table, a chair and an oil drum to sit on, with a gaping hole in the floor. What more could a body ask for? In the evening we visited the friendly Dalmunzie Hotel across the glen. Elizabeth, the owner, explained that the hut was named after a shepherd called Heb, who lived there for many years.

After a good warm breakfast we were away at first light with the cloud hugging the glens. An easy pull led us on to the sprawling mass of Glas Tulaichean. This pointed peak is my favourite of this gang of five whose peaceful slumber had been disturbed by my assault from Glen Ey a few days earlier. She boasts some fine corries, and is easiest climbed from Glen Lochsie, reached from Glen Shee by a derelict miniature railway track, a relic of Victorian prosperity. A layer of mist lay inches above the summit but we found that by lying down on the ground, we could just get a view.

Springy turf led down to the lonely watershed by Loch nan Eun, meaning 'the Loch of the Birds'. We chased after an orange survival bag that looked as if it had been blowing around for several winters, and buried it deep. A herd of deer resembling an Indian war party watched us suspiciously from above as we climbed on to Carn an Righ, 'the Hill of The King'. Sitting out from the main group, this grassy rounded Munro is probably named after King James VI who hunted there. To the west lie the largely empty lands of Atholl, stretching for almost thirty miles to the nearest public road. It was in this wild and often inhospitable place that most of my unclimbed peaks were situated. With winter fast approaching I hoped the weather would be kind.

Darkness fell just as we reached the track leading back into Glen Taitneach, ending a well-planned day which made up for the less successful ones.

It had been bitterly cold overnight and the boots had joined us in our sleeping bags. We were away early with headtorches guiding us along the track. Towering out of the bleak dawn was the pointed peak of Carn Bhinnein, known locally as 'the Witch's Tooth.' It didn't count as one of the walk's summits, although it gave us a pleasant approach to Carn a'Gheoidh, 975 metres, meaning 'Hill of the Goats'. Graham jumped for joy at the feel of crisp snow underfoot. His love of mountains is an inspiration, and there is hardly a weekend when he is not on the hills.

Some ptarmigan jumped from our feet as we worked our way east. Suddenly the ground felt very flat. Then came the realisation that we were standing on top of a frozen lochan.

Thoughts of the wilderness at our back soon receded when we arrived at the Cairnwell, 933 metres. A broad track led up to what is probably Scotland's most visited summit, with the chair-lift ending a few feet away. It seems such a pity that the interests of skiing clash so much with the conservation of the wilderness. The sight of creaking machinery, and endless lines across the glen seemed reminiscent of a First World War battlefield. To us it was a depressing sight.

We pendulumed over to Carn Aosda, 917 metres, before descending to the top of the pass. In 1644 a raiding group of Campbells were attacked here and defeated by the Farquharsons. A five-mile walk took us down the glen to the bar at the Spittal of Glenshee Hotel. There were several Australian and New Zealand girls working in the bar, brought in for the forthcoming busy ski season. All our Highland charm would not convince a single one to come back and have dinner at our luxury cottage. So we gave them a couple of songs and worked our way to base for the last time.

A hard frost overnight had left the glen glistening white. Today's climb couldn't have been any handier. It was right behind the hut, Ben Gulabin, 806 metres, meaning 'Hill of the Beak', is a fine wee mountain, seen at its best from the Spittal of Glenshee, where her short green grass rises like a garden lawn to mix with broken crags and heather. A modern bridge has dispensed with the services of this hamlet's humpback bridge, depriving the locals of some of their best entertainment. Every holiday weekend cars would tentatively approach the rise of the bridge, where once they could see daylight over its crest they would accelerate, unaware that the motorist on the opposite side had the same idea. The result was a short sharp bump, usually ending in a broken light or dented wing. One local lass we met had witnessed fifteen bumps in one afternoon.

We found some boulders and little crags to play on until pulling on to the summit, which was as flat as a billiard table. Graham's camera was soon clicking at the scene of the sunlight unrolling like a carpet over Glen Shee. No wonder it is called the Glen of Fairies, with its enchanting woodland and standing stones. It was at Clach na Coileach that a cockerel is supposed to have crowed in victory after the local MacThomas clansmen defeated a group from Atholl.

GLEN SHEE TO PITLOCHRY, 19–25 DECEMBER

After a brew-up we said farewell to the hut. Graham was later to send an inquiry to a well-known double glazing company. I wonder if the representative came to call! We worked our way west into Glen Lochsie. A thick mist had suddenly fallen, making navigation difficult as we picked our way through a new forestry plantation to climb over the shoulder of Meall a'Choire Bhuidhe. This mountain is the highest point of the ten-mile ridge stretching along the western end of glens Lochsie and Shee. However, the short dip that joins the ridge to mighty Glas Tulaichean is not enough to make her a Corbett; she is well worth climbing, nevertheless.

Darkness was falling as we climbed down to Glean Fearnach. Graham stopped for a drink at a burn and let out a horrified yell — a snow-covered stag lay dead in the water. We could only drag the poor beast out. It was bitterly cold as we waded across the Allt Fearnach. Only after reaching the other bank did we see the bridge! Tired legs pulled us up the glen which pierces into the wilds of Atholl.

Today, 20 December, was the first day of winter, and the old witch celebrated her arrival by raking the glen with a blitzkrieg of gales and torrential rain. We were based halfway up the northern slopes of Ben Vuirich, 903 metres, meaning 'the Hill of the

Roaring.' At 2.00 p.m. we grabbed a brief gap in the storm and raced up her slopes. Three-quarters of an hour later found us on her stormy top. It is a shame to have to rush any mountain, and in particular this shapely remote peak rising out of the ancient lands of Atholl. The summit would normally give a fine viewpoint of the Glas Tulaichean 'Gang of Five' and the Atholl peaks.

We disturbed a large herd of miserable cold deer who un-enthusiastically glided off into the mist like ghostly horsemen. Water seemed to stream from everywhere — reminding me of summer as the white burns flowed down the sides of Glen Loch! The loch in the glen was, I suspect, named on the day after Hogmanay or by an Atholl clansman with a stutter, for it is called simply Loch Loch. Soon the stove was hissing happily and a warming brew brought life back to our freezing limbs.

The morning forecast was warning people to keep off the hills, as temperatures of minus 25 and wintry conditions had been reported. Certainly it was out of the question for us to attempt anything other than collecting water from the burn. Even that took some effort in the Arctic gale-force winds, which left us in no doubt what was happening on the summit of Beinn A'Ghlo, 'the Hill of the Mist'. Her three summits were the precious jewel I desperately wanted to climb before Christmas.

It was not to be; in the early hours of the following morning the weather forecast was still abysmal. So we abandoned our base camp and, with headtorches illuminating the track ahead, wove our way south-west on the track leading to Shinagag. Little did I know then that this 'Hill of the Mist' we had abandoned was to be such a thorn in my side in the bitter winter weather to come, delaying my walk for almost a week.

A kestrel swept the ground ahead as we climbed up the thick heather on to the bumpy ridge of knolls leading to Ben Vrackie, 841 metres, 'the Speckled Hill' merely glimpsed by drivers hurtling along the A9 at breakneck speed. Graham's obsession for rock-climbing had us scrambling up an easy crag *en route*. We got some funny looks from the Sunday trippers on the summit dressed in pack-a-macs and welly boots, as we arrived with our massive packs bristling with ice axes and crampons. When we explained to one tourist wearing a beanie hat that we had been in the hills to the north for a few days; he seemed unimpressed.

Our map ended among the woodland just above the holiday town of Pitlochry, but a well-marked tourist track led us down to the 'big city'. After checking in at the hostel, we got our Christmas celebrations off to the best possible start by visiting a *ceilidh* in a local bar.

Graham went home next day and Tom and Doreen arrived, complete with bicycle retrieved from Glen Shee. I was less than a day's cycle ride from my home, but we decided to spend Christmas in Pitlochry and not disturb the rhythm of the journey. The friendly Pine Trees Hotel gave us a relaxing couple of days. Munro made friends with the hotel's two collies and taught them new tricks like digging up the lawn. I feel the owners were probably quite glad to see us depart.

ARCTIC DALWHINNIE, 26–30 DECEMBER

Boxing Day saw me cycling north once more. A large number of guests waved goodbye from the hotel entrance, making me feel as if I were going off to conquer the North Pole. Twenty-eight miles later the little village of Dalwhinnie came into sight. She seemed like an oasis after the bleak moorland of the Drumochter Pass. There was a transport café which was closed, two hotels — both closed — and a bed-and-breakfast — closed. I was obviously going to have a hectic night life during my short stay.

A small wood was the most sheltered place available to camp as a cutting wind blew snowflakes horizontally between the trees. At last the tent was pitched and I could crawl inside my sleeping bag. But I had forgotten the most precious thing a lightweight camper needs — water. I put my boots on again and broke the ice in a nearby burn, fingers sticking to my metal billy-can. However, a piping hot meal and an endless supply of tea kept me warm as I studied the map like a general planning a campaign.

In the morning the water bottle had frozen solid, so another trip was made to the burn; everything from the trees to the tent was frosty white.

Two pairs of gloves kept my hands warm as the bike jerked into life and clanked its way south towards the Drumochter Pass. Above the road lies a huge plateau which is tame and gentle

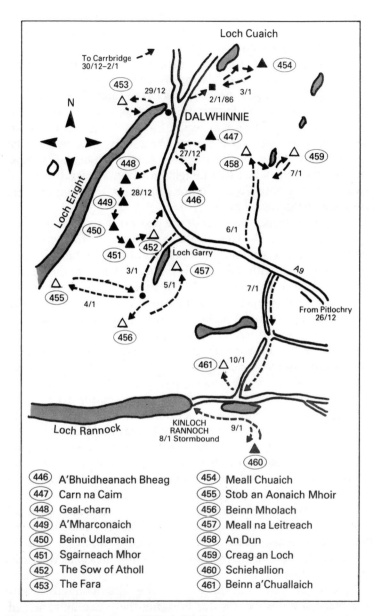

Loch Cuaich

To Carrbridge
30/12–2/1

(454) Meall Chuaich

(453) The Fara
29/12
2/1/86
3/1

N

DALWHINNIE

(447) Carn na Caim

27/12

(458) An Dun
(459) Creag an Loch
7/1

Loch Ericht

(448) Geal-charn
28/12

(446) A'Bhuidheanach Bheag

(449) A'Mharconaich

(450) Beinn Udlamain

6/1

(451) Sgairneach Mhor
(452) The Sow of Atholl

Loch Garry

3/1
(457) Meall na Leitreach

A9

(455) Stob an Aonaich Mhoir
4/1
5/1
7/1

From Pitlochry
26/12

(456) Beinn Mholach

(461) Beinn a'Chuallaich
10/1

Loch Rannock

KINLOCH
RANNOCH
8/1 Stormbound
9/1

(460) Schiehallion

(446)	A'Bhuidheanach Bheag	(454)	Meall Chuaich
(447)	Carn na Caim	(455)	Stob an Aonaich Mhoir
(448)	Geal-charn	(456)	Beinn Mholach
(449)	A'Mharconaich	(457)	Meall na Leitreach
(450)	Beinn Udlamain	(458)	An Dun
(451)	Sgairneach Mhor	(459)	Creag an Loch
(452)	The Sow of Atholl	(460)	Schiehallion
(453)	The Fara	(461)	Beinn a'Chuallaich

Map 41   Dalwhinnie to Kinloch Rannoch

above the A9, but to the east it falls steeply in a mass of corries and avalanche-prone slopes that every winter threaten to block the narrow Gaick Pass.

It seemed a shame to spoil the fresh snow with my tracks as I pulled up on to this misty plateau which lies in the very centre of Scotland. The compass-bearing was taken carefully — this is no place to get lost! The mist started to clear once the summit of A'Bhuidheanach Bheag was reached and I was treated to a fine view down a frozen Loch Garry. These hills come in for a fair amount of criticism as being boring heathery lumps, but in my opinion the critics just lack imagination. An approach from the east via the remote Cama Choire will give an exciting day, and they are perfect for skiing.

A boundary fence led most of the way north to Carn na Caim, meaning 'Cairn of the Curve'. She is the higher of the two hills at 941 metres. The chilling afternoon wind had brought in more snow and it was with relief that I climbed down from the freezing summit towards the roadside. My heart was in my mouth when I saw dozens of footprints around where I had hidden the bike. With it being so cold I hadn't dared to padlock it for the lock would be bound to freeze. I needn't have worried: the bike was still there and it was soon being put to good use bombing back to the tent for a warm meal.

Cold weather plays havoc with my feet, causing nasty hacks sometimes inches long. I wore several pairs of dry socks at night to keep them warm. In the morning the sleeping bag was coated with ice and the billy-cans, filled with water the night before, had mushroomed into mini icebergs. The propane-mixture stove got them melted down and I was soon digging into a breakfast of hot bran, muesli, tea and compo biscuits.

I brushed the snow off my poor frozen bike and we again followed the A9 south towards Drumochter. The same route was followed by Prince Charlie as he marched south to rout the Redcoats at Prestonpans; fortunately for him the roads were a lot quieter in those days!

It was still dark with the stars shining like diamonds against the black sky, a shooting star breaking the peace by racing off on its destructive course. The beam of my torch bounced along the track leading into Coire Fhar at the northern end of the

Dalnaspidal Deer Forest. The four Munros and one Corbett in this group give a fantastic circular walk, justifiably popular with the new A9 making the mountains a couple of short hours away from the central belt of Scotland.

Geal-charn was a very white hill, as I passed the large boulders near the summit that give the appearance of human beings when seen from the glen. Giant Loch Ericht spread out to the south-west like a fiord as I followed the bouldery ridge that climbed on to a now misty A'Mharconaich, 975 metres, meaning 'the Horse Place.' There are two summit cairns, the most easterly being the higher.

A handy fence led up and over Beinn Udlamain, 'the Gloomy Mountain', which is the highest Munro of the group. Time was running short to climb the two remaining mountains. After floundering through waist-deep snow in Sgairneach Mhor's boggy peat-hagged col, I literally ran up her slopes, sprinting for twenty yards then slowing to walking pace, then sprinting again.

Bad weather was coming in from the north, as I tapped the frozen trig point that marked the top of Sgairneach Mhor, 991 metres, meaning 'the Big Stony Hill.' Any stones today, however, were well buried under the snow. The wind was howling around her Coire Creagach, sending spindrift towers spiralling above the mountain and stinging my face. The ridge slipped off to the east and would slide unremarkably to Drumochter, except that nature had other ideas and produced the large knoll known as the Sow of Atholl, 803 metres. The summit cairn of this Corbett gave a superb view of the pass. It was on her slopes that Middelton's tiny ragged army, supporters of Charles II, was ambushed and defeated by General Morgan and his government troops. Was it my imagination that I heard the clink of a sword and a pistol shot? Was the wind playing tricks or were those really the ghostly cries of the clansmen calling through the storm?

Darkness was falling as I climbed down, crossing a frozen Allt Dubhaig. It was a four-mile walk back to the bicycle after a long day, but I was so happy with five more summits under my belt that I sang every song I could think of. Then I walked a mile past where the bike was hidden and had to turn back and retrieve it!

Things were livening up in downtown Dalwhinnie — I found the pub was open. Inside I met an English father and son spending their holidays touring in a caravanette. The youngster had great hopes of getting snowed in somewhere and returning to school about the middle of May! It was another bitterly cold night as I made my way back to the tent.

My last peak of the year was to be The Fara, fifth highest of Scotland's Corbetts. Dawn was breaking as I crossed the dam over a frozen Loch Ericht, the ice creaking eerily in the grim light of day. The Fara sits handily close to Dalwhinnie railway station and can be easily climbed between trains, but she deserves better than that, for she has one of Scotland's finest viewpoints — one few tourists ever see.

A compass-bearing from the side of the wood took me straight to the summit. The snow was sparkling in the bright sunshine. I had heard the peak was a fine viewpoint but nothing could have prepared me for the magnificent panorama displayed before me. The peaks of Ben Alder and Aonach Beag looked so near I could almost touch them, and down Loch Ericht shone the mountains of the Black Mount. North of The Fara lies an empty quarter, seldom visited except to see the remarkable Dirc Mhor, meaning 'Large Dagger', which is a dramatic ravine hemmed in by crags. It shouldn't be missed when climbing this very special mountain.

The frozen tent was packed away to be dried out later as I cycled north to meet the support team at Carrbridge, thirty-seven miles away. The miles sped by as I rejoiced in the knowledge that only 45 mountains now remained unclimbed. It was great to have a couple of days' break with my friends. Hogmanay was a wild occasion as always, with singing and dancing into the wee sma' hours. I would be glad to get back to the hills for a rest.

CHAPTER 11

January 1986

LOCH CUAICH AND LOCH GARRY 2–5 JANUARY 1986

It was cold and snowing lightly as I cycled south towards Dalwhinnie, the thirty-odd miles passing slowly against an icy headwind. I left the main road to cycle up the snow-covered Land Rover track skirting the side of the aquaduct leading to Loch Cuaich. A chilling mist reduced visibility to a few feet.

It was a great pleasure to meet up with Alan and Dave who were staying in the glen. The company of these two cheery walkers was to be a fine tonic for the many lonely days and nights that lay ahead.

The frozen loch creaked and groaned as the ice strained for more room. Dave led the way through the deep snow leading up to Meall Chuaich. The name of this remote Munro means 'Hill of the Quaich', owing to its drinking-bowl shape. She sits in the empty quarter of the Gaick Forest, home to one of Scotland's most dramatic passes, which has a real Khyber feel to it. The pass is renowned for its avalanches, as the snow blown across the plateau builds up on the edge of the steep slopes overlooking this canyon. Deer often upset the delicate balance and are killed by a snow slide, victims of winter's most formidable traits. In the winter of 1800 a Captain Macpherson and four men, staying in a hut near the Gaick Lodge, were all killed by an avalanche.

We were hoping to get a view down Glen Tromie, another interesting approach to the mountain. But mist clung to the summit like candyfloss around a stick. With my ice axe I carved a big 44 on the snowy pyramid of a cairn and had lunch with Alan and Dave while we waited for the mist to clear. It didn't — probably hasn't yet! My companions were working their way east to admire the Gaick Pass, while I retrieved my snowy bike and cycled back down the track and through the Drumochter Pass.

At Dalnaspidal Lodge I met John and Mary Kennedy, who kindly let me use their phone, and with true Highland hospitality gave me sandwiches and a dram as well. Indeed, with their generosity and absorbing conversation, it was dark by the time I left. The Land Rover track leading along the north shore of Loch Garry was thick with snow. The loch looked well frozen, but as it creaked and groaned eerily through the darkness I wasn't going to risk cycling on it with my heavy load. The track ended like a broken drainpipe. Compass and torch led me through the snowy moorland to the bridge across the Allt Shallainn.

It was now bitterly cold and, even with gloves on, my fingers stuck to the billy-can while collecting water from a snow-filled burn.

The blackness of early morning was slowly eclipsed as a grey light ebbed over the moorland. We were now in the heart of the empty lands of the Craiganour Forest. Near by lay three remote Corbetts. My body tingled with excitement at the thought of exploring a new quarter of Scotland's wilds.

The Allt Shallainn twisted its way west towards the most isolated peak, Stob an Aonaich Mhoir, 855 metres. It seemed strange to come out of the wilderness and find a tarmac road leading from Loch Rannoch to lonely Coire Bhachdaidh Lodge on the shores of Loch Ericht. Probably the easiest way to tackle this out-of-the-way mountain is up this road by bicycle, or from Loch Ericht by canoe. There are many hills that can be enjoyably reached by kayak, adding to the pioneering spirit.

A steady pull led up to this 'Peak of the Big Ridge'. This mountain has a dual personality. Her eastern slopes, easy and gentle, cross over her four-mile-long ridge, then plummet into Loch Ericht. I stood by the cairn: surely I was the mountain's firstfoot of the year! Across the loch lay a snowy Beinn Bheoil with her wild eagles' corrie. Beyond the peaceful seclusion of wooded Ben Alder Bay lay the Rannoch hills, climbed in June, and the Mamores and Grey Corries, climbed in September. I had the feeling the walk had turned full circle, or almost so, with only 43 out of the original 499 mountains left to climb.

The stormclouds I had been anxiously watching all morning came over, covering the mountains in a new layer of white, as I worked my way back through the moorland of the Talla Bheith Forest. It was through these lands that a large force of Mac-Dougalls and Comyns came, intent to stamp out the Robertsons, allies of Robert the Bruce. After having spied on the enemy camp as a pedlar, the Robertson chieftain led his clansmen into battle, trapping their foes in some bogland near the site of the present-day Loch Ericht dam.

A herd of deer looked surprised to see a human at this time of year and tried to race off, but the thick snow slowed their progress to a sluggish jog. It was like watching a movie in slow motion as their ponderous plodding led them up the hillside. The icy winds brought a fierce storm that raked the moorland just as the tent was reached. As the snowstorm roared outside, I was glad of the firewood I had cut that morning.

Next morning my boots were warm, having come into the sleeping bag with me the night before. It was a beautiful morning. Although still dark, a glowing red blanket was creeping across the sky. With the prospect of a fine winter's day I hurriedly took off up the snowy slopes of Creag nan Gabhar as the first rays of sunshine reflected on the new snow. Ahead lay Beinn Mholach, 'the Rough Stormy Mountain', who seemed to be in an amicable mood. Her remoteness, combined with perfect weather conditions, were to make this hill one of the finest and most memorable of the walk. A sea of thick snow led up to her fort-like peak which had a huge summit cairn. Mist was low in the glens, covering all the great straths and through routes for miles around. It was like standing on an island looking out on an ocean of mist. To the south, as the summit of Schiehallion emerged like a giant shark's fin, my camera worked overtime. Like many Corbetts this mountain has a superb viewpoint, which on a clear day gives an exhilarating view towards all points of the compass.

The easiest approach to Beinn Mholach is without doubt from Loch Rannoch, where two Land Rover tracks snake towards her lower slopes. The best weather of the day was over as I crossed the moorland to the north-east and started up the broad-sloped hill of Meall na Leitreach, 775 metres. A chilling wind spat snow and mist across the mountain as I raced to reach the summit. She is probably most often climbed from Dalnaspidal, close to the A9. But today's climb fitted in nicely with Beinn Mholach and gave a bird's-eye view of Loch Garry as a bonus. It was on the shores of the loch that a small party of Macphersons clashed with a strong force of MacColls from far off Argyll. After a fierce battle the raiding MacColls were forced to flee, leaving their leader and most of their men slain behind them.

Meall na Leitreach is shaped like a loose-leaf binder: her steep slopes climb from the loch, then fall easily to the east across the empty moorland stretching to Glen Garry, disturbed only by the choppy waters of lonesome Lochs Con and Errochty. Three mountains of an unfrequented part of the Highlands had been climbed. Tomorrow would take me further east, towards the narrow Gaick Pass: an exciting thought as I returned to base, looking forward to the prospect of a warming brew.

THE GAICK PASS AND KINLOCH RANNOCH, 6–11 JANUARY

It had snowed again overnight, and I had difficulty finding the bike which had been abandoned on the side of Loch Garry two nights earlier. At last I spied a handlebar sticking out of the snow and pulled my bike free. Poor thing, I bet it wished it had belonged to a paper-boy. Its thin tyres made heavy weather of the deep snow as we floundered our way along the Land Rover track, sinking into one drift after another. Periodically the wheels would slip on ice sending me flying, only to land gently in the snow. What a mad game this is, but would we have it any other way!

Mary Kennedy again welcomed me to her house with a warming cup of tea, while I phoned Tom to check in. We later sent her a copy of our fund-raising tape, 'The Hills and Glens so Peaceful', as a small token of thanks for her family's kind hospitality.

It seemed strange to be cycling along the busy A9 after the morning's experiences. In the woodland behind Dalnacardoch Lodge the bike was hidden and gear changed over from panniers to rucksack once more. A couple of cross-country skiers whizzed past, their skies making light work of the deep snow. I followed their tracks leading north towards the Gaick Pass. A lonesome cairn lay by the roadside, perhaps in memory of one Highland laddie who left to fight for the cause of the Robertson clan, never to return.

It was now bitterly cold and my right foot began to hurt, though I couldn't understand why. I increased speed as darkness started to fall; ahead, rising like an oasis out of the Arctic, was the woodland surrounding Sronphadruig Lodge. The lodge was deserted. I tried to imagine the rush and hustle during the stalking season with the estate's garron ponies waiting patiently for the tweed-dressed sportsmen to take one last shot at a steel target of a deer before heading to the hills. Meanwhile the housekeeper would breathe a sigh of relief, clear the breakfast away and start to prepare enough food to satisfy mammoth appetites when the shooting party returned.

But this winter's evening the lodge was in mothballs. Snow covered the doorstep and windows. The only sound was the creaking door of an outhouse hanging off its hinges, moving back and forward in the Arctic wind. At least I could camp in the lee of the wind. The pain in my foot was becoming unbearable as I hurriedly collected some water from a frozen burn. Lying on my sleeping bag I tried to take my right boot off. It was jammed solid. At last I prised it off. My socks had frozen to the inside of the boot. Would frostbite now end my journey ... was I now paying the price for lack of experience? I rubbed and rubbed my foot till at last the warmth painfully returned, but it throbbed for ages. However, after three mugs of piping hot tea it did settle down.

Two Corbetts lay on either side of the pass, rough and steep and delightfully remote. With dawn breaking I pulled up the southern slopes of An Dun, anxiously watching for cracks of snow or snowballs rolling down — tell-tale sign of an avalanche-prone slope, for which this area is infamous. There are few happy stories regarding avalanches, but one in this area crashed down the mountain, killing several hares, deer and grouse, till finally delivering them to the doorstep of a starving family.

An Dun means 'the Fort'. If the mountain had been located in more populous parts it surely would have been an incredible hill fortress. As it is, her precipitous slopes are an exciting relief from the rather monotonous plateau stretching west to Drumochter Pass. A herd of deer crossed into the narrow Cama Choire, 'the Crooked Corrie'. It's a place typical of the Gaick, full of surprises and a fine sight in wet weather when her many waterfalls come to life. Leaving the misty summit I descended to the lodge, stopping to admire the pattern made by the broken ice on Loch an Duin below.

Across the glen lay Creag an Loch, 876 metres, 'the Cliff of the Loch'. It is her crags that add drama to the pass as the footpath squeezes between the two mountains. The weather was turning foul as I pushed on to her table-top summit. Frozen snow clattered across the top, and my legs were hidden in a moving fog of spindrift. There were two summit cairns, and it took some effort to visit both, as the arctic wind froze my jacket and beard.

Back at the lodge, my kit now packed, I brewed up before turning my back on the bonnie Gaick, the hidden jewel of the Atholl moors.

It was a happy walker who made his way back down to Dalnacardoch Lodge. The objective was to reach Kinloch Rannoch. There were two routes, one by a good road, for almost thirty miles, or the other, opposite the lodge, by the minor road, which was only nine. I chose the latter and cycled over this snowy toboggan run, originally built on one of General Wade's military roads. The bike slithered on the deep snow. The sight of a Land Rover struggling ahead was scarcely encouraging. The bike began to gather speed as it descended to Trinafour. The brakes were full on, but had no effect on the wheels' icy rims. As the bike hurtled downhill, a wheel slipped from under me. A good kick with my foot luckily corrected the bike's position. Then a hairpin bend came zooming up. Boots were dragged along the road in an effort to try anything to slow the bike's pace. Then, leaning hard over, we screeched round the corner. I don't know to this day how the bike didn't crash, or maybe somebody was looking after me that night.

At Trinafour I joined the B847 leading to Kinloch Rannoch. It had been snow-ploughed so I could relax. Suddenly ahead appeared a huge plot of rutted ice that jerked the bike violently. It bumped on to another patch, skidded, then regained its balance. The cycling was proving to be more dangerous than the mountains! It was a relief to cycle into Kinloch Rannoch for the second time on the journey, and slip into a piping-hot bath.

In the morning the bike crawled out of town but gale-force winds slowed it to a standstill. Snow stung my eyes and an animal feed pack took off like a rocket down the glen. My plans to climb Schiehallion had to be abandoned. I couldn't even reach her lower slopes.

The following day I woke to another foul morning, the strong winds sending snow showers filtering through the streets. As I cycled out of town her buildings disappeared in a white blur behind me. The bike struggled in the fresh snow as I pedalled and pushed the contraption towards the Braes of Foss, the easiest approach to Perthshire's most shapely Munro, Schiehallion. This 'Fairy Hill of the Caledonians' is a beautiful mountain whose cone-like summit is visible like a beacon from most Perthshire peaks. There was no sign of any views today as thick mist reduced visibility to a few feet. I followed the direction of the footpath which was buried under the snow.

Schiehallion has played a large part in helping scientists to understand more about the earth's mass. A surveyor is believed to have originated the idea of map contours while working on the mountain. A huge cross marked the summit, perhaps the work of nearby Rannoch School, a unique boarding school with its own fire brigade and mountain rescue team.

In days of old the woods of Rannoch were a fine hiding place for wanted men. Many of the outlawed MacGregor clan settled here and continued warring with their enemies. If pressed, they would retreat to their stronghold on Loch Rannoch, reached by a narrow causeway from the shore. Their enemies naturally presumed that this would be at the shortest point between the shore and the island on the north side of the loch. This was not the case, as it took a much longer indirect route from near Finnart Lodge on the southern shore, a distance of almost half a mile.

Returning along the ridge I met a cheery group of students who were staying at Pitlochry. Their leader had climbed Schiehallion before and was busy explaining what the mountain and the view would look like if the mist cleared. Optimism is an essential part of a hillwalker's personality. He added that under certain conditions on the mountain a figure would cast a double shadow. Local legend was that this was a fairy accompanying walkers on the mountain. His friends looked unimpressed.

Down in the glen I apologised to my bike for leaving her in a snowdrift all day. On reflection, speaking to bicycles was not a good sign. Maybe it was just as well there were only 38 summits to go!

The heavy overnight rain had left the once snowy hills streaked like a zebra. The mountain's burns had erupted into their familiar white torrents, filling Dunalastair Water to the brim. Above the loch rose a long ridge leading up to Beinn a'Chuallaich, the massive Corbett sprawling between Dunalastair and Loch

Errochty. It was refreshing to see farmland around her southern slopes, although this area has been populated since the earliest of times, as the numerous hill forts or duns bear testament. One is hidden where I had left the bike in the woodland, near Drumchastle Farm. An even stranger form of habitation in the shape of MacGregors' Cave lay across the water. Here was home to some of the poor outlawed heroes of Clan Gregor. Ousted from their ancient lands by Campbell-enforced legislation, they became a landless clan. Only their grim determination and field-craft kept them alive – that and the burning desire to take revenge on their enemies.

> Glen Orchy's proud mountains, Coalchuirn and her towers
> Glenstrae and Glen Lyon no longer are ours
> We're landless, landless, landless, Grigalach!
> But doomed and devoted by vassal and Lord,
> MacGregor has still both his heart and his sword.
> Then courage, courage, courage, Grigalach.

Sir Walter Scott

A strong gale-force wind ripped over the mountain, but by keeping in the lee of her well-defined southern ridge, I avoided most of the blast. Only deer were grazing on the mountain's eastern Fea Corrie. Here gathered the warriors of Clan Robert-son, answering the call of the fiery cross sent round their lands. With broadswords raised, the corrie would echo to the sound of their battle cries before they marched off to fight at Bannockburn for Robert the Bruce, and on countless other times during Scotland's turbulent history.

The wind's blasts forced me on to all fours to reach the summit, where I caught my breath in the lee of the cairn. To the north lay a stormy Loch Errochty, centre-piece of the empty moorland stretching towards the A9. The many ruined shielings there are memorials to the happier days when people lived and worked this land, now forsaken to the deer and the grouse.

The wind blew me back down the hill and whizzing past Loch Tummel. I was whistling happily 'By Loch Tummel and Loch Rannoch and Lochaber I will go', even though I was travelling in the opposite direction, towards Pitlochry Youth Hostel.

It had been a cold night and the weather prophets of Radio Scotland were promising a wild day on the hills. Leaving the A9 at Garry Bridge the bike slipped on some black ice and — wallop! — I crashed to the ground.

The woodland and heather were sporting rich winter colours along the south shore of Loch Tummel, as squirrels made use of the snow-free weather to gather food for the long winter ahead. The Frenich burn was in a stormy mood as I followed her course into a cold misty world. Ahead lay two Corbetts, Meall Tairneachan and Farragon Hill, the two highest points of the Weem Deer Forest. These two mountains make a fine horseshoe route. They had proved to be a formidable barrier to the advancing Roman legions who had not only the ferocious Caledonian tribes to battle with, but the untracked wilderness as well.

A snowstorm had me working by compass, following the course of the burn to a junction, the launching pad for the next turn-off. This is a theory which works fine as long as the terrain agrees with the map and your treasured feature is not buried under snow. The snow flurry stopped for a minute and I spotted two stalkers in beautiful tweed camouflage, waving at me. They signalled they were going up Meall Tairneachan. I pointed to myself then Farragon Hill, a mile and a half further east, to which I got a thumbs-up approval.

Another snowstorm followed, bringing with it a snowy lace curtain that drew tight across the hillside. The poor stalkers would be lucky to see the ends of their gun barrels. Farragon Hill loomed ahead. Smaller of the two Corbetts, she is probably the more interesting, especially if approached over the rocky hillocks to the north. A wailing sound became louder and louder as I approached the summit, where the fury of winter roared down on me. It was a scary experience, crawling on all fours through the storm to the summit cairn.

There was no question, in this weather, of being able to keep to the broad ridge leading west to Meall Tairneachan. A more cunning plan was required. By backtracking to the junction in the burn I took a fresh bearing that led across the snowy moorland to this 'Hill of Thunder' near the summit. The snow was blinding and the roar of the wind made my ears ache, until at last I bumped into the frozen trig point.

It was a relief to backtrack down the mountain and reach

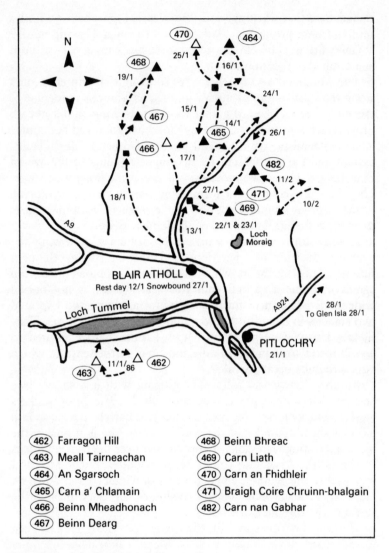

Map 42 Atholl and Loch Tummel

the roadside, ears still buzzing. It took a quarter of an hour to undo a frozen toggle.

The bike's lights lit up the road ahead, the tarmacadam sparkling — a sure sign of black ice. Several times the bike slipped from under me. The most spectacular fall was close to Pitlochry, where the bike collapsed under me and I raced ahead sliding on the rucksack, much to the bewilderment of a car coming in the other direction.

In the morning I cycled north to Blair Atholl and met the support team at the Tilt Hotel. What followed was the usual rush of a rest day as equipment was checked and repacked.

CAM YE BY ATHOLL? GLEN TILT AND THE RING OF TARF, 14–19 JANUARY

In the remote lands of Atholl lay nine mountains. Given the weather, they could all be climbed in three days, but being lucky with the weather was not the trend through this long journey. It had been very cold overnight and at daybreak violent snowstorms rushed down the glen, covering the windows in snow. Glen Tilt stretches for sixteen miles before merging with Glen Feshie in the 'Spaghetti Junction' of paths that meet at White Bridge in the Cairngorms. The glen had been an important through-route since Stone Age times. Yet in 1840 the Duke of Atholl tried to close the glen and verbally clashed with Professor Balfour and a party of botanists. The matter led to a court case which fortunately the Duke lost. The story is told in a famous poem, 'The Battle of Glen Tilt':

> Balfour had a mind as weel
> As ony Duke could hae, man,
> Quo he, There's ne'er a kilted chiel
> Shall drive us back this day, man.
> It's justice and it's public richt
> We'll pass Glen Tilt afore the nicht.
> For Dukes shall we, Care a'e bawbee?
> The road's as free, To you and me,
> As to his Grace himself, man.
>
> Sir Douglas MacLagan

North of Marble Lodge I took the long south-western ridge leading to Carn a'Chlamain, 963 metres, meaning 'The Hill of the Buzzard'. She was the first of six mountains known as the Ring of Tarf, surrounding the remotest area in Europe. They were to be quite a problem over the next few days.

I made a favourite crossing of this mountain one midsummer's night, arriving at the top in darkness, an inky dawn within half an hour allowing a torchless descent. What a difference from today's weather, as an Arctic gale raged across the ridge, sending a sea of spindrift swarming around my knees. With compass in hand I tried to fight around the tight bend that leads this meat-hook-shaped ridge to the summit. But it was impossible, as time after time I was knocked down by the wind. Even crawling was unsuccessful. A quarter of a mile from the summit I gave up and retreated north to a snow-covered bothy known humorously as the Tarf Hotel.

This 'howf' was a welcome refuge in a wild and inhospitable area — it has surely saved many lives. Unfortunately it is now under threat of demolition by Atholl estates as it is being used by walkers during the stalking season. When it was built, the bothy was fitted with central heating pipes and running water. Some comedian had brought along an AA hotel sign. The place was deserted. I was delighted to find a rickety bed to keep me off the frozen floor. It was early to bed, as the door creaked in the wind and snow plastered the windows.

> I sift the snow on the mountains below,
> And their great pines groan aghast;
> And all the night is 'tis my pillow white,
> While I sleep in the arms of the blast.

Percy Bysshe Shelley, 'The Cloud'

It had been the coldest night I had ever experienced — my sleeping bag was coated with ice. Teeth chattered as I put on the boots that had shared the bag with me. My Gore-Tex jacket, which had been hanging on a nail, was frozen solid like a piece of hardboard. It made horrible noises as it was forced into a wearable shape, before I ventured out into the blizzard raging outside.

Collecting water from the frozen burn only a few yards from

the door was an exciting experience, as the bothy disappeared in a white blur of snow. Any attempt at the hills today would be suicidal. It took me all my time to find the bothy again.

The day was spent shivering in my sleeping bag, writing a speech for a Rotary Lunch in Pitlochry in six days' time. I thanked my lucky stars there was a bothy here for I would have been in dire straits without it.

The storm had blown through overnight, leaving a snowdrift against the door. I wove my way east through the endless desert of snow-covered dunes for two miles to the east. Here lies a bridge across the Tarf Water, 'bridge' being a rather generous word for the two strands of wire between the two telegraph poles on either side of the river. To the north lie two of the remotest Munros in Scotland, An Sgarsoch and Carn an Fhidhleir.

I was looking forward to a view of the Cairngorms and snowy Glen Feshie from the summit of An Sgarsoch. But the deep soft snow slowed my progress. By the time the top was reached the scenery had disappeared under a mantle of mist. With the weather worsening I took a bearing to the col of her sister peak, Carn an Fhidhleir, 'the Hill of the Fiddler'. The storms of the last couple of days had taught me a healthy respect for this wild area. When a snowstorm came flurrying, backed by menacing clouds, I decided to head back to the bothy. I cursed myself for being a wimp but was later to be glad of my decision, for a blizzard beat me to the bothy door and raged for hours. The price of reaching that far-off peak might just have been too high.

I was now in the ridiculous situation of having climbed the more accessible of the two Munros. If the weather kept like this, Carn an Fhidhleir might as well be on the east coast of Greenland for all the chances I would have of reaching it. Tomorrow I would have to phone in to the support team so my route would lead me south, hopefully over Carn a' Chlamain — which had been in such a winter rage yesterday — and Beinn Mheadhonach, a Corbett. If so, it would be a great improvement on my pathetic attempts so far to conquer the mountains of wildest Atholl. For during the last two days I had been forced to retreat from the summit ridge of two mountains and managed to climb only one. Fourteen miles of walking for a summit less than three miles from the bothy!

A thick mist covered the glen, requiring a compass-bearing to be taken from the bothy door. The next time I was to see the cottage again was early one summer's morning with the sunlight beaming on the corrugated iron roof and deer grazing contentedly on the green grass: a little different from today's Ice Station Zebra.

As soon as I was a few feet from the door the building vanished, swallowed up in the fog. My route wound its way south towards Carn a'Chlamain, the mountain that had been so inhospitable two days earlier. Snowy hillocks appeared out of the mist like mammoth peaks. The burn was buried deep under the snow which meant I was struggling chest high to cross it. The compass-bearing didn't seem to make any sense at all as my route veered off across some steep ground. But patience paid off, for at last the cairn appeared inches from my face.

Sandwiched between this peak and Beinn Dearg in Glen Bruar is Beinn Mheadhonach. Probably never has a mountain been better named 'the Middle Hill'. The compass led me west to Gleann Mhairc with the view restricted to my red bootlaces. The glen forms a deep trench from Glen Tilt to the remote Loch Mhairc where only the keenest of fishermen would be found. The glen was flat and the peaceful waters no doubt flowed under the ice at my feet before charging down through its southern part, a deep gorge in contrast to this tamer higher level. There was not a sound except for snowflakes gently falling, as I pulled up on to Beinn Mheadonach's comb-like summit. This peak is the Corbetts' equivalent to Aonach Mor in Glen Nevis, whose flat crest of a summit hides the precipitous slopes on either side.

Sadly there was not enough time to push further west for Beinn Dearg, as the narrow ridge led down to a stone bridge over the bubbling Allt Mhairc, a sad relic of the Clearances. The path leading to Glen Tilt was frozen over and my feet slipped from under me. A quick jab with the ice axe prevented me taking a frozen bath in the burn below. The glens over the centuries had carved huge gorges leading to Glen Tilt. It must be a nightmare to descend this way in the dark.

A stalker with his pony was about half a mile in front, his shot cargo sadly dropping blood on the crisp white snow.

At Blair Atholl it was bliss to slip into a warm bath and have a good meal.

Simon Strachan and Ron Waddell arrived in the morning. It was good to have some company on the hill as we followed the fine track from Blair Atholl to Glen Bruar. The path was frozen and slippery, one concrete-covered bridge being like an ice rink. Allt Scheicheachan bothy was deserted. We gathered some firewood and settled down to cook a Burns Supper: whisky, haggis and more whisky. What more could a body ask for? It was a happy night with songs and jokes cracked into the small hours.

With dawn breaking we took to the slopes of Beinn Dearg, 1,008 metres. It was hard work ploughing through the deep snow. The red-tinged granite boulders that give this peak its name, 'Red Hill', were buried under winter's snowy carpet. Beinn Dearg is the highest Atholl peak west of Glen Tilt. Although many will climb her in a smash-and-grab raid up Glen Bruar, she is best appreciated as part of the fine circuit of the Ring of Tarf, taking in the four Munros, with two Corbetts added for a bonus.

The frustrating thing about this stage of the journey was that success or failure was dictated by the weather. In the foulest of summer weather progress can be made on the mountains, but when a blizzard reduces visibility to a few feet, venturing on the hills is only for the insane and over-insured. Today we were lucky. The mist cleared as we descended to the empty moorland towards Beinn Bhreac. Although lacking in drama this remote Corbett is enhanced by its position in the backwoods of Europe's most isolated wilderness. The conditions were perfect for cross-country skiing as we made our way up to this, the loneliest of Corbett summits, my 468th peak.

We made our way west to Glen Bruar down the side of the ravine of the Allt Beinn Losgarnaich. The path shown on the map was well buried under the snow and we inched around the nasty steep slopes, while the burns roared below. It should have been dark by now, but a full moon lit up the glen. No headtorches were required for the return walk to Blair Atholl. The miles whizzed by as the glen echoed to our voices singing 'Wha Wadna Fecht for Charlie', Simon giving support with an admirable imitation of the bagpipes he loves to play.

The most energetic part of an outing with Simon lies at the end of the day, when his ancient Cortina refuses to start and requires a helping hand. However, as if by magic, the engine chugged to

life. But problems had only just begun, for the road from Old
Blair had become an ice rink. Crampons were put on to push the
vehicle up the hill. Simon kindly offered to take my heavy gear in
the car and drop it off at Pitlochry Youth Hostel, while I followed
on the bike.

The moonlight danced on the snowy slopes of Creag Eallaich
overlooking the A9. In 1689 my ancestors stood on the hillside
with Bonnie Dundee and the other Jacobite clans. They waited
for General Mackay and his government troops to filter through
the Pass of Killiecrankie, outnumbering the Highlanders almost
two to one. When the order to charge came, the clansmen lost
600 men in the first few minutes, victims of the enemy's volley
fire. The troops' success was short-lived, for as they struggled to
fit the new-fangled bayonets issued to them, the clansmen were
among them wielding their great claymores, killing 2,000 in three
minutes. Mackay's army had been routed, but the Highlanders'
leader, Bonnie Dundee, had been mortally wounded, so the most
promising of all the rebellions fizzled out.

'THE DIEL'S AT KILLIECRANKIE—O': THE SECOND FIGHT FOR ATHOLL, 20-26 JANUARY

In the morning I met Alan Thomson, a freelance journalist from
Glencoe. He interviewed me for *The Scotsman* newspaper, the
first of several articles his magic pen was to write. His insistence
on referring to me as 'bachelor Craig' convinced the support team
he was trying to marry me off. Later he took dozens of photographs of this most unsightly male model, on and off the bike,
then on the slopes of Beinn Vrackie. There, among the rich
colours of the Pitlochry woodland, I sported the latest in colourful climbing jackets, which looked more at home on a ski slope
than a Scottish peak. Alan's camera clicked like a machine gun,
his encouraging words promising that the photos might appear in
the company's new brochure. However, they must have decided
my shaggy beard and woollen 'bunnet' weren't quite sophisti-
cated enough for the French *piste*. Alan's parting gift was some
tinned goodies which were to be an enjoyable treat in the cold
nights ahead.

Climbing the Inaccessible Pinnacle unroped would be a frightening experience, but not as much as the prospect of giving a speech to Pitlochry Rotary Club. I had been invited by the club's convener, Peter Malloch, who owns the town's camping shop. The club had its biggest attendance in months, and they seemed to enjoy my humorous talk. Or maybe it was the spectacle of this dishevelled 'cateran' addressing them with a speech written in the dark of a bothy under siege from Arctic blizzards outside. They probably had few speakers blowing emergency whistles and throwing bags of dehydrated food over their shoulders in the course of their talks. Tom had travelled up from Glasgow and Bill Roy made a welcome appearance from Edinburgh.

After meeting so many friendly people, it seemed strange to cycle back alone to Blair Atholl, and in the darkness follow the snowy road up Glen Tilt. The wilds of Atholl still had four unclimbed mountains, including Beinn a'Ghlo, the walk's jinx mountain.

I woke to a stormy morning with snow flying horizontally down the glen, reducing visibility to a few feet. There seemed no possibility of climbing any hills in these Arctic conditions. At 11.00 a.m. the storm started to recede. It was all the encouragement I needed, and I set off up the snowy slopes of Carn Liath, the most southerly of the three Munros that make up the Beinn a'Ghlo group.

Glen Tilt soon disappeared in a flurry of snow. The glen was once popular with royalty: the remains of wolf pits can be seen to this day near Forest Lodge. Mary, Queen of Scots, attended deer drives here. On one unhappy occasion, her favourite hound charged at a herd of deer before the beaters could get out of the way, resulting in two men being trampled to death.

A blizzard raged on Carn Liath's summit ridge as I crawled to the top. The biting snow stung my face. It was very frightening but at least there was a safe retreat to the west if required. I struggled for breath at the summit. It would be madness to try to reach the next Munro summit, so a retreat was made down her western slopes. The wind knocked me over several times, giving excellent ice-axe-breaking practice. The storm was worsening and I counted my blessings in managing to reach at least one summit that day.

If the weather was bad that day, it was even worse the next. It snowed heavily all day, ruining any hope of climbing any mountains. A ten-mile round trip was made to Blair Atholl to buy more supplies and to phone the support team to tell them that I would not be able to check in for three days. As usual my plans were at the mercy of the weather conditions. We had found new friends with the Aberdeen Met Office who gave us tremendous support in supplying accurate reports rather than the general information on their answering machine. Hugh Cumming advised that there should be an improvement by Saturday, two days away.

The sound of the wind roaring outside and the snow pelting against the tent was not encouraging. I rolled over in my sleeping bag and cooked breakfast. The hills were definitely out of the question, but perhaps I could make it to the Tarf Hotel bothy and be ideally poised to take full advantage of tomorrow's expected fine weather conditions.

The track up Glen Tilt was well buried with snow as it swung over the shoulder of Dun Mor. At this desolate spot I was ambushed by the full force of a winter blizzard as if, lying in wait, the old witch Cailleach had let rip her fury. Snow and ice clattered across the moorland like heavy cavalry as the wilds of Atholl erupted in a frenzy of Arctic madness.

Ahead lay a small lean-to stable, offering little shelter, though a smaller shed to the side looked more promising. I tried the door which was jammed with ice and snow. The ice axe cleared most of it away and it swung open. Inside were a couple of hay bales. There was just enough room to squeeze in safely from the tempest outside. With all my clothes on I snuggled into my sleeping bag to face a cold night as the snow forced its way through a gap in the roof, covering the bag in snow from time to time. After several brew-ups I felt snug in my warm bag as the little shed creaked in the Arctic winds.

The stove chugged into life, its fiery jets brightening the dark little shed as the tea simmered. I left a card thanking the estate for leaving the shelter unlocked, but ticking them off for the poor room service. It had been a night of Siberian harshness: boots and stove had joined me in the sleeping bag.

The deep flowing Tarf Water appeared frozen solid except for a black shadow down the centre. The daunting wire bridge across the river is a sort of initiation test. It consists of two simple strands of wire, one for your feet, the other for your hands. This one is well made, although others I have come across can be nightmares if the wires are slack. As a result of the sub-zero temperatures the strands had frozen white. Even with two pairs of gloves my hands were numb. To have fallen into the river in these conditions could have been fatal.

It was a relief to reach the other side where my poor hands painfully thawed out. Aberdeen Met Office seemed to have got their sums right, for over the horizon came a beautiful crimson dawn, the most welcoming red carpet imaginable. Being in Europe's remotest corner I expected to have the hills to myself, but was surprised to see two cross-country skiers leaving the Tarf bothy and crossing in front of my route, their magic slippers making short work of the hard snow. In the brilliant sunshine it was a pleasure to cross this snowy desert towards Carn an Fhidhleir, 'the Hill of the Fiddler'. What a difference in the weather from a few days earlier, when snowstorms had turned me back, only a mile from the summit of this remote Munro.

Even Sir Hugh Munro found these hills a handful on occasions. With his friend Walter Garland, they endured an overnight epic traversing neighbouring An Sgarsoch in terrible conditions, to limp into Braemar the next day. There was nothing 'soft' about these Victorian mountaineers. I wonder how today's brightly coloured 'Crag Rats' would cope, emulating some of their long days, dressed in baggy tweed breeches and tacketty boots. The world is fortunately full of characters: I have heard of one young climber who dresses exactly like a nineteenth-century mountaineer, right down to the last detail.

At last the summit cairn came into sight — the last Atholl peak west of Glen Tilt had been conquered. There was satisfaction in reaching my 470th peak, but the real pleasure was the view. To the north the Cairngorms rose like white giants, while all around stretched endless ranges of white-laced mountains from Lochaber to Schiehallion. This made up for the unbearable conditions of the last few days. Skiers, climbers and walkers everywhere would be smiling today.

The tell-tale tracks in the snow of a hunting wild cat could be seen in the morning. After a brew-up at the shed I shouldered my pack for the return journey down Glen Tilt. Opposite Dun Mor, I spied a fox, its red coat sticking out like a sore thumb against the white background of the hillside. I barked twice at it and it replied! I barked again. It yapped back but retreated up the slopes and yelped again. I waved my friend goodbye. How inadequate we are, needing our sleeping bag, stove and food to survive, while our cunning friend lives off the land, often sharing his den with badgers and other animals. I once witnessed a fox pretending to chase its tail in a playful manner, the way puppies do, but with every whirl it got slightly closer to the unsuspecting rabbits bemusedly watching him.

Down in Glen Tilt I was welcomed by members of the Corriemulzie club who had rented a bothy for the weekend. A fun evening was had among their pleasant company.

The glorious weather was short-lived. We woke to a grey threatening sky spitting snow down the glen. I was soon racing up the slopes of the Munro's biggest mouthful, Braigh Coire Chruinn-bhalgain. This was the middle mountain of the Beinn a'Ghlo trio. These popular mountains normally give a relatively easy day from Glen Fender. They seemed deserted today, as a biting wind and stinging snow welcomed me to the top of this unpronounceable mountain. Visibility was restricted to inches rather than feet in the sea of mist and snow. Only one more summit to climb — Carn nan Gabhar — and I could put a big line through the wilds of Atholl on my planning map.

The compass led me down towards the col but I could scarcely tell which way was up or down. The slopes seemed to be terribly steep as I tottered to keep my balance, ice axe at the ready. Did the snow move just then? Where is this slope going? I imagined it slipping over the steep escarpment into Coire Lagain, taking me with it, the story of my walk ending as a fatality item in the Sunday papers. My nerve cracked. It was too dangerous — why throw away your dream journey when the mountain could be safely climbed another day?

I was soon lost, and grateful to stumble down wild Glas Leathad. There was still time for one last try. A spur led up from the glen. It was covered in ice near some broken crags, less than three-quarters of a mile from the summit. But then the roaring sound of the wind from the glen became a reality, racing over the mountain and knocking me over time after time. It was impossible to continue. Tail between my legs I followed the Allt Fheannach, preferring to keep to the bed of this wild rough burn than the steep slopes that hemmed it in from either side.

Mrs MacGregor kindly let me phone the support team from Forest Lodge. Before returning to the bothy most of the party had gone home, although a couple were waiting rather anxiously for two cross-country skiers, a little overdue. By the time my rucksack was packed they had returned. Beinn a'Ghlo had beaten me again. My wandering journey had given me an eleven-mile walk to climb one summit less than two miles from the glen.

With everybody accounted for we made our way down to Blair Atholl. I retrieved my long-suffering bike from a snowdrift. But it was impossible to cycle on the road which had frozen solid. The bike had to be pushed, and was a perfect nuisance as it repeatedly slipped and fell over. It was a long and tiring journey to the Tilt Hotel.

GLENS ISLA AND CLOVA 27–31 JANUARY

Tom and Doreen arrived in the morning and we had a busy day reorganising the next stage. The weather report for next day reckoned there would be a brief spell of calm weather in the morning, followed by winter storms. Would this give me enough time to climb the last of Bheinn a'Ghlo's peaks? It was still dark as I left Loch Moraig and followed the path towards Coire Lagain. After a couple of miles, however, a moving mass of snow showers pelted the glen, leaving little doubt what was happening two thousand feet higher. My resolve was broken. Jinx mountain would have to wait to be fought another day.

Other, hopefully less troublesome, mountains lay further east as the bike clanked the 40 miles to Glen Isla. Snow and ice-covered roads slowed progress till at last the welcoming sight of the hotel appeared ahead. Moira and Lillian Ferris welcomed me in. The smoky old-fashioned bar was a happy place that evening, with the local people of the glen mixing with a visiting platoon of Welsh Guardsmen. A bird's nest fell down the chimney, filling the

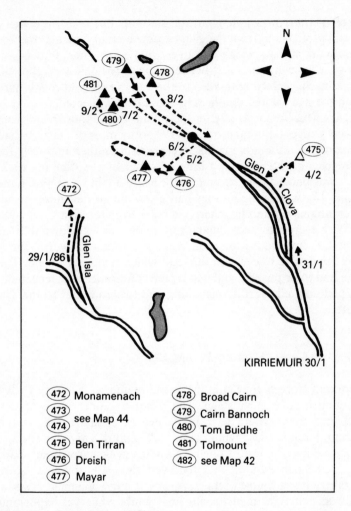

Map 43   Glens Isla and Clova

bar with smoke, which added to the atmosphere. Fortunately I met the stalker Peter Grant, whose hill, Monamenach, I planned to climb in the morning. Although busy shooting hinds at that time, he kindly gave me a free hand on the mountain.

The snow-covered road was tediously slow as the bike slithered up Glen Isla, past the ruins of little Forter Castle, ravaged by

Argyll in 1640. From Auchavan an easy climb led up to join a line of fence posts that stretched through the mist to the top of Monamenach, 'the Middle Hill'. My short direct route scarcely did justice to the mountain, which would be far more interestingly climbed from the path leading into Glen Beanie or from Glen Brighty to the north. The mountain seemed alive with mountain hares which would skip off into the distance and disappear down their burrows.

To the west lies Glen Shee, 'the Fairy Glen'. Here lived McComie Mor, the legendary hero of Clan MacThomas, who won great fame in leading his clan in many frays, particularly against their enemies in Atholl. He was greatly upset when a local prophet told him he would die with his head under a certain boulder in wild Caen Lochan. McComie Mor visited the glen, took away the boulder and mounted it in the wall above his head so the prophecy could come true in a more civilised manner.

The Caen Lochan Glen is actually an extension of Glen Isla, and gives a far more exciting ascent of Glas Maol than ever could be enjoyed from the Cairnwell roadside, so spoilt by ski developments. The glen boasts an array of paths which the walker can enjoy, taking him to the high tops amid spectacular scenery, or exploring the beautiful cul-de-sac of Canness Glen. It's all worth while.

The bike was soon in action again as I started cycling the 32 miles east towards Glen Clova. The miles sped by that winter's afternoon as I rode through the pleasant woodland of Glen Isla. But while struggling up a steep hill into Kirriemuir disaster struck: I pulled a muscle in my knee. It was impossible to continue and I had to rest it for a day.

After the rest my knee felt strong enough for me to continue. Kirriemuir sits at the mouth of 'The Glens', for Isla, Prosen, and Clova all fan out from the town through a maze of country roads. My route led into Glen Clova, to my mind the prettiest of the Angus Glens. I was taking it very easy so as not to aggravate the injury. Glen Doll is a pretty wooded valley surrounded by impressive crags, a popular stamping ground for east coast climbers and walkers.

John was the new warden for Glen Doll Youth Hostel. I was his only customer. We spent the evening chatting about Ferniehurst Castle in the Borders, which is the hostel he looked after before transferring here. The fortress was built by the Kerr family, who were seemingly all left-handed. Interestingly, they built the staircases in the towers in an anti-clockwise direction, so their sword hands would have a tremendous advantage over any enemies who managed to breach the castle's defences.

It was a cold night as I stared out on the bleak mountains. January — the killer month — was over. The weather could have been worse, though not a lot. Would February be kinder?

> Days lonely and gregarious,
> Grim days and hilarious,
> Days of delight, most various,
> I've sampled every one.
>
> 'Mountain Days' by Barclay
> Fraser and the SMC Journal

CHAPTER 12

February 1986

Retreat to Glen Esk

———

'Forward' to the lands of Ogilvy (Glen Clova)

———

West to the Hill of Mist and Glen Almond

———

The Ardtalnaig Corbetts and Glen Vorlich

———

At home among the Children of the Mist: Balquhidder

———

The home run: Ben Ledi to Loch Lomond

———

The final peak: Ben Lomond

RETREAT TO GLEN ESK, 1–3 FEBRUARY

> The brightest hour or unborn spring,
> Through the winter wandering
> Found, it seems, the Halcyon morn
> To hoar February born . . .

Unfortunately I could not share Shelley's romantic description of the new month, as an attempt on the hills was beaten back by driving wind and snow. Aberdeen Met Office had promised more was on the way, though there was a possibility of escaping the worst of the weather further east. Early afternoon found me cycling down the glen with the snow filling the road behind. Thirty cold miles led me within sight of the twinkling lights of Edzell, a small town at the foot of Glen Esk. The journey had reached its most easterly point; there was nowhere else to run. A fifteen-mile road would lead to the head of the glen. From here a five-mile walk would reach Mount Keen, one of our easiest Munros. This could be the most demanding part of the walk if the falling snow succeeded in blocking the glen. I imagined myself stuck in Edzell for weeks. A phone call was made to Tom who was to drive to Edzell the next evening and come up to meet me – hopefully – coming down the glen. It was discouraging that, after all the bad weather last year, the trip was still plagued with atrocious conditions, where the easiest of hills had to be fought for by hook and claw.

It was still dark when I left the following morning. A bleak dawn broke slowly over the twisting road leading up Glen Esk, a place once renowned for her illegal whisky bothies. More recently it appeared in the news regarding its huge population of rabbits, doubtless snug in their burrows in today's raw weather. The car park at the head of the glen was deserted. Soon my boots were crunching across the crisp frozen snow. To the west lay a frozen Loch Lee hemmed in by snowy crags, a wild place of great beauty and surprises. Only a thousand years ago brown bears, wolves

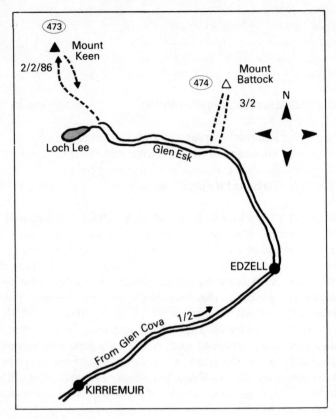

Map 44   Glen Esk

and boar lived in these wilds, now long gone . . . or have they? It is quite conceivable that some small forgotten corner of Scotland is home to a family of wolves or wild pigs.

Hungry deer pawed at the deep snow in Glen Mark, ravenously searching for some grass below. There is a monument at the Queen's Well in memory of Queen Victoria, who was quite a mountain wanderer herself, after years of visits to her second home at Balmoral. Ahead lay Scotland's most easterly Munro, Mount Keen, 939 metres. Admittedly she is not our most spectacular peak, sitting among the surprisingly least-visited hills of the eastern Mounth. However, a fine day can be had combining the summit with a through route over Glen Tanar and the Mounth Road, following the ancient trail used by cattle drovers, and the armies of Macbeth, and later Bruce. To the west, where Water of Mark squeezes its way between the crags on either side, lies Balnamoon's Cave, named after a prominent Jacobite who lived here in hiding after Culloden.

My beard was soon frozen in the Arctic winds, as I climbed through the mist and deep snow to the summit. The weather was deteriorating by the minute, as snow fell incessantly, backed by strong icy winds clattering across the frozen waste of the Mounth. It was a relief to have climbed this mountain before the glen was blocked up with snow.

It was a weary but happy cycle down the glen. A car's headlights beamed ahead and came to a halt. It was great to see Tom, even better to see the bottle of whisky he proffered. Three swigs later the magic water had restored body and soul ... I can scarcely remember the twelve-mile cycle to Edzell!

It was snowing next morning as I cycled out of Edzell, the bike's wheels leaving a snake-like trail behind as it led me up Glen Esk once more. It was at the peaceful hamlet of Tarfside that Robert the Bruce defeated his enemies, the Comyns, in one of their many battles. The bike slithered to a halt at Milden Lodge where I pushed it among some woodland. A few feet away lay a brown snow-covered heather knoll, then nothing — just a whirling mass of snow. That was all that could be seen of Mount Battock, the most easterly mountain of the walk.

What a miserable scene it was as snow fell heavily, backed by angry gusts of wind. Out of the blur I could just make out a stationary Land Rover a few yards away. I tapped gently on the window and a tall stalker in heavy tweeds stepped out. I asked politely if I could climb the mountain, hoping it would not interfere with any deer-stalking. The stalker's tough weather-worn face cracked into a big smile: 'Nay, laddie, you'll nae be interfering with any stalking the day. I wouldn't set foot on those hills in this weather, but I admire you for trying, anyway.' I was waiting for him to ask me for my next of kin, but in an instant he had shaken my hand and driven off, leaving me staring at the swaying mass of snow dancing before me, his discouraging words ringing in my ear: 'I wouldn't set foot on those hills in this weather.' These were the words of a man who must know the hill inside out, so what chance had I against the winter frenzy, inches from my eyes? But if my ancestors could march forty-four miles through mountains raked with blizzards as bad as these, when they fought with Montrose at Inverlochy, surely I could manage six snowy miles in daylight?

I took a careful bearing and set off. A faint outline of the Land Rover track buried under the snow was a help. Mount Battock inches above the other hills of the Forest of Birse, a land of high moorland and peat hags, delightfully wild and remote, yet just over twenty miles from the oil-rich city of Aberdeen. An array of Land Rover tracks approach the mountains from the south and west. A longer approach by the Fungle Road, an ancient pass between Esk and Deeside, could be more rewarding.

The outline of the white burn led me uphill. Nothing could be seen through the snowstorm except the odd black boulder, looking huge through a veil of mist and snow. The progress was sluggish; in the knee-deep snow it was more like swimming than climbing. Close to the summit I stumbled into a battered fence that led to the trig point. My frozen mitts triumphantly touched the top of my 474th summit, the most easterly point of the walk. But what a barbaric welcome she gave me, as a freezing wind swirled around the summit. Glen Esk had been won before it could be blocked with snow. Now for the second attempt on the mountains of Glen Clova.

The Arctic weather continued as I backtracked on my route, my footprints made on the ascent almost totally covered by the new snow falling.

A 30-mile cycle ride took me back down the glen and along the snowy roads leading to Kirriemuir, passing the incredibly preserved white and brown Caterthun hill forts, sitting astride the gentle pass breaching the Menmuir Hills. These incredible fortifications are well worth a visit. Apart from their historical interest they give a bird's-eye view of the low lands of Angus. I wondered what the Vacomagi tribe would have thought of this strange 'horseman' passing their strongholds. In ancient times Scotland would have been a lot warmer than now, yet in the heyday of the clans it was colder. We are left with the happy medium — the bitter summer of 1985 being an exception!

At Kirriemuir it was a delight to relax in a warm bath and have a good meal. After the Arctic struggle in Glen Esk, would the weather in Glen Clova be kind? Aberdeen Met Offic didn't think so.

FORWARD TO THE LANDS OF OGILVY (GLEN CLOVA), 4–9 FEBRUARY

The winding road led out of Kirriemuir and zig-zagged north towards Glen Clova, passing Cortachy Castle, ancient stronghold of the Ogilvies. The castle is reputed to be haunted by the ghost of a drummer boy who fell from the battlements, perhaps taking the clan's motto 'Forward' too literally! A freezing wind slowed the bike's progress north until it slid to a halt at the foot of Ben Tirran, Glen Clova's only Corbett. White hares seemed to be everywhere as I struggled through the deep snow. The mountain is best climbed from the roadside where it's well worth a diversion to explore her two spectacular hill lochs, perched on the hillside, carved out by the Ice Age. Both have excellent paths leading to them. The larger Loch Brandy once had a fine stock of trout, until a poacher who had a score to settle with the local landlord put some pike in. Ben Tirran may mean 'Hill of Escape' or 'Rescue'. Certainly the Ogilvies who lived in the glen suffered badly from cattle raids by marauding clansmen. Their loyalty to the many doomed rebellions of the Stuart cause found them too close for comfort to avenging government troops, while other clans were safe in their remote mountain lairs further west.

The strong winds produced a moving sea of spindrift, making navigation difficult. This was no place to get lost. The little-visited hills of the Eastern Mounth look as if they could give you days of happy wandering just trying to find the way down! North-west lies the table-top summit of Lair of Aldararie. Here the local clans would meet and compete at Highland Games. In recent years some mindless people stole from the summit the stone putts they used to throw.

Mountain hares were my constant companions on the descent. Dozens of them ran from cover, racing downhill, only to be disturbed again a few minutes later.

In the morning the bike was pedalled and pushed over the snow-covered road leading to its off-shoot Glen Doll. A fox jumped over a wall, raced ahead, then sprang up the hillside. Perhaps it was the same cunning animal with a keen interest in archeology who dug up two Bronze Age arrowheads here several years before. Glen Clova ranks with Ben Lawers as being the richest source of wild flowers in Scotland. Many a botanist has forced a new route up the glen's crags in search of an isolated ledge with rare specimens.

The weather was as unsettled as ever, an inky clear sky one minute, a violent flurry of winter madness the next. The path that leads to the ruins of Kilbo in Glen Prosen goes through the forest, the trees laden with snow. I tottered, trying to keep balance on the steep slopes of Shank of Drumfollow, with the track buried under several feet of snow. Ahead lay the twin peaks of Mayar and Driesh. These two gentle Munros have something for everyone, gentle hillwalking or exciting climbing in Driesh's Winter Corrie or Mayar's spectacular Corrie Fee.

The compass led me to the trig point of Driesh, meaning the Thorn Bush, before backtracking to the col and up to Mayar. Here the mist cleared to reveal the long plateau stretching for three miles to Tolmount and Tom Buidhe. Both these Munros can be added to the last pair. They make a pleasant horseshoe route descending back to Glen Doll via Jock's Road, that ancient byway between Clova and Braemar. That was my plan today but, as I started crossing towards Dun Hillocks, I noticed some strange cloud movements to the north. I hurried my pace as a huge billow of clouds, thousands of feet high, moved like a wave crashing on a beach, swirling and twirling as it boiled above Lochnagar. Trouble was coming — big trouble. This was no place to get caught by a blizzard, with the escape route to Glen Doll blocked by Coire Fee. I raced back towards Mayar as the slopes erupted into a moving sea of spindrift. A whirlwind of winter wrath was at my heels. I reached the Shank of Drumfollow when the blizzard hit the mountain. My trusty compass led down to the woodland but the Arctic tempest was fighting there too, crashing through the firebreaks, the trees creaking and groaning in agony above.

The old witch Cailleach had beaten me again. Tail between legs, I retreated to the bar at the Ogilvy Arms Hotel. What a pleasant surprise it was to see Simon Stewart, the young Dundee climber whom I had met in Strathfarrar in the summer of 1984. It was our conversation by the fireside that planted the seeds of my plan to attempt the Munros and Corbetts. Interestingly enough Simon joined Martin Moran for a few days during his lightning winter tour of the Munros.

The snow was falling heavily. With difficulty we pushed his car free and he disappeared down the road, hand waving from the window in a moving mass of snow. With the youth hostel closed for the night I took a room at the hotel. It snowed continuously next day, ruling out any prospect of achieving anything on the hills.

The morning forecast was: clear at first with bad weather making an unwelcome appearance in the afternoon. Mrs Brown gave a cheery wave from Acharn Farm as I plunged through the fresh snow on Jock's Road, winding between the trees under the stern frown of rocky Craig Rennet. Suddenly the woodland stopped and I plunged into the narrow snowy glen like a bull let into the ring. A lengthy diversion avoided an avalanche-prone slope before climbing over the shoulder of Cairn Lunkard. There is a shelter near here, built in memory of five climbers who died in a savage blizzard while trying to cross the pass. It was a mournful spot to stand by as the threatening clouds delivered the expected snow storm. For half an hour I waited for it to clear, but it didn't. In reality I had lost my bottle only one mile from the summit of Tom Buidhe. I turned back, the snowflakes following me all the way to Acharn Farm. Suddenly it stopped snowing, the sky cleared and the sun came out to taunt me. It was even more sickening when somebody passing asked, 'You will have had a good day today?' Sometimes you need to be braver to turn back than to go on.

The Ogilvie Arms Hotel has a bunkhouse, and it was there I had a rendezvous with Graham Moss and his friends from Strathclyde University Mountaineering Club.

The road was still thick with snow as I cycled north towards Acharn Farm. I didn't want to leave the bike in full view by the roadside, so I carried it up the hillside and left it among a green square of woodland. A car pulled up with most of the passengers bound for Glen Doll. Graham joined me as we went further up Glen Clova towards Bachnagairn. Ahead lay Broad Cairn and Cairn Bannoch, the two Munros overlooking the southern slopes of Lochnagar. It was almost exactly this time of year — the 11 February 1746 — that the Ogilvie clansmen gathered here and marched to Glen Muick to join Prince Charlie. The men wore thin leather brogues and slept out in the snow in their plaids, with only a handful of oatmeal to sustain them.

The woodland around Bachnagairn was waist-deep in snow, and the Burn of Gowal sported the most beautiful icicles I have ever seen. They were about twenty feet long. It was good to climb higher and reach firmer snow leading to Broad Cairn. We could see right down Glen Muick, her snowy pines stretching to Ballater; it seemed a lifetime since I had been there in December. A skier puffed up behind us, struggling on the frozen surface, as we pushed on for Cairn Bannoch, 1,012 metres.

There were some awesome cornices creeping over the edge of Creag an Dubh Loch. One false step in a white-out would send you on a high dive into the frozen lochan a thousand feet below. Small wonder these hills were such an inspiration to Captain Scott and Dr Edward Wilson, the famous Antarctic explorers. At their favourite viewpoint in Glen Prosen is a memorial to these two stalwart heroes. After reaching the South Pole on 17 January 1912, they both expired on the great ice barrier in March of that year. 'For the journey is done and the summit attained and the barriers fall.'

There were not enough daylight hours left for climbing south to Glen Clova's two remaining peaks, Tolmount and Tom Buidhe. This was frustrating, but nevertheless had to be accepted. Soon we were in the deep soft snow in the glen. A party of skiers raced by, tauntingly shouting: 'This is the way to travel, lads.' However, we gained sweet revenge by overtaking them when they hit a frozen stretch. Their faces were a study when they passed by, just as I had retrieved my bike from its snowy hiding place and cycled down the hillside. Back at the bunkhouse I was invited to join the club for their annual dinner, which as always was a fun event, with humorous speeches followed by a rousing *ceilidh* in the bar afterwards. A friendly snowball fight ended the evening on a high note, except for one poor lad who jumped for cover knee-deep into an icy burn.

Two friendly students were my companions as we followed the now well-beaten trail up Glen Doll. In the late nineteenth century the landowners tried to close this ancient pass, but were firmly defeated by the Scottish Rights of Way Society, a fine band of dedicated people who give the wilderness some muscle to fight back against the lunacy of man.

Cross-country skiers were soon racing past us. This wonderful mode of transport is ideal for the gentle rolling Angus Hills.

Tom Buidhe was reached with ease in today's clear weather, making a mockery of my previous failed attempts. Certainly turning back at Cairn Lunkard two days previously was embarrassing beyond belief, yet it was the correct decision at the time. Having survived the journey for so long I wasn't prepared to throw it away taking unnecessary risks. A fine bum-slide brought us to within a few hundred feet of Tolmount. From the summit we enjoyed a brief view of Glen Callater below, before a familiar veil of mist blocked it from view. The last of the Angus hills had fallen; only seventeen peaks remained unclimbed.

Close to Cairn Lunkard there had been some small slab avalanches. Incredibly the slopes were little over twenty degrees steep, a reminder that gentle inclines are prone to avalanche just as easily as steep ones. My two companions, both called David, waved goodbye as they worked their way north towards Cairn Bannoch and Broad Cairn. Darkness was creeping over the Angus Hills as I cycled down Glen Clova for the last time. The warmth and friendliness of the members of the Strathclyde University Mountaineering Club had been a great morale-booster as I prepared for the final push home. It seemed that what had started out as an impossible dream would, with luck, become a reality.

WEST TO THE HILL OF MIST AND GLEN ALMOND, 10–16 FEBRUARY

It was a cold misty morning as I cycled out of Kirriemuir for the last time. Ahead of me was a 25 mile run leading to Straloch in Strath Ardle. A lengthy detour was being made to reach the last peak of my jinx mountain of Beinn a'Ghlo. The tarmac road into Gleann Fearnach was thick with snow as the bike slipped and slid on the packed snow. What a difference from my last visit, before Christmas!

Unbelievably, a cycle was following behind, ridden by a Welshman on a foray to climb Ben Vuirich. My bike was abandoned in the woodland behind Daldhu farm.

Having established a base, I settled down to cook a dehydrated meal. Earlier on in the trip I had given back the most tasteless flavours to the support team. This plan was now backfiring as they were getting short of fresh supplies and now I was receiving them all back again! It was bitterly cold outside, but tomorrow, come hell or high water, jinx mountain would be climbed, if only the weather would be kind.

The studies of Alexander Buchan, the famous Scottish meteorologist, showed that the 10 February is usually the coldest night of the winter. Cold was an inadequate description for the freezing night. In the morning my sleeping bag was coated in ice. The boots which had joined me in the sleeping bag the night before were taken out, while I cooked my breakfast on the struggling propane gas stove. Within ten minutes the boots were frozen again and had to be returned to the bag for another heat.

The wind was howling outside, but it was clear. I listened to the morning forecast like a condemned man waiting to hear the jury's verdict. The report was vague in the extreme, the weathermen covering themselves for almost any eventuality except a heatwave.

Armed with crampons and ice axe I drew closer to my old adversary. Shrouded in mist, the hillside seemed to shiver in the wind, fresh from Siberia. I pushed on up the slopes towards Airgiod Bheinn. It was a frustrating, clumsy climb, one step up and two steps down. At last I pulled on to the ridge, now only one mile from the summit of Carn nan Gabhar, 'the Hill of the Goats', the last unclimbed summit of Beinn a'Ghlo. I raced along the ridge before the weather could change and hurl me down the mountain, as it had done on many previous attempts.

A veil of mist crept in, reducing visibility to a few feet. Compass in hand, like a wolf closing on its kill, I inched nearer the summit, heart pounding with excitement. Ignoring the trig point I sprinted on for the summit cairn. My cheers could be heard in Pitlochry. This troublesome mountain's three summits could easily have been climbed if given just one good day. No such luck — three days had me stormbound on either side of the peak. It had taken a further three days to climb the rest of her summits, two of those in dreadful conditions.

After so much goating around, the temper of 'the Hill of The Mist' was calm today. There is an old stalking story that a rifle fired in one of her nineteen corries could not be heard in any of the rest. Certainly she is a massive mountain and, although I cursed her on occasions, the view today was reward enough.

Stretched out before me were the crisp snowy peaks of Atholl and the Grampians, all white and beautiful, all climbed.

With only sixteen hills to climb it was a happy hillwalker who made his way down to Coire Lagain, disturbing a huge herd of deer who swam through the deep snow to the sanctuary of Beinn Bheag, where they eyed me suspiciously. After a celebratory brew-up, I headed back down the glen, but already the Arctic weather was closing in. I had been lucky and grabbed the few mild hours of the day for the climb, but an attempt now would certainly be unsuccessful.

The road down Gleann Fearnach was like a toboggan track. The bike slipped several times, once straining my groin. It was a relief to reach the main road at Straloch and celebrate the success on Beinn a'Ghlo with a stay at the friendly Altchappie Hotel.

Andrew, the hotel owner, refused to take any form of payment for my accommodation, which was a kind gesture, typical of the warmth of the people I met. In the morning I went to visit the local primary school, where Mrs Dutch introduced me to the children. I told them how tough it had been climbing their local hill, Beinn a'Ghlo: almost six days of atrocious weather, fighting and crawling through blizzards. My description would have done Captain Oates proud. Then one little boy put his hand up and said, 'My Grannie's climbed that hill.' I only wish she had been with me!

The children presented me with a donation for Erskine Hospital. Then they all came outside to see their hero depart. All the children waved as I mounted my bike like John Wayne — but it wouldn't move, the chain was frozen solid. How embarrassing! Only after a great deal of oiling could I get it going once more. Sixty little hands once more waved goodbye as the bike limped out of the playground.

A 30-mile cycle ride led me west through Blairgowrie and Dunkeld to the Amulree Hotel in Strathbraan. Two members of the support team were there, and it was pleasant to have an afternoon's rest while we planned the next stage to Crieff. The hotel owner had phoned the keeper in Glen Almond, who kindly arranged that a wee bothy, normally locked, would be left open. I spent the evening in the company of a cheery tweed-bonneted Highlander who was celebrating the recent sale of his farm and his new move into a bungalow, ideally situated next to the hotel bar!

It was 6.00 a.m. The boiling kettle had filled the kitchen full of steam. In front of me was a breakfast tray kindly left out by the cook, and an envelope with a generous donation to Erskine Hospital. The warmth of the kitchen was left behind as I stepped out into a cold misty morning. On the roadside was a tweed 'bunnet' frozen solid. I recognised it, as belonging to my drinking companion from the night before. I left it on his doorstep with a note saying, 'Try Super Glue'.

The road running south runs parallel with General Wade's old military road. The bike clattered over the pass to Newton Bridge, entrance to the last remote quarter of the walk. It is said that 400 men marched out of this distant head of Glen Almond to join the 1715 Rebellion. The glen's population is now only a meagre six. The track to the lodge at Auchnafree was thick with snow. The chambered cairn of Clach na Tiom-Pan, 'the Stone of the Timid People,' looked more like an igloo in today's weather.

Mr and Mrs Inglis, the caretakers of Auchnafree Lodge, offered to shelter my bike in a garage and invited me to lunch next day. How quaintly civilised their gesture seemed, as the snowflakes fell on the Glen Almond hills. I crossed the river and took to the easy slopes of Auchnafree Hill. Mist clung to the hill-side, thick in her winter coat. There was not a sound except the crunch of my boots, for the normal bubbly burns were frozen solid, paralysed in winter's arctic grip. This remote mountain was used as a fine hiding place in days gone by. In Coire Chultrain, close to Thief's Cave, lies the Kirk of the Grove, where Cove-nanters, persecuted for their religious beliefs, held their out-of-door services, known as Conventicles. Here they would worship while a few sentries kept a careful watch for the oppressive dragoons. To this day, soldiers of the Cameronians, the famous Covenanters' Regiment, are allowed to take their rifles into church.

Glen Almond was an important route leading from Loch Tay to the cattle trysts in Crieff and Perth. This fine route still exists today, as do several other delightful walks, such as the one directly north from Auchnafree, through pretty Glen Lochan to Loch Freuchie. Other routes partly disappeared under the waves when the loch was dammed to make the Loch Lednock reservoir. It was bitterly cold on the summit and I took a bearing west towards Ben Chonzie, the area's only Munro. The frozen surface

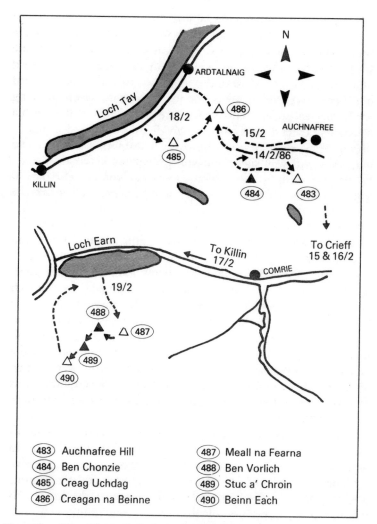

Map 45   Glen Almond, Ardtalnaig and Glen Vorlich

of Loch Turret appeared like crazy paving from above, as I closed
with the mountain's impressive Coire Uaine, whose black crags
glowered from the snowy slopes. The ice axe was put to good use
on the steep pull that led to the summit ridge above Moine Bheag.
At the cairn a thick veil of mist cheated me of a view of Crieff and
the handful of peaks in the Southern Highlands still unclimbed.

Dozens of mountain hares, almost invisible in their white coats, raced to their burrows, as my route wound north to Lechrea. The bridge there consisted of a single iron girder. John Pollock, the stalker, had kindly left an outhouse at Dalriech unlocked. The door creaked open. Most of the room was full of animal feedstuff but there was plenty of space for a sleeping bag, which was aired while the tea boiled. This was a five-star bothy — it even had electricity. Later I took a look outside and disturbed a herd of deer grazing right outside the door. Gleaming stars lit up the black sky. All was silent and still except for a shooting star. I hoped this clear weather would continue for the climbing of tomorrow's two Corbetts further up the glen. The mountains were still and quiet.

Despite the optimistic clear sky the night before, I woke to a miserable morning with snow flying horizontally down the glen. Not much of a welcoming sight for my anniversary morning. I had now been on the hills for one full year. Hoping for a favourable break in the weather, I walked head-down to the ruined house at Dunan. To the north lay the easy slopes of Creagan na Beinne, 887 metres. However, even the gentlest of slopes was impossible today. I gained a few hundred feet, but visibility was down to a few inches and the driving snow forced me back time after time. It was impossible to continue, so I backtracked down the glen: not a very encouraging start to my second year in the mountains.

Back at Auchnafree John Pollock, the stalker, welcomed me into his house and gave me a warming mug of coffee. John had worked here for many years and dearly loved the glen. He liked nothing better on a fine summer's evening than to play a round of golf on the six-hole course he'd built close to the lodge. The warmth and hospitality of this small community was quite unbelievable. Like an honoured guest I was shown to the Inglises door and invited in for lunch.

This cheery couple, caretakers for the lodge, treated me to a superb lunch. Their cuisine and company were both enjoyed immensely, but I was beginning to get very concerned about the heavy snow falling like a rain of white cricket balls outside. I had arranged to see the support team in Crieff the following morning — it would be a disaster to get stuck in the glen. The Inglises showed me round the lodge, the smoking room, and master bedrooms, while gently I tried to hint it was time I was on my way. But my hosts would not be put off. They reminded me of a colonial couple in India calmly making tea, not in the least concerned that 30,000 tribesmen were storming the front gate. But I soon lost my selfish attitude for Crieff was only eleven miles away and their conversation was fascinating.

My hosts came to say farewell, and a small congregation of stalkers and shepherds gave me a generous donation for Erskine Hospital. The party waved goodbye as I disappeared into the white blur and pushed the bike to the road. The contraption was a lot lighter, for John Pollock, who had been going into Crieff, had kindly taken my heavy cycle bags ahead. The weather was closing in badly now as I wheeled into a very white Crieff and relaxed in a hot bath at the Murray Park Hotel.

It was a surprise at breakfast to read about the walk in a small entry in the *Scottish Daily Express*. The support team arrived for the last rest day meeting of the trip.

THE ARDTALNAIG CORBETTS AND GLEN VORLICH, 17–19 FEBRUARY

It had snowed almost continuously for the last two days. I hoped for a spell of clear weather, although that didn't seem very likely as the bike wove along the icy shore of Loch Earn and over Glen Ogie to Killin, for a fresh attempt on the Ardtalnaig Corbetts.

Not a sound came from the sleepy village as the bike wheeled out into the darkness of a February morning. Suddenly it came to a halt and refused to move. The chain was frozen solid. Aching fingers painfully replaced the problem chain. But the bike would still not budge: the gear wheels had frozen too. The coldest February in decades had been too much for my faithful old Peugeot. I wheeled it back into town just as dawn started to break; hot water provided by a newsagent managed to thaw the gear wheels, but in a few seconds they froze up again.

It was developing into a beautiful clear day and I couldn't get to my hills! I phoned Tom and asked him to pick up a spare wheel and deliver it that night. The town's fishing shop hired bikes in the summer, and I was busy helping the owner retrieve one from his shed when a police Land Rover stopped. A big constable said,

'Are you the laddie on the charity walk requiring a bike? Well, it's just coming behind you.' Tom had phoned the local rescue team and asked if anyone could lend me a bike. Duncan Macdonald, a mechanic and keen Triathlon competitor, arrived with a sleek machine. It was a lightweight double-butted 531 frame, which in cycling jargon basically means 'Rolls Royce'. I thanked him profusely and cycled out of town. The bike was a dream and went like a rocket. Once again, a mountain rescue team had come to my aid.

At Ardeonaig I took the faint path leading up Fin Glen, once a popular path although the damming of Loch Lednock had reduced its use considerably. The race was really on to beat the approaching darkness. I walked and ran up the snowy slopes of Creag Uchdag, 879 metres, 'the Crag of the Hollows'. The summit was thick with mist, but for once clear of the blizzards and gale-force winds I had come to accept as normal. A hurried bearing led me down the winding glen to the ruined house of Dunan before springing up Creagan na Beinne, 887 metres. Both these Corbetts give a pleasant round from Loch Tay-side through a wild and little-visited part of Perthshire, so watch you don't break a leg. It was through these hills that an avenging group of MacNabs — described in Chapter 5 — came hauling their boat for an amphibious assault on their enemies, the MacNishes, living on an island on Loch Earn. Soon they got fed up hauling a small galley across these wilds and abandoned it in Glen Beich. The boat's remains could still be seen last century.

The night's stars were appearing as the summit cairn of Creagan na Beinne was reached, and it was a happy hillwalker who descended to Loch Tay-side and sang all the way along to pick up the bike at Ardeonaig. My headtorch was a poor substitute for the lack of bicycle lights, although it mattered little, for a fit body and a sleek bicycle were a perfect combination as the miles to Killin slipped by. Tom was waiting at the Coach House Inn with the spare wheel for my old bike. It was put on, tested, and found to be perfect.

The support team had experienced a traumatic time recently. The last two winter months had them very worried about my whereabouts. Now, as we approached the end of the walk, it was they more than me who bore the pressure as the glare of publicity increased. Tom explained that the press and TV needed to know a finishing date. Could the walk be completed by the end of the month? If so it would have to be done on Thursday 27 February, rather than Friday, a poor day for media coverage. It was all a bit of a strain for a guy who had left home a year earlier to enjoy a long-distance walk, never dreaming it would be completed. But how could I, who had taken six days to climb Atholl's Beinn a'Ghlo, give my word that the last twelve peaks would be climbed within the next nine days? Given good weather, it would be no problem, but that particular factor had hardly been on my side throughout this journey.

With fingers crossed I decided to agree to the finishing date, hoping that the old witch Cailleach, the goddess of winter, who had been so angry this year, had wielded the worst of her Arctic wrath.

Spurred on by the urgency of the journey I cycled out of Killin before the milkman was awake. At the top of Glen Ogle the moonlight glimmered on the lochan at the top of the glen. Legend has it that some children drowned here under tragic circumstances.

The grey walls of the Glen Ogle railway viaduct appeared out of the gloaming, a monument to a bygone age. It was in this narrow pass that my ancestor Rob Roy MacGregor, with a handful of men, ambushed thirty government cavalry sent to arrest him.

> Instant through copse and heath arose,
> Bonnet and spear and bended bow,
> On right and left above below,
> Sprang up at once the lurking foe.

> Sir Walter Scott

At 8.00 a.m. I abandoned the bike in some bushes near Ardvorlich and started up a very snowy Glen Vorlich. The weather forecast was favourable today which was just as well, for a long day lay ahead. In the deer forest of Glen Artney, between Loch Earn and Callander, lay two Munros and two Corbetts, giving fifteen miles of walking over their summits. With luck the walk could be won today, although I had my doubts when waist-deep in snow at the top of Glen Vorlich. Meall na Fearna, 809 metres, is the most easterly mountain of the range. I wonder how many visitors she gets, compared with the popular Munros Ben Vorlich and Stuc a'Chroin in the centre of the group. The summit was like an ice rink; crampons were strapped on for a slip-free life. Adrenalin was now flowing as the race continued over the Bealach Dearg to gain the narrow ridge leading to Ben Vorlich. It was clear on top and the mountains of Loch Tay sprang up like pins in a bowling alley. But my eyes were drawn south-west to the impossible dream: Ben Lomond, my final summit.

The line of fence posts leading over the ridge was buried under the snow. On a previous climb, one May evening, I heard them buzz with electricity, which led to a hurried descent as a thunderstorm broke, sending lightning crashing across the mountain.

Opposite lay Stuc a'Chroin, this Munro's sister peak, meaning 'Hill of Harm' or 'Danger'. The drifting snow had narrowed the ridge to a beautiful knife-edge as I followed it down to Bealach an Dubh Choirein, tripping over my crampons as I went. Then came a steep climb by the gap between the crags at Creag Dubh, to push along the summit ridge to Stuc a'Chroin. With just over two hours of precious light left I followed the knobbly ridge west, running and walking to the steep slopes of Beinn Each. Opposite, perched on the south side of Stuc a'Chroin, lay a frozen Lochan a'Chroin, a perfect campsite – in the calm of a sunny summer's evening.

With a shout of 'Ard-choille!', the battle cry of the MacGregor clan, I raced up the last hundred feet, the ice axe acting as a third leg on the mad sprint to the summit, from which they must have heard my cheers in Glasgow. If the walk had not been won today, at least it had taken a great leap forward. A joyful descent was made to Bealach nan Cabar and Glen Ample beyond. A multitude of songs soon passed the eight dark miles back to the bike. With a celebratory pint in the Rob Roy bar I couldn't have felt more at home!

AT HOME AMONG THE CHILDREN OF THE MIST: BALQUHIDDER, 20–22 FEBRUARY

The Braes of Balquhidder have always been a special place for me. Since my early schooldays I would cycle up here from Glasgow and enjoy a day's walk, exploring the homeland of the MacGregor clan, even if my idea of holidays didn't quite agree with the school's timetable! The glen rings with countless tales, many connected with the legendary Rob Roy MacGregor, who is buried at the kirk. However the real pleasure of the glen comes from the beautiful grassy braes, the wooded shores of Loch Voil and the white dramatic peaks rising to the west. The sun always seems to shine in Balquhidder

As the bike whizzed along the shore of the loch, squirrels doing a far better imitation than Tarzan, leapt from tree to tree. From Blaircreich I took to the slopes of Stob a'Choin, meaning 'Dog Peak'. This shapely pointed Corbett is one of the finest hills in the Southern Highlands. Yet she is forgotten, hidden among the empty lands between Balquhidder and Loch Katrine, where very few walkers go. Soon I was in a world of snow and mist, as the rim of the corrie was reached. A strong wind blew across the bumpy ridge that rose and fell like a roller coaster as it worked its way west. It was alarmingly steep in places, the precipitous northern slopes thankfully hidden by the thick veil of mist. Imagine if I had an accident now! New-found energy had my ice axe arm working double time as the final push was made up the ramparts of this spectacular mountain.

South from the summit, across a lonely forgotten glen, lies a ridge of small mountains stretching north-west through wild country towards Parlan Hill. Here lies Bealach nan Corp, meaning 'the Pass of the Dead'. It was once an old coffin route, and cairns mark the places where the burial parties would rest while carrying the coffins for burial on Inchcailloch, an island on Loch Lomond.

It had been my plan to traverse further east to climb Ceann na Baintighearna, which lay six empty miles to the east. She is a forgotten mountain in every sense of the word. Even the Ordnance Survey omit naming her highest point. However, the weather had deteriorated. After an hour of floundering through a sea of mist and moving snow, with the only view being my frozen

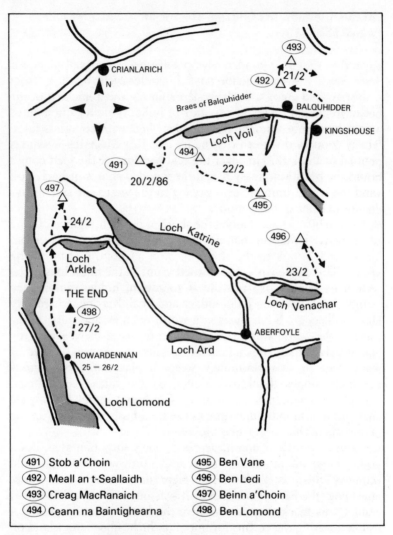

Map 46   Balquhidder to Ben Lomond

mitt holding the compass, I gave up trying to reach that remote peak. The snowflakes followed me all the way down to the glen.

It had been a bitterly cold night, and the snow fell heavily as I cycled north towards Lochearnhead. The chances of a successful day on the hills looked very slim, and my mind filled with thoughts of an emergency plan to reach Ben Lomond by the twenty-seventh. Suddenly it stopped snowing. A hint of blue sky appeared. Within minutes it was a gorgeous warm winter's day. There are few things as fickle as Highland weather.

At the head of Glen Kendrum towered two fine Corbetts, lying between Glen Dochart and Balquhidder. I was soon eating snow as refreshment on the approach to Meall an t-Seallaidh, meaning 'Hill With a Wide View' or 'Hill of the Sight'. Strangely, in all my previous visits to this green mountain I had enjoyed perfect conditions similar to today's. A favourite route is up through the woodland of Kirkton glen, where the forestry road gives way to a delightful path weaving up the hillside to a pretty lochan, over-shadowed by the spectacular cliffs of Leum an Eireannaich. There is reputed to be the remains of a Pictish hill fort nearby, known locally as 'The Trenches'. This and other titbits of history of the area are well recorded in Elizabeth Beauchamp's book, *The Braes of Balquhidder*, published by Heatherbank Press.

It had developed into a perfect winter's day, the like of which I had not experienced for weeks. The mountain's slopes fell gently south to Balquhidder, by now no doubt bustling with activity. In medieval times the highlight of the social calendar here was the Angus Fair. One particular year the main inhabitants of the glen, the MacLarens, were enjoying the merriment of the Highland Games, when suddenly the glint of sunshine gleaming on armour and swords was spotted approaching from Kingshouse. An army of Buchanans had come to wage war on the peaceful glen. There was panic at first. A few MacLarens went to fight the foe but were steadily driven back. However, the fiery cross had been sent round the glen. Over the hills and through the bracken came hundreds of MacLarens, aided by the warlike MacGregors. They crashed headlong into the Buchanans, trapping them against the River Balvag. The fighting was furious as claymores clashed. Not one of the invaders survived.

A herd of deer, stark against the snowy background, raced over Cam Chreag as I climbed down to the col of the next Corbett, Creag MacRanaich. The southern approach is guarded by a girdle of crags but I found a gap between them and pushed on to the summit.

There were now only five peaks left to climb: my dream was

coming true. Meanwhile I enjoyed a pint at the Kingshouse Hotel. The lads there were bound for a *ceilidh* in Stirling and kindly invited me to join them. Much as I wanted to go, the thought of cycling 60 miles there and back in the dark was just too much. Instead they treated me to a few tunes on their pipes before leaving.

The freezing night had left the roads coated with ice. This became apparent as the bike slipped from under me while I was cycling through Balquhidder. The village has seen more than her fair share of history. The gallant Montrose was here in April 1645 with 500 men, no doubt recruiting before travelling on to Doune. Queen Victoria came to visit on one of her many Highland tours.

I wheeled south into Glen Buckie, once a popular route for whisky smugglers. This was no small-time operation: on one occasion as many as sixty men made up a long convoy of whisky-laden ponies through this glen to Glasgow.

With only a handful of peaks left to climb there was a new spring in my heels as I climbed up through Fathan Glen to the eastern ridge of Ceann na Baintighearna. This Corbett lies in the empty land of the small mountains between Balquhidder and the Trossachs. When Loch Katrine was dammed, extending her length, it created an impenetrable barrier which has produced this empty quarter, a wild and unremembered land only 30 miles from Glasgow. Even the Ordnance Survey print the name of this peak in the wrong position.

The hills were under thick mist. It was a complicated series of bearings that led me south, then east through knee-deep snow to the high moorland leading to Moine nan Each, 'the Bog of the Horses'. Suddenly the mist cleared to reveal a white flowing sea of mountains, still and silent. No one was in sight — I could just as easily have been at the North Pole. It was a fitting approach to my 495th mountain, Ben Vane, 821 metres, from 'bàn' meaning 'white', an apt description for this snowy peak. I suspect this hill is rather thrown in as an extra jaunt from popular Ben Ledi to the south. But just as worthy a route can be enjoyed from Glen Finglas Reservoir, where some easy scrambling can be found on Creag an h-Airigh.

From Glen Buckie a nice path leads over the shoulder of the fairy hill of Beinn an t-Sithein to Strathyre. In 1846 this bonny village was doomed to disappear under the waves of Loch Lubnaig, as the Glasgow Water Company planned to dam the loch. Fortunately the project was dropped and Loch Katrine was dammed instead.

With only three mountains left to climb, I skipped down to Glen Buckie, and cycled down to Balquhidder for the last time. Before leaving this special place there was something I wanted to see once more. Boots crunched across gravel in the churchyard until I stood silent in front of Rob Roy's grave: a simple memorial to a great man, the hero of the clan that refused to be stamped out. Someone had left a heather bouquet tied with MacGregor tartan on his slab. I said a little prayer, then laid on the slab the card that I placed on every mountain top, and whispered the words 'Ard-choille Grigalach', the battle cry Rob would have known all too well. My boyhood hero was a fearsome warrior but kind, too. He earned himself a reputation as a real-life Robin Hood, stealing from the rich and giving to the poor and starving. He had a fine sense of humour and often played pranks on the clan's enemies.

It was dark when I wheeled the bike into Callander. The support team were waiting in a nearby pub where we enjoyed a premature celebration in training for the *ceilidh* planned at the end of the walk.

THE HOME RUN: BEN LEDI TO LOCH LOMOND, 23-25 FEBRUARY

Today was like a holiday, for surely now the pressure was off, as the bike whizzed out of Callander under the slopes of the Pictish-built Dunmore hill fort, tauntingly close to the Roman base in Callander. Soon I was weaving between the yellow broom creeping up on Ben Ledi. This Corbett is justifiably popular with its eagle-eye view of the central belt of Scotland. Across the low Menteith Hills to the south lies Flanders Moss, once a huge, treacherous bog, quite impenetrable. Perhaps not quite so for the MacGregors, who would escape through the mire by a secret route with their stolen Lowland cattle, while their pursuers dared not follow.

We drive the cattle through the glens,
Through the corries, woods and bens,
Through the sleet or misty rain,
When the moon is shin-ing low,
By frozen loch and drifted snow,
Stealthily and bold we go,
Though small our hope of gain.

'Thogail nam Bo' (Lifting the Cattle)

This mire and Loch Lomond formed a formidable barrier to any invading armies, who were forced to keep to the east near Stirling: hence the famous battles of Stirling Bridge and Bannockburn.

With adrenalin flowing I was soon enveloped in a world of mist. The most popular route up this peak is from the Falls of Leny at the foot of Loch Lubnaig. Here you can climb up on to the eastern shoulder or by Stank Glen and enjoy some scrambling on the boulders and pinnacles above the treeline. A circuit by Ardnandave Hill is also rewarding. I climbed her once just simply to test a tent, erected it in teeming rain, made a mug of tea, then packed it up again. Munro, my collie, thought this was very strange. From the south-east the ridge has as many bumps as the Loch Ness Monster. Each one has you thinking it is the summit.

Ben Ledi means 'Hill of God', although many who toil, cursing, up her slopes every summer are probably unaware of it! The mountain was once an important place for the Druids who are believed to have practised sacrificial rites and ceremonies on the mountain. Close to the summit a sweetie paper blew out of my pocket. I chased it and eventually, by diving on it, stopped its wanderings, much to the amusement of Fred, from Callander Mountain Rescue Team, who was standing by the cairn. It was a pleasure to have some company on a top, for a change, as I had not met anyone on the mountains since Tolmount in Glen Clova a fortnight ago.

Fred pointed to the frozen col to the north. Here lies Lochan nan Corp, a macabre-like name, meaning 'the Loch of the Dead'. He explained that the pass was once a popular 'Coffin Road'. One winter a party laid down their casket at the top of the pass, not realising they were standing on the lochan. The ice cracked and the party drowned.

Fred was heading down by a different route while I back-tracked down to the shore of Loch Venachar.

The sun was now shining brilliantly as the bike toiled over the Duke's Pass in the heart of the beautiful Trossachs, the area which so inspired Victorian writers and poets. It is a magical spot, bristling with forests and dramatic little mountains. If you are travelling through the Duke's Pass, don't be surprised if you see a clan battle taking place for 'The Clan' (officially the Scottish War and Heritage Society) often re-enacts battles here, following in the footsteps of Rob Roy who ambushed a company of Redcoats near by.

A thirteen-mile cycle ride took me to Loch Ard which sat like a piece of glass, the forest to the south resembling an Alaskan scene, requiring only a howling wolf to complete the picture.

It was a beautiful morning as my poor suffering bike, which was reaching the end of her days, clanked through the golden wood-land of the Loch Ard forest. It was strange to be cycling through such familiar ground for the round of Loch Katrine and back to Glasgow was a popular summer evening jaunt on the bike. Free of the woodland, the bike climbed to the top of the pass and then braked so the rider could admire the view. There at last was Loch Arklet, a sight I had dreamed about, with the hills of Loch Lomond beyond. My year-plus journey had now turned full circle. Bits were falling off my poor bike regularly, but still it kept going. At last we stopped at the hamlet known as the Garrison of Inversnaid.

This place got its name from the Redcoats who were under the impression that, by building a fort here, they would be able to control the wild MacGregor clansmen, a naive thought. Rob Roy was always keen on explosives. It was a sort of hobby of his, even though it made him unpopular with his clansmen, for his experiments with gunpowder affected the cattle's milk production! The MacGregors waited till the fort was built then blew it up. It has been a ruin ever since.

Boots were donned for the second last hill of the walk, Beinn a'Choin, 769 metres, meaning 'Hill of The Dog'. It seemed fitting that the hill was a Corbett, leaving the last mountain, Ben Lomond, to take precedence as a Munro. The Snaid burn lay somewhere buried under the thick snow as I climbed higher under the shadow of Stob an Fhainne, the small mountain named in praise of Fionn's legendary warriors. In the mist it took some time to reach the summit, which in typical Corbett fashion seemed to have a variety of tops. It was satisfying that this mountain should lie in the wildest quarter of the Southern Highlands, my last real sole experience with the wilds before the expected jamboree on Ben Lomond.

As if by magic the grey veil lifted like a curtain and peak after snowy peak stretched into the distance, each one climbed. Glen Gyle below was the very heart of the lands of MacGregor. With burning pride I raised my arm and shouted, 'Ard-choille Griga-lach!' The battle cry echoed across the glen and I could distinctly hear voices replying. Were the ghosts of the MacGregor clansmen cheering too? Listening intently I heard a ghostly voice calling through the mist: 'Get off the hill, you. We're stalking'!

With only one last peak remaining I climbed down to the bike which at Inversnaid had reached the end of her journey. The hotel owners there agreed to look after it till the support team picked it up. I patted my faithful Peugeot goodbye. During a journey of 4,152 miles through good roads, rough tracks, and mountain burns, two front wheels had been replaced and four rear ones, but the trusty machine had brought me safely to my destination.

The path wound south towards Rowardennan. Many other long-distance walks had ended this way, walking down the shore of Loch Lomond. Last year's heavy rainfall had taken its toll on the steep banks of the loch. Two massive landslides had gouged great firebreaks in the forest, a quarter of a mile of trees and soil plummeting into the loch. I met up with a couple of lads from Clydebank returning from an overnight trip. Their cheerful company made the journey pass more quickly. Eventually the story of my year-long adventure unfolded. They left me with two small bottles of whisky to celebrate with, on the final summit. Such kindness was refreshing, and was typical of the people I met on my walk.

Rowardennan Youth Hostel was open, even if I was only their second guest that night.

THE FINAL PEAK: BEN LOMOND, 25–27 FEBRUARY

In some ways it was a bit of an anti-climax to reach Rowarden-nan. For now, ahead of schedule, I was forced to sit around for two days for the sake of my appointment with the publicity machine on the twenty-seventh. However, it gave me a rest, and time to prepare answers to seventeen of the most likely questions the media were likely to throw at me.

On the second evening the support team arrived. Tom explained that BBC and STV cameras would be coming, plus the popular press. Erskine Hospital were kindly supplying a caravan to serve food and hot drinks. It was all rather frightening. The climbing party would have to be down by 11 a.m. which would mean an early start. We tried to imagine where the television cameras and press would stand, and realised if we descended by the normal path, the interview would take place outside the gent's loo, which hardly added to the environmental setting!

Slightly north, a scenic track wound its way through the trees to come to a dead stop behind a hillock. The only way this could be reached from the main path down the mountain was by fighting through several acres of young forestry. But it gave what we and the media would be looking for: a scenic descent from the mountain. All we were concerned about was that our charity would gain maximum impact from the publicity.

The following evening my friends who would take part in the climb arrived: Angus Cameron, Graham Moss, Julie Watson and Alan Comrie. More stalwarts were to arrive in the morning. Murdo Macpherson and Cameron MacNeish arrived from Radio Scotland's 'Leisure Trail' programme. Their idea was to produce two programmes from the interview, one about my walk, intermingled with a story about fishing in the Highlands. The expert on this subject was sitting beside me in the shape of the amiable Roderick McMenemy. The interview was quite hilarious, although I think Roderick was quite hurt that the only fish I had managed to catch on my year-long journey were two baby trout in a dixie pan.

At 5 a.m. the hostel was bustling with activity as sleepy walkers downed mugs of coffee and sorted out their kit. I made an early phone call to Heather Fraser of Radio Clyde who did an interview over the phone. It was a remarkable occurrence that throughout the trip, even from the most remote telephone boxes in Knoydart and the outer islands, I had enjoyed crystal-clear lines home. However, now, only 30 miles from Glasgow, the interference on the lines was chronic. Poor Heather switched the record button on her tape recorder and lost me in a fuzz of atmospherics. I could understand she was asking me a question but had no idea what it was. It must have sounded very strange.

'Did you have any problems on your trip, Craig?'

My now deaf ear was replying, 'Oh, yes, the support team visited once a fortnight.'

It was pitch black as we left the hostel and met Alan Thomson, who arrived at Rowardennan car park hot-foot from Glencoe. The merry party made its way up the path singing 'Whisky in the Jar'. A crimson sky heralded the arrival of dawn as we reached the halfway point at Sron Aonaich. Loch Lomond stretched out like a sheet of glass below us, her forested islands bristling like hedgehogs. We pulled up the long easy ridge that climbs steeply to Ben Lomond's bulky summit. The path, of course, was buried under the snow, but during the summer months the track is almost wide enough to cycle up; indeed, a jeep was driven up here after the war.

We gave a big cheer for Alastair Conkie, who arrived at our tail. He had been running a little late and missed our start, but had now caught us up. We certainly would not be celebrating today without his support on the Cuillins of Skye. At last we pulled on to the summit ridge and there ahead stood the snowy pointed peak that marks the top, her slopes falling steeply to Gleann Dubh below. Instead of rushing to reach the top I felt reluctant, for I knew it would mean the end of this journey and the way of life I had learnt to love so much. A few minutes later we were on top, popping champagne, while Alan Thomson sat me on top of the frozen triangulation point with ice axe in one hand and a bottle of champagne in the other. He ran through rolls of film while an Arctic mist moved in, freezing our beards solid.

Then suddenly the mist cleared and we looked north at the endless ranges of mountains glistening in their white coats. People may talk about Scotland's assets being her oil, whisky and industrial capacity. To my mind there is no doubt that our finest jewel lies in these lovely mountains, wild and untamed, proud and beautiful. Let's keep them that way.

As we turned to climb down to face the media, a strange confusion of thoughts filled my mind. Among these beloved mountains I may have been alone at times, but I was never lonely. The many colourful characters whom I met on my travels and who cheered me on my way made sure of that. Now, all the thoughts, hopes, disappointments and achievements of the happiest year of my life were going to vanish under a barrage of questions — back to civilisation.

I turned and winked goodbye to the 498 mountains who had been my companions for a year and two weeks, and fancied that maybe Rob Roy, the greatest mountain man of them all, was winking too.

> Farewell ye hills of storm and snow,
> The wild resort of deer and roe.

> Duncan Ban MacIntyre

Gaelic Glossary

It is a delight to be able to pronounce the name of a mountain properly and to understand its meaning. This is not so easy in Scotland where most of the mountains are named in the ancient Gaelic language. The mountains were usually christened after their shape, so you can be given an idea of what terrain to encounter on your climb. The translation of Gaelic place names in the wilds can unfold a rich tapestry of life in yesteryear and a history often forgotten. Malcom MacLennan's *Gaelic Dictionary* (1985) by Acair and Aberdeen University Press is the only one I could find that translated from Gaelic to English *and* vice versa. There is a handy introduction to mountaineering Gaelic in *Munro's Tables*, the bible of the game, published by the Scottish Mountaineering Club. Detailed below are some of the most popular Gaelic descriptions:

abhainn	stream	breaghad	beauty
aighenan	hinds	buchaille	shepherd
airde	stature, height	buidhe	yellow
airgid	silver	cailleach	old woman
allt	burn, stream	caisteil	castle
aonach	mountain ridge	cam	crooked
auch	field	carn, cairn	pile of stones
ban	light-coloured	cateran	cattle thief or
beag	small		Highland marauder
bealach	pass	cath	battle
beinn, bheinn	hill	chaoruinn	rowan
bhuiridh	bellowing	chlaidheimh	sword
bidean	peak, summit	citheach	mist
binnein	pointed peak	coille	wood
bo	cattle	coinneach	moss
bodach	old man	coin, choin	dog
breac	speckled	creag, craig	crag

criche	spoil, raid
cuaich, quoich	drinking cup
cuilean	holly
daingeann	strong, tight
damh	deer
dearg	red
diollaid	saddle
dubh	black
dun	hillfort
eala	swan
eas	waterfall
eun	bird
fada	long
fearna	alder
fhidhleir	fiddler
fhuarain	well
fhudair	gunpowder
fionn	white
fraoch	heather
freiceadain	to watch, look
gabhar	goat
garbh	rough
geal	white, bright
giubhais	pines
glas	greenish grey
gorm	blue
gualainn	shoulder
iaruinn	iron
innis	meadow
iolaire	eagle
iubhair	yew
lair	mare
lairig	a major pass
laoigh	calf
leac	slab
leitreach	slope
leum	leap

liath	grey
lochan	small loch
meall	hill
meirleach	thieves
mhadaidh	foxes, wolves
mhaighdean	maiden
(also maighdean)	
mhanach	monk
mheadhoin	middle hill
monadh	moor, hill
mor, more	big
muc	pig
nathrach	adders
odhar	dapple-coloured
oighreag	cloud berry
raineach	fern
ruadh	red
rubha	point, cape
sail	heel
saoibhaidhe	fox's den
sgiath	wind
sgurr, sgorr	rocky peak
shasuinn	Englishman
shionnaich	fox
(also sionnaich)	
siath	fairies
socath	snout
spidean	summit, ridge peak
tairneanaich	thunder
tarmachan	ptarmigan
teanga	tongue
tigh	house
tom	hill
tuirc,torc	boar
uaine	green
uamh	cave
uisge	water

Statistics

Month	Hills climbed	Miles cycled	Miles walked	Mountain weather conditions (days)			Active days
				Clear	Damp/Misty	Wet or Snowing	
Feb 1985	12	282	90	6	2	4	12
Mar 1985	21	591	153	8	4	13	27
Apr 1985	41	405	286	6	8	12	26
May 1985	55	214	352	8	10	7	25
Jun 1985	55	421	279	6	6	14	26
Jul 1985	62	306	282	2	5	16	23
Aug 1985	43	137	286	1	8	16	25
Sep 1985	64	278	265	1	8	13	22

Oct 1985	38	252	237	3	13	6	22
Nov 1985	24	352	158	2	8	9	19
Dec 1985	38	268	218	2	12	9	23
Jan 1986	19	255	213	3	8	13	24
Feb 1986	26	391	211	7	10	9	26
Total	498	4152	3030	55	102	187	300

An interesting feature of the above statistics was the constant battle against the weather. This was a bitter pill to swallow, especially in the summer months when ambitious days were planned. No amount of planning could have prepared us for the summer of 1985, the wettest since 1897.

It should be noted that the above table does not include rest days or days when ill.

Equipment

There can be few sports where such a keen interest is shown in the equipment available, for the nomadic hillwalker counts every ounce of weight that goes into his pack. Not a few have been forced to desperate measures such as photocopying maps on to lightweight tissue paper, or cutting the ends off their tooth-brushes. It would be possible to spend a fortune on buying the lightest of equipment, but few have such funds available. While appreciating that no two people would use the same equipment, I list below the gear that was used, and which the severe weather put firmly to the test — particularly boots, waterproofs and tent.

CLOTHES

Breeches
My faithful Harris Meyer breeches, after many years' use, dis-integrated on the Isle of Skye. Two pairs of Craghoppers were then bought which are still in use.

Shirt

Two pairs of tartan woollen shirts lasted the trip. One pair was being used while the other was being washed by the support team. Underneath was worn either a Brynje thermal string vest, or a TOG 24 thermal Merkalon vest. The TOG 24 had the added advantage that it could also be used as a spare sweater.

Socks

Polisox supplied six pairs of their excellent Rambler socks, one pair of which was worn underneath a thick pair of Star socks. Despite their being wet for most of the time, I suffered only one blister on the whole journey.

Jacket

Two TOG 24 jackets were used throughout the trip, except during the summer when I switched to a lighter Helly Hansen type. All were ideal for the wet conditions experienced, forming a second barrier in the unlikely event of rain penetrating through the waterproof shell clothing.

Waterproofs

Berghaus kindly supplied two Mistral Gore-Tex jackets and over-trousers. I was most impressed with this breathable waterproof material. It kept me dry through the most incredible downpours, without any build-up of condensation on the inside of the garments. I am certain that if I had stuck to nylon or Neoprene shell clothing I would have got a good soaking on several occasions.

Yeti Gaiters

These gaiters are designed to fit round the boot, giving all-round protection. Their only drawback is that the rubber band which goes under the instep of the boot tended to wear fairly quickly, with rocks and scree tearing the rubber. However, when the snow was on the ground there was scarcely any wear at all.

FOOD

The saying 'You are what you eat' could not be more appropriate for the long-distance walker. Lightweight dehydrated food was used in the wilds and full use was made of local shops and youth hostel stores. A food drop was delivered by the support team or sent ahead to a hotel or guesthouse which kindly agreed to look after it till I arrived. My original idea was to have a large number of biscuit tins hidden throughout the Highlands. Fortunately this idea was dropped due to lack of time ... which was just as well, for, once the bad weather started ripping my ambitious plans to shreds, they probably would have been in the wrong locations.

Normal Day Ration

Breakfast
Alpen Muesli
Powdered scrambled egg or bran muesli
Tea and compo biscuits

Lunch
Jelly
Bag of nuts and raisins
Six bars of chocolate
One oatmeal block

Dinner
Dehydrated main meal
Instant custard or Angel Delight
Compo biscuits
Tea or coffee

This was a similar diet to what I had used on previous walks. I soon got fed up with oatmeal blocks, Kendal Mint Cake and jelly bars. When they were taken out I could live on £2.36 a day. With one or two exceptions the dehydrated main meals were quite palatable. Towards the end of the journey I did start to suffer from lack of fibre, and on returning home suffered a long bout of the energy-sapping disease, delayed viral syndrome. This could have been due to the high amount of chocolate eaten during the journey.

OTHER EQUIPMENT

Rucksack

A Berghaus Cyclops Roc was the ideal rucksack for the trip. It comfortably carried loads of about 55 lb, although I normally carried about 25 lb. It could be packed down to be used as a day sack, and when almost empty was comfortable to use when cycling. I liked its one big compartment, detachable pockets and inside zipped pocket.

Sleeping bag

A Mountain Equipment Four Season bag was used for the colder months, and my faithful old Blacks Norseland in the summer. Both were lovingly packed in a squeezable stuff bag and wrapped in several poly bags. Because duck down is useless when wet, both were a lot lighter and less bulky than the synthetic hollofill types available. A half-length foam Karimat was used for most of the trip, a Five Season mat in the winter.

Stove

Epi Gas kindly supplied a Backpacker Stove with enough propane mixture cartridges for the walk. Unlike butane, which struggles to work properly in cold weather, the propane gas was reliable even in the coldest weather experienced. Two billy-cans from a Camping Gaz Globetrotter Stove were used. A plastic mug, baby can opener and one spoon completed my cooking utensils.

Map case

A fold-up map case from Survival Aids kept maps dry, while its useful pocket held log book and other maps required.

Water carrier

A roll-up water carrier was very useful and I hardly noticed its 4 oz weight.

Emergency

A bivy bag, first aid kit and a small flare pack were carried throughout the trip. Ice axe and crampons were required for both winters.

Torches

A Petzel headtorch with focusing beam was used, as was a Tekna super eight-beam torch. This hand-held torch gave an incredibly strong beam and was useful for finding tracks or huts in the dark.

Camera

A Minolta automatic camera was used throughout the walk. It was powered by alkaline batteries that had to be kept in a warm pocket in very cold conditions to prevent them freezing.

Bike

My faithful Peugeot 10-speed was used throughout the journey. Poor bike, it could have belonged to a paper-boy who would have regularly oiled and polished it. Instead it was abused, expected to carry loads in excess of 40 lb, taken over rough tracks to a lonely spot, then abandoned in soaking bracken or snow-filled woodland. The ice axe rested on the rear luggage carrier, held in place by a tennis racket clip. Dales (Cycles) Ltd., Glasgow, supplied replacement parts, at express speed, throughout the walk. No hold-ups took place, owing to their excellent back-up.

Boots

I have always liked heavyweight mountain boots, and have not been able to find any of the modern lightweight types available that offer anything like the same protection and support. A pair of Scarpa Monte Rosas fitted perfectly after being well broken in before the start. They lasted an incredible ten months of almost continuous use. John Macfarlane, the cobbler in Dalmarnock Road, Glasgow, performed miracles by resoling them three times and repairing the toe cap twice. Eventually, in January 1986, they started to leak and were retired. The reserve boots, Scarpa Bronzos were used to the end of the walk.

Tent

Throughout the walk, I tried to make as much use as possible of the caves, bothies and youth hostels I came across. So I wanted to carry a tent that would be as lightweight as possible and pack down to a very small size. The answer was a Vango Zephyr Solo, which weighed about 3 lb and packed into the bulk of a couple of sugar bags. It was a good sturdy little tent, if a little tight for room inside. During the winter months I used the excellent Winter Gear Gemini, a Gore-Tex single-skin tent which was dome-shaped with a tunnel-type entrance. It weighed only 5 lb 8 oz and stood up to some fierce Arctic weather.

Radio

A small transistor radio was carried during the winter months for weather reports. I was tempted to carry a CB radio for safety reasons but the cost and weight were prohibitive.

Charity Involvement

It wasn't until the walk was underway that I realised my efforts could benefit some worthy charity. Erskine Hospital is home for over 400 ex-servicemen, all suffering from wounds inflicted in their country's wars from the First World War to the present struggle in Northern Ireland. Those who gave so much themselves have to rely on donations for their welfare. The hospital requires over £3.5 million a year to keep open. My walk, through public donations and over thirty slide shows and talks, raised £18,000 for what is surely the most deserving of all charities.

If you would like to make a donation, or receive further information, please contact The Commandant, Erskine Hospital, Bishopton, Renfrewshire, PA7 5PU.

Bibliography: A Useful Guide for Further Reading

Note No date of publication has been given for the Scottish Mountaineering Club (SMC) guides, as these are updated regularly.

Abbey Press, *Tales and Truths of the Central Highlands*.

Andrew, K.M. and A.A. Thrippleton, SMC District Guide *The Southern Uplands*, Scottish Mountaineering Club.

Atkinson, Tom, *South West Scotland*, Luath Press, Barr, Ayrshire, 1986.
The Lonely Lands, Luath Press, 1986.
Road To The Isles, Luath Press, 1986.

Beauchamp, Elizabeth, *The Braes of Balquhidder*, Heatherbank Press, 1978.

Bennet, Donald, SMC District Guide *The Southern Highlands*.
SMC Guide *The Munros*, 1985.

Brown, Hamish M., *Hamish's Mountain Walk*, Gollancz, 1978.
Hamish's Groat's End Walk, Gollancz, 1981.
(Both available from Paladin in paperback)
Climbing the Corbetts, Gollancz, 1988.
Poems of the Scottish Hills, Aberdeen University Press, 1982.
The Island of Rhum, Cicerone Press, 1988.

Campbell, M. *The Enduring Heartland* (Argyll) Turnstone, 1977.

Carrell, C. and M. Maclean *As an Fhearan, A Pictorial View of the Clearances*, Mainstream, 1986.

Cunningham, A., *A History of Rannoch*, pub. the author, 1984.

Donaldson, G. and R.S. Morpeth, *A Dictionary of Scottish History*, J. Donald, Edinburgh, 1977.

Donaldson, J.C., *Munro's Tables*, (the bible of the game) SMC, last revision 1981.

Donaldson, M.E.M., *Further Wanderings Mainly In Argyll*, Paisley, 1926.

Feacham, Richard, *Guide to Prehistoric Scotland*, B.T. Batsford, 1977.

Firsoff, V., *In The Hills of Breadalbane*, Hale, 1954.

Fraser, D., *Highland Perthshire*, Standard Press, Montrose, 1971.

Fraser, Macdonald, *The Steel Bonnets*, Pan Books, 1974.

Gilbert, R., *Memorable Munros*, Cordee Publishers.

Gordon, Seton, *Highways and Byways in the Western Highlands*, Macmillan, 1935.

Hawke, E.L., *Buchan's Days*, Lovat Dickson, London, 1937 (rare work).

Hogg, James, *Highland Tour* (The Ettrick Shepherd).

Johnstone, S.G., SMC District Guide *The Western Highlands*.

Kilgour, W.T., *Lochaber in War and Peace*.

Linklater, E.G., *The Prince in The Heather*, Hodder, 1966.

Linklater M., *Massacre, The Story of Glencoe*, Collins, 1982.

Logan, James, *The Clans of the Scottish Highlands*, Ackermann & Co. reprinted 1980.

McCowan, R., *Ben Nevis, Story of Mountain and Glen*, Lang Syne, 1986.

Macdonald, M., *Historic Hill Routes of Lorn and Lochaber*, West Highland Publications, 1982.
  Fort William and Nether Lochaber, West Highland Publications, 1985.

Macgregor, A., *Feuds of the Clans*, Stirling, 1907 (rare work).

MacLennan, M., *Gaelic Dictionary*, Acair and Aberdeen University Press, last reprinted 1985.

Macrow, B., *Kintail Scrap Book*, Oliver and Boyd.

Merrill, John, *Walking My Way*, The Hogarth Press, 1984.
  From Arran to Orkney, Spur Books, 1981.

Moir, D.G., *Scottish Hill Tracks: Southern Scotland*, Bartholomew, 1975.
  Scottish Hill Tracks: Northern Scotland, Bartholomew, 1975.

Moran, Martin, *The Munros in Winter*, David and Charles, 1986.

Murray, W.H., *Rob Roy MacGregor, His Life and Times*, Richard Drew, 1982.

Nature Conservancy Council, *Isle of Rhum Nature Trail Guide*.
  The Parallel Roads of Glen Roy

O'Reilly, K.J., *What To See Around The Kyle of Tongue*, pub. by the author.

Orrell, Robert, *Saddle Tramp in the Highlands*, Robert Hale, 1983.

Prebble, John, *The Highland Clearances*, Penguin Books, 1963, reprinted 1985.

Salter, Mike, *Discovering Scottish Castles*, Shire Publications, 1985.

Scott, Sir Walter, *The Poetical Works of Sir Walter Scott.*
Rob Roy, J.M. Dent, 1962.

Slesser, Malcolm, SMC District Guide *The Island of Skye*, SMC.

Smith, Robin, *Grampian Ways*, Melvan Press, 1980.

Steven, Campbell, SMC District Guide, *The Central Highlands*, SMC.

Strang, Tom, SMC District Guide, *The Northern Highlands*, SMC.

Tennant, Norman, SMC District Guide, *The Islands of Scotland*, SMC.

Thompson, F., *Murder and Mystery in the Highlands*, Hale, 1977.

Tranter, Nigel, *Robert the Bruce Trilogy*, Hodder and Stoughton, 1971.
Also *The Wallace, The MacGregor Trilogy* and many more.

Underwood, P., *A Gazetteer of Scottish and Irish Ghosts*, Souvenir Press, 1973.

Watson, Adam, SMC District Guide, *The Cairngorms*, SMC.

Weir, Tom, *Highland Days*, Cassell, 1948, reprinted 1985.
The Western Highlands, Batsford, 1973.

Useful Addresses

John Muir Trust, 5 Gray Street, Broughty Ferry,
Dundee DD5 2BH.
Promotes the conservation of wild areas of Britain.

The National Trust for Scotland, 5 Charlotte Square, Edinburgh
EH2 4DU.

Scottish Rights of Way Society, 1 Lutton Place, Edinburgh
EH8 9PD.

Scottish Sports Council, Caledonia House, South Gyle,
Edinburgh EH12 9DQ.
(Glen More Lodge, National Outdoor Training Centre)

Scottish Wildland Group, 93 Queen Street, Alva,
Clackmannanshire FK12 5AH.
Promotes the conservation of the wildlands of Scotland.

Scottish Youth Hostels Association, 7 Glebe Crescent, Stirling
FK8 2JA.

L. Whittome, Achinreir Farm, Barcaldine, Argyll.
Horse riding holidays through the Highlands.

Index